D0811953

# A History
## of Economic Thought:
### From
### Aristotle
### to Arrow

CHARLES E. STALEY

# A History of Economic Thought

# A History of Economic Thought

## From Aristotle to Arrow

Charles E. Staley

BLACKWELL
Cambridge MA & Oxford UK

Copyright © Charles E. Staley 1989

First published 1989
First published in paperback 1991
Reprinted 1992

Blackwell Publishers
3 Cambridge Center
Cambridge, Massachusetts 02142, USA

108 Cowley Road, Oxford, OX4 1JF, UK

All rights reserved. Except for the quotation of short passages for the purposes of
criticism and review, no part of this publication may be reproduced, stored in a retrieval
system, or transmitted, in any form or by any means, electronic, mechanical,
photocopying, recording or otherwise, without the prior permission of the publisher.

Except in the United States of America, this book is sold subject to the condition that it
shall not, by way of trade or otherwise, be lent, re-sold, hired out, or otherwise circulated
without the publisher's prior consent in any form of binding or cover other than that in
which it is published and without a similar condition including this condition being
imposed on the subsequent purchaser.

*Library of Congress Cataloging in Publication Data*

Staley, Charles E.
A history of economic thought.
Bibliography: p.
Includes index.
1. Economics — History. I. Title.
HB75.S6878    1989        330'.09        88–36028

ISBN 1-55786-031-9
ISBN 1-55786-295-8 (Pbk)

*British Library Cataloguing in Publication Data*

A CIP catalogue record for this book is available from the British Library.

Business
HB
75
. S6878
1989

Typeset in 10 on 11½pt. Times
by Footnote Graphics, Warminster, Wilts
Printed in the USA

# Contents

# Acknowledgments

I wish to thank the following for their helpful comments on the book in various stages of its preparation: Edward Ames, Bernard Semmel, and Mark Walker, all of State University of New York at Stony Brook; Gavin Reid and Innis Smith of the University of Edinburgh; and William O. Thweatt of Vanderbilt University. Some read parts of the manuscript, some read it all; the final product is much improved by their efforts and I am grateful to them all.

# 1
# Introduction

Economics has a long history, stretching back to ancient Greece. This book deals with the major figures in economics, their ideas, their lives, and their influences on subsequent writers and developments of thought. We shall meet people of all kinds – philosophers, theologians, stock-brokers, physicians, mathematicians, and full-time economists – and from many countries. What they had in common was a desire to understand and explain economic phenomena. In the process they contributed to the body of knowledge which exists today and which is ever growing as the presses continue to roll out journals and books on economic theory.

Different approaches and different theories predominated at various times. These central concerns, which some historians of science call paradigms and others scientific research programs, are a major part of the history of economics. The Scholastics were interested in what economic behavior was compatible with the teachings of the church. Classical economics, from Adam Smith through John Stuart Mill, was concerned with the growth of the wealth of nations and its distribution among functionally defined economic classes. Neo-classical economics dealt with the allocation of resources in a static society. Keynesian economics was devoted to macroeconomics and the problems of employment. Modern economics is heavily mathematical, with the general equilibrium model as a focus.

One purpose of the study of the history of economics is to learn how knowledge (I do not say wisdom) grows, both in factual content and in the theories used to organize and understand the facts. This requires learning both what the content of the theories was and the process by which they changed into the next major set of concerns. This growth of knowledge is not in a straight line and it was not a painless process; there have been and there are plenty of arguments and debates.

Another purpose of courses in the history of thought is to broaden the awareness of students. Modern economics is so technical and mathematical that a heavy investment in technique is required. In the process there is a danger that technique for its own sake, divorced from both current social problems and from the past, may become the complete program for study. Jacob Viner, a distinguished historian of economic thought, once wrote a charming piece called "A Modest Proposal for Some Stress on Scholarship in Graduate Training" as an antidote for such excessive specialization.[1] Knowing what the ancestors said provides perspective that can be acquired in no other way.

One approach to the history of economics which commands distinguished support is the "Whig history." Macaulay in the nineteenth century judged the past as to whether it led to the present, particularly to the type of society favored by the Whig Party. A Whig history of economics would therefore study the past from the standpoint of the present state of economic science.[2] Much of this book is Whig history – the diagrammatic analysis of some of Adam Smith's ideas, and the canonical classical growth model, for example. But parts of the past of economics do not lend themselves to the Whig approach – many of the ideas of the Scholastics, which were normative, or some of the wilder ideas of the nineteenth-century American economist Henry C. Carey, for example. These are included in this book because it is not a good idea to believe that wisdom is exclusively concentrated in the present. If that were true, economics would never have progressed past Adam Smith.

And finally there is the same reason to study the history of economics that Professor Jonathan Hughes gives for studying American economic history – "so you won't be so ignorant." College education is a combination of learning specific skills and general culture. Most economics courses emphasize the former. But since the history of economics is part of general culture (maybe not a widely known part, but one with some importance), this book deals with both.

## *Notes*

1 Reprinted in Jacob Viner, *The Long View and the Short* (Glencoe, Ill., 1958).
2 Paul A. Samuelson, "Out of the Closet: A Program for the Whig History of Economic Science," *History of Economics Society Bulletin*, Fall 1987.

# 2
# The Scholastics and the Mercantilists

## *The Scholastics*

Before Adam Smith, discussions of economics were often part of other concerns. While there were some independent writers, three important groups stand out in the landscape of early economics. These groups are the Scholastics, the Mercantilists, and the Physiocrats. Each group had its own distinct interest, and in the course of discussing that interest each developed an area of the emerging subject of economics.

The Scholastics were medieval writers, which is to say that they were churchmen. Their economics was developed in the course of applying their philosophic and religious principles to the problems of commercial life. For example, the famous school man St Thomas Aquinas (1225–74) asks and answers such questions as whether in trading it is lawful to sell a thing for more than was paid for it, and whether the trader may lawfully sell it for more than it is worth. (In Roman civil law, a thing was said to be worth what it could be sold for. The Scholastics turned the principle around out of ethical reasoning.) Another hotly argued medieval question was whether interest (called usury) was something "peculiarly & inherently vicious . . . , more than in unjust, deceitful sales, or other similar kinds of fraud."[1]

Their interest in the justice of economic actions ranged over the distribution of income and wealth as well as the exchange of goods. To answer their questions, the Scholastics used reasoning applied to principles derived from the Bible, from Greek philosophers (especially Aristotle), and from Roman law. The fundamental consideration was that the price charged should be a just price, for, according to St Thomas Aquinas, "to sell dearer or to buy cheaper than a thing is worth is in itself unjust and unlawful."[2] What is a thing worth? Aristotle's discussion in his *Nichomachean Ethics*, Book V, chapter 5, of justice in economic exchange is monumental in its vagueness and gave generations of scholarly commentators ample scope for imaginative reflection. Aristotle said that in trading the sort of justice which holds men together is reciprocity in accordance with a proportion and not on the basis of precisely equal return. For it is by proportionate requital that the city holds together ... Now proportionate return is secured by cross-conjunction. Let $A$ be a builder, $B$ a shoe-maker, $C$ a house, $D$ a shoe. The builder, then, must get from the shoemaker the latter's work, and must himself give him in return his own ... For it is not two doctors that associate for exchange, but a doctor and a farmer, or in general people who are different and unequal; but they must be equated. This is why all things that are exchanged must be somehow comparable. It is for this end that money has been introduced, and it becomes in a sense intermediate, for it measures all things ... The number of shoes exchanged for a house must therefore correspond to the ratio of builder to shoemaker. For if this be not so, there will be no exchange ... And this proportion will not be effected unless the goods are somehow equal. All goods must therefore be measured by some one thing, as we said before. Now this unit is in truth demand, which holds all things together ... This is why all goods must have a price set on them; for then there will always be exchange, and if so, association of man with man. Money, then, acting as a measure, makes goods commensurate and equates them ... Now in truth it is impossible that things differing so much should become commensurate, but with reference to demand they may become so sufficiently.[3]

It may help the student puzzled by the Aristotle fragment to note that the ancient Greeks did not have a theory of market price. If the commodity had a uniform quality, like grain, it was typically sold by a monopolist or by government regulation. (Greek commentary was typically concerned with public administration, or the use of public discussion to arrive at a fair price, rather than with market determination of price.) If it varied in quality, like clothing, individual bargaining was the common means of setting the price. In this connection, there is the interesting suggestion that because the Greeks in general thought the harmonic mean, which is derived from the ratios of octaves and therefore derives from the "music of the spheres," had ethical priority over the arithmetic and geometric means, Aristotle may have applied it in the case of barter. If the carpenter offers his table for 12 pairs of shoes, while the shoemaker says he will give 6 pairs for the table, what is the just price? The harmonic mean is 8 pairs of shoes, which is one-third lower than 12 and one-third higher than 6, and a typically Greek idea would have been to say that was just compared to the arithmetic mean (9) or the geometric mean (the square root of $6 \times 12$, which is nearly 8½). However, since Aristotle's actual number has been lost in copying, this is conjectural.[4]

In trying to make sense of Aristotle, medieval scholars pursued several different lines of inquiry.[5] One of the earliest was Robert Grosseteste (1168–1253). He struggled with the idea that economic exchange requires a common unit of measure. He suggested three measures: usefulness, need in the sense of necessity, and need in the sense of craving. Subsequent writers took the last sense and eventually related value to demand.

A second problem in the passage quoted from Aristotle is what he meant by a "cross-conjunction" relating the value of the producers and the value of the product. One solution is that the value of the product depends on the amount of the producer's labor tied up in the product (what was later known as the labor theory of value). Albertus Magnus (d. 1280) made this idea sophisticated by stating that (1) if the builder does not get a just exchange society will perish and (2) the measurement which is essential in exchange is labor and expenses. This led to the idea that value in exchange must comply with the cost of production. Some followers of Albertus Magnus made the labor element mean the number of labor hours involved, as Marx did later. Others related producer worth to the differing values of labor time in different markets, while still others insisted that production would stop if costs were not covered. This line of thought develops the supply side of price theory, just as Grosseteste's developed the demand side.

Albertus's student St Thomas Aquinas was a brilliant expositor of Scholastic doctrine. He accepted Albertus's proposition that the just price had to cover labor and expenses, but made a contribution of his own in pointing out the difference between "natural valuation" and economic valuation. For example, in spite of his human superiority, a slave was often less valuable than a jewel or a horse. Human wants or human need is the measure of value, since price varies with human need. Later writers, commenting on St Thomas, expanded need from personal to market demand. Market demand itself, they said, meant ability to pay, not simple desire. This development, however, took many centuries. The seventeenth-century writers Grotius and Pufendorf explained it in its mature form, and in turn passed the ideas on to Adam Smith. This is the "filiation of economic ideas" which fascinated Joseph Schumpeter in his long, erudite *History of Economic Analysis*.[6]

While need in relation to value immediately invokes a demand curve to the modern student, in the Scholastic model need comprises supply as well as demand. "Demand may be heavy, but as long as there is sufficient supply, *indigentia* does not raise price, only if there is scarcity. . . . It is not that crop failure and famine raise the price of bread, *indigentia* being given; it is rather they increase *indigentia*, which raises price."[7] This interpretation entered Scholastic economics in the early 1300s in the teaching of Henricus de Fimaria. It enabled the church fathers to answer the question, is it just to sell at a higher price to the poor in greater need than to the rich in less need? Since value was related to need, it is just, provided that the price is set in a market free of fraud and of greed.

An interesting notion rising from the need-based rule of the just price is this: if the seller of a good suffered a great cost he could sell at a higher price, assuming the buyer would pay it; but, assuming the same need on the part of the buyer as in the previous case, the seller could not raise the price if his costs were not extraordinarily great. This was to prevent taking advantage of a buyer's great need. A buyer's price was to be tied to the aggregate market need, not to his individual situation or to a monopoly market.

An important strand of Scholastic economics was contributed by Gerald Odonis (ca. 1300), writing on the labor and expenses side of the just price. Skilled labor has a higher value than unskilled labor because it is rarer. Its product is therefore more scarce, and, being more scarce, is more valuable.

So we have arrived at the conclusion that the just price must consider the buyers' needs (i.e., the demand curve), the sellers' costs (i.e., the supply curve), the scarcity of the product, and the condition of the market (absence of monopoly). Toward the end of the Scholastic period a Belgian priest, Venerable Leonard Lessius (1554–1623), made a more sophisticated statement about monopoly, distinguishing among different cases of monopoly pricing. Conspiracy on the part of sellers, force, and fraud are unjust monopoly practices. (Notice that the anti-trust laws are relatives of the just price doctrine.) But a monopoly created by a ruler for a just reason (such as to raise funds for the public welfare) or by a speculator who buys at harvest time and sells later at a higher price is quite just. The speculator has been exercizing an entrepreneurial function and should be rewarded for it.[8]

There are Scholastic writers who took an entirely different tack. Their position is that it is a sin to make a worldly success by moving out of the social position into which one is born. Hence a just price will be the one which allows maintenance of social status, but no more. The experts now believe that this idea was a minor part of Scholastic economics, although the commentators of seventy years ago put it forward as *the* dominant theme. Sweeping reversals of opinion such as this are not rare in the study of history.

The history of economic thought is not only an investigation of what writers of the past have said (with all the problems of interpretation suggested in the previous paragraph). It is also a study of what has caused these writers to develop their ideas in the particular way they did. There are two methods of approaching this problem, which have come to be known as the "relativist" and the "absolutist" approaches. The relativist attempts to relate economic ideas to the social form existing at the time and says that earlier economic systems are not simply young versions of modern capitalism. Earlier thinkers should not be judged according to the compatibility of their reasoning with our contemporary economic life. Another less Marxist version of relativism is the creed of institutional economist Wesley C. Mitchell that to a large extent the important developments in economic theory were made in response to changing current economic problems, rather than being the outcome of "the forthright process of logical excogitation."[9]

The absolutist approach is to regard the history of economic ideas as an intellectual development. One of the clearest examples of this method is seen in Frank Knight's essay on classical economics, which begins with the assumption that our primary interest in our ancestors is to learn from their mistakes, and proceeds to list the main deficiencies of the Ricardians in a sort of check list before tackling their doctrines in detail. The absolutist is often willing to grant that a particular theory may be explained by prevailing circumstances, but will differ from the relativist in insisting that the theory cannot be *justified* by any such historical considerations. Error is error and must be noticed when it appears. Actually both approaches are illuminating and neither should be given complete dominance.[10]

It is easy to find both interpretations of the Scholatistic just price. The relativists say that it was a response to an economy facing chronic low-level stagnation and changing social forms. Both features make for price wars and upset markets, needing some arbitrator like the church. The imperfect markets and common presence of oligopoly rather than competiton added to the need for an arbitrator. Much time and effort would have to go into bargaining without the standard price provided by the just price; this bargaining effort was converted into useful economic activity (or at least potentially could have been converted). The absolutists look at Scholastic economics as an intellectual development, the process of puzzling out the meaning of Aristotle's philosophy in the light of Judeo-Christian religion.[11]

Another major question which occupied generations of Scholastic writers was usury, which one expert called by far the most important and most debated issue in Catholic doctrine.[12] Usury was defined as *any* payment of interest on loans, and was regarded as unjust because it was a payment for "a sale of what does not exist," as St Thomas Aquinas put it.[13] Scholastics thought that lending and repaying money involved something which did not exist because, following Aristotle, they thought that the proper use of money was in making exchanges or spending it. Repaying the original sum of money borrowed was the exchange of the borrower's money for the lender's money and was perfectly in order, since it was in accord with the exchange function of money. The payment of interest, however, was not in exchange for anything in the Scholastic view, and hence cheated the borrower. Of course this is entirely contrary to modern interest theory, which says that the borrower is paying for the privilege of consuming goods sooner than he otherwise could or of acquiring capital goods or inventory which could yield a net income. Furthermore, the lender must get a payment for parting with his cash, because there are benefits to liquidity. It gives the ability to meet emergencies, to take advantage of unexpected bargains, and to avoid capital losses. But all this was completely outside Aristotelian teaching.

There were two interesting developments from the usury doctrine. One was in the world of business affairs. Since the collection of interest was held by the church to be unjust, it was forbidden. But practical men looked for a way around the prohibition. In the field of banking, foreign exchange dealers set prices which allowed for the long time which it took in those days to collect from foreign countries; by paying less than the face price for foreign bills of exchange (i.e., by discounting) the dealers earned what was in effect interest. But they argued that the transaction was a purchase of foreign funds, not a loan, so they brought it into the approved category of exchange. The result was that banking became an institution devoted to foreign exchange.[14]

The other contribution of the usury discussion was in the field of economic theory. Joseph A. Schumpeter, an enthusiastic devotee of Scholastic economics, claimed that the theory of interest was launched at that time, particularly in the proposition of St Antoine (ca. 1400) that the fundamental factor raising interest rates above zero is the existence of business profits. Since this was not followed up by any discussion of what is involved in business profits (risk, a return to entrepreneurship, or the productivity of the owner's capital), most commentators are not as impressed as was Schumpeter. However, in the course of debate over what compensation a lender could legitimately claim, a modern theoretical idea was developed. All agreed that an extra charge for tardy repayment and for damage suffered by the lender was just. But could the lender claim that he suffered damage if he did not earn the same return he could have by using the money himself in an alternative investment? The learned fathers said no, but the idea itself is equivalent to the doctrine of opportunity cost – one of the most important and fundamental building blocks of modern economics.[15]

Scholastic thought continued to flourish in the sixteenth century, but then it increasingly became "a frozen and lifeless relic of an earlier age, still studied reverently in theological seminaries but steadily losing its influence on social behavior in the outer world.... By the seventeenth century, mercantilism, as a political and economic doctrine which stressed national power and national prosperity, dominated the lay world."[16]

## The Mercantilists

Adam Smith devoted more than 200 pages of the *Wealth of Nations* to an exposition and demolition of what he called "the commercial or mercantile system." Most of these pages describe English mercantilistic trade restrictions and explain why free trade would be better, in his opinion. In the years since 1776, mercantilism has been studied both by economists as a system of economic thought and by economic historians who try to appraise mercantilism as a "significant sequence of events," in the words of Alexander Gershonkron.[17] As this distinguished historian and others have pointed out, to some extent the two approaches to mercantilism have been separate enterprises, with different features emphasized. In large measure this is the result of the fact that economic policy as actually formulated and carried out is not simply the outcome of an intellectual debate, but responds to political and economic forces. The British debate in the years 1820–40 over eliminating tariffs is a good case in point. A modern student of that debate has concluded that the politicians were the best informed, the merchants the least informed, and that economic principles, considerations of equity, and most especially matters of national power all played a role.[18] A similar mixture of motives prevailed during the preceding centuries when mercantilism was in flower.[19]

Viewing mercantilism as a set of ideas rather than as a historical policy-making episode, the basic belief was that it was necessary to accumulate gold and silver through foreign trade in order to foster national wealth and power, and therefore a variety of restrictions on imports and subsidies to exports was needed. These propositions were defended in England during the fifteenth through eighteenth centuries by a series of writers, many of whom were merchants or who were connected with the great trading company, the East India Company. The French writers were likely to be administrators (e.g., Jean Baptiste Colbert, 1619–83, the one most often cited). German contributions came from bureaucrats and their teachers. As economics, two of the great experts of recent years give mercantilistic writing poor marks from the absolutist point of view. Schumpeter said that the bulk of the literature is essentially preanalytic, crude, written by unprofessional or uneducated people; and Viner called it essentially a folk doctrine, the doctrine of practical men not used to subtle analysis.[20] (As a practical argument, however, Schumpeter felt that mercantilistic policies were adequate to reach defensible ends, considering the circumstance and opportunities of the times. Thus he applied relativism to practice but not to theory, an interesting example of schizophrenia.)

One of the most famous mercantilists, Sir Thomas Mun (1571–1641), after observing that "The ordinary means therefore to increase our wealth and treasure is by *Forraign Trade*, wherein wee must ever observe this rule; to sell more to strangers yearly than wee consume of theirs in value," justifies the accumulation of treasure by stating that "those Princes which do not providently lay up treasure, or do imoderately consume the same when they have it, will sodainly come to want and misery."[21] However, the amount of treasure which the king is able to lay up is equal only to the amount of the balance of trade surplus, according to Mun, for if he tried to accumulate more, some of the money in the state would be "drawn into the Princes treasure, whereby the life of lands and arts must fail and fall to the ruin both of the publick and private wealth."[22] These remarks illustrate both central doctrines and the sort of assertions on which they rested.

The mercantilists certainly did not agree among themselves on all points, even if they did share the common notion that trade restrictions were needed to ensure gold and silver imports. There was much controversy and in the process some development of ideas. One debate was whether to control the foreign exchange markets or not; a famous English devotee of control, Gerard de Malynes, argued that control by the government of the rate of exchange was necessary because in unregulated markets bankers would arbitrarily set the price of foreign currency too high. Although we would expect this to generate an export surplus and a gold inflow, Malynes argued that it would actually result in a loss of specie because no one abroad would accept undervalued sterling exchange in payment. Rather they would demand gold or silver.[23] Another English merchant, Edward Misselden (fl.1608–54), argued against Malynes, that "dastardly combatant," that the market value of the exchanges depends on the relative supply and demand of foreign currencies and that in turn on the relative demand and supply of goods in foreign countries. This is clear progress in economic understanding. In addition to Misselden's insight into foreign exchange markets, he was the first to use the terminology of the "balance of trade," which he called an "excellent and politique Invention, to shew us the difference of waight in the Commerce of one *Kingdome* with another."

Similar advance in understanding is shown in the controversy over whether the East India Company should be allowed to export specie. Such primitive mercantilists as Malynes claimed that this impoverished the realm; but both Misselden and Mun argued that the spices and so on purchased with the gold were re-exported to Europe for a larger amount of gold, so that in the end the transactions added to the gold stock. Recently, indeed, some economic historians have used one aspect of this argument as an explanation of why the mercantilists were infatuated with the notion of accumulating gold: neither India nor another important trading partner, the Baltic, provided much of a market for English goods, but did eagerly accept gold. Gold was, in effect, the inventory of goods for sale to these regions.[24]

More than a century later, in 1752, David Hume made himself immortal as an economist by his demonstration that the mercantilists' goal of acquiring specie via the balance of trade was self-defeating: an export surplus leading to a gold inflow would raise prices at home which would correct the export surplus.[25] It is a fascinating fact that the mercantilists had the first part of this theory, that a gold inflow would raise prices, but did not conclude that the price rises would turn the balance of trade against the gold importer, even though Mun had at one point used the relevant tool, the price elasticity of demand. Mun remarks that "It is a common saying, that plenty or scarcity of mony makes all things dear or good or cheap; and this mony is either gotten or lost in forraign trade by the over or under ballancing of the same ..."[26] He had also pointed out that a 25 percent reduction in the price of cloth would increase the quantity sold by 50 percent; a simple reversal of the argument leads immediately to Hume's conclusion, as Mun himself pointed out: " ... for as plenty of mony makes wares dearer, so dear wares decline their use and consumption, as hath been already plainly shewed ..." But the automatic balancing mechanism will not come into play if the specie is used as the merchant's stock-in-trade rather than getting into domestic circulation, and this was Mun's plea: "And although this is a very hard lesson for some great landed men to learn, yet I am sure it is a true lesson for all the land to observe, lest when wee have gained some store of mony by trade, wee lose it again by not trading with our mony."[27] This was Mun's own particular view; in general, most other mercantilists believed that an expansion of money would "quicken trade" (i.e., expand output) rather than raise prices.[28]

A major element of the mercantilists' doctrine was their belief that exports themselves (as distinct from the effects of the specie they might generate) were good for employment and that a large population with low wages was necessary for exports. Some went so far as to argue that policy should be concerned with a favorable balance of labor as well as or instead of a favorable balance of trade; that is, they would calculate the labor content of exports and of imports, and attempt to maximize the difference. This particular calculation was a rather small part of mercantilist thought. Much more common was the insistence on the necessity for low wages to encourage exports. For example, Sir James Steuart, one of the very late mercantilists (his book was published just nine years before the *Wealth of Nations*), advised the notional statesman to whom he addressed his counsel in these terms:

> If he find that goods are not exported, because of high prices, while manufac-
> turers are enjoying superfluity, and indulging themselves in idleness, let him
> multiply hands, and he will reduce them all to their physical-necessary; and by
> thus augmenting the supply, he will also reduce the prices in his markets at
> home.[29]

The narrowness of the mercantilist outlook and its close connection with nationalism is shown by what David Hume called "the jealousy of trade,"[30] the idea that other trading states are one's rivals, or, as modern theory puts it, that trade is a zero-sum game. Few went as far as Theodore Ludwig Lau, a German mercantilist of the early eighteenth century, who welcomed plague, war, famine, and harvest failure in other countries because of the economic advantage to Germany. But the more moderate statements were inflammatory enough. Thus Sir Thomas Mun, referring to the Dutch, said that "there are no people in Christendome who do more undermine, hurt, and eclipse us daily in our Navigation and Trades, both abroad and at home ... More might be written of these Netherlanders pride and ambitious endeavours, whereby they hope in time to grow mighty, if they be not prevented."[31] And so on at great length. The reiteration of the need to build up one's own military, monetary, and economic strength at the expense of others led the nineteenth-century German historians, as well as Eli Heckscher in the twentieth century, to characterize mercantilism as a system of state-building and of power. A brilliant essay by Jacob Viner demonstrates persuasively, however, that economic plenty and political power were both important goals and were regarded as mutually support-ing, progress in each helping to promote the other.[32]

Not all the writing by merchants in mercantilist times developed mercantilist ideas. One of these is a good illustration of the following phenomenon in the history of economics: it sometimes happens that a publication appears, is lost sight of, and then much later is rediscovered with delight in the quality of economics it contains and amazement that it did not have more contemporary impact. One of the most famous examples of this was William Stanley Jevons' discovery of Richard

Cantillon's *Essai sur la Nature du Commerce en Géneral* (1755), which had effectively dropped out of sight even though it was mentioned in the *Wealth of Nations*. The example from mercantilist days is Isaac Gervaise's *The System or Theory of the Trade of the World*, a twenty-four page pamphlet originally published in 1720 and rediscovered by Jacob Viner in the 1930s. Gervaise, a member of the Royal Lustring Company,[33] went against the whole mercantilistic fraternity by declaring that "This consider'd we may conclude, that Trade is never in a better condition, than when it's natural and free; the forcing it either by Laws, or Taxes, being always dangerous ... "[34] What is more remarkable, Gervaise arrived at this conclusion on the basis of a theory that the balance of payments is subject to a self-regulating mechanism. His argument differed from Hume's price–specie flow mechanism, which asserted that the attempt to accumulate gold by restricting imports would be frustrated by the inflationary impact of gold on domestic prices. Gervaise instead anticipated a much later theory. He set up a model very similar to the absorption model much discussed in the 1950s.[35] The absorption model begins with the proposition that national output is purchased (or absorbed) either by a country's residents or by foreigners. This may be expressed by the equation $Y = A + B$, where $Y$ is national income, $A$ is the total amount of spending or absorption by residents of goods and services, and $B$ is the trade balance. Absorption theories analyze what happens to $B$ by looking at the effects of economic variables on $Y$ and $A$. This is what Gervaise did. He reasoned that an increased purchasing power resulting from a gold inflow or from increased domestic credit will add more to spending than it does to output (i.e., $A$ will increase more than $Y$). Hence $B$ will fall, leading to a trade deficit and a loss of gold (or to devaluation). So an initial trade surplus and gold inflow may be corrected by national income effects of the sort emphasized by post-Keynesian economists. *The System or Theory of the Trade of the World* was indeed a remarkable essay, far ahead of its time.

After the *Wealth of Nations* did its hatchet job on mercantilism, mercantilistic ideas became the domain of historians and policy-makers rather than of mainstream economists for the next century and a half. However, in 1936 John Maynard Keynes revived the possibility that mercantilism had been respectable contemporary economics in his chapter "Notes on Mercantilism, the Usury Laws, Stamped Money, and Theories of Under-consumption," which was devoted to these matters of peripheral interest in *The General Theory of Employment, Interest, and Money*. Keynes argued that in the circumstances of mercantilist days the only way to reduce the domestic rate of interest to combat unemployment was to increase the amount of gold and silver via the trade balance, and also that an improved trade balance could serve as an outlet for excessive domestic savings. Keynes thought the mercantilists displayed practical wisdom in their economic policy recipes and distinctly saw an important problem without being able to solve it analytically. Most of the controversy generated by the Keynesian revolution had to do with the economics of contemporary domestic national income problems and policies, but Heckscher, in the revised edition of his *Mercantilism* criticized the "Notes on Mercantilism." Among several points the most cogent was that the kind of unemployment which Keynes analyzed – industrial unemployment caused by too high a rate of saving compared to investment spending at full employment – was not the problem at all in mercantilist days. Economies of the time had primarily an agricultural base and the unemployment problem was seasonal or frictional. Changing the rate of interest via gold imports is hardly the indicated policy for that sort of unemployment.

Economic policy in many countries today has a bias toward protection of import-competing industries which is analogous in some ways to mercantilism. Contemporary mercantilism argues that protection will increase real income, not the gold stock. But such episodes as the formation of the European Common Market and British–French financing of the Concorde airplane have been cited as modern mercantilism which reflects the faith in trade controls and the concern with unemployment of the writers of three centuries ago.[36] This in turn may reflect a feeling common to many generations that one should turn to the government to get things done. Keynes refers to the mixture of rage and perplexity with which Bonar Law (a British Conservative politician of the early twentieth century) regarded the "classical" economists' denial of his (Bonar Law's) mercantilistic ideas, and Jacob Viner relates an incident from 200 years ago when Horace Walpole told with amusement how his aunt had read about a distiller who was burned when the head of his still flew off. She thought an Act of Parliament should be made against the heads of stills flying off.[37]

## Notes

1 Carolus Molinaeus, *A Treatise of Contracts and Usury*, reprinted in A. E. Monroe, *early Economic Thought*, (Cambridge, Mass., 1924), p. 105.

2 St Thomas Aquinas, *Summa Theologica*, reprinted in Monroe, *Early Economic Thought*, p. 55.

3 *The Works of Aristotle*, vol. 9, *The Nichomachean Ethics*, trans. W. D. Ross (Oxford, 1930), pp. 1132b–3b.

4 The suggestion is that of S. Todd Lowry, "Aristotle's Mathematical Analysis of Exchange," *HOPE*, 1969, pp. 44–66. (*HOPE* is the acronym for the journal *History of Political Economy*, which specializes in the history of economic thought.) His article "Recent Literature on Ancient Greek Economic Thought," *Journal of Economic Literature*, 1979, pp. 65–86 has a bibliography of 124 items and is a gold mine for students looking for term paper material.

5 The following exposition is based on an impressive piece of scholarship, Odd Langholm, *Price and Value in the Aristotelean Tradition*, (Bergen, 1979). Warning: much untranslated Latin appears in this book.

6 While Schumpeter traces Scholastic teaching in Adam Smith, Langholm

claims that Nassau Senior, writing in the 1830s, brought the exchange model of the *Nichomachean Ethics* into his teaching far more than did other early modern economists.

7 Langholm, *Price and Value*, p. 113.

8 Barry Gordon, *Economic Analysis before Adam Smith* (New York, 1975), has a detailed discussion of Lessius, and is a good reference on the Scholastics generally.

9 Wesley C. Mitchell, *Types of Economic Theory*, vol. I (New York, 1967), p. 20. For a Marxist version of the relativist approach see Paul M. Sweezy, *The Theory of Capitalist Development* (New York, 1968), pp. 35–6.

10 Knight's essay is in *On the History and Method of Economics* (Chicago, 1956), p. 37. Mark Blaug, *Economic Theory in Retrospect*, 4th edn (Cambridge, 1985) pp. 1–9, has a good exposition of the absolutist–relativist approaches.

11 A series of articles in *History of Political Economy*, develop these positions. These include George W. Wilson, "The Economics of the Just Price," *HOPE*, 1975, pp. 56–74; Stephen T. Worland, "*Justum Pretium*: One More Round in an Endless Series," *HOPE*, 1977, pp. 504–21; and David D. Friedman, "In Defense of Thomas Aquinas and the Just Price," *HOPE*, 1980, pp. 234–42. Langholm's book, on which this chapter relies, is very much in the absolutist tradition.

12 Jacob Viner, "Religious Thought and Economic Society," *HOPE*, 1978, p. 85. The most detailed survey of usury doctrine is John T. Noonan, Jr, *The Scholastic Analysis of Usury* (Cambridge, Mass., 1957).

13 Monroe, *Early Economic Thought*, p. 66.

14 See Raymond de Roover, "Ancient and Medieval Thought," *International Encyclopedia of the Social Sciences*, vol. 4, (New York, 1968), p. 434.

15 Other economic issues commented on by the Scholastics include the quest for individual wealth, property as an institution, charity, proper coinage, and taxation. Viner, "Religious Thought", discusses these issues. A mystery novel published in 1983, Umberto Eco's *The Name of the Rose*, gives a vivid picture of the life of people such as the Scholastic writers referred to here. The author is himself a professor in Italy; his detective hero is a monk very similar to Sherlock Holmes. The extremes of Scholastic life are well portrayed: the devotion to religion, the reliance on the literature and opinions of Aristotle and Aquinas, the ability and willingness to reason at greath length and with hair-splitting intensity on the basis of just a few words from the past (for example, the monks in the story argue for pages over whether Christ ever laughed), all are brilliantly laid out. Unfortunately, in the story the monks never got to arguing over the just price or usury.

16 Viner, "Religous Thought," p. 12.

17 "History of Economic Doctrines and Economic History," *American Economic Review Papers and Proceedings*, 1969, p. 2.

18 W. D. Grampp, "Economic Opinion when Britain Turned to Free Trade," *HOPE*, 1982, pp. 496–520.

19 A new theory in the field of the economic regulation of industries has led to the suggestion of another aspect of the mercantilistic era. Regulation creates a monopoly profit if competition from other nations is prohibited; this profit (called a rent in this theory because it is not a return to useful activities) adds to

the income of businessmen. It also adds to the revenue of governments if they tax the business profits or force the entrepreneurs to bid for the right to conduct business. Mercantilist states vigorously supplied monopoly rights to meet their revenue needs, and the merchants had to pay for them. In this interpretation, mercantilism declined in England when Parliament won the right to supply monopoly legislation, because it is much more expensive to lobby a legislative body for special favors than it is to pay off a central executive. This interpretation also explains why regulation was much more extensive in France, where the system was much more centralized. It also explains why merchants favored mercantilism; they were not interested in whether mercantilism was self-defeating, as such economists as David Hume contended, because what they wanted was a share of the regulatory rent. This interpretation is explained in detail by Robert B. Ekelund, Jr, and Robert D. Tollison, *Mercantilism as a Rent-Seeking Society: Economic Regulation in Historical Perspective*, (College Station, Texas, 1981). For other historical analyses of mercantilism as a problem in economic policy, see D. C. Coleman (ed.), *Revisions in Mercantilism*, (London, 1969).

20 Schumpeter, *History of Economic Analysis* (New York, 1954), pp. 337 and 348; Jacob Viner, "Mercantilist Thought," *International Encyclopedia of the Social Sciences*, vol. 4, (New York, 1968), p. 436.

21 Sir Thomas Mun, *England's Treasure by Forraign Trade*, reprinted in J. R. McCulloch, *Early English Tracts on Commerce* (London, 1956), pp. 125, 186–7. Mun's book was published in 1664 but written about 1626–8.

22 Ibid., p. 189.

23 Lynn Muchmore, "Gerrard de Malynes and Mercantile Economics," *HOPE*, 1969, pp. 336–58, suggests that Malynes's idea that bankers could set the price of foreign currencies at will resulted from Malynes's not inconsiderable experience with financial intrigue.

24 C. Wilson, "Treasure and Trade Balances: the Mercantilist Problem," *Economic History Review*, 1949, pp. 152–6 was one of the first economic historians to present this idea.

25 Hume's analysis is in his essay "Of the Balance of Trade"; the edition most helpful for students of economics is Eugene Rotwein (ed.), *David Hume: Writings on Economics* (Madison, Wisconsin, 1970). Modern monetary theory points out that prices of home goods could not increase above the prices of the same goods abroad by more than the cost of transportation if they are traded, but that equilibrium will be restored because consumption spending becomes greater than output at constant prices for the country whose money supply has increased. This leads to an import surplus and an outflow of excess gold. See Paul A. Samuelson, "A Corrected Version of Hume's Equilibrating Mechanism for International Trade," in John S. Chipman and C. P. Kindleberger (eds), *Flexible Exchange Rates and the Balance of Payments* (Amsterdam, 1980).

26 Mun, *England's Treasure*, p. 141.

27 Ibid., p. 138.

28 See the detailed discussion in Jacob Viner, *Studies in the Theory of International Trade* (New York, 1937), pp. 33ff. The first two chapters of Viner's book, together with Eli Heckscher, *Mercantilism*, rev. edn (New York, 1955), are the great modern works of scholarship on mercantilism.

29 Sir James Steuart, *An Inquiry into the Principles of Political Oeconomy*, vol. 2, ed. Andrew Skinner, (Edinburgh, 1966), 2, p. 693.
30 The title of one of his essays, published in 1758.
31 Mun, *England's Treasure*, pp. 202–3.
32 Jacob Viner, "Power versus Plenty as Objective of Foreign Policy in the Seventeenth and Eighteenth Centuries," reprinted in his book *The Long View and the Short* (Glencoe, Ill., 1958).
33 Lustring is a type of silk cloth.
34 Isaac Gervaise, *The System or Theory of the Trade of the World* (Baltimore, Md, 1954), pp. 17–18.
35 See Sidney S. Alexander, "Effects of a Devaluation on a Trade Balance," *IMF Staff Papers*, 1952, pp. 263–73.
36 See Harry G. Johnson, "Mercantilism: Past, Present, and Future," *The Manchester School*, 1974, pp. 1–17.
37 John Maynard Keynes, *The General Theory of Employment, Interest and Money* (London, 1936), p. 350; and Jacob Viner, "The Intellectual History of Laissez-Faire," *The Journal of Law and Economics*, 1960, p. 56.

# 3
# One Foot in the Mercantilist World and One in the Classical

John Locke stood with "one foot in the mercantilist world and with one foot in the classical world," according to John Maynard Keynes. This chapter deals with the major figures of the late seventeenth and early eighteenth centuries – John Locke, Sir William Petty, Bernard Mandeville, Richard Cantillon, and Sir James Steuart. They all contributed in one way or another to changing the concerns of scientific writing from the moral concerns of the Scholastics and the bullionist ideas of the early mercantilists to "scientific economics."[1]

Naturally, and speaking in a relativistic tone of voice, had the world itself not changed from medieval to modern there would have been no development of economics. "Adam Smith might have been a great moral philosopher in that earlier age, but he could never have been a great economist; there would have been nothing for him to do."[2] The medieval world was one of the manor, of the divine right of kings, of many small principalities, of little trade, of the dominance of the Catholic Church, of guilds, of serfs tied to the land. Over the centuries following 1400 the capitalistic market system gradually evolved. Many changes in social life, in politics, and in the philosophic basis of society were involved. Some outstanding features of the change process included the enclosure movement, in which large landholders, the lords of the manor, fenced in what had been common ground to raise sheep for the rapidly growing woolen industry. The peasants, who had depended on the commons for grazing land and for firewood, could no longer survive as agricultural workers. They became landless proletarians, many of them paupers and sturdy vagabonds, who were the basis of an eventual urban labor force. Another major change was the rise of Protestantism, particularly the Calvinist variety, in which the drive for wealth became an accepted goal for a religious person. Exploration and the inflow of New World gold and silver helped the rise of money economies. Oliver Cromwell and the victory of Parliament in the English Civil War, with the later Glorious Revolution of 1688, reduced the divine right of kings in Britain to a memory, and throughout Europe nationalism replaced the hundreds of petty principalities with different laws, customs duties, and consequent restraints on trade. Towns developed, roads connected them, inventions such as the printing press, the windmill, the clock, cannon and gunpowder were made. The end result of all these changes was that the market replaced medieval rigidity and the "just price"; land, labor and capital replaced the manor, the serf, and the hoards of medieval money lenders, and economics replaced theology as an explanation of how the society worked. Samuel Johnson said that "There is nothing which requires more to be illustrated by philosophy than trade does." The people discussed in this chapter were prominent in developing the new "philosophy."

We begin with Sir William Petty (1623–87), an extremely colorful and versatile man. He went to sea at age 13, and found himself left in France with a broken leg. There he went to college, and later studied medicine in Holland. When he went to Oxford in 1646 to study medicine he gained entry to the circle of scientists that later became the Royal Society; and after he became a doctor he became professor of anatomy and of music (in the latter post he apparently taught applied mathematics). But he soon left the university to go to Ireland as physician-in-chief to Cromwell's army. Then he took over the survey of the Irish lands; this survey was necessary to be able to give forfeited land to the soldiers and those who put up the money for the army. From the survey Petty made a sizable sum in cash plus some land; he bought other land outright and wound up with some 100,000 acres. The rest of his life he then devoted to science and to politics.[3]

In science he tried his hand at a variety of projects, including designing a "double-bottomed" ship (i.e., one with two keels connected together). The science for which he was best known in his day was "political arith-metick," the application of what he called "number, weight, and measure" (actually a biblical phrase) to problems of current policy. His first essay on political arithmetic was designed to prove that the power and wealth of England had not been declining since 1650, and that England was as powerful as France. Others dealt with the growth of London, comparisons of the populations of London, Paris, Rome, and other cities, and so on. The intellectual effort in political arithmetic was not in statistical methods; the arithmetic mean was the only statistical method used. The scientific interest was in the attempt to use scanty statistical data to give clues to the questions under investigation.

Here is an example of "political arithmetick" in action. The problem is to estimate the population of the city of London. There are three ways of doing this, says Petty. One is to estimate the number of houses, and the number of people living in each; the second is to find the number of burials in healthy times, and the proportion of those who live to those who die; the third is to use the number of those who die in a plague year, in proportion to those who escape. To find the number of houses, he takes the number reported to be burned in the great fire of 1666 (13,200 houses). The people who died in these houses comprised one-fifth the total deaths, so there must have been $5 \times 13,200 = 66,000$ houses in 1666. There were 4/3 the number of burials in 1686 than there were in 1666, so the 1686 housing was 4/3 the 1666 housing, or 4/3 × 66,000 = approximately 88,000.[4] The final calculation holds only if the death rate had not changed in the period, but since 1666 was a plague year this seems unlikely; also it requires that the average population of the houses that burned was the same as those which did not, and that the death rate in 1666 out of those two sets of housing was the same. Since the houses that burned were in the center of London, and more crowded and unhealthy than those outside the city walls, this part of the calculation also seems unlikely.[5] Adam Smith, after reporting calculations on the grain trade made by a later author, remarked that "I have no great faith in political arithmetick ..." (*Wealth of Nations*, Book IV, chapter V). Some interpret this as meaning that he did not credit numbers arrived at by a process of guessing and fiddling. Others are more severe on Smith and, with Schumpeter, attribute the wilting of an inspiring message and a suggestive program to the wooden hands of the Scottish professor.[6] It seems more likely that political arithmetic foundered because of inadequate data on which to base calculations.

Petty had two followers in political arithmetic who should be mentioned. One was Gregory King (1648–1712), who presented data from which a demand curve for wheat can be constructed; for example, if price is nearly five times above normal, only half the normal amount will be demanded. (King's demand curve is $q = -2.33p+0.05p^2-0.00167p^3$, a calculation made by G. U. Yule on the basis of the five points on the curve presented by King.) Another was Charles Davenant, who, in particular, presented a very clear definition of national income, subtracted out expenditure on clothing, feeding, defending, and ornamenting the people, and put the difference into "wealth or national stock," i.e., investment. This improved both over the mercantilists, who regarded money as the national stock, and Petty, who calculated national income as equal to national expenditure but made no allowance for investment – only for consumption.

Petty's modern reputation rests less on his political arithmetic than on his analytical approach. It has been well said that "It is not the correctness of its analysis, but the method of analysis that defines a work as scientific. One of the chief elements of the scientific method is a taste for economy in analysis, an abhorrence of ad hoc explanations, a determination to explain as wide as possible a range of phenomena in terms of a few simple principles. The *Treatise* [i.e., Petty's *Treatise on Taxes*] meets this test brilliantly ..."[7] One of these "few simple principles" is that any tax which reduced output should be avoided. Another is that land rent is a surplus, the amount of corn left over after paying the subsistence of labor and other expenses of cultivation. This was in advance of the general literature of the time, which regarded rent as a money expense and a cost of production. These principles are applied repeatedly throughout Petty's discussion of taxation. Other points for which Petty is famous include the following.

1   Petty made an early statement of the benefits of the division of labor,

and its relation to the extent of the market. He observed that in so vast a city as London each manufacture can be divided into as many parts as possible, so that the work of each artisan can be simple and easy; he illustrated with watches rather than with a pin factory as in the *Wealth of Nations*, but he concluded, as Adam Smith would have done, that the watch would be better and cheaper than if one man made the whole thing.[8]

2    Another basic economic concept which Petty was among the first to discuss is the velocity of money. He asked, "How much money is necessary to drive the trade of the nation?", and answered that if the expense of the nation is 40 million pounds, and if the revolutions of payment are weekly, as they are for poor people, then 1/52 of 40 million is enough money. But if the circles of payment are quarterly, as for rental payments, then 1/4 of the total is required. Since the economy is a mixture of the two velocities, he decided that 5½ million pounds would be enough to drive trade in that instance.[9] Since he did not analyze the effects of changing velocity on the price level or the expenditure level he cannot be credited with the quantity theory of money, but his clear exposition of the income velocity of money is an excellent example of his theoretical ability.

3    Petty emphasized labor in his theory of value, and was rewarded by the title of "the father of poiitical economy," granted to him many years later by Karl Marx. But unlike Marx he did not believe that labor was the sole source of value. One of his colorful statements was that labor is the father and active principle of wealth, as lands are the mother.[10] One of his preoccupations was to determine the "natural par" between a land measure of value and a labor measure of value. Since a ship, for example, is the creature of both land and labor, "we might express the value by either of them alone as well or better than by both and reduce one into the other as easily and certainly as we reduce pence into pounds" (*Works*, vol. I, p. 45). The par is the amount of land needed to produce the subsistence for a laborer. Cantillon in the next century developed this approach further. Indeed, Schumpeter believed that few sequences in the history of economic analysis are so important as Petty–Cantillon–Quesnay, as a result of the overall influence of Petty on Cantillon. We shall go into this in more detail later in this chapter.

The next transitional economist we shall look at is John Locke, who is probably better known as a philosopher and a political theorist. Locke had a classical education (i.e., Latin and Greek, and the Greek philosophers) at Oxford in the 1650s, and taught there until 1667. While teaching he studied medicine, and in 1667 he became the personal physician of Lord Ashley. This evolved into service as personal secretary and political assistant to Ashley, who was Chancellor of the Exchequer; and this connection led to an appointment as Secretary to the Council for Trade and Plantations. When his patron lost his position, Locke lost his also in 1674. He travelled about Europe, spending some years there in exile just before the crown was handed over to William and Mary in 1688. It was during this time he did his philosophical writing, publishing *Treatises of Civil Government* and *Essay Concerning Human Understanding*. In 1690, in connection with a controversy over whether the legal rate of interest should be reduced, he published *Some Considerations of the Consequences of the Lowering of Interest and Raising the Value of Money*. This book dealt not only with the rate of interest but also with recoinage: should coins which contained less than their face value in silver be called in, melted down, and reissued with full weight of silver in them? Debate on this issue continued during the 1690s, and Locke published more on this subject as the controversy went on.[11] Although Locke's economic writings are far from extensive, they were based on twenty years of practical experience with problems of trade and money, and on his years of study of Aristotle, the Scholastics, the natural law theorists, and the experimental sciences that began to flourish around 1650, and they had a lasting influence. In particular, he argued that economic affairs are governed by natural laws, and thereby set economics apart as a science with a body of fundamental laws.

Locke's position as a transitional figure appears in his discussion of the value of goods. Like philosophers since Aristotle, he distinguished between value in use ("the intrinsic natural worth of anything"), which was its fitness to contribute to our well-being, and value in exchange, which was the quantity of other goods that it can be exchanged for. Value in exchange was no naturally settled value but depended on the proportion of the "quantity to the vent." The quantity is the stock of goods supplied, the vent is the flow of goods purchased for consumption – actually a point on the demand curve, depending on the price, but although Locke talks about substitution between goods and the way vent reacts to price he does not give an unambiguous formulation of a demand curve. Rather his stress on the proportionality between quantity and vent reflects both Aristotle's use of proportionality and also the popularity of proportions in contemporary science – Boyle's inverse proportions between pressure and volume of a gas, for example.

One application of Locke's theory of value was in his approach to the quantity theory of money. Money is a special case. It originates in a social contract which enables men to agree on a commodity (actually gold and silver) to serve as a store of value. It is then also used for exchange. Once agreed on the contract should not be broken (which was the basis for his objection to reducing the weight of silver in a coin in the recoinage dispute). But money is a commodity and subject to the law of value of all commodities – the proportion between quantity and vent. If one assumes that money is demanded only as a medium of exchange, the vent for money is constant, and then all changes in the value of money result from changes in quantity. For example, if a country lost half its money and kept the same output, either half the goods would be unsold or the price level would fall to half the previous level.

Like Petty, Locke tried to estimate the amount of money needed to drive trade, and thereby calculated the velocity of money. As one historian comments,

> Should this appear truistical at present, it should be recognized that in the last decade of the seventeenth century, at the beginning of a tradition of scientific analysis of economic and monetary afairs, Locke's codification of ideas undoubtedly represented a major step forward ... It became important to the century that followed that, by stating the case in the way he did, Locke opened the way to the development of a theory of monetary balance and economic equilibrium.[12]

Another of Locke's concerns and contributions was the theory of the rate of interest. Late in the sixteenth century interest was accepted as an economic phenomenon and not a moral or church matter. During the seventeenth century there were periodic controversies over whether to lower the legal rate of interest. One of these controversies occurred around 1690, which was the occasion of Locke's writing on the subject.[13] There were some who argued that the prosperity of Holland was the result of the low interest rate in that country, and that therefore the government should lower the legal rate in England. Locke was opposed, on the ground that lenders would avoid the legal rate and in fact would charge the market rate. The market rate, like any price, depended on the proportion between vent and quantity. The vent or demand for money loans is derived from the merchants' needs for circulating capital and the manufacturers' needs for intermediate goods. The quantity or supply of money loans comes from savers, who must be compensated for the risk that their loans will not be repaid. The market rate might be either the natural rate, which would be set in a competitive market, or a monopoly rate if competition did not prevail. Locke's argument was that the legal rate should be the natural rate, both, as already mentioned, because only the natural rate would be effective, and because to the extent that loans were actually reduced because people would hoard rather than lend at the low legal rate, there would be a "stopping of the Current of money, which turns the Wheels of Trade."[14] Notice that the assumption that money is demanded only as a medium of exchange, used in developing the value of money, has been changed; if people hoard, money must be demanded as a store of value as well. This leads Locke into considering the relation of the value of money as determined by the rate of interest with the value of money as determined by the quantity theory of money. Keynes considered that Locke had not been able to make a synthesis between the two values; according to recent research, this was because Locke considered the two values of money to be separate things, with the rate of interest having an effect on prices only if changes in the rate affected the foreign trade sector, thereby changing the quantity of money in the country through imports or exports of specie.[15] Locke, in fact, like the mercantilists, wanted the trade balances to be favorable so that gold and silver would be imported; but he did not value the gold and silver for themselves, but because they would drive more trade.

Locke's final foray into economics was in connection with the great recoinage crisis of the 1690s. Before 1663 coins did not have a milled edge; this enabled people to clip a little silver off and pass the coin along. After 1663 there were thus two varieties of coin circulating, the milled-edge coins at full weight and the lightweight, clipped coins. Because the market price of silver bullion was higher than the mint price there was an incentive to melt down the full-bodied coins, so that few of them were actually circulating. The point at issue in the 1690s was whether to call in all the old coins and recoin them at full weight, in which case there would be only about half as many coins circulating as before, or whether to recoin with a lower silver content.[16] Locke objected to reducing the silver content of the coins. He claimed that gold and silver had come to be used as money by common consent, and that what was valued as money was a certain amount of metal. Only the quantity of silver in a coin is the measure of its value, not what it is called. Originally the pound sterling was actually a pound of silver. Locke argued that if you still call the coin a pound but put in only two-thirds of a pound of silver, people would value the coin at only two-thirds of its previous value. Recoinage at a lower weight would be defrauding the public in the first place and would not change the standard of value in the next place. Locke's view ultimately was accepted and the recoinage took place at full weight; the result was a reduction in the amount of money (i.e., coins of a given denomination) circulating, and a deflation – exactly as Locke's quantity theory of money would predict.[17] Locke's belief that the intrinsic value of a coin was the silver it contained, which value could not be changed, arose from his belief in the "Law of Nature." This doctrine, which comes down from Aristotle, is that if a thing is natural it is right; furthermore, Locke believed that the natural law could be known by deductive reasoning from the nature of God and man. Scientific laws as well as moral laws come from divine law and both are inevitable; the laws of economics are as inevitable as the laws of physics. A recent study puts it this way: "he left us something much more important than any one particular theory: he bequeathed to economics an attitude and a method of approach which did much to make our discipline into a science."[18]

Our third figure standing partly in the mercantilist and partly in the modern world was Bernard de Mandeville (1670–1733). He was born in Holland, educated there as a physician (a specialist in the "hypocondriack and hysterick passions"), and moved to London in the 1690s. In 1705 he published a little poem, *The Grumbling Hive: or Knaves turned Honest*. The beehive in this fable was a prosperous place as long as there were the usual criminals, cheating lawyers, doctors charging extortionate fees, politicians robbing the treasury, and lazy clergy. Also everyone displayed a love of luxury, prodigality, pride, and vanity, which kept the economy prosperous. But as soon as everyone turned honest the level of employment dropped drastically, and the change from vanity, etc., to sober respectability further cut the level of spending. Mandeville reissued the poem several times with a prose commentary which grew larger each time; the new issue in 1714 was called *The Fable of the Bees: or, Private Vices, Publick Benefits*.[19] It became the object of vigorous objection by clergymen, philosophers, and critics, and its defence of vice and luxury earned its author many enemies.

Its importance for economics was not its technical contributions – there were none – but its discussion of institutions. Mandeville argued that the economy would function properly only if a "skilful Politician" made sure that the pursuit of selfish interest advances the public welfare. This is to be done not by detailed intervention, but by establishing wise laws which channel selfish human nature away from harming fellow citizens into actions beneficial to them. Mandeville says these laws develop over time, in a trial and error process, and all he wants is for politicians to pay ample attention to selfishness and self-interest in framing them.[20] But if this is the message, why did his book create so many enemies for him?[21] It was because of Mandeville's style. He says, for example

> a considerable Portion of what the Prosperity of *London* and trade in general, and consequently the Honour, Strength, Safety, and all the worldly Interest of the Nation consist in, depends entirely on the Deceit and Vile Stratagems of Women; and that Humility, Content, Meekness, Obedience to reasonable Husbands, Frugality, and all the Virtues together, if they were possess'd of them in the most eminent Degree, could not possibly be a thousandth Part so serviceable ... "[22]

This is scarcely the way to make friends and influence people.

But if Mandeville's promotion of a legal and institutional framework that lets people function according to self-interest within that framework points in the direction of *laissez-faire*, in some of his recommendations Mandeville clung to mercantilist doctrines: he favored low wages, child labor, and government control of foreign trade. His reason for trade control was not to accumulate gold and silver in the tradition of high mercantilism, but to make sure that imports equalled exports, so that the country would not lose specie.

Adam Smith did not think Mandeville was so bad as did the shocked readers of Mandeville's day. Smith said that Mandeville's system "once made so much noise in the world, and which, though, perhaps, it never gave occasion to more vice than what would have been without it, at least taught that vice, which arose from other causes, to appear with more effrontery, and to avow the corruption of its motives with a profligate audaciousness which had never been heard of before."[23] On the other hand, he was not sure of Mandeville's economics, claiming in his lectures that spending £1,000 on luxury would reduce the stock of the country by that much, while if the £1,000 were invested the wealth of the nation would increase.[24] Obviously Smith was thinking of a fully employed economy, along the Say's Law approach he used in the *Wealth of Nations*.

While Bernard de Mandeville was penning his cynical remarks on private vices, across the Channel in Paris an Irishman named Richard Cantillon was gaining the banking experience that made him his fortune and gave him the background for his *Essai sur la Nature du Commerce en Général*. Many call him the "first economist" for his emphasis on the price system and its autonomous, self-adjusting features. As a banker, Cantillon was astute enough to profit from the Mississippi Bubble that wiped out so many others. This episode is important enough to merit a brief description. John Law (1671–1729), a Scot, had studied banking and proposed banking schemes in France, Edinburgh, and Italy; his banks were to issue paper money against bank stock, East India Company Stock, and government bonds. Oddly enough, he considered all these stocks and bonds to be part of the money supply. Eventually, in 1716, he got a bank charter in Paris. At first the bank was conservatively managed. Then Law formed a company to take over the management of the colony of Louisiana. This company acquired the French tobacco monopoly, the Senegalese Company, the French East India Company, the China Company, the Africa Company, the right to run the mints, and the right to collect taxes on behalf of the government. All this with its vast potential for profits led to a speculative boom in the Mississippi Company stock. But when the speculative fever began to ebb, Law pegged the price of the Company stock by having his bank buy it with newly issued bank notes. The result was a disastrous inflation; his notes lost favor, and eventually both the bank and the Mississippi Company went bankrupt. But long before that Richard Cantillon had bought stock in the Company cheaply and had sold out near the peak. Cantillon now quit banking and travelled in Europe until 1734, when he moved to London. He worked on his book between 1730 and 1734, but in 1734 he was murdered by his discharged cook, who set the house on fire, destroying many of Cantillon's manuscripts. His book was not published until 1755, but a man with the magnificent name of Malachy Postlethwayt used a great deal of it in his *Universal Dictionary of Trade and Commerce* (1751–5). Adam Smith referred to Cantillon in Book I, chapter VIII of the *Wealth of Nations*, and the Physiocrats were influenced by him. But the book essentially dropped out of sight until it was accidentally rediscovered by William Stanley Jevons, who wrote an enthusiastic article entitled "Richard Cantillon and the Nationality of Political Economy" in 1881.[25]

Cantillon, like his fellow financier-economist David Ricardo, wrote a brisk book, quite different from the leisurely style of Adam Smith or the bloated style of Mandeville. He made contributions to three fields in particular: population theory, price theory, and monetary theory. He had a Malthusian population theory; his comment that "Men multiply like Mice in a Barn if they have unlimited Means of Subsistence" is surely one of the memorable phrases of economics. It was his thesis that the great landed proprietors determined the size of the population by their habits of consumption and spending. If the proprietors lived in cities, spent largely on luxury and ornament, and required the produce of the land to support

the job for the statesman, for the economy was not likely to maintain its due proportions naturally.

One application of this idea was Steuart's analysis of the progress of the economy in the exchange stage. There were three sub-stages: infant, foreign trade, and inland trade. The infants were the less-developed countries, who needed to promote their manufactures; once they were established, they could trade with other economies, with the statesman holding down their price levels so that their exports could continue. But because people liked luxury it was hard to keep prices down, and when they got out of line, markets would be lost and the home economy would have to be protected from imports to keep full employment. This simple outline was overlain with historical and contemporary examples, with detailed analyses of what could go wrong at each stage and what the statesman should do. For example, there might not be enough money to sustain growth. This led to a long detailed statement of monetary dynamics, the advantages of paper money and credit, the role of money as a unit of account and as a means of payment, and the relation of money to economic activity.[28]

However, this emphasis on intervention[29] was out of tune with subsequently developing economics, while Smith's "invisible hand" was in tune. Steuart's book also lacked the analytical neatness of the organization of the *Wealth of Nations*, even though it did have a scientific approach in that he used principles common to each part of the economy.

## Notes

1 William Letwin, *The Origins of Scientific Economics* (Garden City, NY, 1964) is a very readable book contrasting the "old style" and the "new style."
2 Robert L. Heilbroner, *The Worldly Philosophers*, 4th edn (New York, 1972), p. 17.
3 Petty's life is covered by Lord Edmond Fitzmaurice, *The Life of Sir William Petty* (London, 1895), and E. Straus, *Sir William Petty: Portrait of a Genius* (Glencoe, Ill., 1954).
4 C. H. Hull (ed.), *The Economic Writings of Sir William Petty* vol. 2, (Cambridge, 1899), p. 533. Hereafter cited as *Writings*.
5 See Letwin, *Scientific Economics*, pp. 141ff, for a critique of Petty's cavalier way with numbers.
6 Joseph Schumpeter, *History of Economic Analysis* (New York, 1954), p. 212.
7 Letwin, *Scientific Economics*, p. 154.
8 Petty, *Writings*, vol. II, p. 473.
9 Petty, "Verbum Sapienti," in *Writings*, vol. I, pp. 112–13.
10 "Treatise of Taxes", *Works*, vol. I, p. 68.
11 For details on Locke's life, see the chapter on Locke in Letwin, *Scientific Economics*, and Karen I. Vaughn, *John Locke, Economist and Social Scientist* (Chicago, 1980).

12 Douglas Vickers, *Studies in the Theory of Money 1690–1776* (Philadelphia, 1959), p. 60.
13 Marian Bowley, *Studies in the History of Economic Theory before 1870* (London, 1973), has a chapter on "English Theories of Interest in the 17th Century Reconsidered" that gives a survey of the development of the ideas.
14 Ibid., p. 48.
15 Vaughn, *John Locke*, pp. 65–6.
16 Joyce Appleby, *Economic Thought and Ideology in Seventeenth-Century England* (Princeton, NJ, 1978), has an excellent chapter on the crises over money.
17 Sir Isaac Newton, the great physicist, was Master of the Mint during the recoinage, from 1696 to 1727. A study of his papers dealing with his duties concluded that "the truth is that Newton never realized, even with his acute analytical mind, the limitations and implications of Gresham's law" (G. Findlay Shirras and J. H. Craig, "Sir Isaac Newton and the Currency," *Economic Journal*, 1945, pp. 127–41). Gresham's Law is that bad money drives out good (bad money is light-weight; good is full-bodied). Sir Thomas Gresham wrote during Elizabethan times; Raymond de Roover, *Gresham on Foreign Exchange* (Cambridge, Mass., 1949) is the best source on Gresham.
18 Vaughn, *John Locke*, p. 137.
19 The standard modern edition, edited by F. B. Kaye, was published by Oxford University Press in 1924. Of the nearly 900 pages in this edition, only twenty are the original poem.
20 See Nathan Rosenberg, "Mandeville and Laissez-Faire," *Journal of the History of Ideas*, 1963, pp. 183–96, and A. F. Chalk, "Mandeville's Fable of the Bees: A Reappraisal," *Southern Economic Journal*, 1966, pp. 1–16.
21 Philip Harth, in his introduction to the Penguin edition of *The Fable of the Bees* (Hammondsworth, England, 1970), gives a good discussion of the controversy the book aroused.
22 *Fable of the Bees* vol. I, (Oxford, 1924), p. 228.
23 Adam Smith, *Theory of Moral Sentiments* (Oxford, 1976), p. 313.
24 Adam Smith, *Lectures on Jurisprudence* (Oxford, 1978), pp. 393–4. By the way, the seal of the Royal Economic Society displays a large honey bee in its center. Its founders must have thought the *Fable of the Bees* quite important.
25 This article is reprinted in Richard Cantillon, *Essai sur la Nature du Commerce en Général*, edited and translated by Henry Higgs (London, 1931). It is an interesting article because of its enthusiasm, but much of the information in it had to be corrected by later writers. See Higg's article "The Life and Work of Richard Cantillon," in Cantillon, *Essai*, pp. 363–89, and J. J. Spengler, "Richard Cantillon: First of the Moderns," *Journal of Political Economy*, 1954, pp. 281–95, 406–24. On John Law, see E. J. Hamilton's article in the *International Encyclopedia of the Social Sciences*, vol. 9 (New York, 1968).
26 Professor Vickers argues that Cantillon did not notice, or at least did not describe, the possible inconsistency between the microeconomic adjustment in one market and macroeconomic adjustment; in particular, he did not allow for possible changes in "intrinsic values" as the level of macroeconomic activity changed (Vickers, *Theory of Money*, p. 213). But in spite of this he agrees that Cantillon "combines in a highly developed form many of the propositions which had emerged in the earlier literature and anticipates also some of the best

theoretical traditions which developed during the two hundred years following its publication" (ibid., p. 185). In a similar vein, Michael Bordo argues that Cantillon has many affinities with modern monetarists, including his emphasis on the quantity theory of money, the dynamic path of the return to equilibrium, his emphasis on a general equilibrium, and his emphasis on the role of the quantity of money in determing the state of the balance of payments and the exchange rate. See Bordo, "Some Aspects of the Monetary Economics of Richard Cantillon," *Journal of Monetary Economics*, August, 1983.

27 The edition published by the Scottish Economic Society (Edinburgh, 1966), edited and introduced by Andrew S. Skinner, is recommended; Skinner provides a detailed biography as well as an analysis of the book.

28 Vickers, *Theory of Money*, has a long and detailed chapter on Steuart's theory of money. He regards Steuart as having summed up the work of the authors from Petty and Locke on down.

29 The emphasis on intervention and full employment classifies Steuart as one of the precursors of John Maynard Keynes in the judgement of S. R. Sen, *The Economics of Sir James Steuart* (Cambridge, Mass., 1957).

# 4

# The Physiocrats

Adam Smith devoted eight chapters of the *Wealth of Nations* to mercantilism but only one to the Physiocrats. His explanation for this disparity was that although Physiocratic thinking was the product of men of great learning and ingenuity, it contained errors that were not worth examining at great length since Physiocracy probably would never do any harm anywhere in the world. Two hundred years later, interest in Physiocracy flourishes considerably higher than the tepid praise of Adam Smith would suggest. It was the first school of economics, with a recognized leader and disciples, complete with the first journal of economics (the *Journal Oeconomique*). Its famous model of the circular flow of goods and money through the economy, the *Tableau Économique*, was the basis for Wassily Leontief's Nobel prize-winning concept, the input–output table.[1] Earlier, Karl Marx had been excited by the *Tableau*, calling it "incontestably the most brilliant idea of which political economy had hitherto been guilty." He developed his own scheme of capitalist reproduction from it.[2]

Physiocracy means literally something like "doctrine of natural order," and reflects the idea of the Physiocrats that their theories were innate, "evident principles of the most perfect constitution of society," which "manifest themselves, of themselves, to man," as du Pont de Nemours said.[3] Alternatively, they referred to themselves as *les économistes*. The man who developed these self-evident ideas was a Frenchman, François Quesnay, a surgeon who took up economics in the 1750s. Quesnay's self-evident code of justice included private property, freedom of contract, and freedom of trade. (The Physiocrats opposed mercantilism and originated the slogan "*Laissez faire, laissez passer,*" i.e., "let them do it.") In economics his basic ideas were that agriculture is the crucial sector of the economy because it produces a net surplus over the cost of production whereas industry does not. This surplus must be circulated through the economy by the expenditure of the landlords who get the surplus from the farmers as rent. Finally, the health of agriculture and hence of the whole economy depends on employing sufficient long- and short-term capital in farming, as well as removing mercantilistic restrictions on farming and subsidies to manufacturing.

Quesnay, who was said by Schumpeter to belong to the select circle of the four most important economists of all time, spent his early years as a surgeon. It has been suggested that his medical experience gave him the idea of the circular flow of economic life, analogous to the flow of blood in the body. Indeed, Quesnay was an expert on the circulation of the blood. He was involved in a controversy with a physician who claimed that the flow of blood away from a wound was greater than the flow toward it. One conclusion from this hypothesis was that an inflammation in the head should be treated by opening a vein in the foot, since blood would rush away from the foot toward the head, where it was needed. Quesnay, properly dubious, investigated the hypothesis by constructing a tin model of the circulatory system and making a hole in it. He demonstrated that the flows to and from the wound were equal, and hence that the vein should be opened in the head.[4] His medical reputation became so high that eventually he was appointed to the exalted post of physician to the King's mistress, Madame de Pompadour, and took up residence in Versailles. He was not a typical member of the court, perhaps because he was sixty-two years old; Marmontel describes Quesnay formulating his axioms and calculating the *produit net* of agriculture, as indifferent to the frivolity and intrigue of the court as if he had been a hundred leagues away.[5]

Quesnay's concern with agriculture, it has been suggested, came from his rural background; but wherever it arose, it was well-founded. French agriculture was partly carried on by peasants whose plots were very small and who carried a heavy burden of taxation, and partly by large landlords (nobles and clergy) who had no interest in emulating the progressive British agriculture but who continued the old ways of farming. Agriculture lacked capital and the prospect for accumulating capital was very dim, given the propensity of the court to war and to live luxuriously. The tax system was a mixture of direct taxes from which the nobles and the church were exempt and indirect taxes on items such as salt, beverages, and imports. These taxes and the use of forced labor to built roads (the *corvée*) were a heavy burden on the rural sector.

Quesnay began his study of agricultural economics with a series of institutional and statistical studies which were published in the *Encyclopédie*, the great expression of eighteenth-century French enlightened thought. Here he gave detailed data about the great increase in returns made possible when agriculture had enough capital to work with – a 100 percent return on circulating capital when advanced techniques were used compared to only 36 percent return in peasant farming.[6] On the other hand, competition would keep profits in industry equal to the wages of management, with a zero return on capital. This is the origin of the famous Physiocratic notion that industry and commerce are sterile (or unproductive) while agriculture produces a net surplus. Because of the Physiocratic concern with agriculture it is tempting to think of this surplus as Ricardian land rent, but it is really a return to capital. It is, however, paid to the landowners, since farm labor earns only subsistence wages. (The Physiocratic distinction between productive and unproductive activity was taken over and modified by the classical economists; in their hands productive labor became labor which produced something tangible, be it agricultural or industrial, while unproductive labor produced only services. Since Adam Smith picked up this idea from the Physiocrats, some of whom he met while earning his pay as the young Duke of Buccleuch's tutor on the grand tour of Europe, Professor Stigler once quipped that this shows there is no such thing as a free trip to Paris.)

The next cornerstone of Physiocratic doctrine is that the spending of the surplus by the landlords generates the circulation of demand in the economy. Quesnay probably got the idea from Richard Cantillon; chapter XII of Cantillon's *Essai sur la Nature du Commerce* is entitled "All Classes and Individuals in a State Subsist or are Enriched at the Expense of the Proprietors of Land," and chapter XV develops the theme that "The Increase and Decrease of the Number of People in a State Chiefly Depend on the Taste, the Fashions, and Modes of Living of the Proprietors of Land." (Another physician, Bernard de Mandeville, had earlier insisted that one type of spending was the engine which drove the economy in his *Fable of the Bees* (1714), but he identified the role of luxury spending in general rather than the spending of landlords in particular as crucial.) Quesnay developed the theory much more fully than Cantillon had, turning it into a formal model which he set out in his *Tableau Économique*.[7] The *Tableau* went through several versions, one of which was lost and not rediscovered until 1965 when it turned up in family papers of the Du Pont family in Delaware.[8] (One of Quesnay's disciples was Pierre S. Du Pont de Nemours, who eventually wound up in the United States, a penniless refugee of the French Revolution, and who founded the great Du Pont chemical company.) The versions are actually rather similar; a schematic drawing is presented in figure 4.1.

Figure 4.1 shows the zig-zag version of the *Tableau*, tracing out the transactions among the three sectors into which Quesnay divided the economy. (The l. following the numbers is the abbreviation for livres, the French monetary unit of that day.) The numbers are illustrative rather than being actual data; they reflect Quesnay's belief about the propensities to spend and the ratios among types of spending in the economy which would be observed if France made use of the best available techniques and social organization. The *Tableau* begins by listing the "annual advances" required in agriculture and industry; these advances are the short-term investment in seeding and cultivation of the farms and in the provision of an inventory of raw material for industry. (Quesnay also recognized the importance of investment in fixed capital such as machines, animals, buildings, clearing, and so on, but did not list it in the *Tableau*.) The middle column refers to the proprietors of land. They receive 2,000 livres as rent (called "annual revenue" in the *Tableau*) from last year's produc-

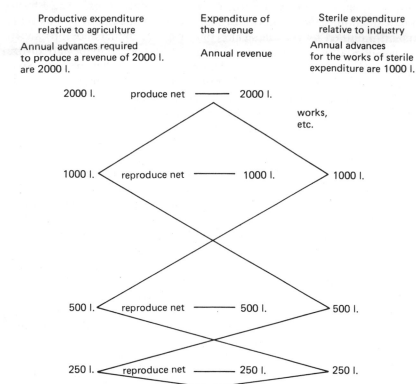

**Figure 4.1**

tion. Their spending of this income initiates the flow of spending in the economy. It is assumed that they spend half their income on agricultural products, half on industrial products. The other classes have the same propensities to consume. Thus, the farmers spend 500 livres of the money they receive from landlords on industrial products, and 500 on farm goods (the latter amount, like other intrasectional flows, is not explicitly shown). Then the sterile or industrial sector respends half of the 500 livres it has just received from the farmers in purchasing agricultural goods. As shown in the diagram, the flows continue back and forth through the economy, falling by one-half each time. Assuming that the time consumed by each round trip through the economy is short enough that the amount involved in a given transaction becomes negligibly small by the end of the year, the total earned by the industrial sector in that year will be 2,000 livres; 1,000 livres of this will be spent on industrial products during the year and 1,000 livres will be used to reconstitute the annual advances so that industrial production can continue next year. The farm sector also receives 2,000 livres from the rest of the economy during the year but because of the surplus produced by agriculture 2,000 livres is generated in rent. At the end of the year the 2,000 livres rent is paid to the landlords, and the farmers are left with 2,000 livres of seed, food, etc., to serve as annual advances for the coming year. The *Tableau*, it will be observed, does not prove that a net surplus is generated in farming; it simply assumes that it is.[9]

Quesnay used the *Tableau Économique* to demonstrate the effects of various events and policies on the economy. He showed that a change in the direction of spending by the proprietory class from agriculture to industrial products reduced net revenue in subsequent years and hence reduced the prosperity of everyone. He showed how increased trade coming from a reduction of trade restrictions would raise farm prices and hence increase the net revenue and the prosperity of all classes. And he argued that taxes on either the productive or the sterile class would decrease the annual advances and hence reduce the production in following years; the Physiocrats preferred a "single tax" on rent in order to relieve farmers of the tax burden which was inhibiting the sort of investment needed to modernize French agriculture.

Two of the major contributions of the Physiocrats are prominently displayed in the *Tableau*: the circular flow of income and the idea that capital is a series of advances. The advances theory of capital became one of the most fervently held concepts of the classical economists, as exemplified in their theory of the wages fund. One enthusiastic commentator went so far as to call Quesnay's capital concept "the single greatest analytical contribution made in the history of economic thought."[10]

The zig-zag formulation of the *Tableau* illustrates the circular flow of income, but it is not as good a foundation for analysis as the Leontief-type input–output table which may be derived from it. The input–output table shows immediately the interdependence of the sectors of the economy, with the amounts purchased by each sector from the others entered as a total rather than having to be calculated as a sum of transactions. Table 4.1 sets up the Quesnay transactions in input–output form; the columns show where each sector makes its purchases, while the entries across the rows show where each sector sells its output. For example, landlords sell their output (rental services) only to farmers. The entries for the landlords' purchases, 1,000 livres each from agriculture and industry, and the farmers' purchases of 1,000 livres from the artisans are immediately obvious from the zig-zag form of the *Tableau*. The farmers' use of 2,000 livres of their own output is the annual advances listed in the first column of the *Tableau*, and the artisans' purchases of 2,000 livres from the farmers are composed of 1,000 livres of raw material for annual advances and the

**Table 4.1**   The Physiocratic input–output table

|               |           | Inputs (purchases) | | | |
|---------------|-----------|---------|-----------|----------|-------|
|               |           | Farmers | Landlords | Artisans | Total |
|               | Farmers   | 2,000   | 1,000     | 2,000    | 5,000 |
| Output (sales)| Landlords | 2,000   | 0         | 0        | 2,000 |
|               | Artisans  | 1,000   | 1,000     | 0        | 2,000 |
|               | Total     | 5,000   | 2,000     | 2,000    | 9,000 |

All quantities are in livres.

1,000 livres of food purchases shown in the zig-zag. Intra-industry flows, apart from the farmers' annual advances which are an input rather than a final consumption item, are not shown. The Physiocratic vision of the interdependence of the economy is indeed brought out in a striking way when it is presented in the input–output form.[11]

One offshoot of the Physiocratic emphasis on the flow of demand among sectors of the economy was the mark it left on the debates centering around Say's Law of Markets. This proposition and the debates about it were a prominent part of early nineteenth-century classical economics. There was a very spirited controversy over whether there could ever be a general glut (i.e., excessive aggregate supply in the economy as a whole as opposed to excessive supply in a single market, which everybody agreed was possible). Physiocrat Mercier de la Rivière had stated very clearly that one must be a seller in order to be a buyer, which is close to the Say's Law proposition that supply creates its own demand. Further, he went on, aggregate equilibrium can be upset only accidentally.[12] Also the basic Physiocratic idea that money served only to circulate goods was in the spirit of Say's Law. But Physiocratic tenets were used also by the opponents of Jean-Baptiste Say and his co-originator of Say's Law, James Mill. If spending by the landlords is inadequate, said William Spence, national income will fall (in other words, there will be a general glut of the sort denied by the Say–Mill faction). This was generalized by Lord Lauderdale into an insistence on the importance of consumption generally and the danger of parsimony – the savings might not be invested. All this will be discussed in detail later; the point to notice here is that the Physiocrats were the source of ideas on both sides of this important economic controversy.

Physiocracy began to decline in the 1770s; Quesnay dropped economics and began writing on mathematics (maintaining his interest in circular flows by writing, naturally enough, on the mathematics of the circle), and critics began rising on all sides. The last hurrah proved to be the appointment of Anne Robert Jacques Turgot, a man with considerable sympathy with the Physiocrats, as minister of finance in 1774. Turgot had previously been a distinguished provincial administrator, but he was unable to carry out his Physiocratic reform program successfully when he got to Paris. He was allowed to start a number of reforms simultaneously:

he removed controls on the internal grain trade, abolished the guilds, substituted a tax for the *corvée*, and tried to control the spending of Louis XVI. Each of these actions aroused much opposition, and he was dismissed in 1776. His reforms – necessary as they were – were overturned. But his opposition to government controls made him a hero to a group of *laissez-faire*, free-trade French economists in the middle of the nineteenth century who, reacting to socialist experiments of the revolution of 1848, drew on many of Turgot's papers for justification of their position. For example, Turgot advanced a very French argument against protection by tariffs:

> To persist in opposing . . . [the advantages of free trade] from a narrowminded political viewpoint which thinks it is possible to grow everything at home, would be to act just like the proprietors of Brie who thought themselves thrifty by drinking bad wine from their own vineyards, which really cost them more in the sacrifice of land suitable for good wheat than they would have paid for the best Burgundy, which they could have bought from the proceeds of their wheat.[13]

At the same time as he was playing his role in the history of France, Turgot also contributed to the development of economics. His most famous book is *Réflexions sur la Formation et la Distribution des Richesses* (1770), a guide to economics written for the benefit of two Chinese students who were supposed to keep their French patrons informed about developments in China after they returned home.[14] The *Reflections* are a generalization of Quesnay's ideas. Turgot added a class of capitalist entrepreneurs to Quesnay's division of society into farmers, landlords, and artisans. He pointed out the necessity of advances not only to agriculture but also to large-scale manufacturing, which Quesnay had ignored, and the need for a return to capital which covered trouble and risk. Like the Physiocrats generally, he favored placing taxes only on land rent, but for a different reason: rather than arguing that rent is the only "disposable" or surplus form of income, he said that a tax which reduced the net rate of interest below the market rate would be passed on to borrowers. The higher rate to borrowers would reduce the demand for capital; since capital is essential for wealth, it is unreasonable to interfere with it. In a sense it is the same argument, but Turgot's version is more sophisticated.

Although the busy public administrator drew on and generalized ideas of the Physiocrats, he contributed sufficient new and important elements of his own to warrant from Schumpeter the title of "one of the greatest scientific economists of all times." His strong points as a theorist were his analysis of interest and his work on diminishing returns. Turgot's interest theory was that the rate of interest did not depend on the quantity of money (a favorite dictum of earlier economists such as John Locke), but upon the demand of borrowers and the supply of accumulated savings. In addition, he showed how the returns in such different investment outlets as land, industry, and portfolio loans come into an equilibrium reflecting the amount of risk and trouble; if returns in one investment outlet exceed the risk premium, capital is attracted to it and the returns fall. This is an excellent example of competitive market theory applied to the capital market. It is regarded as Turgot's major original work, and had considerable influence on the late nineteenth-century capital theorist Eugen Böhm-Bawerk.[15] His remarks on diminishing returns were tossed off in an evaluation of a prize essay on indirect taxes in a contest of which he was a judge. In his comments on the essay he began with a situation where annual advances bring a 25 percent return; then says "It is more than probable that if the advances were increased by degrees from this point up to that at which they would bring in nothing, each increment would be less and less fruitful."[16] Turgot thus at one stroke formulated both incremental analysis and the law of diminishing returns. But his formulation did not take hold; later economists had to rediscover it, and indeed, Turgot did not use it in his own later work.

The French government made a gesture toward applying Physiocratic principles, abortive though it proved to be; but they got considerably further than Russia (which at that time was heavily influenced by France), possibly because the wrong Physiocrat was sent to help Catherine the Great at her invitation. Mercier de la Rivière, the *économiste* in question, was more interested in the proposition that Physiocracy was the expression of natural laws than he was in the details of Physiocratic theory or policy. His interview with Catherine the Great, it is reported, went like this:

"Sir, can you tell me the best way to govern the state well?"

"There is only one way, Madame, namely to be just, that is, maintain order and enforce the laws."

"But on what basis should the laws of a kingdom rest?"

"On one only, Madame, on the nature of things and men."

"Certainly, but if one wants to give laws to a people, what rules should one follow?"

"Madame, to make laws is a task which God has reserved for Himself. How can man be considered competent to impose laws on beings of whom he has no or only imperfect knowledge? And by what right would he impose laws on beings whom God has not placed in his hands?"

"To what then do you reduce the science of government?"

"To the study of the laws which God has so evidently engraven in human society when He created man. To seek to go beyond this would be a great calamity and a destructive undertaking."

"Sir, it has been a great pleasure to listen to you, and I wish you good day."[17]

## Notes

1 Wassily Leontief, *The Structure of American Economy 1919–39* (New York, 1941), p. 9.

2 Paul M. Sweezy, *The Theory of Capitalist Development* (New York, 1968), appendix A by Shigeto Tsuru, is a very clear exposition of the relation of Marx's scheme to the *Tableau*.

3  T. P. Neill, "The Physiocrats' Concept of Economics," *Quarterly Journal of Economics*, 1949, is a good source for the natural order theories of the Physiocrats.

4  See V. Foley, "An Origin of the *Tableau Économique*," *History of Political Economy (HOPE)*, 1973, pp. 121–50.

5  Marmontel, *Memoires*, livre cinquième (*Oeuvres Complètes*, Paris, 1818), p. 292.

6  W. A. Eltis, "François Quesnay: A Reinterpretation," *Oxford Economic Papers*, 1975, pp. 167–200 and 327–51. This essay is highly recommended for a short, careful introduction to Physiocracy. A. L. Miller, "Quesnay's Theory of Growth: A Comment," *Oxford Economic Papers*, 1978, adds some detail to Eltis's paper. For a longer modern study, Ronald L. Meek, *The Economics of Physiocracy* (London, 1962) is the best reference.

7  An interesting example of changing fashions in the history of economic thought is Sir Alexander Gray's comment, made as recently as 1931, that the *Tableau* had better be reduced to an embarrassed footnote, since he doubted that it would ever be more than a vast mystification. (*The Development of Economic Doctrine*, London, 1931, p. 106). This attitude is to be contrasted with the sizable contemporary interest which comes, says Meek, from the revived attention of economists to aggregative and general equilibrium analysis (*Economics of Physiocracy*, p. 266). Elizabeth Fox-Genovese, a historian rather than an economist, believes that the current popularity of the *Tableau* is too technical; by disregarding the political and ideological preconceptions of the Physiocrats the meaning of the *Tableau* is distorted, she asserts. See her book, *The Origins of Physiocracy* (Ithaca, NY, 1976). Her book is written from a Marxist perspective.

8  See Marguerite Kuczynski and Ronald L. Meek, *Quesnay's Tableau Économique* (London, 1972).

9  Quesnay intended the *Tableau* to be a visual interpretation of his conception of essential economic relationships. As a technical economic device, however, Paul A. Samuelson terms the zig-zags a chimera. He thinks they are not useful in illustrating a dynamic sequence of spending, although they can be given an interpretation as showing all the past years' inputs which have contributed to this year's output. Quesnay himself, of course, had no such notion. See Samuelson, "Quesnay's '*Tableau Économique*' as a Theorist Would Formulate it Today," in Ian Bradley and Michael Howard (eds), *Classical and Marxian Political Economy* (New York, 1982), pp. 60–1.

10  Robert V. Eagley, *The Structure of Classical Economic Theory* (New York, 1974), p. 20.

11  The input–output table can be converted into a tool to analyze the effects on the economy of such things as a change in the mix between agricultural and industrial goods in total national output if the standard Leontief assumptions are made. These included fixed output coefficients (e.g., farmers need 0.2 livres' worth of industrial input for each livre of agricultural output, and this is fixed for relevant ranges of farm output), and the assumption that each sector spends its income in the period in which it is received. The first presentation of the *Tableau* as an input–output table was Almarin Philips, "The *Tableau Économique* as a Simple Leontief Model," *Quarterly Journal of Economics*,

1955, pp. 137–44. An expanded version, a 9 × 9 rather than a 3 × 3 table, was concocted by T. Barna, "Quesnay's *Tableau* in Modern Guise," *Economic Journal*, 1975, pp. 485–96, with further dynamic interpretation in T. Barna, "Quesnay's Model of Economic Development," *European Economic Review*, 1976, pp. 315–8.

There is a technical debate about the best form of a Quesnay input–output table. Table 4.1 shows a closed-end system; there is no input provided from outside the system or output disposed of outside it. Professor Samuelson, however, prefers an open-ended system, where land is treated as a primary input and the landlords' consumption is not an input into the system but is an item dictated by exogenous tastes. Samuelson, "Quesnay's '*Tableau Économique*'."

12 See the excellent presentation by Thomas Sowell in *Classical Economics Reconsidered* (Princeton, NJ, 1974), pp. 35ff. A more difficult reading is Joseph J. Spengler, "The Physiocrats and Say's Law of Markets," *Journal of Political Economy*, 1945, pp. 193–211 and 317–47.

13 Peter Groenewegen, "Turgot's Place in the History of Economic Thought: A Bicentenary Estimate," *HOPE*, 1983, p. 91.

14 W. J. Ashley's translation of the book is available in a recent reprint by Augustus M. Kelley, and there is a new translation by Ronald L. Meek, *Turgot on Progress, Sociology, and Economics* (New York, 1973). Turgot's other writings on economics are discussed in P. D. Groenewegen, "A Reappraisal of Turgot's Theory of Value, Exchange, and Price Determination," *HOPE*, 1970, pp. 177–96 and most of them are translated in P. D. Groenewegen, *The Economics of A. R. J. Turgot* (The Hague, 1977).

15 This influence, and a controversy involving such major figures as Marshall, Wicksell, and Cassel as well as Böhm-Bawerk, are explained in Groenewegen, "Turgot's Place." The controversy was over the correctness of Böhm-Bawerk's interpretation of Turgot.

16 See Edwin Cannan, *A History of the Theories of Production and Distribution in English Political Economy from 1776 to 1848* (London, 1917), p. 116.

17 The story is reported in H. W. Speigel, *The Growth of Economic Thought*, revised edn (Durham, NC, 1983), p. 198. The Physiocrats' use of maxims led Lionel Robbins, one of the deans of the history of economic thought, to refer to Quesnay as a "very gnomic commentator," and Voltaire to write one of the classic satires of economics in "The Man of Forty Crowns."

# 5
# Adam Smith

It was Joseph Schumpeter's contention that Adam Smith stood at the confluence of two streams of thought, that of the philosophers (including the Scholastics) on the one hand, and that of practical men of affairs, government administrators and their teachers on the other. Smith's *Wealth of Nations* (1776), says Schumpeter, was a synthesis and organization of the material he derived from these streams, contributing nothing that was analytically new. Schumpeter's rather ungenerous view of Smith's merits is not typical, however; it is more usual to think of him as George Stigler does: "he was as great an economist as has ever lived."[1]

Adam Smith lived – and enjoyed – the life of a scholar. Born in 1723 (on June 5, so that he shares John Maynard Keynes's birthday) in Kirkaldy, Scotland, he was raised by his widowed mother. When he was only fourteen years old he went to Glasgow University, where he stayed for three years, and then went on to Oxford for six years on a scholarship to prepare for the ministry. Oxford was an educational disaster, for "the greater part of the public professors have, for these many years, given up altogether even the pretence of teaching."[2] Smith was not alone in his criticism of Oxford; Edward Gibbon in 1752 said of the dons that "From the toil of reading, or thinking, or writing, they had absolved their conscience. . . . Their dull and deep potations excused the brisk intemperance of youth."[3] Unlike the dons, Smith read widely, and when he returned home he organized and presented a series of lectures on rhetoric and *belles lettres* in Edinburgh, for which the public paid a fee. These lectures were so successful that he was appointed to the Chair of Logic at Glasgow University in 1751, and promoted to Professor of Moral Philosophy in 1752. He was a successful professor, and his first major publication, *The Theory of Moral Sentiments*, came in 1759.

This book, which gave Smith a great reputation, is concerned with the nature of man in society: motives for behavior, and the rules of ethics and of justice. The main hypothesis is "sympathy." People are born with capacities both for self-love and for fellow feeling. They are able to put themselves in another's place, to imagine his or her circumstances and feelings, and to judge whether a response to particular circumstances is proper or not. They are also able to imagine how their own actions appear to an outside spectator, and because they desire the approval of others, they tailor their actions to what they believe the "impartial spectator" would approve of. Because man also has an inborn selfish motive, however, the desire for approval may not be strong enough to prevent actions which harm others. The formation of general rules of morality, based on long experience of the observation of proper behavior, and of rules of justice with legal sanctions prevent disruptive behavior and allow man to form a society.[4] Because *The Theory of Moral Sentiments* emphasized sympathy and the later *Wealth of Nations* emphasized selfishness ("It is not from the benevolence of the butcher, the brewer, or the baker, that we expect our dinner, but from their regard to their own interest"), there grew up a considerable literature about what German scholars called "das Adam Smith-problem": was there a conflict between the two books? Had Smith changed his mind? Careful recent scholarship holds that because the *Wealth of Nations* is narrower in scope and is largely about economic activity, it concentrates on self-interest but does not therefore rule out sympathy.[5]

*The Theory of Moral Sentiments* made such a splash that Charles Townshend (famous for imposing the tea tax that led to the Boston Tea Party) arranged for Smith to supervise his young stepson, the Duke of Buccleuch, on a grand tour of France, as mentioned in chapter 4. Smith was to tutor the Duke in return not only for a stipend during the tour but also for a lifetime pension thereafter. They were in France for two years, and although they stayed for a while in Paris, where Smith met some of the Physiocrats, most of the time was spent in Toulouse. As the social life there was not especially active, Smith had time to begin writing the *Wealth of Nations*. Economics had long been one of his many interests (others were history, law, government, language, the fine arts, astronomy, ancient logic, and metaphysics), and the subject was covered in his lectures on Moral Philosophy at Glasgow University. (Two copies of students' notes have survived and are published in the Glasgow Edition of *Lectures on Jurisprudence*.) On his return to Scotland in 1766, Smith went to ground in Kirkaldy for ten years completing the *Wealth of Nations*, which he finally published in 1776. It became, according to Schumpeter, "the most successful not only of all books on economics but, with the possible exception of Darwin's *Origin of Species*, of all scientific books that have appeared to this day."[6]

The balance of his life Smith spent not as a scholar but as a public servant, being appointed (oddly enough for a man who had devoted hundreds of pages to attacking restrictions on trade) Commissioner of the Customs and Salt Duties in Scotland. Although Schumpeter called the job a quasi-sinecure, it must have interfered with his project to "give an account of the general principles of law and government, and of the different revolutions which they had undergone in the different ages and periods of society; not only in what concerns justice, but in what concerns police, revenue, and arms, and whatever else is the object of law," as he wrote in the advertisement to the sixth edition of *The Theory of Moral Sentiments* (1790). Smith's death in 1790 left this project uncompleted.

The *Wealth of Nations* comprises 903 pages of leisurely writing consisting of, in the words of the complete title, an inquiry into the nature and causes of the wealth of nations. In the process Smith covers an immense amount of ground: theoretical analysis, reviewed below; history; current problems and affairs. The index notes such subjects as "Abassides, opulence of Saracen empire under"; "Cash accounts at Scotch banks explained"; "*Corvée*, a principal instrument of tyranny"; "Ireland, supplies strong porters and beautiful prostitutes, fed on potatoes, to London." It is not a stripped-down book of rigorous analysis such as David Ricardo later wrote. Smith believed in piling illustration upon illustration.[7] Not only his penchant for historical illustration but also his belief that the institutional structure had to be right if market forces were going to foster the growth of the wealth of the nation led him to amplify his theories at great length.

The *Wealth of Nations* is divided into five books. Book I deals with the productive power of labor and the distribution of the national product. It deals at length with the division of labor, develops the theory of atomistic competition and the price system as the guide to resource allocation, and goes into the distribution of income among the factors of production. Book II is a discussion of capital as the fundamental element of economic growth. Book III covers the different economic growth experiences of different nations, emphasizing the different experiences with agriculture, cities, and commerce. Book IV is mostly about mercantilism, a short chapter on theory and eight long chapters on policy, showing the evil effects of restrictions on trade. The last chapter discusses Physiocracy. And Book V is a long book about taxes and the proper sorts of government expenditures.

The division of labor is an essential concept both in the microeconomic price theory and in the macroeconomic growth theory of Smith. His famous example was the pin factory. He conjectures that one man, without specialized machines, could not make more than twenty pins a day; but that in fact a small factory employing only ten people doing specialized operations such as cutting the wire or putting on heads can produce 48,000 pins a day.[8] Not only do people specialize on tasks within a factory, but also factories specialize in making individual parts of the final product, with corresponding gains in productivity.[9] The implication for the theory of growth is obvious: the more specialization, the more growth, although there are limits to be noticed later. For Smith, there is a social cost for this economic benefit. If a person does only one or two simple things all the time he loses his mental agility and becomes "as stupid and ignorant as it is possible for a human creature to become" (*Wealth of Nations*, p. 634). The public should be required to acquire some reading, writing, and arithmetic, in little schools, with the master partly but not wholly paid by the

government, to offset this. The idea that the workers are the victims of the
machines was to be developed by Karl Marx in his concept of "alienation."

The division of labor is important both for growth and for the operation
of the price system. With each person specializing it is necessary to
exchange what he or she makes in order to be able to acquire all the other
things consumed. This is made possible by an inborn "propensity to truck,
barter, and exchange." Another inborn propensity, the propensity to
pursue one's own self-interest, makes exchange produce the maximum
income under the proper institutional arrangement, which is competition
rather than monopoly. This is the famous "invisible hand:" the pursuit of
self-interest guides resources into their most profitable uses, which maxi-
mizes both individual and national income. (Smith adds, in a characteristi-
cally tart comment, that "By pursuing his own interest he frequently
promotes that of the society more effectually than when he really intends
to promote it" *Wealth of Nations*, p. 423.) Carrying out this process, in
equilibrium the return to a resource in all its various uses will be equal, an
idea which has been called "still the most important substantive proposition in all of economics."[10]

Exchange in a competitive market is rarely done with barter; generally
money is used and prices are set. Smith saw several problems for the
theorist in the matter of what he called "exchangeable value." One was the
well-known diamond–water paradox: water has a high value in use but a
low value in exchange, but diamonds with scarcely any value in use have a
high value in exchange. (Here Smith means by value in use objective
usefulness, not subjective utility or, to refine it further, marginal utility.)
This paradox was resolved by such marginal utility theorists as Jevons, who
set up the theory that relative price ratios equal ratios of marginal utility in
a consumer's equilibrium. Since water is plentiful it has a high total but a
low marginal utility and hence a low relative price. Although Smith had
told his class at Glasgow that "Cheapness is in fact the same thing with
plenty. It is only on account of the plenty of water that it is so cheap as to
be got for the lifting, and on account of the scarcity of diamonds (for their
real use seems not yet to be discovered) that they are so dear,"[11] the
emphasis had shifted in the *Wealth of Nations* to a cost of production
theory of value.

Another problem Smith perceived was that of how to measure value,
and a third was what is the cause of value. The cause was divided into
"natural" or long-run price and "market" or short-run price theory, and
into the "early and rude state" and the advanced society where stock has
accumulated and land is all private property. In the rude state, with labor
the only factor of production, goods exchange according to their ratios of
the labor time embodied in them (the deer and beaver example used by
Smith is one of the famous passages in the book; see Book I, chapter VI).
But in the advanced state the price must cover not only the wages of labor
but also the rent of land;[12] goods can then not exchange in proportion to
labor time.

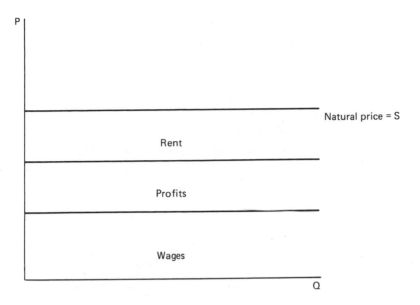

**Figure 5.1**

Figure 5.1 shows Smith's ideas about natural price. Natural price is cost-determined because of the implicit assumption of constant costs; the long-run supply curve (S) is horizontal, and the role of demand in the long run is to determine how many resources the industry must support. The component parts of long-run supply are the returns to the three factors of production, taken to be data in the discussion of the prices of goods.[13]

Smith regarded the natural price as the central price to which the prices of commodities gravitate (Book I, chapter VII), but the actual or market price might be above or below it, depending on the relation between the current amount supplied and the amount demanded at the natural price.

In figure 5.2, *A* is what Smith calls the effectual demand – the demand of those willing to pay the natural price. It exceeds the quantity brought to market at the natural price; the competition among buyers raises the market price. This attracts more resources into the industry (following the principle of self-interest); short-run supply (SRS) shifts to the right, and the market price falls back to the natural price shown as equal to the long-run supply (LRS). If *A* had been to the left of *B* (effectual demand less than current supply at the natural price), the market price would be lower than the natural price, resources would leave the industry, and the market price rise. All this is very clear in Smith and was judged by Schumpeter to be by far the best piece of economic theory he turned out.[14]

But Smith's discussion of the way to measure value is something else again. This discussion (Book I, chapter V) claims that what a good is really worth to a person is the toil and trouble it saves him, that value is equal to

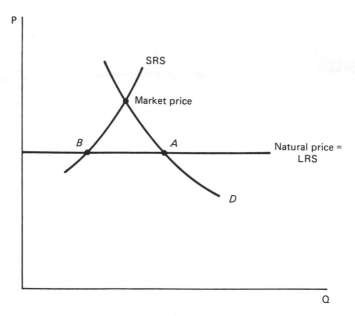

**Figure 5.2**

the quantity of labor that can be commanded by the good. Measuring value by money runs into the trouble that the value of money itself is changeable; the virtue of measuring by quantities of labor is that labor is always of equal value, says Smith.

It is easy to compute labor commanded by a good. If the money price of the good is $10, and labor is $2.50 per hour, the good commands four hours of labor. (How do you know whether to use the wages of unskilled labor, skilled labor, or whatever other category you can think of? By the "higgling and bargaining of the market," a sort of rough equality is arrived at, so that a wage of $5 per hour for a skilled worker means that his time is equivalent to two hours of unskilled labor paid at $2.50 per hour. This allows for hardship, ingenuity, training, etc. Hence a representative wage unit may be constructed.) This technique is fine for the short run, says Smith, when money wages (called silver wages) do not change much; but if you are computing real value over a span of centuries, the changes in the value of silver make the calculation worthless. It turns out, however, that over a period of centuries, corn (i.e., wheat, in the usage of the times; what we now call corn was called maize or Indian corn) commands nearly equal quantities of labor, since corn is the subsistence good. Therefore if you compute real value by dividing the money price of the good by the money price of the amount of corn a worker buys with his wages you have the long-run real price of the good. Although the basic ideas are simple, Smith's presentation is extremely complex. Subsequent developments of the labor theory of value by Ricardo and Marx formed a major part of classical economics.[15]

A cost of production price theorist will naturally pay attention to the component parts of cost. Smith began by considering wage costs. He mentioned many influences which were developed by later writers in considerable detail. In particular, in the long run wages will be at subsistence (what he calls the lowest rate consistent with common humanity; he is not as hardboiled as was the first edition Thomas Robert Malthus in 1798). This level will actually be observed only if the economy has not been accumulating more capital for a long time; if it has, the long-run tendency will be masked by the short-run effects of an increasing demand for labor running ahead of the short-run supply. This follows from Smith's notion of what was later to be called the wages fund, which he held applied in the short run. He envisaged masters who advanced materials and wages to workmen out of their savings (or out of the savings of other people, who loaned the money to the masters). The size of the wages fund related to the number of workers determined real short-run wages. This notion, as we shall see, lasted nearly 100 years, until John Stuart Mill's famous recantation in 1869.

Mixed in with these subsistence and wages fund considerations were several other influences which could have been (and later were) developed into wage theories: bargaining between masters and workers, with the master having all the advantages; the productivity theory, where the productive power of the worker determines wages (presented in particular for the rude state of society before capital was accumulated; after that, the wages fund theory becomes dominant); and a residual theory, where the worker gets what is left after rent and profits are deducted. In this area of economics Smith was more important as a stimulus to later work than as the author of a polished piece of analysis.

In addition to his rather unfinished theory of the general level of wages, Smith talked about the structure of wages. Here he was much better. The basic idea is that the monetary return to different types of labor varies so that the net advantages (of money on the one hand compared to aspects of the job on the other) are equalized. Thus, a person with long training has to receive higher wages to recover the cost of the investment in education (what is now called human capital formation). Other differences among jobs which lead to different money wages include the ease, the dirtiness, or the honorableness of the employment; *ceteris paribus*, a dirty job will pay more than a clean job. Alas, *ceteris* generally is not *paribus*, and the dirty jobs wind up paying less because there is a low demand or a lack of alternative employment for unskilled, untalented people. Another occupational difference pointed out by Smith was that seasonal employment paid more per day because the worker had to save to cover the periods when he was unemployed. Those whose job has much responsibility must be paid more, he says, because responsibility is an irksome burden (others say that really the high rewards come because of a low supply of those suited to assume responsibility). The last factor is risk. Actually the risky job should pay more, but because of "the overweening conceit which the greater part of men have for their abilities," as well as the fact that the chance of gain is over-valued (see the experience with lotteries), risky professions actually are paid less than the amount of risk suggests they should be (e.g., seafaring). In Professor Stigler's accounting of the successes and failures of Professor Smith, this analysis of wage differentials (Book I, chapter X) is counted as an "enormously successful application of the theory of competitive prices."[16] The relation of this labor market theory to competitive price is stressed by Smith; in this chapter he spent a good many pages recounting and deploring the policy of Europe which prevented the achievement of the equality of net advantages because it prevented people from changing jobs, and because it sometimes limited the number of people in one job and sometimes artificially expanded the number of people in others. One of the faulty aspects of the policy of Europe was that many of the regulations required people in the same trade to register or to tax themselves, which led to one of the most famous of statements made by Smith: "People of the same trade seldom meet together, even for merriment and diversion, but the conversation ends in a conspiracy against the public, or in some contrivance to raise prices" (*Wealth of Nations*, p. 128).

The second part of the cost of production is the profits of stock (i.e., of capital). It was clear to Smith that not all the return to the employer was profits; part of it was really wages for the labor of inspection and direction. The part that actually comprised profits was hard to measure; Smith judged that the rate of profits was about twice the market rate of interest in Great Britain in his day, and profit was thus made up of the interest return on capital plus a premium for risk, since business sometimes made extraordinary losses. As to the determinants of the level of profits, Smith argued that as more capital was accumulated profits would fall because of the competition of the owners of stock (Book I, chapter IX), and because it gradually becomes more and more difficult to find profitable ways to employ the extra capital (Book II, chapter IV). Many business records survive from Smith's day, and modern accounting and econometric techniques show that some of Smith's ideas about profits were factually correct, while others were not well founded. The profits of the seventeen firms whose records still exist did move up and down together, and they equalled twice the rate of interest. But profits did not fall after the repeal of the Navigation Acts, as Smith predicted, and the East India Company did not have the highest profits, as Smith said.[17]

The costs of production are rounded off with rent, the last of the trilogy. In the chapter on price (Book I, chapter VI) Smith says it is a cost of production and helps determine price, but when he comes to the chapter on rent (Book I, chapter XI), he says it is different from wages or profits. The latter two are the cause of price, but rent is the effect of it. A high rent does not cause a high price, but results from it. This conflict is resolved by looking at the context. In the earlier chapter he is talking about individual commodities, where rent is in fact an opportunity cost. If the grower of oats cannot pay as high a rent as the grower of cattle, the owner will rent to the cattleman; so rent is indeed an inescapable cost element. But in the later chapter he is talking about rent for land as a whole, where there is no opportunity cost.[18] It was this concept which Ricardo developed, and which became famous as "Ricardian rent." Smith's notion was that rent increased as society progressed, so that landlords could be trusted to be on the side of the public welfare in decisions affecting the growth of the economy; not so businessmen, for profits fall with economic growth, and therefore business is likely to be on the side of measures narrowing the market, restricting growth, and deceiving and oppressing the public (*Wealth of Nations*, p. 250). Smith, the glorifier of the market, was no glorifier of individual merchants and manufacturers.

The *Wealth of Nations* is not just a study of price, markets, and incomes. Smith was interested in the grand sweep of history, the rise, growth, and decay of nations. In his examination of this, he emphasized three things: the division of labor, the accumulation of capital, and the institutions necessary to promote unimpeded growth. As we have seen, the more finely labor is divided, the greater the output per worker. But at any one time the division of labor is limited by the extent of the market. The extent of the market depends on the growth of cities, the development of transportation (particularly water transportation because it is cheap), the extent of foreign trade, and of course on the size of the national income. The division of labor also requires capital, for machines, for advances to workers, for the money to circulate the product, and for the goods in process. There is an upward spiral at work; more division of labor leads to more income, which leads to more saving and capital formation, which supports more division of labor.

The whole of Book II of the *Wealth of Nations* is devoted to capital. Outstanding features of this discussion include, to begin with, the distinction between fixed and circulating capital. The former, which includes machines, buildings, and "acquired and useful abilities" (what we now call human capital), earns the owner an income without being sold (since these are used in the production of things which are sold, but themselves remain in the owner's possession). Circulating capital, however, must be sold before it earns any income. This is really inventories of finished goods or goods in process or of foodstuffs. Because of the necessity to maintain capital, Smith distinguishes between gross and neat (i.e., net) revenue for the nation as a whole, which is similar to the GNP and NNP concepts we use today.

Money, which Smith regarded as part of the capital stock of society (after all, we have to refrain from consuming part of our income in order to acquire the gold or silver which circulates as money under a metallic standard) received a very long discussion (Book II, chapter II). Although metals are durable and divisible, and hence make good money, paper is much less costly and just as convenient. If a country with a gold standard begins issuing paper money, no more money in total will be needed to circulate the goods produced; the excess gold and silver will flow abroad and bring more goods home, leaving the total money supply constant but with a larger proportion of it consisting of paper money. At this point what Professor Viner called a "minor mystery" arises. Smith knew David Hume's price–specie flow analysis,[19] according to which the increased money supply would raise prices at home, causing the home country to lose exports and to import more from abroad where prices are lower, this in turn leading to the gold outflow. But Smith does not refer to the price effects of the increased money supply; instead he uses an anology, the channel of circulation, and says the increased money supply will overflow the channel. Several writers have tried to resolve the mystery; for example, it has been suggested that Smith disapproved of one application of Hume's monetary theory, in which Hume suggested that one country could not progress permanently, because when it began to progress its poorer neighbor would become a cheaper place in which to buy and the rich country would lose gold with an adverse effect on its economy. Smith's theory of growth had no room for such impacts.[20]

As part of his discussion of money Smith examined thoroughly the banking practice of his day. He thought banks were a good thing,.because they freed dealers from having to keep idle cash on hand as a precautionary reserve; dealers could borrow from the banks when there was a sudden need for cash, and could turn their reserves into real capital. At the same time banking regulations were needed, even if they were a violation of "natural liberty," in the interests of the security of the whole society. Smith pointed out that banks could, and did, overissue paper money, as indicated by people constantly trying to redeem it in metallic money. Smith's rule for the proper amount of paper money is just the sum which merchants feel obliged to keep unemployed in ready money for answering occasional demands (what Keynes called the precautionary demand for money); any greater amount would exceed the demand of the economy for money. Smith thought that by restricting loans to "a real bill of exchange drawn by a real creditor upon a real debtor, and which as soon as it becomes due, is really paid by that debtor" (p. 288) he would achieve his goal. The notion that banking practice is neutral if loans are only for short-term financing of inventories, which is what Smith was referring to, was very important in the banking and currency controversies of the nineteenth centuries. It became part of the Federal Reserve Act of 1913, even though Henry Thornton showed that it was fallacious in his book of 1802, *Nature of Paper Credit of Great Britain*.[21]

As influential as Smith's ideas on money were his theories of what he called the accumulation of capital, or "productive and unproductive labour." Smith believed that capital accumulation resulted from saving, since banking financed only circulating, not fixed capital. He also believed that there was no problem in getting the saving invested: "What is annually saved is as regularly consumed as what is annually spent, and nearly in the same time too" (p. 321). Thus Smith was an early propounder of Say's Law. But the puzzling part of the chapter (Book II, chapter III) is the

concept of productive and unproductive labor. The terminology is reminis-
cent of the Physiocrats, who called agricultural labor productive and labor
in the manufacturing sector sterile, but the concept is quite different.
Capital (except human capital) takes the form of material things, and it is
the producers of these things who are called productive workers. Other
workers – menial servants, judges, generals, physicians – may be honor-
able and useful, but they are unproductive. The notion of productive
workers is muddied, however, by an alternative definition: these workers
add value to the materials with which they work. Modern commentators
argue that what Smith was warning against was the employment of
retainers in the feudal manner and the expansion of government workers,
but his exposition is not very clear.

The owners of capital do not always use it themselves and earn profit on
it; they may lend it to others and earn interest. (Recall from the earlier
discussion that Smith regarded profit as interest plus a risk premium.)
Smith had a real theory of interest, as contrasted to the monetary theory of
earlier writers which he criticized. Capital to him was not money but real
goods, and, although loans were generally made in money, what the
borrower really wanted and paid for was a part of the annual produce.
Marian Bowley, who provides a very helpful survey of "English Theories
of Interest in the Seventeenth Century," believes that the difference
between Smith and such earlier authors as Barbon, North, and Locke is the
result of the different economic universes they were contemplating. The
seventeenth-century writers lived in "an economy in the early stages of
potentially rapid economic development without appropriate financial
experience or institutions," and they were trying to find the right questions
to ask.[22] In any event, in light of Smith's general preference for competitive markets, it is noteworthy that here was one he wished regulated; he
did not want spendthrifts driving up the rate of interest and acquiring loans
at the expense of productive borrowers.

Having accumulated capital, it is necessary to decide what to invest it in.
Smith classified the types of investment as agriculture, manufacturing,
wholesaling, and retailing, and said that in each occupation the quantity of
productive labor put in motion and the value added to national product by
equal investments were very different. He gave agriculture the priority of
putting into motion the greatest quantity of productive labor, then
manufacturing, then wholesaling (with variants depending on whether it is
all done within one country, or between the home and a foreign country, or
between two different foreign countries using the home country's ships).
Ranking investment outlets in this way rather than by profitability, and, in
particular, emphasizing agriculture on the basis of labor put in motion, is
generally regarded as an error.[23] One interpretation is that Smith regarded
the mercantilists such as Colbert who favored manufacturing and the ones
who fostered foreign commerce as being wrong, and was trying to find an
argument against them.

Smith's favoring of agriculture is also apparent in Book III, "Of the

Different Progress of Opulence in Different Nations." This is a historical study, which opens with a theory of the way progress occurs naturally – agriculture first, which provides a surplus from which towns grow up and manufacturing is supported, with foreign trade occurring later only when there is a surplus to sell. But the burden of Book III is that governments had forced development out of this natural order, with towns artificially built up by the ruling monarch for security against the barons. Capital then flowed out of the towns into the country, and of course the growth of the towns widened the market, while the power of the king brought security to the farmers. Thus progress occurred even if it was not done in the natural sequence.

Security was only one of the institutions that fostered growth. Security included both property and the tenure of farmers who rent from landlords. Control of the techniques which perpetuated large landed estates – primogeniture and entail upon a particular line of succession – was needed, because small proprietors were generally the most industrious, intelligent, and successful (*Wealth of Nations*, p. 392). And freedom of trade (with exceptions) was an important institution – indeed, it received 229 pages in the section on the "Mercantile System," as Smith called it, plus many other references throughout the book.

In Book IV, Smith presented a simple version of mercantilism: wealth consists of gold and silver, and this is to be acquired by restrictions on foreign trade. Smith countered that "it would be too ridiculous to go about seriously to prove, that wealth does not consist in money" (p. 406), and as for restraints, in general if you let people follow their own self-interest to produce the greatest value in their own businesses then the annual revenue of society will be as great as it can be. Following the principle of division of labor, a family does not make for itself what it can buy more cheaply than it costs to make it. "What is prudence in the conduct of every private family, can scarce be folly in that of a great kingdom" (p. 424).

The trade theory which Smith used to back up his argument has two parts. One is called absolute advantage, and consists simply in comparing the cost of acquiring the good abroad with the cost of making it at home (his grapes in Scotland versus wine purchased abroad is a famous example). Ricardo and others around 1817 pointed out that it might be best to make a good at home even if it cost more than it costs to make abroad, provided there was another good in which you had a still greater cost disadvantage (the theory of comparative costs). This part of Smith's trade theory was then a stepping-stone to a more sophisticated theory. But he also had a "vent for surplus" theory, which ties in neatly with his growth model. By means of trade the extent of the market can be widened, facilitating the division of labor and allowing capital to be used more productively than in a closed economy.[24]

Smith did not present his free trade case as holding all the time. "As defence, however, is of much more importance than opulence" (p. 431), the Navigation Acts, which promoted British shipping, were said to be perhaps the wisest of commercial regulations. A tax on foreign goods when there is a tax on the domestic industry is reasonable. A retaliation against foreign tariffs when there is a chance to make them repeal their tax is good policy. The repeal of existing high tariffs should be done by slow stages to prevent excessive disorder, although the economy can reabsorb displaced workers rather easily, as the experience with the veterans of the war of 1763 showed. A particular manufacture may be acquired sooner than it would otherwise have been if it gets protection (an acknowledgment of the infant industry argument, famous in nineteenth-century American tariff debates). But in general Book IV argues against restrictions and in favor of the invisible hand.

One aspect of mercantilism was the control of colonial trade, which was opposed by Smith, as was the whole idea of colonization. "To found a great empire for the sole purpose of raising up a people of customers . . . [is] extremely fit for a nation whose government is influenced by shopkeepers" (p. 579). Colonies would not cover their costs, which are high in blood and treasure. They distorted capital into the carrying trade, which puts in motion less labor than agriculture and industry, in Smith's view. While they do widen the market, this can be done without forcing them to remain in colonial status, and indeed the American colonies should have representation in Parliament, said Smith in 1776. This was one doctrine of Smith's which later classical economists did not follow; they thought the colonies were valuable as outlets for surplus population, and some ingenious schemes for organizing colonies and planning their growth, such as those of Edward Gibbon Wakefield, were proposed.

The last, long book of the *Wealth of Nations* is about public finance – expenses, taxes, and public debts. Defense, the administration of justice, and public works (good roads, bridges, navigable canals, etc.) are the functions of government because they are advantageous to society without affording a profit to a small group. Private enterprise therefore would not produce them. (He believed education, however, was better done as a private enterprise, a reflection of his unhappy years at Oxford.) To support these activities taxes are needed. Here Smith provided four famous maxims:

1  The subjects should support the government in proportion to their ability.
2  The tax should be certain, not arbitrary.
3  It should be convenient to pay.
4  It should not cost much to collect.

He then somewhat tediously reviews taxes on a great variety of things.

Schumpeter provides a fitting conclusion to this review of the *Wealth of Nations*; "from about 1790 on, Smith became the teacher not of the beginner or the public but of the profession, especially the professors.[25] The thought of most of them, including Ricardo, started from him and most of them again never got beyond him."[26]

# *Notes*

1 Stigler, "The Successes and Failures of Professor Smith," *Journal of Political Economy*, 1976, p. 1200. The 1976 bicentenary celebration of the publication of the *Wealth of Nations* brought forth a monumental reappraisal of all aspects of Smith's thought; a review with a bibliography of 175 items is provided by Horst Claus Recktenwald, "An Adam Smith Renaissance *anno* 1976? The Bicentenary Output – a Reappraisal of his Scholarship," *Journal of Economic Literature*, 1978, pp. 56–83.

2 *Wealth of Nations*, Modern Library edition (New York, 1937), p. 718. This edition, edited by Edwin Cannan, was for long the standard; a new edition, called the Glasgow edition, edited by Campbell, Skinner, and Todd, was published by Oxford University Press in 1976. (Oxford is no longer in the condition described by Smith!) All the works and correspondence of Smith are available in the Glasgow edition. The Modern Library edition is used for all citations in this text.

3 John Wain, *Samuel Johnson* (New York, 1975), p. 51.

4 A good brief summary of the basic ideas of *The Theory of Moral Sentiments* is given in Andrew S. Skinner's introduction to the Pelican Classics edition of the first three books of *Wealth of Nations* (Penguin Books, 1979).

5 See the editors' introduction by D. D. Raphael and A. L. MacFie to the Glasgow edition of *The Theory of Moral Sentiments* (Oxford, 1976).

6 Schumpeter, *History of Economic Analysis* (New York, 1954), p. 181.

7 C. R. Fay, *Adam Smith and the Scotland of his Day* (Cambridge, 1956), explains many obscure references such as Scotch pebbles, an example of an industry using no capital.

8 Today in the United Kingdom one employee can make 800,000 pins a day; see C. F. Pratten, "The Manufacture of Pins," *Journal of Economic Literature*, 1980, p. 93.

9 Smith's account of the gains from specialization led M. Prony to draw up a plan whereby a large number of completely untrained people could do the computations for the mathematical tables produced by the French revolutionary government. See Charles Babbage, *On the Economy of Machinery and Manufactures* (London, 1842).

10 Stigler, "Successes and Failures," p. 1201.

11 Adam Smith, *Lectures on Jurisprudence*, eds R. Meek, D. Raphael, and P. Stein (Oxford, 1978), p. 478. This book includes lecture notes from Smith's classes in the 1760s. The diamond–water paradox was mentioned by John Law in 1705 and by J. Harris in 1757; see *Lectures on Jurisprudence*, p. 333.

12 Another tart remark of Smith's comes at this point: "the landlords, like all other men, love to reap where they never sowed" *Wealth of Nations*, p. 49.

13 The commentators differ in their interpretation of Smith at this point. Mark Blaug, *Economic Theory in Retrospect*, 4th edn (Cambridge, 1985), p. 39, says that a cost of production theory is meaningless if the prices of the productive services are not determined, but Smith had no consistent theory of wages and no theory of rent or profits at all; hence Smith had no theory of value. Paul Samuelson, "A Modern Theorist's Vindication of Adam Smith," *American Economic Review*, 1977, pp. 42–9, presents a mathematical formulation in

which goods prices and factor prices are simultaneously determined, which he claims represents Smith's theory. Samuel Hollander, *The Economics of Adam Smith* (Toronto, 1973), summarizes as follows: "given labour market conditions the money or silver price of corn (governed by the principle of specie distribution) determines the money wage rate and thus labour costs throughout the economy and – taking for granted nominal profits – the silver price of all commodities produced without land. And given the conditions of scarcity and productivity relating to land, the same silver price of corn together with the money wage rate (and profit rate), will govern the rent per acre on corn land and thus the alternative cost that must be met by all other land-using products" p. 179. In other words, he agrees with Samuelson and disagrees with Blaug.

14 Schumpeter, *History of Economic Analysis*, p. 189.

15 Blaug, *Economic Theory*, pp. 49ff, presents Smith's labor-commanded theory of value as an index of economic welfare. D. P. O'Brien, *The Classical Economists* (Oxford, 1975) pp. 84ff, contends it was not a national welfare standard, but attempted to measure the sectional interests of the rent receivers. But all agree that Smith did not view labor as being the *cause* of value, but rather the *measure*.

16 Stigler, "Successes and Failures," p. 1201. Otto Mayr, "Adam Smith and the Concept of the Feedback System," *Technology and Culture*, vol. 12, 1971, claims that Adam Smith was the first to present the self-regulating theory of markets in a form that could be analyzed by engineering feedback loops (although Hume's price–specie flow mechanism, described in chapter 2, was the earliest economic feedback loop, it was monetary rather than market analysis). A feedback mechanism is like a thermostat, which regulates the room temperature by measuring the temperature and sending commands to the furnace when the actual temperature deviates from the desired temperature. Like Stigler, Mayr presents Smith's theory of the equilibrium rewards among different types of occupations as a special case of the functioning of a market system. Mayr speculates on possible connections between Smith's analysis of self-regulating mechanisms and the increasing use of such mechanisms in eighteenth-century technology; here is an illustration of the relativistic approach to the history of economic thought, specialized to technology rather than the usual social organization context.

17 The data are analyzed in Philip Mirowski, "Adam Smith, Empiricism, and the Rate of Profit in Eighteenth-Century England," *HOPE*, 1982, pp. 178–98.

18 A very clear exposition is given in D. H. Buchanan, "The Historical Approach to Rent and Price Theory," *Economica*, 1929, pp. 123–55. An alternative interpretation is that rent arises because a small group of wealthy people own all the land, and keep it scarce for cultivation because of the amenity value of unimproved land. The demand for luxuries on the part of the rent-earning landowners results in a small wages fund. Rent arises as a payment for the scarcity value of agricultural land, and because the cost of production of corn (governed by the small wages fund) is less than its price. See J. M. A. Gee, "The Origin of Rent in Adam Smith's *Wealth of Nations*: an Anti-Neoclassical View," *HOPE*, 1981, pp. 1–18.

19 Smith referred to it in the 1760s in the lectures reproduced in *Lectures in Jurisprudence*.

20 This is the interpretation of J. M. Low, "An Eighteenth-century Controversy in The Theory of Economic Progress," *The Manchester School*, 1952, pp. 311–30. Another explanation, emphasizing Smith's neglect of the short-run aspects of the balance of payments, is that his concern with paper money was with its beneficial effects on economic activity; see David Laidler, "Adam Smith as a Monetary Economist," *Canadian Journal of Economics*, 1981, pp. 185–200. For other suggestions see F. Petrella, "Adam Smith's Rejection of Hume's Price–Specie Flow Mechanism: A Minor Mystery Resolved," *Southern Economic Journal*, 1968, pp. 365–74. Robert V. Eagley, *The Structure of Classical Economic Theory* (Oxford, 1974), pp. 72–8, and Thomas M. Humphrey, "Adam Smith and the Monetary Approach to the Balance of Payments," *Federal Reserve Bank of Richmond Economic Review*, Nov./Dec. 1981.

21 A very clear brief discussion of this may be found in Blaug, *Economic Theory*, pp. 201ff.

22 Bowley, *Studies in the History of Economic Theory before 1870* (London, 1973), p. 62. Others who criticized the idea that the rate of interest depended only on the supply of money included Hume, Turgot, and Cantillon.

23 Professor Hollander has a very subtle and complicated defense of it, however, in *The Economics of Adam Smith*.

24 Hla Myint explains this very thoroughly in "Adam Smith's Theory of International Trade in the Perspective of Economic Development," *Economica*, 1977, pp. 231–48.

25 An interesting specific example has recently been carefully analyzed. In 1830 Thomas Robert Malthus, then Professor of History and Political Economy at the East India Company's College at Haileybury, gave his class 564 questions on the *Wealth of Nations*, which one student put into his copy of the book. Questions on Smith's treatment of the Physiocrats were the most extensive of any topic, reflecting Malthus's own personal interests. See J. M. Pullen, "Notes from Malthus: the Inverarity Manuscript," *HOPE*, 1981, pp. 794–811.

26 Schumpeter, *History of Economic Analysis*, pp. 193–4.

# 6
# Thomas R. Malthus

Thomas Robert Malthus[1] was a major figure in intellectual history generally as well as in the development of classical economics. In particular, Malthusian population doctrine has generated far-ranging controversy and its influence has extended far beyond economics. Malthus attended Cambridge University and taught there between 1793 and 1804, which enabled Keynes to give him the honorific title of "The first of the Cambridge economists." Malthus had many interests; he won an award in mathematics at his college, and was a church minister and hence used the title Reverend as well as Professor. He eventually came to specialize in economics; indeed, he became the first professor of political economy in England when he was appointed to the faculty of the East India Company's College at Haileybury, an institution formed to train managers for the company.

Malthus's position in economics is unique. The principle of population (in a modified form) became one of the cornerstones of classical economics, but in other areas of the subject he had to uphold his unorthodox opinions strenuously and at length, particularly in discussion with his good friend David Ricardo. On subjects ranging from the theory of value to the policy of free trade to Say's Law Malthus's views were anti-classical.[2]

Malthus's first and most famous book, *An Essay on the Principle of Population* (1798), arose out of a debate he had with his father, Daniel Malthus. Daniel agreed with the French mathematician and philosopher Condorcet that mankind was capable of infinite perfectibility by virtue of the unlimited application of reason and science, and with the English social philosopher William Godwin that the "extensive diffusion of liberty and happiness" was possible.[3] Thomas Robert claimed that these philosophers were wrong. Mankind, he said, would inevitably breed itself into misery because population outran food supply, or else would be unhappy because it indulged in vice in order to keep population down. His father, duly impressed by this argument, capitulated and suggested that his son publish his ideas, which he did, anonymously at first. When the book became popular he published an expanded and somewhat changed edition in 1803 under his own name, and continued to revise the book throughout his life.

Although as Malthus himself said his ideas were not new (he cited Hume, Adam Smith, and Robert Wallace)[4] his presentation was so effective that his name became attached to the overpopulation idea forever after. His theory was that food is necessary for existence, and that the "passion between the sexes" is also necessary and will remain about constant.[5] These two necessary aspects of life follow different patterns of growth: population (if unchecked) would grow in a geometric progression, doubling every twenty-five years according to the evidence provided by the experience of the American colonies. But he decided by mental experiments that food would grow only in an arithemetic progression, adding the same constant amount to the total food supply every twenty-five years. (Malthus's illustrative numbers for population growth are 1, 2, 4, 8, etc., and for food are 1, 2, 3, 4, etc.) Even if one starts with an ample food supply, the more rapid rate of growth of population soon means that the poor are "reduced to severe distress." People die early of malnutrition and disease. This Malthus calls, alternatively, misery or the positive check.

The human race, however, has options not available to other animals. It can practice birth control, patronize abortionists, or refrain from marriage but gratify the passion between the sexes by means of the services of prostitutes. Malthus named these practices preventative checks or vice.

In the second edition of the *Essay* in 1803 he added another preventative check: moral restraint, which is the postponement of marriage without irregular gratification. This addition to the list of population restraints is sometimes said to have marked a change in Malthus's attitude from hard-boiled to soft-boiled. Along with the softening of the restraints came a more mellow attitude toward the possibility that economic growth would help the poor. In the first edition he claimed that industrial growth could not raise the population limit, since food is the binding constraint. Gradually, as the *Essay on Population* was revised, he admitted that industrial growth is a normal feature of economic development, that it raises the standard of living of the poor who consume not only food but "some conveniences and even luxuries," and that the shift of labor from agriculture to manufacturing does not reduce the food supply because it "would be made up, and indeed more than made up, by the beneficial effects of improved skill and economy of labour" in farming. Malthus had discovered both the Industrial Revolution and the Green Revolution![6]

Before tracing out the reactions to Malthus's dismal prediction that the human race (except for the few who can follow moral restraint) is doomed to vice or misery, it is worth looking at the modern status of this theory. According to one prominent view, the difference between science and metaphysics is that science makes a prediction about future events that can be falsified by testing against the evidence. In this view Malthus's population theory is not science because it allows no room for falsification: if a given country is not facing starvation then the population must be practicing moral restraint or vice. In Malthus's own view, however, the really important "ultimate" check to population is the food supply, even if it is not the "immediate" check. He did not predict the drop in birth rates which began later in the nineteenth century in industrialized countries; instead he focused on death rates. Kingsley Davis, an eminent modern population expert, calls this a great empirical mistake, the result of the inadequacy of Malthus's theory.[7]

Something very striking to the modern observer is the strong component of morality mixed with Malthus's positive theory. Calling birth control and "irregular connections" vice is to make a moral judgment. He did not believe such things wrong solely from a puritanical point of view about sex, however; he thought that if fertility could easily be controlled, man's natural indolence would surface and that underpopulation would be a problem.[8] While some writers, such as Gunnar Myrdal, insist that standard economics is shot through with value judgments (see especially his book *The Political Element in the Development of Economic Theory*, 1953), most economists try to keep positive economics separate from normative judgment. But not Malthus. In fact he used his theological ideas as the framework for his *Essay*, and in his own mind it seems to have been an exercize in theology rather than a study in economics; he discussed the problem of evil and how to reconcile human suffering from overpopulation with divine benevolence (suffering would stimulate moral growth and benevolence); the purpose of man on earth (for the growth of his mind); the optimum population in the eyes of God (as much as the means of population will support, qualified in the second and later editions by the statement that the people should be healthy and happy, not half-starved). Theologically speaking, Malthus had an optimistic approach to the population problem, however dismal the outcome from the perspective of economics.[9]

In his own day, it must be said that Malthus's theory was a huge success: but it generated a controversy as to whether he was right or wrong that continues to this day. The prediction of misery led Carlyle to call economics "the dismal science". Economists of Malthus's day agreed with him, however, and David Ricardo made subsistence wages part of his theory.[10] John Stuart Mill reports in his *Autobiography* how the principle of population was a banner and point of union for him and the Utilitarians with whom he associated in his youth, but they made a significant change. Whereas Malthus regarded birth control as vice, the view of J. S. Mill, Francis Place, and others, was that only through birth control could population be controlled and wages raised. Mill distributed pamphlets explaining the technique of a primitive birth control device (using sponges in the same way that modern diaphragms are used), and was arrested for doing so.[11] Indeed, it was not until 1877 that contraception could be publicly discussed in England.

In the 1830s professional opinion began to turn against Malthus. In particular, Nassau Senior claimed that Malthus had made one important error. He claimed the standard of living tended to rise faster than population because of a desire that Malthus had overlooked: the desire to better one's condition, which is as natural as the wish for marriage. Many others took up this idea, and also emphasized the empirical evidence against Malthus, so that his doctrine went into eclipse as a tool of economics.[12] In 1893 Edwin Cannan called the *Essay on the Principle of Population* a "chaos of facts collected to illustrate the effect of laws which do not exist."[13] But the work still possesses an incredible vitality, with a new edition in 1970 and another in 1976.

Karl Marx mounted a somewhat different and extremely vehement charge against Malthusian population economics. Since Marx was convinced that poverty is the result of the inexorable working of the capitalist system, in which part of the labor of the proletariat is expropriated by the capitalist simply because the latter hires the former, he was adamant in his belief that overpopulation could not be the cause of working-class misery. Malthus, he said, was a superficial, schoolboyish plagiarist; and he was, in addition, a Protestant parson – a group which roused Marx's easily awakened ire (see *Capital*, vol. I, chapter 25, section 1). Marx's colleague Friedrich Engels called Malthusianism "a vile and infamous doctrine, a repulsive blasphemy against man and nature".[14] Engels's disproof of the Malthusian doctrine of geometric population growth and arithmetic food growth harks back to Condorcet, whom Malthus had originally attacked. Science, according to Engels, will progress in a manner just as limitless and at least as rapid as population. If it were not for capitalist exploitation, the world could move away from misery, poverty, and crime.[15]

While founders of Marxism were repelled by Malthus, another influential thinker found in him the key to his own path-breaking idea. Charles Darwin relates in his *Autobiography* how on reading Malthus it struck him that the geometric increase of a species means that there must be a struggle for existence, and that during this struggle favorable variations for survival would be preserved while unfavorable ones would be destroyed. The favorable ones would result in the formation of a new species. Darwin worked on this idea, which he formulated in 1838, for many years, and eventually published it in *The Origin of Species* in 1859. Malthus had thus unwittingly contributed to the theory of evolution.

Before moving on from the general subject of population, it is convenient to mention at this point the major role that population doctrine played in the life of the great Swedish economist Knut Wicksell (1851–1926). He became a neo-Malthusian in his twenties, advocating birth control at a time when this was extremely unpopular in Sweden. He did not take up the study of economics until he was in his thirties, gaining a professorship only when he was nearly fifty, but he always maintained his interest in population problems. In 1909, when he was 59, he wrote up his lectures on population while in jail serving a sentence for blasphemy. (He had challenged the authorities as a test case in the freedom of speech by his remarks on the Virgin Birth. Clearly Wicksell was no retiring academic economist but an activist worthy of the late 1960s.) In this pamphlet, whose English title is *The Theory of Population – Its Composition and Changes*, he introduces the idea of the optimum population. This he defines as the level at which further increase leads to a reduction in prosperity, and he argued that Europe at that time had passed the optimum. Factually European incomes have risen considerably since Wicksell's time, but his idea of the optimum population has continued as a tool of welfare analysis (see, for example, J. E. Meade, *Trade and Welfare*).[16] In general, however, population theory has not formed a major part of economics, the general consensus being that the nineteenth century had disproved Malthus.

Turning to Malthus the economist, naturally one finds that some of the interests of Malthus the population theorist are carried over. In particular Malthus was an agrarian. He claimed that commerce, including of course international commerce, was inferior to agriculture as a source of wealth because commercial prosperity would only be temporary while agriculture was more permanent. It was also more moral, as trade was exploitative. As an agrarian he opposed the importation of corn, arguing for tariffs on imports, bounties on production, and for Britain to become a corn exporter rather than an importer. Many of his doctrines were similar to those of the Physiocrats, such as the necessity of a high price for grain and the superior productivity of agricultural pursuits compared to industrial. But his agrarian bias did not come from reading the Physiocrats; he rather had this bias first and used what he believed valid from Physiocratic literature after discovering the similarity of their views.[17] The origin of his agrarian bias was his fear that cheap corn would ultimately harm the workers by inducing excessive population growth.[18] They would be better off working hard to earn their food and postponing the formation of their families. The argument that workers would be better off with cheap food did not impress him; he believed it was unwise to rely on foreign sources which might suffer either short-run interruptions, as in war time, or long-run contractions and adverse terms of trade.

Malthus backed his argument that workers were better off with high grain prices than low ones with a piece of technical analysis. If the worker's wage is regulated by the price of corn, when the corn price rises so does his wage. He can then either consume the same amount of corn, and actually buy more of other things because their price has not risen although his wage has; or he can substitute some of the relatively cheaper things and increase his welfare still more.[19] Francis Horner, a leading intellectual of his day and one of the founders of the *Edinburgh Review*, said this idea had the look of a paradox, and, like most of Malthus's ideas, was revolting to the common belief. The foundation of the paradoxical-seeming idea is that wages are regulated by the price of corn; by a slight change, converting his attention to Ireland and claiming that wages are regulated there by the price of potatoes, Malthus was able to argue that the chief cause of Irish poverty was that potatoes were the staple rather than corn. The reason is that as potato prices rise wages also rise, but there is nothing cheaper than potatoes to substitute in the Irish diet so that (unlike corn consumers) higher prices do not make Irish workers better off.

Not only were workers better off with high grain prices than low, they were better off with a shortage of housing. In 1807 Malthus argued against a scheme to build cottages, partly to remedy the housing shortage, partly to create jobs. His argument was that the housing shortage was the reason why the poor laws do not encourage early marriage as much as they otherwise would. If there were more houses the population would grow so rapidly "as to render the condition of the independent labourer absolutely hopeless." Keynes's laconic comment on this proposition was that "Economics is a very dangerous science."

While chapter 7 below covers Malthus's long debate with his friend Ricardo over Say's Law, it is appropriate to complete this chapter on Malthus's general economic ideas by noting that he disagreed with Ricardo on practically everything else as well. He thought that Ricardo's theorizing was too abstract and that "the frequent combination of complicated causes, the action and reaction of cause and effect on each other, and the necessity of limitations and exceptions in a considerable number of important propositions, form the main difficulties of the science."[20] On the other hand, he also disagreed with the inductive method, in which one first observes facts and then makes theoretical generalizations. The two prominent inductivists in economics in Malthus's day were the Reverend Richard Jones, who took over Malthus's chair at the East India College and who wrote an inductive study of rent called *An Essay on the Distribution of Wealth* (1831), and William Whewell. Whewell, although he wrote some papers on economics, was primarily a mathematician and historian of science; he gave much support and encouragement to Jones.[21] But Malthus was not in sympathy with the exclusively inductivist approach; he wrote to Whewell that the tide was setting too strong against Ricardo and that Mr Jones was "carried a little out of the right course by it." A judicious mixture of deduction and induction seems to have been Malthus's approach.[22]

Another source of dispute with Ricardo was over the use of supply and demand analysis. In chapter 30 of his *Principles of Political Economy and Taxation* (1817) Ricardo states his position: "It is the cost of production which must ultimately regulate the price of commodities, and not, as has been often said, the proportion between the supply and demand ... The opinion that the price of commodities depends solely on the proportion of supply to demand ... has been the source of much error."[23] In fact, by demand Ricardo usually meant the quantity demanded rather than demand in the schedule sense. Malthus, however, had a rudimentary notion of a demand schedule, and he distinguished between what he called the extent and the intensity of demand. The extent of demand was the quantity actually purchased (i.e., the point on the demand schedule equal to the current supply). Intensity was the price people would pay for the quantity, and it depended on the number, wants, and means of the consumers (which determined the position *of* the demand curve) or on the abundance or deficiency of supply (which determined the position *on* the demand curve). Malthus thus did not distinguish between movements of the demand curve itself and movements along it. In spite of his ambiguity, Malthus has been given the accolade of devising the best explicit *theoretical* conception of demand among British classical writers of his day.[24] If his was the best, then after all there has been some progress in economics. Malthus used his supply and demand analysis for both long- and short-run situations and in his debates on Say's Law, and tried to make intensity of demand, reflecting wants and tastes, the active force in determining the national income. But this is taken up in detail later.

A further disputed notion with Ricardo was the measure of value. Ricardo, as we shall see, favored an abstract measure, an invariable standard which was a commodity produced with the economy's average ratio of labor to capital, using capital which was of the average durability of capital in the economy. By assumption, he declared that gold had these properties. But Malthus preferred an imperfect usable measure to a perfect hypothetical one; at first he favored the average between the price of corn and the price of labor as a good approximation, but later decided that the labor commanded by a product was the best measure of its value. This was because command over labor showed how well the good was suited to people's desires and how abundant the supply was compared to the desires of consumers, and how efficient capital was in increasing wealth and population by setting people to work. Modern readers have different reactions to Malthus's formulations.[25] The debate over the measure of value consumed a great deal of the time and energy of Malthus and his friend Ricardo, but had they not been arguing about that, they would surely have been arguing about something else. However, as Ricardo said in the last letter of their correspondence, "I should not like you more than I do if you agreed in opinion with me."

# Notes

1 According to John Maynard Keynes's biography (reprinted in his *Essays in Biography* (London, 1933)), the name Malthus derives from Malthouse; presumably his ancestors were in the brewing business at some time. Patricia James, *Population Malthus: His Life and Times* (London, 1979), is now the standard biography; William Petersen, *Malthus* (Cambridge, Mass., 1979) is a shorter biography by a demographer. Donald Winch, *Malthus* (Oxford, 1987) combines both biography and analysis of Malthus's ideas in a very short book in the Past Master Series.

2 A biographical essay on the contentious aspect of Malthus is W. D. Grampp, "Malthus and his Contemporaries," *History of Political Economy* (*HOPE*), 1974. Salim Rashid, "Malthus' *Principles* and British Economic Thought 1820–1835," *HOPE*, 1981, pp. 55–79, examines the substance of the controversies, giving both Malthus's views and others' reactions to them.

3 The relevant writings of these philosophers are in a very handy collection of articles which include background, contemporary opinion, and critical essays as

well as the text of the 1798 *Essay* itself: T. R. Malthus, *An Essay on the Principle of Population*, edited by Philip Appleman (A Norton Critical edition, 1976).

4 Schumpeter, who loved to puncture reputations, says that the Malthusian population doctrine sprang fully developed from the brain of Giovanni Botero in 1589, and that his path-breaking performance is the only one in the whole history of the theory of population to deserve any credit at all. *History of Economic Analysis* (New York, 1954), pp. 254–55.

5 He was a practitioner as well as a theorist raising a family of three, the first born after eight months of marriage. "It is not difficult to guess the ribald comments that must have been made . . . ," James, *Population Malthus*, p. 165.

6 Geoffrey Gilbert, "Economic Growth and the Poor in Malthus's *Essay on Population*," *HOPE*, 1980, pp. 83–96, traces in detail the evolution of Malthus's ideas on this aspect of population.

7 See Blaug, *Economic Theory in Retrospect*, 4th edn (Cambridge, 1985), chapter 3, and Kingsley Davis, "Malthus and the Theory of Population," in P. Lazarsfeld and M. Rosenberg (eds), *The Language of Social Research* (New York, 1955).

8 The moralistic aspects of Malthus's population theory are discussed by Davis, "Theory of Population," and in a more technical manner by David Levy, "Some Normative Aspects of the Malthusian Controversy," *HOPE*, 1978, pp. 271–85.

9 J. M. Pullen, "Malthus' Theological Ideas and their Influence on his Principle of Population," *HOPE*, 1981, pp. 39–54, is a fascinating source for this topic. It appears that in many parts of his theology Malthus was as unorthodox as he was in economics.

10 See chapter 8 for details on how Ricardo modified the basic Malthusian doctrine.

11 The episode is discussed and the "diabolical handbills" for which Mill was arrested are reprinted in Pedro Schwartz, *The New Political Economy of J. S. Mill* (London, 1972).

12 The discussion is summarized by Mark Blaug, *Ricardian Economics* (New Haven, Conn., 1958), chapter 6.

13 Cannan, *Theories of Production and Distribution* (London, 1893), p. 113.

14 Malthus, *Essay* (Appleman, ed.), p. 148.

15 R. Meek, *Marx and Engels on Malthus* (New York, 1954) has rounded up their comments on all aspects of Malthus, his economic theory as well as his population doctrine.

16 Meade, Oxford, 1955, chapter VI. Wicksell's population doctrine is presented in a translation of his pamphlet by Monica S. Fong, "Knut Wicksell's 'The Two Population Questions,'" *HOPE*, 1976, pp. 311–23. Wicksell's lifelong interest in population is detailed in Torsten Gärlund, *The Life of Knut Wicksell* (Stockholm, 1958), and summarized by P. A. Samuelson in his Wicksell lecture, "Stability and Growth in the American Economy," reprinted in his *Collected Scientific Papers* (Cambridge, Mass., 1966), vol. 2. Professor Samuelson's amateur psychological analysis is that Wicksell's fixation on population questions came from an early emotional crisis involving religion and sex.

17 Bernard Semmel, "Malthus: 'Physiocracy' and the Commercial System," *Economic History Review*, 1965, pp. 522–35, traces out the connections between Malthus and the general doctrines of the Physiocrats.

18 J. J. Spengler, "Malthus the Malthusian vs. Malthus the Economist," *Southern Economic Journal*, 1957, pp. 1–11, goes into considerable detail on this. An alternative explanation is provided by W. D. Grampp; he suggests that Malthus believed that agriculture should be protected because the owners of agricultural land were the protectors of political liberty. See Grampp, "Malthus and his Contemporaries," *HOPE*, 1974, p. 297.

19 W. D. Grampp, "Malthus on Money Wages and Welfare," *American Economic Review*, 1956, pp. 924–36, shows how all this works using budget lines and indifference curves. There was however a slip in his geometric interpretation which was corrected by Louis A. Dow, "Malthus on Sticky Wages, the Upper Turning Point, and General Glut," *HOPE*, 1977, pp. 303–21. Spengler, "Malthus the Malthusian," claims that Malthus held this view only temporarily and that it was not fundamental to his desire for a high grain price.

20 Malthus, *Principles of Political Economy* (London, 1820), p. 8.

21 In fact, he was so busy with his various scientific activities that like some teachers in all ages he did not give much time to his students. It is reported that he once gave his servant a list of names of those of his pupils whom he wished to invite to a wine party. Among them was that of an undergraduate who had died some weeks before. "Mr. Smith, sir; why, he died last term, sir!" said the servant. "You ought to tell me when my pupils die," replied Whewell sternly. The anecdote is in James Sutherland (ed.), *The Oxford Book of Literary Anecdotes* (Oxford, 1976), pp. 257–8.

22 N. B. de Marchi and R. P. Sturges, "Malthus and Ricardo's Inductivist Critics: Four Letters to William Whewell," *Economica*, 1973, pp. 379–93, is the best brief survey of this methodological controversy. Two references for students interested in Jones and his criticism of Ricardo are the articles by William L. Miller, "Richard Jones: A Case Study in Methodology," *HOPE*, 1971, pp. 198–207, and "Richard Jones's Contribution to the Theory of Rent," *HOPE*, 1977, pp. 346–65.

23 Schumpeter's remark on this passage is that it reflects little credit on Ricardo as a theorist. *History of Economic Analysis*, p. 601.

24 The accolade was awarded by R. B. Ekelund, Jr, E. G. Furubotn, and W. P. Gram, *The Evolution of Modern Demand Theory* (Lexington, Mass., 1972), p. 11. Other good explanations of Malthus's demand theory are in V. E. Smith, "Malthus's Theory of Demand and its Influence on Value Theory," *Scottish Journal of Political Economy*, 1956, pp. 205–20, and, by the same author, "The Classicists' Use of 'Demand'," *Journal of Political Economy*, 1951, pp. 242–57.

25 D. P. O'Brien, *The Classical Economists* (Oxford, 1975), p. 106, called the debate over the measure of value "unprofitable"; Lilia Costabile, "Natural Prices, Market Prices and Effective Demand in Malthus," *Australian Economic Papers*, 1983, p. 168, thinks that Malthus provided a correct formulation of the classical theory of value and distribution, and that the full significance of his book *The Measure of Value* (1823) has not been appreciated yet.

# 7
# David Ricardo, Classical Monetary Theory, and Say's Law

David Ricardo (1772–1823) is generally credited with the invention of the technique of economics. Adam Smith dealt with history, current affairs, laws, and philosophy along with his economic theory. Ricardo, the man of affairs, took all this for granted. As he said in a letter to his friend Thomas Malthus, "My object was to elucidate principles, and to do this I imagined strong cases, that I might show the operation of these principles." Imagining strong cases is what economic theorists do.

Ricardo was an energetic, capable man whose formal education ended at the age of fourteen – a rather skimpy intellectual background for a great economist, one would think.[1] He entered the family stock-broking and stock-jobbing business with his father, where he remained until 1793. Then he broke with his family, who were Sephardic Jews, because he married a Quaker girl. He was forced to go into business for himself, but his chances for success were good as this was just at the start of a period of twenty-two years of war with France, with all which that implied for deficit finance and activity on the financial markets. Such a success was he that when he retired in 1815 (aged forty-three) he had capital of about a half-million pounds. He had in the meantime become intrigued by economics as the result of picking up a copy of Smith's *Wealth of Nations* while on vacation in 1799. He studied economics as a hobby but did not become professionally involved until 1809, when he wrote letters to the newspapers about the monetary controversies of the day. This led to his association with the active group of economists in London, including Malthus and James Mill.[2]

At about the time of his retirement a major public policy issue was boiling up: British agriculture, which was losing its comparative advantage as the Industrial Revolution progressed, had been protected from competition by the Napoleonic Wars. The question now was whether to continue the protection by means of tariffs, in this case the famous Corn Laws. Ricardo opposed the policy, and wrote a pamphlet explaining his reasons. This pamphlet, "An Essay on the Influence of a Low Price of Corn on the Profits of Stock," was expanded into the *Principles of Political Economy and Taxation* under the urging of James Mill. It was soon recognized as a classic.

Ricado's next project, again at the urging of friends, was to get himself into Parliament through the recognized technique of purchasing a rotten borough (Portarlington, in Ireland; he paid Lord Portarlington £4,000 for the seat and loaned him £125,000 on a mortgage). Ricardo took his seat in 1819, and was an active and influential member.[3] He died, apparently of a mastoid infection, in 1823, having accomplished a remarkable amount in his fifty-one years.

## Ricardo and his Contemporaries on Money

Ricardo's first publications on economics dealt with monetary problems arising from financing the Napoleonic Wars. The discussion of these problems resulted in much important monetary work. People were accustomed at this time to a metallic standard, either gold or silver; and following John Locke they were generally opposed to any tinkering with the metallic content of the currency. Locke, in his book *Further Considerations Concerning Raising the Value of Money* (1695), had argued that the state guaranteed the performance of legal contracts, and that changing the quantity of silver in a pound sterling was essentially a breach of contract. Richard Cantillon and David Hume continued the emphasis on the importance of metallic money, from fear of excessive circulation, high prices, and balance of payments deficits. Adam Smith added his authority to the metalist position. However, not all eighteenth-century monetary theories were metallic; in particular John Law and Sir James Steuart had argued for paper money, or cartalism, as it was called.[4]

At the beginning of the Napoleonic War period England was on the gold standard, with the Bank of England holding the nation's reserves. In 1793 there was a run on the bank, arising from a fear of invasion by the French. This was handled without abandoning the gold standard, but a more serious panic in 1797 reduced the Bank's holdings of gold from £5 million to £1¼ million. The government ended the redemption of bank notes in specie, and England remained off the gold standard until 1821. During this time the government had to do some deficit spending and to borrow from the Bank of England, and naturally there was some inflation. Since index numbers were in their infancy and current price index numbers were not computed, it is not easy to be precise about how much inflation there was. A good estimate seems to be that if 1790 prices are set equal to 100, then 1801 prices were about 166, 1810 prices about 182, and 1815 prices about 200.[5] But the problem that really exercized the monetary controversialists was the reaction of foreign exchange markets. From 1799 to 1804 England made substantial payments abroad, both for military expenditures and for payments for corn imports resulting from harvest failures. This increased the supply of pounds abroad and led to a fall of about 13 percent in the number of (Hamburg) marks it cost to buy an inconvertible or "paper" pound. Along with this discount on the paper pound went a rise in the price of gold. Before the restriction on specie payments by the Bank of England each pound sterling was exchangeable for 123 11/24 grains of 22-carat gold; by 1801 this much gold cost about 8 percent more. The 8 percent premium on gold bullion, added to about 5 percent shipping cost from England to Europe, meant the cost was similar whether one bought marks either directly with paper pounds which had depreciated 13 percent or indirectly by first buying high-priced bullion, shipping it to Hamburg, and selling it for marks.

After 1804, with normal harvests, the pressure on the paper pound eased and the premium on gold bullion vanished. But between 1809 and 1815 the supply of paper pounds increased again, and they fell to a discount of 20 percent while gold bullion went to a premium of 16 percent. (Edwin Cannan, in his introduction to *The Paper Pound of 1797–1821*,[6] says this was started by the opening up of South America to British commerce which caused a wave of optimism – called "speculation" at the time – among traders.) During the first period of currency misbehavior Henry Thornton wrote the *Nature of the Paper Credit of Great Britain* (1802) (called by Professor Blaug "the greatest single work on monetary theory produced in the classical period"). Ricardo's publications on money and the famous *Bullion Report of 1810* (the report of a select Parliamentary committee to inquire into the cause of the high price of bullion) came during the second episode.

Henry Thornton (1760–1815) was both a banker and member of Parliament, but in his day he was perhaps better known for his religious activities. He was an Evangelical, on the low-church wing of the Church of England, and was a leader in the abolition of the slave trade, the founding of Sierra Leone as a homeland for liberated slaves, and was active in various missionary and tract societies. He was famous for his charity, giving away some six-sevenths of his income before he was married.[7] As an economist, he was especially active in the decade 1800–1810, publishing *The Paper Credit of Great Britain* early in the decade and participating in the drafting of the *Bullion Report of 1810* at its close. He also worked on the Irish Currency Committee in 1804.

During the course of the nineteenth century orthodox, classical monetary theory rested on the quantity theory of money and on Hume's price–specie flow mechanism (see chapter 2). The implications of Hume's analysis were that the balance of payments corrected itself through price-level changes and that, in Ricardo's phrasing, the amount of gold and silver in the world would accommodate itself among nations so that trade would take place on the same basis as if it were purely a trade of barter.[8] This was the theory that led Edwin Cannan to his recipe for correcting the inflation of World War I: "When the scales at last fall from the eyes of the people of Europe, groaning under the rise of prices, they will no longer cry to their Governments 'Hang the profiteers!' but 'Burn your paper money, and go on burning it till it will buy as much gold as it used to do!'"[9] Thornton's *Paper Credit* is intriguing because it is much more subtle than that, introducing ideas which were rediscovered and developed by Wicksell and by Keynes many years later. His version of the ideal gold standard was a modified one which had fixed exchange rates and the use of gold internationally but a domestic paper money supply not necessarily regulated by the gains and losses of gold. For example, in the 1797 balance of payments crisis, he argued against the wisdom of deflating the economy in the orthodox gold standard fashion because sticky wages, lagging behind price cuts, would cause unemployment. Since the crisis was caused by harvest failure as well as war-time interferences, cutting imports by cutting spending was not the proper policy; instead he recommended filling the balance of payments gap by exporting gold, replacing it by paper money at home. This is not the only modern-sounding part of his analysis. He introduces the Keynesian notion of liquidity preference in his discussion of the way people's confidence influences the ratio of cash to short-term bills they will hold at a given rate of interest. Like Wicksell, he made investment decisions depend on a comparison of the money rate with the real rate of interest. In his writing, velocity of money is not a crude concept of a constant rate of turnover of money but is related to the rate of interest, the type of asset considered (total velocity being a weighted average of the velocity of different assets used to make payments), and to institutions.

A decade later, in the *Bullion Report of 1810*, Thornton helped analyze a different monetary crisis, and concluded that the Bank of England had issued too much paper money, and that it should reduce the note issue and restore the gold standard. In this case, as well as in some of the analysis in his earlier book when he referred to long-run problems, his approach was like that of Ricardo: the Bank of England had printed too much paper money when the market price of bullion exceeded the mint price and when the foreign exchange value of the pound had fallen below the pre-war level *permanently* (i.e., for more than two years or so).[10] Ricardo wished to use this criterion for the over-issue of paper money on every occasion, long run and short, whereas Thornton used it only in the long run. We shall see the precise meaning of the criterion as used by Ricardo later. Meanwhile it should be re-emphasized that in this period, where the point at issue was really inflation, good tests for inflation were hard to come by. Index numbers were not yet well developed, and it was recognized that the simple test of seeing whether more paper money had been printed was inadequate (the total volume of spending would not necessarily increase if more paper were printed, as liquidity preference might change so that velocity would fall, or the paper money might simply replace bills of exchange or others means of payment).

Ricardo's approach was the opposite of the subtlety of Thornton. In a series of newspaper articles and pamphlets in 1809–10 Ricardo argued that the rise in the price of gold which began in 1808 was entirely due to the over-issue of bank notes by the Bank of England. He would have nothing to do with the idea that the rate of exchange or the price of gold was related to war-time payments to European allies or extraordinary purchases of food in a bad harvest. His theory was that the foreign exchange needed to pay for such extraordinary needs could be quickly earned by sending goods such as cloth, unless money happened to be a cheaper commodity to send. As he put it, "The exportation of the coin is caused by its cheapness, and is not the effect, but the cause of an unfavorable balance: we should not export it, if we did not send it to a better market, or if we had any commodity which we could export more profitably."[11] The inflation caused by excessive paper money prevents selling our products abroad and forces us to close the balance of payments gap with gold, in his view. The remedy is to reduce the circulation of paper money by forcing the Bank of England to redeem its bank notes in gold. Professor Sayers concluded that the fact that Ricardo, whose influence both on monetary thought and on policy was destined to be so powerful, took this simple quantity theory of money view was a major disaster for nineteenth-century monetary theory.[12]

After the Napoleonic Wars ended Ricardo continued to push for a return to a gold standard. His version of the gold standard, as outlined in his *Proposals for an Economical and Secure Currency* (1816), was to drop the coinage of gold and use a paper currency, but to require the Bank of England to buy and sell to the public twenty-ounce gold ingots at the mint price and to allow free export and import of gold. This would limit the circulation of paper money to the same level of currency that a gold coin standard would provide, since over-issue of paper would lead to an import surplus. This payments deficit would be paid for by gold obtained by exchanging Bank of England notes for gold ingots. To prevent the loss of gold the Bank would have to limit the issue of paper money.

The ingot plan was tried for two years but in the monetary turmoil of returning to the gold standard it was dropped, not to be revived again in Great Britain until 1925. It turned out that Ricardo's monetary theory proved a poor forecaster of what would happen when the gold standard was resumed around 1820. He thought that since bank notes had depreciated 4 percent below par (it took £104 to buy the same quantity of gold that £100 bought at the pre-war gold standard price), a contraction of bank notes and of prices by 4 percent was needed. But actually prices in England fell by much more than 10 percent by 1822, along with all the hardships of a major depression. Ricardo attributed this to the inept management of the Bank of England. He claimed that under his ingot plan the Bank would have had to buy no gold, but rather to sell it; instead they scrambled for gold, raising its price, which required a much more extensive appreciation of paper money (i.e., lowering of the price level) than would have been necessary had not people who were "notoriously ignorant of the most obvious principles of political economy" been in charge of the Bank.

Ricardo was thus the founder of that element of classical monetary theory which said that the way to run the monetary system was to make paper behave like gold. But this was not all there was to Ricardo, or to classical monetary theory either. Thornton and, later, John Stuart Mill represented the part of classical monetary theory which said that money had to be managed. The debate is not even yet resolved, as is shown by the urging of Milton Friedman that money be controlled by means of a rule specifying a given percentage rate of growth in the money stock rather than by leaving decisions up to the central bank.

For the other strand in Ricardo's monetary thinking which was important for economics, we must turn to his controversy with his friend Thomas Malthus over Say's Law, or the "general gluts" controversy, in their terminology.

## Say's Law

In the Say's Law debate the issue was whether over-saving could be the cause of depressions. As we saw in chapter 4 above, the Physiocrats had presented ideas on both sides of this question, but on balance they believed that the circular flow of income could be upset by inappropriate policies or patterns of spending. Quesnay had urged that money not be hoarded and that savings be promptly invested.[13] Adam Smith put his authority on the side of those who believed that saving caused no problems: "What is annually saved is as regularly consumed as what is annually spent, and nearly in the same time too; but it is consumed by a different set of people."[14] Saving is promptly invested in his view; as a Scot he thought that "A man must be perfectly crazy who, where there is tolerable security, does not employ all the stock which he commands, whether it be his own or borrowed of other people . . ."[15] Although Smith was high authority, some challenged his view. One of the major pre-Malthusian challengers was James Maitland, Eighth Earl of Lauderdale.[16] He believed that "deprivation of expenditure, and consequent accumulation, far from being a means of increasing the wealth of the nation, must . . . by discouraging production, inevitably tend to its diminution. . . ."[17] Why? Because in every society there is a maximum amount of capital which can profitably be formed, determined by the existing state of knowledge. More capital than this will mean an excess quantity relative to demand so that its value will fall and check accumulation. More saving than the optimum amount does not result in hoarding or a Keynesian-variety reduction in income because for Lauderdale saving is transformed into investment. What happens is that there is the destruction of a certain amount of spending on consumer goods on the one hand, as expenditure is diverted from consumption to parsimony, and the creation of an amount of capital of a smaller value than the foregone consumption on the other. In a normally working society there was no problem of excess saving, because the parsimony of one person was counteracted by the prodigality of another. The problem came because legislators took Adam Smith's eulogy of parsimony too seriously and forced people to contribute taxes to a sinking fund which was used to retire public debt. This over-saving caused by law must be as fatal to the progress of public wealth as was over-saving caused by the depraved taste of individuals. Thomas Sowell remarks that Lauderdale's writings were seldom marked by analytical rigor and the rational parts were interspersed with gross errors.[18] But he was the first, as Malthus was the most notable, in the line of dissenters from the classical orthodoxy of Say's Law.

Jean-Baptiste Say (1767–1832) took an active part in the French Revolution but disapproved of Napoleon and spent the years of the Napoleonic wars running a cotton-spinning plant. After 1815 he returned to Paris and became a teacher, running the first course of political economy ever given in France and eventually becoming France's first professor of political economy. His *Traité d'Économie Politique* (1803) went through many editions and was translated into several foreign languages; the Kelley reprint is a reproduction of the 1880 printing of the 1821 first American edition, which indicates the longevity of the book. It was used at Harvard in 1850 and at Dartmouth in 1870. One of the important influences of the book was the way Say systematized and organized economic principles into the broad categories of production, distribution, and consumption. This order was followed by later major writers such as John Stuart Mill (who also added the categories of the progress of society and government). He draws his modern preeminence, however, from the "law of markets," expressed by (and attacked by) Keynes in this form; "supply creates its own demand; – meaning by this in some significant, but not clearly defined, sense that the whole of the costs of production must necessarily be spent in the aggregate, directly or indirectly, on purchasing the product."[19]

What Say said in his chapter "Of the Demand or Market for Products" (Book I, chapter XV), was "it is production which opens a demand for products . . . Sales cannot be said to be dull, because money is scarce, but because other products are so . . . a product is no sooner created, than it, from that instant, affords a market for other products to the full extent of its own value."[20] James Mill made a similar statement in a pamphlet he wrote in 1807 called *Commerce Defended*:

> but if a nation's power of purchasing is exactly measured by its annual produce, as it undoubtedly is; the more you increase the annual produce, the more by that very act you extend the national market, the power of purchasing and the actual purchases of the nation. . . . It may be necessary, however, to remark, that a nation may easily have more than enough of any one commodity, though she can never have more than enough of commodities in general.[21]

Both Say and Mill did not simply give a statement of what we now call Say's Law, they also developed a number of related propositions in their discussion.[22] But the major point is that while they said it was possible for people to purchase production from the incomes earned in producing, it was not until Say's second edition in 1814 that Say said people would in fact do so.

This brings us to Ricardo and Malthus. Almost from the beginning of his career as an economist Ricardo was a devotee of Say's Law. During the controversy over bullion in 1810 Malthus had critically reviewed Ricardo's essay *The High Price of Bullion*; Ricardo published a refutation of this review including the flat statement that "no country ever produced a general glut of all commodities. It is evidently impossible" (*Works*, vol. III, p. 108). In chapter XXI of his *Principles* he reaffirmed this position:

> M. Say has, however, most satisfactorily shewn, that there is no amount of capital which may not be employed in a country, because demand is only limited by production. No man produces, but with a view to consume or sell, and he never sells, but with an intention to purchase some other commodity.... Too much of a particular commodity may be produced, of which there may be such a glut in the market, as not to repay the capital expended on it; but this cannot be the case with respect to all commodities. (*Principles*, pp. 290 and 292).

This did not mean that Ricardo thought there would be full employment all the time; in chapter XIX, "On Sudden Changes in the Balance of Trade," he pointed out that there are "temporary reverses and contingencies," particularly in manufacturing industries, caused by changes in demand coming from the tastes and caprices of customers, from new taxes, and from the effects of war; but he regarded these as temporary until capital could move from the over-supplied industries to others. Malthus and Ricardo argued in correspondence for years about whether there could be a general glut; and eventually in his turn Malthus published his *Principles of Political Economy* in 1820 (the Kelley reprint is of the second edition, 1836). Here Malthus set down as carefully as he could his objection to Say's Law. He assumed that capitalists decided to be more parsimonious, fire their menial servants, and hire productive (i.e., agricultural or factory) workers instead. Consequently total output of goods would rise but total demand would fall, since the total demand of workers is constant (there is simply a shift from unproductive to productive employment, with total wages the same) but the demand of capitalists for conveniences and luxuries has fallen as they are saving, not consuming. Then the price of goods would fall, maybe even below cost, profits would be lowered almost to nothing, production would fall – there would be a general glut. Ricardo, who made an extensive set of notes on Malthus's *Principles* which are reprinted as volume II of his *Works*, replied that capital formation would cease but that if the composition of output changed to allow a higher proportion of wage goods and a smaller proportion of luxuries then prices need not fall. The debate continued in correspondence between the two for the rest of Ricardo's life without their coming to any agreement except that each thought the other was misunderstanding him and that if the other would simply pay attention he would be convinced.

In addition, Ricardo suggested that one source of the controversy was that Malthus looked only at immediate and temporary things, whereas he himself wished to focus on the permanent state of things. This led Keynes in his biographical essay on Malthus (in his *Essays in Biography*, 1933) to comment that the obliteration of Malthus and the domination of Ricardo's views on Say's Law "has been a disaster to the progress of economics." Such a comment reflected Keynes's marked predilection for short-run analysis ("In the long run we are all dead," he once wrote). Keynes in his polemical enthusiasm overestimated the extent to which Ricardo conquered Malthus in the nineteenth century; in those days quarterly and monthly periodicals such as the *Quarterly Review*, *Blackwoods*, the *Edinburgh Review*, and the *Westminster Review* were very influential, and a long series of articles appeared in them attacking Ricardo. In addition, there were a number of books stressing over-saving as an economic problem; two such were written by members of the armed services during active and strenuous careers. General Sleeman, who eliminated the Thugs in India (a sect whose religion involved strangling travelers) and Captain Pettman, a naval officer, both published books containing theories similar to those of Malthus and Lauderdale. And there were others. But Keynes may have been thinking of the neo-classical period, when "discussion of Say's Law practically disappeared from the writings of the leading economists."[23]

An interesting offshoot from the debate was to use general gluts as a theoretical basis for colonization projects. Edward Gibbon Wakefield concocted a scheme of "systematic colonization" (involving land sales rather than free land as on the American frontier, selective immigration, and self-government) as a way to relieve both surplus labor and excess saving. In this he was joined by Robert Torrens, another military man (this time a Colonel of Marines), who figured in the circle of London economists – in fact he took the chair at the first meeting of the London Political Economy Club, founded by Ricardo and James Mill in 1821. Although he has been called by Lionel Robbins the co-originator of "some of the most characteristic doctrines of Classical Political Economy" (for example he participated with James Mill and Ricardo in developing the theory of comparative advantage),[24] when it came to colonies he became anti-classical. Colonies, he said, could provide the outlet for saving which otherwise would result in a general glut.[25]

During the early days of the Keynesian revolution it was fashionable to regard Malthus and his concern for over-saving as a forerunner of Keynes, but the fact that Malthus had his excess saving going directly into investment, whereas in Keynes excess (ex ante) saving is eliminated by a fall in income, marks their theories as being very different. As for the extent to which Malthus was simply wrong, or was formulating a post-Keynesian capital-stock adjustment model, or was talking about economic development, there is a long literature with a range of opinion which is considerably wider than usual among commentators on a topic concerned with the history of economic thought.[26] There is no sign of convergence yet.

# Notes

1 The biographies of Ricardo are Jacob H. Hollander, *David Ricardo, A Centenary Estimate* (John Hopkins University Studies in Historical and Political Science, Series 28, No. 4, 1910), and David Weatherall, *David Ricardo: A Biography* (The Hague, 1976).

2 The correspondence among these people and other economists, through which Ricardo's developing thought can be traced, is in the eleven-volume *Works of David Ricardo* edited by Piero Sraffa (London, 1951), hereafter cited in the text as *Works*.

3 Barry Gordon, *Political Economy in Parliament 1819–1823* (London, 1976) is a detailed study of Ricardo's parliamentary experience.

4 Douglas Vickers, *Studies in the Theory of Money: 1690–1776* (Philadelphia, 1959), p. 195, reviews the metal–cartalism controversy.

5 See Vincent Bladen, *From Adam Smith to Maynard Keynes* (Toronto, 1974), p. 159.

6 London, 1925.

7 F. A. von Hayek's introduction to Thornton, *An Inquiry into the Nature and Effects of the Paper Credit of Great Britain* (New York, 1939), is an excellent account of the life and a somewhat disputed account of the work of Thornton.

8 *Principles of Political Economy and Taxation*, in *Works*, ed. Piero Sraffa, p. 137. Herafter cited in the text as *Principles*.

9 Cannan, *The Paper Pound* p. xli.

10 *Paper Credit*, p. 221. An excellent study of Thornton is available in Charles F. Peake, "Henry Thornton and the Development of Ricardo's Monetary Thought," *History of Political Economy (HOPE)*, 1978, pp. 193–212.

11 *The High Price of Bullion*, in *Works*, vol. III, p. 61.

12 R. S. Sayers, "Ricardo's Views on Monetary Questions," in T. S. Ashton and R. S. Sayers (eds), *Papers in English Monetary History* (Oxford, 1953), p. 79.

13 See Maxim 5 of Quesnay's *Tableau Économique*, eds M. Kuczynski and R. L. Meek (London, 1972), p. 4.

14 *Wealth of Nations* (Modern Library edition, New York, 1937), p. 321.

15 Ibid., p. 268.

16 His book, *An Inquiry into the Nature and Origin of Public Wealth* (1804), included comments on consumer choice and demands as well as the contentions about saving and investment which are the source of most of the current interest in him.

17 Ibid., Kelley reprint edition (New York, 1962), p. 222.

18 Analyses of Lauderdale are to be found in B. A. Corry, *Money Saving and Investment in English Economics 1800–1850* (New York, 1962); Thomas Sowell, *Say's Law* (Princeton, NJ, 1967); and Morton Paglin, *Malthus and Lauderdale* (New York, 1973).

19 J. M. Keynes, *The General Theory of Employment, Interest and Money* (London, 1936), p. 18.

20 *A Treatise on Political Economy* (Kelley Reprint edition, New York, 1964), pp. 133–4.

21 Donald Winch (ed.), *James Mill: Selected Economic Writings* (Chicago, Ill., 1966), pp. 135 and 137. Modern analysis distinguishes two versions of Say's Law: (1) Say's Identity, which says that no one wants to hold idle cash; the result is that the supply of goods automatically is a demand for other goods of equal value. (2) Say's Equality, which says that the supply of goods may temporarily exceed the demand for goods (implying an excess demand for money), but that when it does the price level will fall. This raises the real value of the money supply and eliminates the excess demand for money; the equality

of supply and demand for goods is restored. A very clear exposition is in Gary Becker and William Baumol, "The Classical Monetary Theory: The Outcome of the Discussion," reprinted in J. J. Spengler and W. R. Allen (eds), *Essays in Economic Thought* (Chicago, Ill., 1960). Professor Patinkin has pointed out that the Say's Identity version implies what he calls the invalid dichotomy: since the amount of money does not make any difference in the supply and demand for goods, the goods markets determine relative prices, while the money market (which is supposed to determine the absolute price level) is always in equilibrium so that any absolute price level will do. By contrast, Say's Equality allows prices in the goods market to be affected by the supply and demand for money, and for every relative price structure there is a unique absolute price level. There is an interesting literature on which, if any, economists believed in the invalid dichotomy. See Becker and Baumol, cited above; Don Patinkin, *Money, Interest and Prices*, 2nd edn (New York, 1965), and P. A. Samuelson, "What Classical and NeoClassical Monetary Theory Really Was," *Canadian Journal of Economics*, 1968, pp. 1–15.

22 See Sowell, *Say's Law*, and William J. Baumol, "Say's (at Least) Eight Laws, or What Say and James Mill May Really Have Meant," *Economica*, 1977, pp. 145–61; William O. Thweatt, "Early Formulators of Say's Law," *Quarterly Review of Economics and Business*, vol. 19, Winter 1979, pp. 79–96, points out that James Mill presented all the elements of Say's Law between 1804 and 1808, and that it was not until 1814 that Say provided a complete presentation. He suggests the name should be changed to the Smith–Mill Law, in recognition of the many contributions of Adam Smith to the ideas involved (see chapter 5 of this text).

23 Sowell, *Say's Law*, p. 191.

24 See William O. Thweatt, "James Mill and the Early Development of Comparative Advantage," *HOPE*, 1976, pp. 207–34 for a thorough analysis of why it is a mistake to credit Ricardo alone with comparative advantage theory.

25 On the colonization debate see Bernard Semmel, *The Rise of Free Trade Imperialism* (Cambridge, 1970), and Donald Winch, *Classical Political Economy and Colonies* (Cambridge, Mass., 1965). On Robert Torrens, Lionel Robbins, *Robert Torrens and the Evolution of Classical Economics* (London, 1956) is a highly recommended study.

26 For references see R. D. C. Black, "Parson Malthus, the General and the Captain," *Economic Journal*, 1967, pp. 59–64.

# 8
# David Ricardo's *Principles of Political Economy*

David Ricardo's attention was diverted from monetary problems to more general economic issues by developments in the grain trade as the Napoleonic Wars drew to a close. Wheat had risen from 51 shillings a quarter (i.e., eight bushels which is a quarter of a ton) in 1793 to 152 shillings in 1812. The rising price of grain led to a large increase of domestic output, the enclosure and conversion to farming of much previously unfarmed (often inferior) land, high profits, and high rents. As the price began to fall and imports to build up as the conflict wound down, agriculturalists began to demand protection in the form of a revision of the tariff rates set forth in the Corn Laws. There were hearings before the Houses of Lords and of Commons, and in 1815 the Corn Laws were amended to allow free imports at prices above 80 shillings per quarter and no imports at prices below that. The debates in Parliament, the press, and among economists had all the energy to be expected from an issue with major consequences for the incomes of urban wage earners and manufacturing employees on the one hand and for the politically over-represented farm-owning class on the other.

February 1815 was the high point of the economists' contribution. Malthus, Ricardo, and Sir Edward West[1] all published pamphlets and Robert Torrens brought out a book in that month developing the idea of diminishing returns from the application of labor and capital to inferior land as well as from the more intensive use of superior land.[2] From this they deduced that rent resulted from the fact that lower productivity as output expanded meant higher costs and therefore higher prices. Since the low-cost wheat sold for the same price as the high-cost, the high-productivity land earned a surplus. Since all farmers earned the same rate of profit on their capital as the highest-cost farmer, the surplus was paid to the landlord as rent. (This step of the argument requires some institutional knowledge; typically in England at this time the farmer did not own the land, but rented it on a long-term lease from the landowner. The farmer rather than the landlord provided the capital.) Ricardo, West, and Torrens concluded that restricting imports would increase the price of grain and result in higher rents and therefore was undesirable. Malthus reached the same conclusion about the economic effects but thought the outcome, on the contrary, was desirable: high rents and high grain prices were the most certain sign and necessary consequence of a wealthy society, and in such a society the demand for labor would be high enough that wages would rise even more than corn prices.[3] Malthus's conclusions in this pamphlet have, with justice, often been criticized.

Most but not all modern interpretations of the *Essay on Profits* explain that Ricardo used a "corn model".[4] In this model, agricultural capital consists of wheat, which is the working capital advanced to the farm laborers. Agricultural output is wheat, so that the rate of profit may be computed from the ratio of net output to input in quantity terms without any problem of calculating value. Industry and commerce employ wheat as inputs but produce other outputs; the profits in these sectors of the economy are regulated by the rate of profits in agriculture, according to the *Essay*. As more land is cultivated the net product falls while more capital is used so that the rate of profit on marginal land falls. Since rates of profit must be equal, and since Ricardo assumes corn wages are constant, some of the output on the superior land is transferred to the landlord as rent. The more capital is accumulated, the higher rents rise and the lower the rate of profits becomes.

This theory is easy to show graphically. Since production is a function of the fixed amount of land and of the amount of capital and labor inputs, and since capital and labor are used in fixed proportions in the simple model, we can plot the average and marginal product of capital and labor as in figure 8.1.

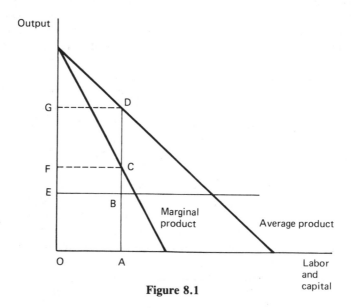

**Figure 8.1**

If labor is available in the amount OA, the marginal product of a dose of labor and capital (which is its return per unit) is AC. If we assume that subsistence wages are equal to AB, then the return to capital is BC. The rest of the average output of labor, CD, is the rent residual. Expressed as the returns of product to the factors of production, land gets the rectangle FCDG, capital gets EBCF, and labor gets OABE. As labor grows, the rent rectangle expands and so does total wages, but the profits rectangle falls. From this Ricardo concluded that, in the first place, the interest of the landlord is opposed to that of the rest of the society; and in the second place, that to increase profits it would be necessary to reduce corn wages, get improvements in agriculture, or import corn at a cheaper price than it could be grown at home. Since the Corn Laws would prevent the importation, they would be responsible for high rents and low profits, and, since accumulation depends on profits, they would be also responsible for halting the progress of wealth and the growth of population. To be consistent in its protection of agriculture Parliament should also outlaw agricultural improvements, said Ricardo, in a concluding rhetorical salvo.

While Ricardo lost the Corn Laws battle – they were not repealed until 1846 – he did have the framework for his *Principles of Political Economy*. To his mind, Adam Smith, in particular, with Say, Turgot, and others, had solved the problems of economics except for the laws which determine the distribution of the product. Smith, he thought, was wrong on rent, and on the future of wages and profits (which meant the future of the economy). But he did not simply repeat in the *Principles* what he had said on the rewards of factors of production in his *Essay on Profits*. He expanded the model. In particular, although the model remained very abstract, the problem of valuation reared its head when a more general model than the corn model was written down. If wages include manufactured goods as well as wheat, it is necessary to have a measure of value in order to find what the value of real wages is. As usual with the classical economists, Ricardo's starting-point on the value problem was with Adam Smith. To review Smith's theory of value as explained in chapter 5 of this text, in the "early and rude" stage of society commodities exchange according to the number of hours of labor embodied in each. In later stages they exchange according to the cost of production, including wages, land rent, and profits. But although prices are determined by the total cost of production, value is measured as the number of hours of labor a commodity will command (i.e., exchange for), on the argument that "what everything is really worth is the toil and trouble it can save ... " To see how many hours of labor a commodity will exchange for, divide the price of the good by silver wages in the short run and corn wages in the long run (where the corn wage is the cost of the subsistence amount of corn consumed).

Ricardo started with Smith in the "early and rude stage" where labor was the only input, and agreed that commodities would exchange according to the number of hours of labor input. But he convinced himself that Smith was inconsistent in the more complicated cases in using labor commanded as a measure of value, where labor was measured in units of money wages or corn wages. He concocted an example[5] where wages go up in corn and down as measured in the total quantity of goods other than corn which the money wage would command. Ricardo was looking for an "invariable measure of value" in order to solve this problem: if the relative value of two goods changes over time, can you tell whether the source of the change is in one good or the other, or in both? Smith's measure, being inconsistent, would not do. But the hours of labor embodied in a good would be such an invariable measure. (Suppose wine takes one hour per bottle to make; the labor embodied is one hour. This may well be different from labor commanded however; if wine costs $3 per bottle and the wage rate is $1.50 per hour, labor commanded is two hours. The difference would be made up of rent, interest, and profits.)

Ricardo goes on to explain that by labor embodied he means the labor tied up in producing the capital used in making a good as well as the quantity of labor used directly in production. As long as the value of capital and its longevity is the same in two industries, computation of their relative value by means of labor embodied gives no problem. But Ricardo then proceeded to knock the props out from under his labor theory of value by analyzing three cases in which the relative prices of goods would not be proportional to the amounts of labor time involved in them: when different proportions of fixed and circulating capital are used; when it takes longer to produce one good than another; when the fixed capital is of unequal durability. In each case the commodity with the most fixed or durable capital or which takes longer to make has a higher price relative to the other one than the relative amount of labor time involved because of payment of interest (called profit by Ricardo) on the capital. Ricardo assumes that a farmer spends £5,000 on labor to grow corn by hiring 100 workers at £50 each, and a manufacturer also spends £5,000 on labor to make a machine. Including profits at 10 percent, the corn and the machine have the same total value, £5,500. But suppose that next year the farmer again spends £5,000 on labor to grow corn, while the manufacturer spends £5,000 on labor which uses the machine to make cloth. With profits still at 10 percent, the corn again has a value of £5,500, while the value of the cloth is £5,000 labor cost plus £500 profit on the investment in labor plus £550 profit on the investment in the machine. So although the quantity of labor required for corn and for cloth is the same, the value of corn and cloth is different: £5,500 compared to £6,050. Hence Ricardo concluded that relative price is not proportional to labor time when capital (in this case, in the form of the machine) is involved. (Notice that Ricardo did not take account of depreciation in this example.)

What worried Ricardo about capital was not that relative prices at any given time would not be proportional to labor embodied, but that it would not be possible to attribute changes in relative prices to changes in the amount of labor inputs involved. Under the labor theory of value, if labor becomes less productive in producing corn, the relative price of corn must rise. But when capital is in the picture, another possibility becomes apparent: the relative price of corn may rise simply because wages have risen, if corn uses less capital and more labor than does cloth. Suppose the wages for the 100 men producing corn and cloth rise to £5,046, while profits fall to 9 percent or £454 so that the total value of corn remains at £5,500. However, the value of cloth, which was £6,050 in the example above, now falls to £5,995. That is because the cost of the 100 men making the cloth, plus 9 percent profits on the circulating capital, is £5,500 (exactly as in corn); to this must be added 9 percent profits on the fixed capital, or £495 (since the value of the fixed capital is £5,500). (This example not only demonstrates that corn has risen in relative value; it also uses Ricardo's proposition that a rise in wages must entail a fall in profits, which we shall develop later.) The theorem that a rise in wages must raise the relative value of the labor-intensive good, which is called "the Ricardo effect," received very heavy emphasis; as a theoretical point it obviously bothered Ricardo, but as a practical matter he was willing to ignore it on the ground that after all labor was the most important component of production; a variation of profit could not be expected to vary relative prices by more than 6 or 7 percent, while inputs would generally vary by much more. Professor Stigler calls Ricardo's theory of value a 93 percent labor theory of value to emphasize that Ricardo's use of the labor theory was empirical, not analytical.[6]

Ricardo went through much the same process in discussing the invariable measure of value – money (i.e., gold), being a produced object, is subject to variations in value because of different quantities of labor it may need for production or because of a change of wages. But it would be so handy to have an invariable measure that he decided to ignore the theoretical difficulties and to suppose that money was invariable. Invariability meant that it always took a constant amount of labor to mine gold and that its capital requirements were the average for the economy; hence gold would not be subject to the Ricardo effect. He could thus give absolute value to goods, by contrast with neo-classical economists' use of relative values in their theories.

Armed with his theory of value, Ricardo was ready to tackle the problem of how the produce of the earth is distributed among classes in the progress of society. Rent he took over from his *Essay on Profits* as the difference in product between grades of land or the difference in product of successive applications of capital and labor to one grade of land. Wages were essentially a datum: the long-run or "natural" wage was the price necessary to keep population stationary, but this level depends on the habits and customs of the people, and varies among countries as well as over time in a given country. In the tables Ricardo constructed illustrating his theory wages were taken to be constant in the sense that a worker could buy the same quantity of corn and of manufactured necessities at all times. Since the price of corn rises with increasing costs of producing it as more capital and labor is applied to land, the money wage must rise in order to be able to afford the same market basket of consumption. It is noteworthy that the market basket is fixed and that no substitution against the more expensive corn is considered by Ricardo. Short-run wages may be above or below the natural wage, and in either case a Malthusian population mechanism restores wages to the long-run level by increasing or reducing population. (Since natural wages are customary rather than physiological, the Malthusian starvation mechanism seems inappropriate, but like all classical economists Ricardo devoutly believed in it.)

We now have a theory of rent and of wages. Profits on marginal land are equal to total product minus total wages (since rent equals zero on this land), and because of competition the rate of profits everywhere will be the same as on marginal land. The basic conclusion about profits – what is called "the fundamental theorem of distribution" – is that "a rise of wages . . . would invariably lower profits" (*Principles*, p. 127). To see why a rise in wages would lower profits rather than raising prices, leaving profits unchanged, let us work through part of the example concocted by Ricardo. We start with ten men and appropriate associated capital on land of a given grade. They produce 180 quarters of wheat which sells for £4 per quarter, or a value of total output of £720. The wage rate per man is £24, which is enough money for him to buy his subsistence real wage of three quarters of wheat (costing £12) plus £12 worth of manufactured necessities. The total wage bill for ten men is £240, and, since there is no rent, profits equal £720 less the wage bill, or £480.

As population grows it is necessary to use less fertile land. Suppose we add ten men, and they cultivate land which returns them only 170 quarters. The price of wheat rises since it costs more to produce; the first grade of land collects rent; wages must rise to enable workers to subsist; and, from the fundamental theorem, profits must fall. Let us see exactly how these qualitative results work out. Table 8.1 shows the quantitative details. The key to the table is that the labor theory of value, expressed in units of the invariable measure of value, gives the 170 quarters on grade 2 land the same total value that the 180 quarters on grade 1 land had in the first step, since the value of the output of ten men is constant. Dividing 170 quarters into the total value of £720 gives the price per quarter of £4 4s 8d. Alternatively, still using the labor theory of value, wheat on grade 1 land has 1/18 unit of labor embodied, wheat on grade 2 has 1/17 unit. The ratio of the prices in the first situation with ten men only on grade 1 land, to the the second situation with ten men on each grade, is then 1/18 divided by $1/17 = 17/18 = £4/£4$ 4s 8d. The new price of wheat leads to the wage rate shown in line 2, the wage bill shown in line 3, and the profits in line 4. Finally, the rent on the best land is shown as line 5. Notice that competition assures that the wage bill and the profits on the two grades of land are equal. Finally, and crucially, notice that the table shows the fundamental theorem on distribution: profits have fallen as wages have risen. (Adam Smith had what seems to be the same theorem in a much more tentative fashion: "The increase of stock, which raises wages, tends to lower

**Table 8.1** Ricardo's model of income distribution

|  | Grade 1 land | Grade 2 land |
|---|---|---|
| 1  Value of product | 180 quarters at | 170 quarters at |
|  | £4 4s 8d = £762 7s 6d | £4 4s 8d = £720 |
| 2  Wage rate | (3 quarters × £4 4s 8d) + £12 = £24 14s | |
| 3  Wage bill | £247 | £247 |
| 4  Profits | £473 | £473 |
| 5  Rent | £42 7s 6d | 0 |

The pound sterling was divided into 20 shillings(s) and each shilling into 12 pence(d).

profits."[7] But Ricardo objected to Smith's formulation, since Smith did not refer to the increasing difficulty of producing food as the cause of the fall of profits; the latter instead traced it to increased competition from the owners of capital (*Principles*, p. 289).) If the reader finds this sticky going, let him consider Thomas de Quincey, who attributed his cure from opium addiction to the exhilarating effects of reading Ricardo!

It is possible to turn Ricardo's theorem and the argument illustrating it into a model of economic growth. (See the appendix to this chapter for a diagrammatic version.) In this model, population grows and capital accumulates over time, with rent gradually absorbing more of the national income and profits falling until they reach a level so low that capitalists would no longer have any incentive to save. Wages remain at the "subsistence" level in terms of commodities consumed, or fall if they are above subsistence, but rise in terms of the invariable measure of value. When saving stops, the economy has reached the stationary state. But Ricardo did not simply make a mechanical application of his model. He argued for policies which would prevent Britain suffering a decline into the stationary state: "a small but fertile country, particularly if it freely permits the importation of food, may accumulate a large stock of capital without any great diminution in the rate of profits, or any great increase in the rent of land" (*Principles*, p. 126). Other policies were important in keeping society progressive. Taxes on capital, wages, raw materials, and necessities should be avoided, and the Poor Laws[8] should be repealed because the taxes required to support them reduced profits, either directly or because wages would be increased, and by the fundamental theorem of distribution, profits thereby lowered.

It is also possible to turn this growth model into a theory of exploitation, as the Ricardian socialists did; they are discussed later (see pp. 104).

A neat example of the way Ricardo's model works is provided by his discussion of what would happen if workers shifted to a potato diet (*Principles*, pp. 332ff). Since it would only require one-third the land to support a given labor force if they ate potatoes rather than wheat, much land would become idle and rents would fall. Wages would also fall as the cost of a potato subsistence wage is lower than a wheat one. By the fundamental theorem of distribution, profits would rise. After the population had grown until the original amount of land under cultivation was once again being used, rents would go back to their orginal level (assuming fertility differences in the two crops remain the same). But profits would be higher, so more capital could be accumulated, and the margin of cultivation extended into less fertile land with potatoes than with wheat. Hence ultimately rents would be even higher than their original level.

Ricardo relied on foreign trade to provide cheap corn in order to avoid the fate of the stationary state, as was noted above. He is also usually credited with that fundamental piece of classical trade theory, the law of comparative cost.[9] Eighteenth-century economists knew that it paid to import a good if it cost less in resources to make the export good which was traded than it cost to make the import good at home. The theory of comparative advantage demonstrates that it is profitable to trade even if it costs more to make both goods at home than it costs to make them abroad. By specializing in the good whose relative cost is the lowest, both countries gain. Ricardo used this example: suppose it takes 100 men to make a given quantity of cloth in England in a year, and 120 men to make a given amount of wine; in Portugal the cloth takes ninety men while eighty men make the same amount of wine. The cost ratios of wine to cloth are 1.2 in England and 0.88 in Portugal; these ratios are the upper and lower limits of exchange ratios within which trade benefits both countries. England gains by specializing in cloth and trading at less than 1.2 units of cloth per unit of wine. Portugal gains if one unit of wine brings back more than 0.88 units of cloth. In Ricardo's example, trade is at a one-to-one ratio. England puts 100 men into cloth and with it buys wine which would have cost the labor of 120 men at home; Portugal uses 80 men to make wine which trades for the cloth that it would have cost 90 units of labor to make herself. John Stuart Mill later added the demand considerations which determine where the ratio of international exchange falls within the comparative cost limits. The theory of comparative advantage when developed with constant cost ratios is called Ricardian to this day.[10]

Just as comparative advantage theory is associated with Ricardo, so is the classical theory of rent, although as already explained Ricardian rent is really an example of multiple discovery. It is worth emphasizing that the classical theory wherein rent is a residual and is not a cost element which must be covered in determining price is true only for the case where land is in inelastic supply. Whenever land has an alternative use the farmer must pay the landlord the amount which the land could earn in its best foregone opportunity; rent then becomes a cost. Adam Smith had treated rent from both points of view, but with Malthus, West, and Ricardo the price-determined view became dominant. It was not unchallenged, however. Richard Jones (1790–1855), Malthus's successor at Haileybury College, was one of the first of the historical and institutional economists who thought that standard economic theory was too abstract. In particular, he made a detailed study of rent around the world. This appeared in 1831 in *An Essay on the Distribution of Wealth and on the Sources of Taxation*. It is the polar opposite to Ricardo's approach, being a historical survey with little analysis; Jones and his friend William Whewell of Cambridge University thought that looking at facts would suggest the proper theory, but they progressed no further than the accumulation and cursory analysis of the facts.[11] Whewell was a leading scientist of his day (called by Schumpeter an "Academic Leader"), a devotee of inductive reasoning, and the author of the first mathematical Ricardian model.[12] Another attack on Ricardian rent was launched in America by Henry C. Carey (1793–1879), a Philadelphia publisher who wrote some thousands of pages on economics after he retired. Carey thought Ricardo had it backward: cultivation in the United States began on inferior hilltop soil and gradually moved to superior bottom land, because the superior soil took more clearing.

Taxation was an applied field of enormous interest to the classical economists. Ricardo included twelve chapters on various kinds of taxes plus two chapters on bounties (which are negative taxes) on trade. He explained that "Political economy ... is only useful as it directs Governments to right measures in taxation" (*Works*, vol. VIII, p. 131). A brief summary of his analysis of taxation should emphasize the following points.

Taxes on wages are equivalent to taxes on profits, since in the short run the supply of labor is fixed. With real wages at the subsistence level, wages net of tax cannot be reduced; hence gross wages must rise when wages are taxed. Since population is fixed, the margin of cultivation does not change, and therefore rent does not change. The rise in gross wages must come out of profits. In the long run, accumulation will be reduced and a smaller population will be sustained than if there were no taxes.

Taxes on agriculture have different effects depending on exactly what the tax is. A tax on pure rent is borne by the landlord (as Henry George said in the 1870s in his defense of the "single tax" in *Progress and Poverty*) because rent is determined by price rather than itself determining price. If the tax is levied on corn, which has an inelastic demand given a fixed population, the price of corn rises. In order to keep real wages constant at the subsistence level, money wages must rise, and profits fall. Also rent earners receive a reduced corn rent, since their money rent is constant but corn prices rise.

A tax on profits cannot be shifted. Wages must remain at the subsistence level and rent, as the residual, is not changed. In the long run capital formation is reduced, and a lower population is supported than if taxes were not levied.

Finally, a tax on manufactured goods is shifted to profits if the goods are necessities (or wage goods, as they were called), but rests with the consumer if the goods are luxuries.

Based on this analysis, Ricardo's final recommendation is for a tax on wage goods (which as we have seen is passed on to profits in his model), with taxes on land rent and on the dividends from stock added for equity among owners of property. Thus "all the objects of an income tax would be obtained, without the inconvenience of having recourse to the obnoxious measure of prying into every man's concerns" (*Principles*, p. 161). This is indeed a far cry from the philosophy and powers of the state revenue services of today. [13]

Another important subject was taken up by Ricardo only in the third edition of the *Principles*. All during the Industrial Revolution one of the concerns of labor was that jobs would be taken by machines; for example, the Luddites in the period 1811–16 conducted a systematic campaign of sabotage to prevent the introduction of new machines. Ricardo had originally believed that new machines would benefit all classes of society through the cheapening of goods, and, since no capital would be destroyed by new machines, total employment would be constant although there would be some reallocation of labor into different industries. But John Barton's publication in 1817 of *Observations on the Conditions of the Labouring Classes* changed Ricardo's mind. The theoretical point introduced by Barton which impressed Ricardo was that part of the funds to buy new machines comes, not from new savings, but from converting circulating capital to fixed capital – i.e., instead of hiring workers, machines are purchased. While the same number of workers would be hired while the machines were being built as in pre-machinery days (some workers being diverted from making finished goods to making machines), as soon as the machines are made, some of the labor becomes redundant. The capitalist no longer has the funds needed to employ the workers, as his money is tied up in machines. (This technological unemployment had an important echo in Marx's reserve army of the unemployed.)

The machinery question was one of the doctrinal staples of the nineteenth century, and indeed, as recently as 1969 Sir John Hicks found a use for Ricardo's formulation in his book *A Theory of Economic History*. Generally the nineteenth-century commentators took the position that the unemployment would be only frictional, as the expanded output would allow new savings and an addition to the wages fund to re-employ labor, or that the new machines would be financed from new savings rather than from savings diverted from the wages fund. [14] Ricardo had actually made that point himself a few pages after his unemployment example, claiming that his example was made overly strong to illustrate the principle. But his qualifications made less of an impact than did his short-run theory. Two examples show the continuing interest in the machinery question: Knut Wicksell in the late nineteenth century argued that if the new machines enabled the same product to be produced by a smaller number of workers, the displaced ones could always produce something else so that the total product would increase. He agreed that there might be a reduction in the marginal product of workers and hence wages could fall; but if there was poor relief it would still increase the national income to employ all workers, paying them their marginal product and increasing their incomes to subsistence levels by charity. [15]

More recently, Paul Samuelson concluded that Ricardo was right and everybody else to the contrary was wrong; in Samuelson's version of Ricardo's model he assumes an invention which allows the same output to be produced with the same land and less labor and capital inputs. Then the returns to the labor and capital dose can fall if the marginal product of the dose is sufficiently inelastic. Obviously, he is not making Wicksell's welfare state transfer assumptions that labor will be supported; rather, we can have "short-run or long-run genocide of population and euthanasia of the capitalists."[16] There are few economists whose ideas fascinate their descendants 150 years later in the fashion of Ricardo.

What is it that makes Ricardo so interesting? It is "his great powers of abstraction and synthesis ... he fashioned what is probably the most impressive of all models in economic analysis ... [he] helped to establish a professional frame of mind which did much to reduce promiscuous fact-gathering and *ad hoc* theorizing and to incite order and precision."[17] It is this analytical approach, rather than the specific content of the model, which has led to the mathematical formulations of Ricardian economics by such contemporary theorists as Samuelson, Pasinetti, Brems, Barkai, and Gootzeit. There is debate over the length of time Ricardo's specific ideas were dominant – Schumpeter believed only James Mill, J. R. McCulloch, West, and De Quincey were Ricardians, whereas Professor Hollander argues that many of Ricardo's critics actually accepted his fundamental notions such as the inverse wage–profits relationship[18] – but by 1870 there is no doubt that "there was a narrowing of focus, specifically a greater concern with exchange and allocation in their own right; a sharpening of theoretical tools, particularly those relating to consumer choice; and the algebraic formulation of general-equilibrium relationships."[19] It is still a matter of debate whether this changed focus represented a revolution or a change in what Sir John Hicks calls the concentration of attention.[20]

## Appendix 1   Sraffa's Modern Ricardian Theory

It is an illustration of the lasting power of Ricardo that recent years have seen the launch of "something of a school among the younger generation of economists – with a *tendenz* that could be described as back to the study of Ricardo and Marx ... "[21] A major source for this revival is Piero Sraffa's book *Production of Commodities by Means of Commodities* (Cambridge, 1960). According to Sraffa, the book is concerned with the properties of an economic system which do not depend on the scale of production or the proportion of factors. Commodities are produced by labor and by other commodities. Demand plays no role in the determination of relative prices; prices depend only on technology and on the distribution of incomes between wages and profits. Because there is one more unknown that there are equations in Sraffa's model, it is possible to take either wages or profits as given, and then to determine the relative prices and the remaining distributive share. This differs from the neo-classical general equilibrium formulation, in which all relative commodity and factor prices are determined at the same time. Sraffa's theory appeals to people who believe that power (or the class struggle) determines people's incomes, rather than economic variables such as productivity and derived demand.

In the course of his book, Sraffa formalizes something that Ricardo long searched for, an invariable measure of value. That is, he found a commodity whose price did not respond to changes in the returns to labor and capital. Ricardo wanted to know whether, when $P_x/P_y$ changed, was it $P_x$ that had changed or $P_y$. If $P_y$ was invariant, he could attribute the entire change to $P_x$. Sraffa constructed such a commodity out of his system as a composite commodity made up of commodities which are used in the production of all commodities; the output proportions of the goods in the composite commodity must be the same as the input proportions; and the equations of production of the goods in the composite commodity are the same as those in the economy. Such a good is of course never actually produced or seen; its only purpose is to serve as a theoretical *numeraire*. But it did solve Ricardo's problem.

But this technical point aside, "what is particularly striking (some might say revolutionary) about the Sraffa system viewed as a whole is its rehabilitation of the Ricardo–Marx approach to problems of value ..."[22] In this sense Ricardo is very much alive.

## Appendix 2    The Canonical Classical Model of Political Economy

A canonical model is a fundamental model; Professor Samuelson, in the article whose title this appendix also employs,[23] gives a mathematical and a geometric version of the classical model of equilibrium, growth, and distribution, claiming that Smith, Ricardo, Mill, and Malthus shared it in common. The geometric version is summarized in this appendix.

The economic assumptions behind figure 8.2 are that the output is produced under conditions of diminishing returns by fixed land and by variable doses of labor and capital (the latter two are combined in a fixed proportion). The curve was interpreted by the classical writers as the average product of no-rent land as the external margin. The rent payment is the surplus above the output on the no-rent land; the profit and wage amounts are subsistence wages and minimum profits at the zero savings level (both assumed to be constant). The diagram shows the economy in long-run equilibrium at E.

The classical growth model depends on how fast labor supply adjusts, as the economy can grow no faster than the labor supply does, and as wages cannot remain above subsistence if a higher wage immediately invokes a bigger population. If labor supply responds instantaneously to higher wages, the so-called "short-circuited" case results, as shown in figure 8.3.

Starting from a small supply of labor and capital at point A, the economy

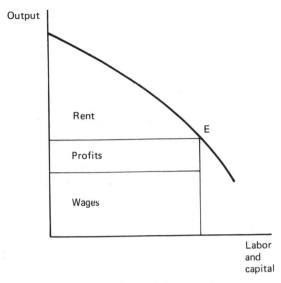

**Figure 8.2**

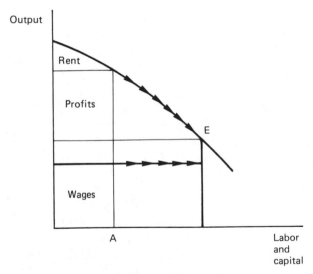

**Figure 8.3**

has low rent, subsistence wages and high profit. The high profit induces capital accumulation and the economy moves to equilibrium at E, with wages always at the subsistence level. But if, as in Smith, wages can be above subsistence for considerable periods of time, a more complicated model results. This is shown in figure 8.4.

The upper curve in figure 8.4 is again the average product of labor and capital on no rent-land. The lower curve is the one that shows the division

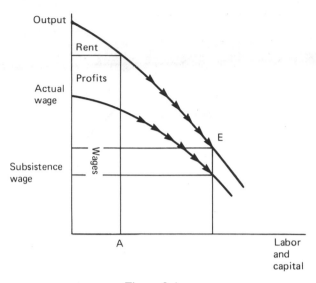

**Figure 8.4**

of the output between profits and wages at the incomes which will provide the same rate of growth in each factor of production. This varies with the saving propensities and the responsiveness of family size to incomes; for example, if family size responds rapidly to pay increases, the lower curve will be close to the subsistence wage. As the economy grows, profit and wages both fall, but both remain above the minima until the stationary state is reached at E.

Recent research shows that figure 8.3, with its labor return remaining at subsistence as the economy grows, although often regarded as the Ricardian growth model, does not really represent Ricardo's thought. Figure 8.4 is much more accurate.[24]

## Notes

1 W. D. Grampp, "Edward West Reconsidered," *History of Political Economy* (*HOPE*), 1970, pp. 316–43, reviews the contributions of Sir Edward West.
2 The sociologist Robert Merton points out that scientific discoveries often come in multiples, when a science has reached a particular stage of development and a problem becomes obvious to several people at the same time. See Robert K. Merton, *The Sociology of Science: Theoretical and Empirical Investigations*, edited by N. W. Storer (Chicago, Ill., 1973). The case at hand seems a very striking instance of this. It also provides an illustration of a common phenomenon, that of the neglected forerunner, i.e. a person who states an idea which is neglected for years and is rediscovered later. In this case, James Anderson published a pamphlet in 1777, *An Inquiry into the*

*Nature of the Corn Laws.* He had the standard classical propositions about rent: that rent depended on price, but price did not depend on rent; he demonstrated the existence and the amount of rent from land of different fertility; he claimed that remitting rents would enrich farmers at the expense of landlords without lowering prices. This was, Schumpeter said, a noteworthy achievement. Part of the pamphlet is contained in J. R. McCulloch, *A Select Collection of Scarce and Valuable Economical Tracts* (1859).

3 T. R. Malthus, *An Inquiry into the Nature and Progress of Rent* (reprint edition, New York, 1969), pp. 46–8. As noted in chapter 7, Malthus has some affinity with the Physiocrats; both he and they favored a high price for grain.

4 For example, Piero Sraffa in the introduction to his edition of the *Principles*, in *Works of David Ricardo* (London, 1951), hereafter cited in the text as *Works*; Samuel Hollander, "Ricardo's Analysis of the Profit Rate, 1813–15," *Economica*, 1973, pp. 260–82 and, more extensively, in his book *The Economics of David Ricardo* (Toronto, 1979), takes exception to the corn model approach. Ricardo's Delphic style has always given room for varying interpretations.

5 *Principles of Political Economy and Taxation*, in *Works*, ed. Sraffa, pp. 19–20. Hereafter cited in the text as *Principles*.

6 Although Ricardo held an empirical labor theory of value, and although he said that the opinion that the price of commodities depends on the proportion of supply to demand has been the source of much error in economics (*Principles*, p. 382), it turns out that his hostility to supply and demand theory rests on a verbal usage common in his day. Supply and demand was used by writers such as Say, Lauderdale, and Buchanan to refer to short-run competitive or to long-run monopoly cases, where price was different from long-run marginal cost. In the long run under competition, the entry of new capital forced price down to long-run marginal cost, whether it was constant (as in manufacturing) or rising (as in agriculture). Ricardo was prone to speak of cost of production as determining price because in the competitive long run, when resources have moved to eliminate excess profits, price equals marginal cost. Demand enters to determine the quantity produced, and indeed, demand is responsive to price. A good source on Ricardo's usage is S. C. Rankin, "Supply and Demand in Ricardian Price Theory: a Re-interpretation," *Oxford Economic Papers*, 1980, pp. 241–62.

7 *Wealth of Nations* (Modern Library edition, New York, 1937) Book I, chapter IX, p. 87.

8 The Poor Laws were the social welfare legislation of the time; the paupers were given relief in the parish in which they were domiciled, and if they moved they lost the right to relief in the original parish and obtained it in the new one only after a full year. The new parish was reluctant to accept outsiders and the workers were reluctant to move; the Poor Laws hampered the mobility of labor and kept agricultural villages over-populated. See T. S. Ashton, *The Industrial Revolution 1760–1830* (London, 1948).

9 W. O. Thweatt, "James Mill and the Early Development of Comparative Advantage," *HOPE*, 1976, pp. 207–34, discusses the history of the idea. He notes that Robert Torrens expressed it in his 1815 *Essay on the External Corn Trade*, thus establishing a two-year priority over Ricardo, and he argues that

James Mill was responsible for including it in Ricardo's chapter on foreign trade as well as for publicizing it in various articles. Subsequent developments, particularly the making and correcting of errors in the analysis of the division of the gains from trade by James and John Stuart Mill, are covered by W. O. Thweatt, "James and John Mill on Comparative Advantage: Sraffa's Account Corrected," in H. Visser and E. Schoorl (eds), *Trade in Transit* (Dordrecht, 1987).

10  See, for example, Richard Caves and Ronald Jones, *World Trade and Payments*, 3rd edn (Boston, 1979).

11  For references on Jones and Whewell, see chapter 6, n. 22.

12  This paper, reprinted by Augustus Kelley in Whewell, *A Mathematical Exposition of Some Doctrines of Political Economy*, has been explained and evaluated by James Cochrane in *HOPE*, 1970, pp. 419–31.

13  Carl Shoup, *Ricardo on Taxation* (New York, 1960), is a very thorough analysis of the subject, going into all the qualifications and details which cannot be put into a short summary.

14  See D. P. O'Brien, *The Classical Economists* (Oxford, 1975), pp. 224–8. For a lengthy study, consult Maxine Berg, *The Machinery Question and the Making of Classical Political Economy, 1815–1848* (Cambridge, 1980).

15  Wicksell, *Lectures on Political Economy*, vol. I (London, 1934), pp. 133–44.

16  Paul A. Samuelson, "Correcting the Ricardo Error Spotted in Harry Johnson's Maiden Paper," *Quarterly Journal of Economics*, 1977, pp. 519–30.

17  George J. Stigler, *Essays in the History of Economics* (Chicago, Ill., 1965), p. 197.

18  Samuel Hollander, "The Reception of Ricardian Economics," *Oxford Economic Papers*, 1977, pp. 23–57.

19  Samuel Hollander, "On the Substantive Identity of the Ricardian and Neoclassical Conceptions of Economic Organization: the French Connection in British Classicism," *Canadian Journal of Economics*, 1982, p. 587. The burden of this paper is that the narrowing of focus did not mean a fundamental break with the classical economists, who had contributed the essential analysis of a capitalist exchange system.

20  For the advanced student, a mathematical article and a long, densely argued book are recommended. The article, by Paul Samuelson, is summarized in appendix 2 of this present chapter. The book, Samuel Hollander, *The Economics of David Ricardo* (Toronto, 1979), is a major study of Ricardo and the surrounding literature, and has been extensively reviewed. The reviews, by Laurence S. Moss, *Eastern Economic Journal*, 1979, pp. 501–12; D. P. O'Brien, *Oxford Economic Papers*, 1981, pp. 352–86 (with rebuttal by Hollander in the same journal, 1982 pp. 224–46) and E. G. West, *Canadian Journal of Economics*, 1982, pp. 308–26, are in themselves good term paper material.

21  Maurice Dobb, *Theories of Value and Distribution since Adam Smith* (London, 1973), p. 248. For a formal book with the *tendenz*, explaining the linear mathematical models much used in the revival of Ricardo and Marx, see Vivian Walsh and Harvey Gram, *Classical and Neoclassical Theories of General Equilibrium* (Oxford, 1980).

22  Dobb, *Theories of Value*, p. 257. A brief but fairly technical exposition of the Sraffa model is provided by A. L. Levine, "This Age of Leontief ... and Who?

An Interpretation," *Journal of Economic Literature*, 1974, pp. 872–81. A good textbook treatment is E. Ray Canterbury, *The Making of Economics*, 3rd edn (Belmont, Ca.), 1987.

23 Paul A. Samuelson, *Journal of Economic Literature*, 1978, pp. 1415–34.

24 See Sir John Hicks and Samuel Hollander, "Mr. Ricardo and the Moderns," *Quarterly Journal of Economics*, 1977, pp. 351–69, and Carlo Casarosa, "A New Formulation of the Ricardian System," *Oxford Economic Papers*, 1978, pp. 38–63.

# 9

# Classical Economics from Ricardo to Mill's *Principles*

During the period between Ricardo's *Principles* and J. S. Mill's *Principles* classical economics was a lively scene. There was action in both theory and problems of government policy. Because of the large number of personalities, books, and issues involved, this chapter can provide only a sample.[1] We shall feature four men: a Colonel of Marines, two lawyers, and a man who made his living by writing as a journalist as well as on economic subjects. The day of the professionally trained, full-time university economist had still to dawn.

The Colonel was Irish-born Robert Torrens (1780–1864). During the Napoleonic Wars he was stationed on an island near Denmark and there he learned economics from the *Wealth of Nations*. He began writing on economics in 1808. After the wars ended he was at various times a member of Parliament (twice), involved in the colonization of South Australia (a river is named for him there), and a prolific writer on colonization, commerce, and money and banking. He was prominent among the economists of his day; for example, he occupied the chair at the first meeting of the Political Economy Club in 1821. All the leading economists in London met there regularly for debate, including Ricardo, James Mill, Malthus, McCulloch, and others.[2]

As a theorist, Torrens worked within the framework of Adam Smith and David Ricardo. He was one of the four people (along with West, Malthus, and Ricardo) who published papers independently setting forth the idea of Ricardian rent in February 1815. He diverged on the matter of measurement of value, claiming that no absolute measure – especially labor – could be found, and he diverged on the matter of the unimportance of capital in the measurement of value, claiming *au contraire* that value depended on capital in the form of accumulated labor.

A major contribution of Torrens was the first enunciation, traditionally, of the doctrine of comparative cost – that a country could gain from trade even though it was superior as a producer to the other country – in 1815, two years before it appeared in Ricardo's *Principles*.[3] But while he stated the doctrine he did not illustrate by comparing two hypothetical cost ratios as Ricardo did, which is regarded as necessary to give the "ultimate essence" of the problem.[4] However, his influence did not stop there. Since the comparative cost ratios only establish the limits to the price ratios in trade, something else must be called on to find out where within those limits the price ratio ultimately is determined. John Stuart Mill showed it was determined by the principle of reciprocal demand (see chapter 10), but Torrens had long emphasized the role of demand. Although he was in favor of free trade, he was opposed to Britain's reducing her tariffs unilaterally. He believed that she should do it only in return for a reciprocal lowering of tariffs abroad. The reason was that with the proper conditions of demand a tariff can improve the terms of trade of the country which levies it. That is, it will get more imports for each unit of goods exported than it did previously. Torrens's example was Cuba, a sugar exporter which imported hardware from Britain, and which decided to levy a tariff on imports. Because the price of hardware rises in Cuba, that country demands less hardware and consequently offers less sugar to Britain; Britain, with less sugar on the market, pays a higher price per unit; i.e., she offers more hardware for each ton of sugar. Cuba's terms of trade have been improved by the tariff. Torrens did not have a clear idea of demand schedules so his explanations were not complete, but he did have the basic notion. His conclusion was that if both countries had a tariff and then Britain unilaterally removed her tariff, the situation would be the same as if Cuba had imposed a tariff in the free trade case. His policy recommendation was that Britain should remove her tariff only if Cuba also removed hers.[5]

Another of Torrens's long-term interests was money and banking. He began as an advocate of paper currency at the time when Ricardo and the authors of the *Bullion Report of 1810* were claiming that excess issue of the inconvertible pound had caused its depreciation. He claimed, as did many others before and since, that if the paper currency was issued to finance genuine mercantile transactions there could not be too much of it. It financed the needs of trade and was retired when the merchants paid off their debts to the banks. This is known as the real bills doctrine, since the debts (the bills, as the short-term debts were called) were to purchase real goods. Then, many years later in 1833, when he was a member of Parliament he completely reversed his position, claiming that a currency involving both metal and paper was subject to excessive fluctuations, causing distress and eventual national bankruptcy. From then until 1858 he was an ardent, able, and prolific supporter of the Currency School, whose chief principle was that a mixed paper and metallic currency should be made to behave exactly like a strictly metallic currency. The reason, according to Torrens and his fellows of the Currency School (Overstone and Norman) was that only this policy would prevent over-issue of money, price rises, and an unfavorable balance of trade and loss of gold, in the fashion explained long before by David Hume. If each pound in paper currency must have a pound's worth of gold behind it, their goal would be accomplished. But what of bank deposits and checks? This was no problem, because they theorized that the amount of deposits was regulated by the amount of notes kept on reserve behind them.

Their opponents, the Banking School (Tooke and Fullarton), held the position that Torrens had argued in 1812, that if the notes are issued to finance commercial operations there cannot be too many of them. As real bills theorists, they believed in the "law of reflux": the notes would be paid off at the bank when the merchants no longer needed them. Apart from some arguments about what determines the balance of international payments, the other major difference between the two groups was their objective. The Currency School wanted to maintain balance of payments equilibrium by allowing the total volume of currency to fluctuate, falling when there was a gold outflow and rising when there was an inflow. But the Banking School wanted to keep the flow of currency more stable.[6]

As it turned out, the Currency School was successful, in that the Bank Charter Act of 1844 (a bizarre piece of legislation to modern eyes) attempted to put their principles into action. The Act split the Bank of England into the Issue Department and the Banking Department. The former could issue bank notes up to £14 million without gold backing; beyond that, 100 percent gold backing was required. The Banking Department, however, could discount bills as it wished, creating deposits and making loans, on the theory that the volume of bank notes it owned would regulate the deposits in a rigid way – in effect, they would hold no excess reserves and would never change their reserve ratio. (This turned out not to be true; the Bank Act had to be suspended three times in twenty-five years because of the exhaustion of reserves of the Banking Department.)[7]

Why did Torrens change his mind, moving from a champion of paper money to a champion of the Currency School? Apparently he had become convinced that the real bills doctrine was wrong and that currency could be over-issued, from the point of view of balance of payments equilibrium. The change was a gradual one and small changes in his position can be traced out in document after document, eventually resulting in the final 180-degree reversal of his position.[8]

The final topic in this survey of Torrens's career is colonization, a subject in which he took a leading role both in theory and in practice. In 1817 he urged colonization because it would help to relieve the pressure of excess population. Later he said it would help relieve poverty and distress in Ireland. In 1829 appeared the colorful figure of Edward Gibbon Wakefield, who both proposed a specific scheme of colonization and added another rationale. Torrens took up both and was a prolific and forceful advocate. Wakefield claimed that immigrants should not be given free land, for that would lead to scattered settlement, a lack of division of labor and of exchange. In order to encourage concentration he urged that land should be sold to the new immigrants at a "sufficient price" to keep them working for a few years before they could save enough to buy their farms. By working for someone else the immigrant would be adding to productivity through the division of labor. And the money derived from selling the land could be used to subsidize emigration from the mother country.

What Torrens contributed, besides his numerous publications and statements before commissions, was a rationale for supporting emigration different from the Malthusian one he had previously used. The new rationale was that colonization was a means of escape from the stagnation that would occur as the economy approached the stationary state. (Refer to chapter 7 above for a discussion of the idea that colonization could solve the practical problems brought by "general gluts.") Profits and wages would be falling and the terms of trade would turn against the stagnant, mature country. Colonization would allow an outlet for the capital which otherwise would be accumulated and would contribute to the already excess amount. This is an early version of the stagnation thesis popular in the Great Depression of the 1930s.[9]

Torrens's practical work in colonization included membership in the South Australian Land Company, formed in 1831, and chairmanship of the Colonization Commissioners who were to establish provinces in South Australia. He had a stormy time on this commission and eventually resigned.

Torrens was obviously an active man and was of influence in his day; Lord Robbins notes that his influence declined after his death, partly because his publications were issued in small numbers and were hard to find. It was Robbins's contribution to restore him to some standing in the history of economic thought by taking the reader through Torrens's writing and relating it to classical economics generally.

Another busy and influential classical economist of the period was Nassau Senior.[10] Senior was trained as a lawyer and practiced law as a profession, but he saw much poverty among farm workers during the Napoleonic Wars in his youth and this led to his interest in economics. His first published paper was on the Corn Laws in 1821; he was elected a member of the Political Economy Club in 1823; and in 1825 he was appointed Drummond Professor of Political Economy at Oxford. (Henry Drummond was a banker who thought that the prospective future leaders of the country at Oxford should have the same opportunities to study political economy that the East India Company cadets had; it should be remembered that Malthus was the Professor of Political Economy at the East India Company College at Haileybury. Drummond endowed a chair at Oxford, one of the stipulations being that the term of appointment was only five years, and another that the holder had to be an Oxford graduate. Senior held the chair twice, from 1825 to 1830 and from 1847 to 1852.) As Drummond Professor, Senior had to give a stipulated number of lectures per year, many of which he published in his *Outline of Political Economy* (1836). This origin of this book gave Jacob Viner the opportunity for a classic put-down. He commented that Senior's economic writings were "mostly by-products of his duties as a civil servant or – still worse – were prepared for delivery as formal university lectures to nondescript audiences at a then backward university. For such purposes, rigorous and thorough theoretical analysis is not, as a rule, the commodity in most urgent demand."[11] (When Viner calls Senior a "civil servant" he is referring to Senior's membership on various commissions, such as the Commission for Inquiring into the Administration and Operation of the Poor Laws, the Commission on the Condition of the Unemployed Hand-loom Weavers, and the Royal Commission on Popular Education.)

Senior is famous for his distinction between pure and applied economics ("the art of economics"), and his insistence that "theoretical economics is a deductive science based on a group of premises which cover the main data relevant to the specific objects of the science, and which are drawn from the real world by consciousness and observation."[12] These premises are:

1  Economic man. In his words, "Every person is desirous to obtain, with as little sacrifice as possible, as much as possible of the articles of wealth."
2  The Malthusian population principle.
3  The proposition that the power of labor may be indefinitely extended by accumulating and using capital goods.
4  Diminishing returns to capital and labor in agriculture, but not in industry.

Schumpeter used these axioms as the starting point for his analysis of classical economic theory, and gives a detailed and interesting critique of them.[13] With his typical fondness for ranking economists, he thought that Senior's performance as a theorist is "clearly superior to that of Ricardo."

As Jevons noted, Senior was one of the forerunners of marginal utility theory. He wrote that value depends on utility, limitation in supply, and transferableness. Under utility, he said that the important thing was the human desire for variety; otherwise wants would cease when people had provided the simple necessities of life. But because the pleasure of a given class of commodities diminishes in a rapidly increasing ratio (two articles of the same kind rarely give twice the pleasure of one), people demand a wide variety of goods.

The theoretical proposition for which Senior is most famous was his abstinence theory of capital. Production requires three agents: labor, natural agents, and abstinence, defined to be the real cost of waiting or of using a roundabout technique of production. Specifically, he said abstinence is a "term by which we express the conduct of a person who either abstains from the unproductive use of what he can command, or designedly prefers the production of remote to that of immediate results."[14] The reward for waiting is profit, which is necessary because abstinence requires a "painful exertion of the human will."[15] The disutility of labor and of abstinence were known as "real costs" to the classical economists; Mill used the fact that a payment is necessary if abstinence is to be pursued to show that labor did not have a right to the whole product (*Principles*, Book II, chapter 2). Marx attacked it because accumulation was forced on the capitalist by competition; it is a historical necessity, in his view, and the approach of Senior was, he said, the substitution of a sycophantic phrase for an economic category (*Capital*, vol. I, chapter XXIV). Others criticized the idea that abstinence is painful to millionaires; this criticism misses the point that it is really the marginal sacrifice, not the average sacrifice, that determines the supply price of savings. Mill used the abstinence theory, and so did Marshall, changing the name to the more neutral term "waiting" (*Principles*, Book IV, chapter 7). So Senior's idea had a vigorous history.

As noted, a large part of Senior's career was spent in the service of the government, investigating economic problems and recommending solutions to them. These included investigating the laws relating to trade combinations, the problems of Ireland, the poor laws, the hand-loom weavers, and "popular legislation." During this time he made it amply clear that he did not think *laissez-faire* was the normal rule. And he was not hesitant about making radical suggestions; for example, he urged that Church of England property in Ireland be transferred to the Catholic Church, to which the peasants belonged; in the furor over this suggestion he lost his teaching post at the University of London. The *Report on the Hand-loom Weavers* is interesting as an empirical example of the situation Ricardo analyzed in his chapter on machinery. Power looms in the factories had caused great distress among the hand-loom weavers. The obvious answer was for hand-loom weavers to take jobs in other industries or in the textile factories. But the weavers preferred the independence of home employment; and they could employ their children at home. The commissioners rejected taxes on power looms and on imports, and minimum wages; they favored education of the weavers and curbs on trade unions because unions restricted membership and hence reduced occupational mobility. The rejected solutions were not disfavored because they were government interferences; rather they were judged ineffective. Taxes on power looms would drive more workers into hand-loom weaving. Taxes on imports would reduce exports and hence employment. Minimum wages would encourage people to remain in hand-loom weaving, and by raising costs would reduce demand. To this day the problem of what to do with a dying industry remains one not easily solved. American coal miners in Appalachia before the energy crisis and the problems of US and European automobile manufacturers facing Japanese competition would have seemed very familiar to Senior.

Our third hero of this chapter is Scotsman John Ramsay McCulloch (1789–1864). McCulloch can claim to be the first professional economist in the sense of making his living exclusively by teaching and writing on the subject, and he did not do badly. On his death he left £16,000.[16] He started out in life as a lawyer's clerk, but in 1817 he became editor of the *Scotsman*, which is still a major Edinburgh newspaper, and he contributed many economic articles both to that and to the *Edinburgh Review* (one of the major intellectual quarterlies of the day). He began his lecturing career in Edinburgh, and continued this career in London as the Ricardo Memorial Lecturer until 1827. After seeking several university posts, he became Professor of Political Economy at London University from 1828 until 1837, during which time he battled the university because he considered his salary inadequate. He left teaching in 1838 to become Comptroller of the Stationery Office, which he administered, it is said, very efficiently until his death in 1864. But all this time he was scribbling away, not only for the periodicals mentioned above and for the *Encyclopaedia Britannica*, but also for a large number of books: his *Principles* and his edition of the *Wealth of Nations*, the *Commercial Dictionary*, the *Statistical Account of the British Empire*, the *Geographical Dictionary*, the *Treatise on Taxation*, and six collections of scarce and valuable tracts culled from his own fine personal library.

It is difficult to give a short, summary treatment of the work of a man who was active in economics for more than fifty years. Although Schumpeter and Blaug both call McCulloch a Ricardian,[17] O'Brien's detailed scrutiny shows that "McCulloch's work was very Scottish in its general approach. He was firmly in the tradition of Hume and Smith with its mixture of fact and analysis, of theoretical and empirical considerations."[18] Again and again he shows that McCulloch has a basically Smithian approach with Ricardian influences of tone and phraseology which often were gradually dropped as McCulloch grew older and Ricardo's influence receded further into the past. In value theory he tried to produce a cost of production theory rather than using Ricardo's invariable measure of value and his 93 per cent labor cost theory. In international trade he used absolute advantage and factor mobility rather than comparative advantage and factor immobility, as had Ricardo in his famous chapter 7. In public finance he was, like Smith, concerned with growth problems such as the impact of taxes on effort and savings. In his approach to growth he resembled Smith in blending theory and fact, rather than employing Ricardian abstractions; also, he did not accept diminishing returns in agriculture nor did he accept Ricardo's view that machinery would cause unemployment. In money and banking he favored the Currency School with reservations (he did not believe the Act of 1844 had solved all the problems). On social problems he was anti-Malthusian. Unlike Malthus and Ricardo he favored the Poor Laws, to avoid revolution. He favored emigration, to remove population pressure, but did not wish to retain colonies. On colonization he was opposed to Wakefield's scheme of concentrating settlers and selling them land because he followed Smith in arguing that new and fertile land was the great advantage in the growth of a colony, and Wakefield would not make full use of this advantage. On labor, he used the wages fund theory, favored peaceful unionism, and favored regulation of the hours of work of children but not of women if they were to be regarded as responsible adult employees.

In such a brief survey it is not possible to look at all the changes and developments in McCulloch's thought. We can conclude that while he was not among the elite two or three leading thinkers, he was an able practitioner of classical economics and an influential popularizer.

The last major character of this chapter is Mountifort Longfield (1801–84), a lawyer and Ireland's first professor of political economy (at Trinity College, Dublin). This chair was modelled after the Drummond Professorship at Oxford, and not by accident; it was established by Archbishop Whately, who had himself been a Drummond Professor. When Whately came to Ireland and established a similar professorship at Trinity, Longfield competed for and won the chair. (The candidates had to take a written examination prepared by Whately, who was particularly interested in the relationship between Christianity and economics.) While holding the chair, Longfield published three sets of lectures. After his term was over, he became interested in practical problems, serving as a land commissioner and working for legal reform. [19]

Unlike Torrens, Senior, and McCulloch, Longfield was not a famous or influential figure among contemporaries. He was little known outside Ireland, and even there his influence lasted only for a decade or two. He was, however, an original thinker. The standard evaluation has been that he was an early member of the school of utility thinkers which culminated in Jevons. Moss denies this strenuously, claiming that instead Longfield's difference from, for example, Ricardo, was that Longfield had the idea of a demand schedule and used it to analyze price in the very short run. Like Cournot, he had an empirical demand curve, not a utility-based one. Of course he did not speak of a "demand curve"; in his terminology each individual has within himself a series of intensities of demand, each intensity measured by the amount he would pay for a commodity rather than do without it. [20] Ricardo, on the other hand, spoke of the proportion between supply and demand, and had in mind the quantity demanded on the long-run supply curve rather than a schedule. Longfield applied his theory to many situations; for example, he analyzed the "injudicious and injurious species of charity" which was sometimes practiced in years of crop shortage. "Persons of more benevolence than judgment purchase quantities of the ordinary food of the country, and sell them again to the poor at half price." Longfield's analysis was that in the end the poor pay as much as they would have if there had been no interference, because too much is consumed early in the crop year, leaving a greater scarcity and a higher price at the end than would have occurred otherwise. [21]

In common with the classical economists, Longfield dwelt at length on the problem of the distribution of income to the different factors of production. To begin with land rent, he argued that the existence of inferior land kept the rent of superior land from getting more and more exorbitant. If there were only 100 acres of land in the country and it was all of one grade, rents would get very high; however, if there was in addition 900 acres of somewhat inferior land the rent paid on the superior land would be much less. Because Longfield thought that there was much inferior land, relatively speaking, whose productivity was not much less than that of the superior land, he concluded that the rental share of landlords would actually diminish as the society grew, in contrast to Ricardo's pessimistic conclusion. He was also acutely aware of the effect of technology on productivity and rents, and wanted to make legal reforms to make the adoption of new technology easier for Irish farmers who leased from landlords.

Longfield discussed the problem of the returns to the owners of capital, paying much attention to fixed capital in the form of machines as the determining factor in this market. The return to circulating capital (the wages funds) was, he thought, regulated by the return on fixed capital. (Recall that Ricardo thought that the return on capital was regulated by the return to investment in agriculture; Longfield had more of an Industrial Revolution point of view.) The rental price of machines is determined by the price which workers will pay to work with them, which is not the way we usually think of factory employment – we think of employers paying the workers. But Longfield said that workers had the option of not working with the machine (this reflects an early stage in the Industrial Revolution if there was substantial opportunity for workers to produce at home rather than in a mechanized factory). If you think of the total output as accruing to the worker, but that he is willing to accept say only 85 percent of it as wages, letting the employer have the rest, then you can think of the worker as paying 15 percent of his output for the use of the machine. If the labor market is competitive, wages will be equal; since no worker will pay to use a machine unless it raises his productivity, the profits on machines of various degrees of productivity depend on how much more productive each machine is than the least-productive machine a worker will consent to use. (This is in fact the reasoning regarding the rent of land of different grades transferred to machines of different productivity.)

Longfield has thus determined the value of the return to a machine. But he was not able to handle the step of converting the return into a percentage rate of profit, which would be necessary for comparing the return to the cost of borrowing from a capitalist or a bank. As Professor Moss explains,[22] Longfield got himself involved in circular reasoning: the percentage rate of profit is the return divided by the price of the machine, but the price of an investment such as a machine is the return divided by the rate of profit (assuming a perpetual investment for simplicity). The circular reasoning involved in needing to know the price of $x$ before you can find the price of $y$ and vice versa is generally handled in economics by general equilibrium theory;[23] Longfield, as a literary economist of the early nineteenth century without J. S. Mill's amazing logical feel for economic interdependence (see chapter 10), was not able to get himself out of his bind.

Wages, says Longfield, are the share left after rent and profits are paid. Laborers share in this total according to the sort of occupational differences Adam Smith stressed (see chapter 5 above). Unlike Ricardo and Malthus, he did not believe that wages would fall to the subsistence level, but rather that they would rise if productivity growth outran population growth.

Longfield's differences from the classical, Ricardian approach are obvious. In many ways he anticipated the theory of Marshall and other late nineteenth-century writers, but he did not pay much attention to the supply side of labor and capital markets. However, as pointed out earlier, his theory had little impact outside of Ireland and even there was soon forgotten.

Finally, on economic policy, Longfield started out advocating *laissez-faire* and free trade. Over his career, however, he shifted his position to favoring such things as poor relief if it was not so high as to diminish work incentives; state creation of a monopoly bank to protect against fraud and to stabilize the money supply; recognition of tenant rights against arbitrary landlord behavior. In general, throughout his career, he was particularly concerned with the welfare of the working class. It is to be regretted that he did not have more influence than he did.

The intellectuals and some of the politicians of the day did not always greet the analysis and recommendations of the economists with enthusiasm or respect. Some typical comments were: Edmund Burke, "The age of chivalry is gone. That of sophisters, economists and calculators has succeeded; and the glory of Europe is extinguished forever." Carlyle said, "Of all the quacks that ever quacked, political economists are the loudest. Instead of telling us what is meant by one's country, by what causes men are happy, moral, religious, or the contrary, they tell us how flannel jackets are exchanged for pork hams, and speak much of the land last taken into cultivation."[24] Walter Bagehot, although editor of the *Economist* and a journalistic writer on economic subjects, did not like abstract economics; he said that "no real Englishman in his secret soul was ever sorry for the death of a political economist; he is much more likely to be sorry for his life." There was criticism of the methodology, that the premises were too narrow, and of the conclusions; there were complaints that the economists had not enough compassion, and that they perceived the world as a dismal place that should be regulated by the market. Many of the critics were poets and novelists, and what Grampp calls "philosophic idealists," opposed to the liberalism of the nineteenth-century economists. The lively interest of outsiders in economics died away as the subject became more technical, and today objections to economics are usually the result of incorrect forecasts of business cycle and stock market trends. But the critics had their effect; both Alfred Marshall and John Stuart Mill took them seriously.

In addition to the four men reviewed in this chapter, many other economists were active at that time. For example, economists played a larger role in Parliament during this period than in any legislature before or since. Fifty-five people who wrote in an organized way on economic problems (and so were considered economists) were members of Parliament between 1819 and 1868 (i.e., between the year Ricardo was elected to Parliament and the year John Stuart Mill was defeated in a Parliamentary election). In one Parliament in the 1830s, thirty-two members were economists. While this is not large compared to the total membership of 658 in the House of Commons, the speeches, writing, and committee activities of these men gave them much influence. One student of the subject says their influence on things like the Corn Laws and taxation far exceeded the number of votes they represented; they sponsored many reforms which were eventually adopted after being turned down repeatedly.[25] The prominence of economic science in the deliberations of Parliament in the early nineteenth century is in marked contrast to its status in the late eighteenth century. "Even twenty-five years after the publication of the *Wealth of Nations*, the Houses of Parliament were largely indifferent to its tenets, suspicious of its truth, and uncertain of its applicability."[26]

Finally, a survey of economics following Ricardo would not be complete if it ignored a group of writers who have been called "Ricardian socialists." The tag was applied by H. S. Foxwell in an introduction to a book written by Austrian Anton Menger entitled *The Right to the Whole Produce of Labor* (1899). It was Foxwell's contention that Thomas Hodgskin, William Thompson, John Gray, and John Bray had begun with the labor theory of value and drawn from it the idea that since laborers bestowed the entire value, they deserved the entire product and that they were exploited if they did not get it. This characterization of these writers is now regarded as an extreme over-simplification. Hodgskin did not agree that value was determined by labor alone under capitalism; he held that there was a *natural* price (equal to labor embodied) and a *social* price under capitalism, which was the natural price plus the unearned income of landlords and capitalists. And he did not draw socialist conclusions; rather, he argued that only workers should own capital and that they should own only what they needed for production. Their ownership would be individual, not collective. British socialism at that time did not propose nationalization of industry or central economic planning.

Hodgskin's writings were an influence on Marx, as Hodgskin had to prove that capital was not a separate factor of production in order to prove that labor had the right to the whole product. But Marx did not like Hodgskin's approach; "the author should have remembered that revolutions are not made by laws," says Marx in *Capital*.[27]

Another Ricardian socialist was William Thompson. He criticized inequality in wealth and income, on the Benthamite utilitarian ground that since there was decreasing marginal utility to wealth, total social utility would be at a maximum if there was equal distribution. In addition, workers without capital lacked security, so his ideal society had the workers owning the capital. Finally, if such a society were competitively organized, it would have various evils (the public interest would not be served, women would be oppressed, information would be scarce). To avoid this, he urged voluntary cooperative communities. While he held the labor-embodied theory of value, he did not draw from it the Marxian conclusion of the inevitable conflict over the surplus.[28]

## Notes

1 For a more complete story, see D. P. O'Brien, *The Classical Economists* (Oxford, 1975) and A. W. Coats, *The Classical Economists and Economic Policy* (London, 1971).

2 Torrens's life is surveyed in S. A. Meenai, "Robert Torrens – 1780-1864," *Economica*, 1956, pp. 49–61, and his work is given a very detailed analysis in Lionel Robbins, *Robert Torrens and the Evolution of Classical Economics* (London, 1958).

3 As noted in chapter 8, n. 9, W. O Thweatt has argued that it was really James Mill who put it in Ricardo's book and later developed it in detail.

4 Robbins, *Robert Torrens*, p. 23.

5 Naturally this was a controversial position at a time when economists generally were pushing for free trade. Robbins's book reviews the controversy, in particular with Nassau Senior, and judges that Torrens won the debate. John Stuart Mill showed his superiority as a theorist by the way he handled the problem in *Essays on Some Unsettled Questions in Political Economy*.

6 John Stuart Mill played a prominent part in this controversy; his role is explained below in chapter 10.

7 In addition to the material in Robbins, *Robert Torrens*, two excellent sources on the Currency–Banking controversy are Jacob Viner, *Studies in the Theory of International Trade* (New York, 1937), chapters III, IV, and V, and M. R. Daugherty, "The Currency–Banking Controversy," *Southern Economic Journal*, 1942-3, pp. 140–55 and 241–51.

8 See D. P. O'Brien, "The Transition in Torrens' Monetary Thought," *Economica*, 1965, pp. 269–301, which presents an important recently discovered manuscript of Torrens's, written in 1826, and traces out the steps in Torrens's conversion.

9 John Stuart Mill was another supporter of Wakefield's scheme, and even approved of the Wakefield–Torrens idea of excess capital accumulation. But it has been pointed that this was contrary to his general Ricardianism; with Ricardo accumulation stops when the stationary state is reached, with Torrens it continues. See Robbins, *Robert Torrens*, and Donald Winch, *Classical Political Economy and Colonies* (Cambridge, Mass., 1965), p. 139. Winch's book gives a good coverage of Wakefield's ideas and influence.

10 There are two major sources: Marian Bowley, *Nassau Senior and Classical Economics* (London, 1937), an analysis of his economics, and a detailed biography, S. Leon Levy, *Nassau W. Senior 1790–1864* (New York, 1970), which is a reprint edition of a book originally published in 1943 under the title *Nassau W. Senior: the Prophet of Modern Capitalism*.

11 Book review of Marian Bowley, *Nassau Senior and Classical Economics*, reprinted in *The Long View and the Short* (Glencoe, Ill., 1958), p. 419.

12 Bowley, *Nassau Senior*, p. 49.

13 *History of Economic Analysis*, pp. 575ff.

14 Bowley, *Nassau Senior*, p. 143.

15 Ibid., p. 149.

16 The great authority on McCulloch is D. P. O'Brien, *J. R. McCulloch: A Study in Classical Economics* (London, 1970).

17 J. Schumpeter, *History of Economic Analysis* (New York, 1954), p. 470; M. Blaug, *International Encyclopedia of the Social Sciences*, vol. X (New York, 1968).

18 O'Brien, *J. R. McCulloch*, p. 16.

19 Laurence S. Moss, *Mountifort Longfield: Ireland's First Professor of Political Economy* (Ottowa, Ill., 1976) is the book length study of Longfield. Also useful is R. D. C. Black's introduction to the A. M. Kelley reprint of *The Collected Writings of Mountifort Longfield*. I have drawn heavily on Professor Moss's book in the following discussion.

20 Malthus was the originator of the concept of intensity of demand; Longfield developed rather than originated the idea. Recently opinion has been returning to the view of Marshall, the great economist of the late nineteenth century, that Ricardo knew that demand played an essential part in governing value but passed over it lightly because he thought its role was less obscure than that of cost of production (*Principles*, 8th edn, p. 503). S. C. Rankin claims that Ricardo generalized Smith's long-run equilibrium theory by applying it to increasing cost cases, and Hollander claims that Ricardo's treatment of demand was particularly sophisticated. For more detail, see chapter 8. If this revisionism is accepted, Longfield's difference from Ricardo would be more terminological than substantial.

21 Longfield, *Lectures on Political Economy* (New York, 1971) p. 56.

22 *Mountifort Longfield*, p. 82.

23 In the case at hand, William J. Baumol, *Economic Theory and Operations Analysis*, 4th edn (Englewood Cliffs, NJ, 1977), has a highly recommended discussion of the determination of interest rates in the general equilibrium model; see pp. 646–8.

24 These and many other quotations are to be found in Jacob Viner, "The Economist in History," *American Economic Review*, 1963, pp. 1–22. Another related article is William D. Grampp, "Classical Economics and its Moral Critics," *History of Political Economy* (*HOPE*), Fall 1973, pp. 359–74.

25 Frank W. Fetter, "The Influence of Economists in Parliament on British Legislation from Ricardo to John Stuart Mill," *Journal of Political Economy*, 1975, pp. 1051–64. For a more detailed survey see the book by the same author, *The Economist in Parliament, 1780–1868* (Durham, NC, 1980), and Barry Gordon, *Economic Doctrine and Tory Liberalism, 1824–1830* (London, 1979).

26 Kirk Willis, "The Role in Parliament of the Economic Ideas of Adam Smith, 1776–1800," *HOPE*, 1979, pp. 505–44.

27 *Capital* vol. I, (New World paperback edition, New York, 1967), p. 751.

28 The most authoritative articles on these writers are by E. K. Hunt, "Value Theory in the Writings of the Classical Economists, Thomas Hodgskin, and Karl Marx," *HOPE*, 1977, pp. 322–45 and "Utilitarianism and the Labor Theory of Value: a Critique of the Ideas of William Thompson," *HOPE*, 1979, pp. 545–71.

# 10

# John Stuart Mill

The history of John Stuart Mill must start with his father, James Mill, "the consummate utilitarian propagandist and theorist," "the enigma of a man – that intellectual machine that did not know how not to work," and we begin here not simply because of biological paternity.[1] James Mill was born in Scotland in 1773 and was educated at the University of Edinburgh under the patronage of Sir John Stuart. But he made his career in London, at first as a writer and later as an important official of the East India Company (his title was the Examiner of the India Correspondence).[2] Among the friends he made in London two were particularly important, both in James Mill's life and for the influence they later had on his eldest son, John Stuart Mill. One of these was David Ricardo, and reference has already been made in chapter 8 to James Mill's influence in urging and cajoling Ricardo into writing and publishing his *Principles*. Mill had long been interested in economics, publishing several pamphlets between 1804 and 1808.

Of these pamphlets, *Commerce Defended* (1808) is particularly important. In it he has one of the very early statements of Say's Law, an early and incomplete contribution to the theory of comparative advantage, and an anticipation of Ricardo's concern with distributive shares and the downplaying of rent as the significant source of economic surplus (as it was, for example, in the Physiocrats) in favor of an emphasis on profits.[3] As to what he was defending commerce from, it was from an attempt to justify the prohibition of trade by neutral vessels between Britain and the continent during the Napoleonic Wars. The defenders of the prohibition, William Spence in particular, typically used Physiocratic doctrine (wealth comes from the land) and under-consumptionist arguments (the need for high spending by landlords) to justify the proposition that trade was not the source of wealth. The role of Say's Law and the theory of comparative advantage in this dispute are obvious. After these publications, James Mill continued his interest in economics even though he did no more writing in the field until he published *The Elements of Political Economy* in 1821.[4] The book proved to be a very dogmatic and unconditional statement of

Ricardian doctrines and Mill is therefore classed by Schumpeter as forming one of the core of adherents necessary to be able to say that there was a school of Ricardian economics. When J. S. Mill came in his turn to write economics he had a solid Ricardian training to draw on.

The other important friend made by James Mill was Jeremy Bentham (1748–1832). Bentham was the leader of the Utilitarians and the Radical Reformers. He was interested in legal reform, not only of the system of law but of many aspects of government – public education, prison reform, secret ballot, popular democracy, and a long list of other reforms. The philosophic basis for this was Utilitarianism, the doctrine that man operates under the governance of pain and pleasure, with happiness the net sum of the two. People act in response to their interests, which are not exclusively their self-interests but to some extent include the happiness of others. It is necessary to have a government to make individuals act so as to achieve a maximum of happiness, the greatest good for the greatest number; this is the function of both legislation and education. The pleasures to be considered include those of the senses, the mind, and the heart. Bentham laid out a "Felicific Calculus" to help the legislator decide whether his actions were adding to or subtracting from happiness. This was a list of dimensions to consider in determining whether a pleasure or pain would have a greater or less value; it includes such things as intensity, duration, certainty, remoteness, and various feedback considerations.[5] Psychological hedonism, the positive statement that people act so as to maximize their net self-pleasure, is not the same thing as the normative statement that governments should provide the greatest happiness for the greatest number, although James Mill did hold both views.[6]

These were the ideas of the man whom James Mill met in 1808. At the time they met Bentham was very little known by the general public. But Mill became his disciple, editor, and propagator. He also helped Bentham decide that democracy was a desirable form of government. In return Bentham, who was independently wealthy, helped Mill's income by providing a vacation house as well as leasing him a house at half price. Mill wrote a lot of Utilitarian propaganda during this period, including *Essay on Government*, and articles in the reviews and in the *Supplement* to the *Encyclopaedia Britannica*. And when he turned to his son John Stuart's education, James provided the young man with what the latter called in his *Autobiography* "a course of Benthamism."

J. S. Mill's education at the hands of what Viner called his "dour and magerful father" was incredible. Greek at the age of three, along with arithmetic; history (Hume and Gibbon) a couple of years later; Latin at age eight; logic at twelve; but because of their difficulty Ricardo's *Principles* and his pamphlets on money were held off until age thirteen. No wonder that he had a breakdown when he was twenty. His father treated him as an adult, kept him from playing with other boys, and gave him no holidays. At age sixteen he took on Colonel Robert Torrens in print about the labor theory of value (and lost).[7] Before he was twenty he had edited

Bentham's *Rationale of Evidence* and published seven major articles on economics, politics, and the law.

After his mental crisis he decided that Bentham had not paid enough attention to important things such as poetry and art, so he began reading and was influenced by a wide variety of writers – Wordsworth, Coleridge, and Carlyle, for example. One important influence was Auguste Comte, a French philosopher who wanted to create one social science that would study human society in *all* its aspects.[8]

When he was twenty-four he met Mrs Harriet Taylor, whom he later married after a Platonic love affair of twenty years' duration. He attributed fantastic mental, moral, and artistic achievements to her, and claimed that she had an enormous influence on him. This will require attention when we look at his *Principles of Political Economy*, but first we should look at Mill's achievements in fields other than economics.

Mill followed his father into the employment of the British East India Company, and after his day's work at the office he wrote widely on many subjects: logic, philosophy, religion, government, as well as economics. In all these fields he is recognized as an important contributor. In fact, his obituary notices give the impression that in his day people thought his greatest contribution was in logic rather than politics or economics, even though his published output was higher in economics than in any of his other fields. Mill's reputation in philosophy today is that he was the most influential philosopher in Britain in the nineteenth century, and in particular he was very profound and effective in his espousal of the liberal view of men and society. It is agreed that he was not among the greatest of "pure" philosophers; his influence came from his efforts to be relevant to practical matters, even when he was writing of abstract subjects such as logic. And his reformulations of empricism and utilitarianism added to the relevance and vitality of these ideas.[9]

In Mill's *Collected Works* there are twenty-seven essays in the volumes on *Economics and Society*, in addition to his two books, *Essays on Some Unsettled Questions of Political Economy* and *Principles of Political Economy*. The *Essays on Some Unsettled Questions* were written in 1829 and 1830, but not published until 1844. They are papers on economic theory and include some famous and powerful contributions. The first is an extension of the classical theory of international trade (i.e., the James Mill–Torrens–Ricardo theory of comparative cost) to explain exactly how the international price ratio is determined and how the gains from trade are divided. Before J. S. Mill's essay the theory had simply said that a country exported the products in which its costs were relatively lowest, and had set the relative costs of production as the limits of relative prices in the trading countries (e.g., the price of silk in world trade could vary between its cost of production in the low-cost country and in the high-cost country). But Mill set forth the idea of demand as a function of price (the first systematic use of this concept in British economics, although Cournot had used it in France in 1838), and used the demands of the countries to determine where within the cost limits the market price would actually settle. He handled other trade problems with the same concepts; these problems included tariffs and what they do to international prices, the effects of payment of tribute, and the analysis of two countries competing in the market of a third one. When this material was later reproduced in Mill's *Principles*, it won the accolade of Francis Ysidro Edgeworth as "the great chapter,"[10] and in addition, the material Mill added on the existence of equilibrium has recently been called "one of the astonishing achievements of the human intellect."[11] Mill's theory was later put into geometry by Alfred Marshall, and is still presented in international economics texts as "offer curves" or "reciprocal demand curves," which vary from the usual demand curves by having quantities of the two goods traded on the axes rather than having price on one axis. Price appears in these diagrams as the ratio of the amount of one good traded for the other: $P_x/P_y = y/x$. For example, if $P_x =$ \$1 and $P_y =$ \$0.50, then $1x$ exchanges for $2y$.

Mill showed that the equilibrium price depended on the elasticities of demand in the two countries, and so did the answers to the other problems he examined. While he had the concept of elasticity of demand in mind, he did not express it with Marshall's precision; rather he classified the influence of "cheapness" on demand according to whether the quantity demanded would be increased more than, as much as, or less than the cheapness.[12]

The second of Mill's *Essays on some Unsettled Questions* deals with Say's Law under the title "Of the Influence of Consumption on Production." This was a denial of the crude version of Say's Law that there could be no general over-production. When there exists a money economy, the seller does not have to buy immediately. There are times when people demand money rather than goods because they have a "general expectation of being called upon to meet sudden demands" (*Collected Works*, vol. IV, p. 277). Then there is a general excess of commodities and a general but temporary fall in price. Becker and Baumol, in reviewing the literature on classical monetary theory, say that in this essay "It is all there and explicitly – Walras' Law, Say's Identity which Mill points out holds only for a barter economy the 'utility of money' which consists in permitting purchases to be made when convenient, the possibility of (temporary) oversupply of commodities when money is in excess demand, and Say's Equality which makes this only a temporary possibility."[13] (For the distinction between Say's Identity and Say's Equality see chapter 7 on Malthus and Ricardo.) This is one of the great papers of classical monetary theory because of its clarity, although it was not novel in terms of ideas – John Ramsay McCulloch had often made the same points.[14]

In money and banking as in other fields, Mill's concern was typically with the practical as illuminated by theory rather than with theory per se. In this case, the practical issue was the controversy over how to regulate the currency. As explained in chapter 9, the Currency School argued that a paper currency convertible into gold should fluctuate in quantity exactly as would a 100 percent gold coin circulation, to maintain the value of the currency. The Banking School claimed that no regulation of the note issue was needed; bankers could not over-issue since any excess of paper money over the needs of trade would come back to the banks as deposits. Mill agreed with this doctrine when the markets were in a "quiescent" state, but thought that when the markets were in a "speculative" state businessmen would take out excessive amounts of loans (*Principles*, Book III, chapter XXIV, section 2). Thus he was in a somewhat intermediate position, although he claimed that the Banking School was far nearer to the whole truth than was the currency theory.

Other papers in the *Essays on Unsettled Questions* were of lesser importance. After they were written, Mill began putting his major efforts into his *Logic*. Then when he decided to write a "treatise on political economy, analogous to that of Adam Smith," he had been influenced by Comte, so that he did not regard economics as a thing by itself but as part of a larger whole. Thus his *Principles of Political Economy* is subtitled *With Some of their Applications to Social Philosophy*. He dedicated some gift copies of the *Principles* (and indeed wished to dedicate *all* the copies) to Harriet Taylor as the most eminently qualified to appreciate the speculations on social improvement as well as being the originator of many of them; it is therefore appropriate at this point to survey Mill's relations with Mrs Taylor.

As mentioned earlier, Mill met Harriet Taylor when they were both in their early twenties. She was bored with her non-intellectual husband and her social circle; he was ready for a Platonic affair. Twenty years later, John Taylor died, and Mill and Harriet were married, but she only lived seven more years before dying of tuberculosis in 1858. Mill, who was extremely devoted to her and always gave her extravagant praise, bought a house within sight of her grave in France and lived there with Harriet's daughter Helen until his own death in 1873.[15]

Her contributions to his general intellectual interests included the psychology of women (one of his books was *The Subjugation of Women*, 1869) and a deep interest in socialism and radicalism. The latter showed up in the *Principles* in Book 2, chapter I, "On Property," which has been called (by Blaug) the most famous chapter in the book; it was the first time that socialism had been treated in a major book in economics. (Mill managed to cover communism without mentioning Marx or Engels, which shows the negligible impact they had on economics in Britain at the time.) Her other contributions to the *Principles*, according to Mill, included the chapter on "The Probable Futurity of the Labouring Class," which rejects the idea of the elite leading the poor but urges peasant proprietorship, consumer cooperatives and profit-sharing so that the poor can help themselves. She was also given credit for the idea that the laws of production are technological in nature but the laws of distribution are man-made and therefore are of a different order. This is an example of what Dr Pedro Schwartz calls her "sometimes regrettable influence."[16] Actually production and distribution interact; the distribution of income affects production decisions because it influences demand, while production decisions such as the proportions in which the factors of production are used affects incomes. The analysis of both requires the economic theory which Mill put off until Book III of the *Principles* instead of beginning his treatise with it. He does conclude Book III with a chapter, "Of Distribution as Affected by Exchange," which concludes that the Ricardian laws of rent, wages, and profits are not modified by exchange and money, but the arrangement is awkward.

Mill began writing the *Principles* in 1845; it was ready for the press about two years later, even though he had taken six months off from it to write articles on his solution to the Irish potato famine (which was to form peasant properties on Ireland's waste lands). This means that he took eighteen months to write a book that totals 971 pages in the *Collected Works* edition. Professor Stigler disagrees with Leslie Stephen, who remarked in 1900 that this speed of composition shows that Mill did not revise any first principles; since Stephen had made the same criticism of lack of originality about Mill's *Logic*, which took twelve years to write, Stephen should have inferred only that Mill took a course in speed writing after 1842. [17] In any event, his goal was to do in 1848 what Smith had done in 1776: to present economic principles together with their applications and their relationships to social philosophy, but using the best contemporary economic theory and nineteenth- rather than eighteenth-century social ideas. As already mentioned, he did this under the headings of production, distribution, and exchange in the first three books; the other two books studied growth and government. It is an extremely broad book; Schumpeter remarks that "there was room for everything within its spacious folds," and he is right. It is very difficult to summarize so extensive a book; we shall therefore consider some main themes and some problems of interpretation.

One problem is whether Mill, although a classical economist, belongs to the subset of Ricardian classical economists. Schumpeter believed that the qualifications which Mill made to Ricardo's theory affected essentials of theory and of social outlook. Blaug put Mill in a "half-way house" between Ricardo and the marginal revolution, claiming that the reformulation of the Ricardian system which he performed left it emasculated. This reformulation took two avenues: one was the addition to Ricardo of ideas from other people, such as the abstinence theory of profit, the generalization of the rent concept, the effects of different systems of land tenure, and factors influencing savings. The other was original concepts which he formulated; there were so many of these that George Stigler credited Mill with being one of the most original economists in the history of the science. We have already noticed his contributions to international trade theory and to Say's Law. Other ideas that were important include non-competing groups, the analysis of joint products, alternative costs, economies of scale, a clear and accurate statement of the law of supply and demand (this was a contribution to British economics; Cournot had already done it in France), the compensation principle, the substitution effect of price changes, and the derived demand theory of factor prices.[18]

Recently the idea that Mill inhabited a half-way house has been challenged.[19] Professor Hollander distinguished between Ricardian economics in the broad sense (economic progress and the laws of distribution when there are diminishing returns to agriculture; emphasis on cost in determining value; Say's Law) and in the narrow sense – the use of the invariable standard of value to derive the fundamental theorem, which is that there is an inverse relation between proportional wages and proportional profits. Hollander contends that in the *Principles* Mill was a Ricardian in the narrow sense. At the same time he recognizes that many of the innovations of Mill himself and of others which Mill used are incompatible with the Ricardian system. Hollander is unable to find an explanation which satisfies him as to why Mill allowed these inconsistencies to stand, although he examines several possiblities; it remains, he says, a problem. And so we shall leave it, as an (at the moment) unresolved controversy in the history of economic thought.

Along with Mill's highly praised contributions to economic theory are a couple of theoretical propositions which have exerted fascination because of their lack of clarity or because of the extraordinary influence they had on the profession at the time. An example of the former is his "fourth fundamental proposition" about capital. His first three fundamental propositions (Book I, chapter V) are that industry is limited by capital, that capital is the result of saving, and that capital is consumed (either tools are worn out, or material is destroyed when its ultimate product is consumed, or laborers consume their wages. This is the underlying rationale for Say's Law: saving eventually results in consumption or, as Smith put it, in spending.) The fourth proposition, which Schumpeter characterized as "enshrined in a confused and embarrassed discussion,"[20] is that "Demand for commodities is not demand for labour." What does determine the demand for labor is the amount of capital devoted to the payment of labor, says Mill. To the student trained in contemporary micro and macro theory it seems obvious that the demand for labor is derived from the demand for commodities, and so Mill cannot be correct. But in the context of classical economics, the proposition follows from the standard classical model: Say's Law, the wages fund, fixed factor proportions, perfectly mobile productive factors, savings-investment equality, the neutrality of money, and a purely competitive economy.[21] It should be added that the fourth proposition holds in the long run, abstracting from the short-run considerations Mill explained in his essay "Of the Influence of Consumption on Production." In the long-run model the total demand for labor is given by the wages fund, the amount of past production that has been allocated for the support of productive labor as Mill put it (*Principles*, p. 63). And the number of workers demanded is given by the fixed-coefficients technology. If, to take a simple example, each unit of capital in the form of machines requires two workers (one to tend the machine and one to fetch raw material and carry away the finished product), then an economy with 100 machines would employ 200 workers in the productive sector. Suppose further that there are 300 people in the labor force and the wages fund amounts to 1,500 bushels of corn in real terms. Then 100 people will be employed as unproductive workers in Adam Smith's sense (servants and the like) and the per capita real wage will be five bushels of corn. To raise real wages more saving will have to be done this year in order to increase the wages fund next year, or else workers will have to reduce their family size. To increase total employment in the productive sector more saving will have to be done to increase the number of machines. Total employment depends on capital formation; the demand for commodities determines the composition of the basket of goods produced by the economy but not the amount of labor used in producing it. But what if there are different technologies in different industries – one industry using one worker per machine, another using three workers per machine? Then changing the direction of the demand for commodities from the first industry to the second would increase the demand for labor. Implicitly, Mill assumed that such differences in technical coefficients did not exist.[22] Controversy has raged for more than 100 years over the meaning and validity of the fourth fundamental proposition, a tribute to the lack of lucidity and the tortuous nature of the examples Mill used to illustrate the idea.

Because the wages fund was so important in classical economics and in the evolution of John Stuart Mill's thought, a little diagrammatic reinforcement may help. The fundamental equation is that

Real wages per capita × number of workers = stock of wages goods

This is, like the formula for a demand curve of unitary elasticity, the equation of a rectangular hyperbola. The diagram therefore looks like figure 10.1. Given the number of workers, the real wage is determined; to increase real wages, either a larger stock of wages goods must be accumulated or else there must be fewer workers.

Since the wages fund played such a key role in the economics of John Stuart Mill, it came as a great shock to the profession when, in a review of a book by W. T. Thornton, Mill declared that he had been guilty along with the rest of the world of accepting the theory without the qualifications and limitations necessary to make it admissible, which was his circumlocutory way of saying that he was abandoning it.[23] Modern commentators have, naturally, different views as to whether this was a good thing. According to P. A. Samuelson,

> Discussion of the so-called wage fund doctrine constitutes one of the most sterile chapters in that dreary gap between the classical age and the revolutionary neoclassical discoveries of the last third of the nineteenth century. . . . It is one of the characteristics of the history of economic doctrines that whenever Adam Smith let fall a casual remark – perhaps defining a desirable canon of taxation, or

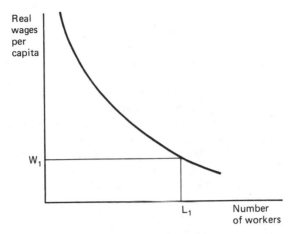

**Figure 10.1**

extolling the superiority of short-term credit, or pointing out the dependence of wages on capital – then throughout subsequent history these casual thoughts have gone reverberating down the corridors of time, ending up in the strangest places and in the strangest forms.[24]

By contrast, George Stigler believes the theory was correct (it made correct predictions), and, while it was not as correct as the marginal productivity theory which had not yet been invented, it was better than no theory at all.[25] But in the 1860s and 1870s what appeared important was Mill's conclusion: the doctrine that trade unions cannot raise wages was deprived of its scientific foundation, and the question of whether or not to support trade unionism became one of prudence and social duty, not political economy.[26] Political economy had said that at the beginning of the technically determined time period of production in the economy (in a farming economy in the temperate zone, it would be one year) there existed a stock of wage goods, the size of which had been determined by the savings of the capitalists. Over the period of production this stock of real goods was expended in hiring labor. Union action could not increase the stock; its size depended on savings.[27] It was this doctrine which Mill abandoned.

While the average wage rate was determined in the short run by the wages fund and the number of workers, within the group of working men unionized labor could raise its wages – but only at the expense of non-unionized workers. Mill thought this presented a problem of morality in the short run but that in the long run, without unions, workers would "people up to the point which will keep their wages at that miserable rate which the low scale of their ideas and habits makes endurable to them" (*Collected Works*, vol. 5, p. 664). Union members, being better educated and more prudent, would exercise population restraint and keep the standard of living up. This is just one example of Mill's constant pre-occupation with Malthusian problems.

The significance of Mill's recantation of the wages fund is that it is taken to be an overt statement of the crumbling of the classical system and of the loss of confidence in it which preceded the marginal revolution of the 1870s. Indeed, Henry Sidgwick in 1883 fixed the date for the passing away of the "halcyon days of Political Economy" as the appearance of Mill's review of Thornton.[28] In England and the United States killing the wages fund notion became a favorite sport, says Schumpeter[29] and was part of the general abandonment of classical economics. But in the interval between the publication of Mill's *Principles* and the rise of Jevons and, in particular, Marshall, the book was the bible of British economists. Viner reports, as evidence that the *Principles* was the longest-lived textbook economics ever had, the fact that it was used in his first college course in economics at McGill University around 1910.[30] And it was still used at Oxford in 1919; it is Professor Lekachman's suggestion that this was because the other possible choice, Marshall's *Principles*, had been written by a Cambridge man.[31]

The unique character of Mill's *Principles* lies in its "pervasive moral tone, at once sentimental and austere,"[32] in its constant attention to the applications of theory and the attempt to make the book practical, and in its insistence that Malthusian population consequences are of the first importance in judging the desirability of economic policies. Contemporary Mill scholarship emphasizes that the "new political economy" Mill espoused was his interest in social justice and his examination of institutions such as trade unions, government, both as a remedy for the deficiencies of *laissez-faire* capitalism and as the potential owner under socialism, and his Utopian vision of a future society of equal, free, and just people.[33] Although Mill originated all the theoretical innovations listed earlier in the chapter, he really thought that "Happily, there is nothing in the laws of Value which remains for the present or any future writer to clear up; the theory of the subject is complete" (*Principles*, p. 456). This famous line did not please Jevons, who concocted a well-known line of his own concerning the basically Ricardian theory which he was trying to upset; he referred to "the noxious influence of authority."[34] But this attitude toward theory on the part of Mill does show that for him the essential thing was economic reform.

## Notes

1  The first quotation is from Donald Winch (ed.), *James Mill: Selected Economic Writings* (Chicago, Ill., 1966), p. 1; the second is from Joseph Schumpeter, *History of Economic Analysis* (New York, 1954), p. 476.
2  Details of Mill's ideas and actions on India are given in a highly interesting book, William J. Barber, *British Economic Thought and India 1600–1858*

(London, 1975). Mill won the job on the strength of a book, *The History of British India* (1817), which he wrote at the same time that he was supporting himself and his nine-child family by journalism and editing.

3 These contributions are surveyed in William Baumol, "Say's (at Least) Eight Laws, or What Say and James Mill May Really Have Meant," *Economica*, 1977, pp. 145–61; William O. Thweatt, "James Mill and the Early Development of Comparative Advantage," *History of Political Economy (HOPE)*, 1976, pp. 207–34; and Ingrid H. Rima, "James Mill and Classical Economics: A Reappraisal," *Eastern Economic Journal*, 1975, pp. 113–18.

4 John Stuart Mill reports in his *Autobiography* how this book was written. He says that James Mill decided to write a didactic treatise of Ricardian doctrines fit for learners. Each day on their walks James gave John a lecture on a portion of the subject, and the next day John had to deliver a written report which had to be rewritten until it was "clear, precise, and tolerably complete." These reports then became the notes from which the *Elements of Political Economy* were written. At this time J. S. Mill was thirteen years old.

5 See chapter 14 for a discussion of the influence this idea had on Jevons. Bentham's discussion is in chapter IV of his book *An Introduction to the Principles of Morals and Legislation* (1789). A detailed analysis is to be found in Wesley C. Mitchell, *Types of Economic Theory* (New York, 1967), chapter III, and also in W. C. Mitchell, "Bentham's Felicific Calculus," in *The Backward Art of Spending Money* (New York, 1937).

6 See Jacob Viner, "Bentham and J. S. Mill," *American Economic Review*, 1949, pp. 360–82. Although Bentham wrote a considerable amount on economics (his *Economic Writings*, edited by W. Stark, London, 1954, fill three volumes), his work on this subject was pretty much unknown and had little influence. For a summary of his economic ideas, and, in particular, a review of the debated question as to exactly how much *laissez-faire* Bentham believed in, see T. W. Hutchison, "Bentham as an Economist," *Economic Journal*, 1956, pp. 288–306.

7 Lionel Robbins, *Robert Torrens and the Evolution of Classical Economics* (London, 1958), p. 71.

8 A good exposition of the details of Comte's theory is W. J. Ashley's introduction to his edition of J. S. Mill's *Principles of Political Economy* (1909). Bernard Semmel, *John Stuart Mill and the Pursuit of Virtue* (New Haven, Conn., 1984) discusses some fascinating aspects of the relations between Mill and Comte, including their disagreements over the "science" of phrenology and the natural superiority of men compared to women.

9 See J. B. Schneewind, article on John Stuart Mill in vol. 5, *Encyclopedia of Philosophy* (New York, 1967); also J. B. Schneewind (ed.), *Mill: a Collection of Critical Essays* (New York, 1968), Introduction. This collection includes an interesting discussion of William Stanley Jevons's criticism of the way Mill treated geometry; Jevons wished to expose the "disconnected and worthless character" of Mill's philosophy. See Reginald Jackson, "Mill's Treatment of Geometry – a Reply to Jevons," in Schneewind, ed., *Mill*. The relation of Mill's *System of Logic* to his approach to economics is discussed in J. K. Whitaker, "John Stuart Mill's Methodology," *Journal of Political Economy*, 1975, pp. 1033–49, who concludes that when Mill comes to put his logical precepts into practice, he "slips frequently from scientist to propagandist" (p. 1047).

10 Palgrave's *Dictionary of Political Economy*, vol. 2 (London, 1926), p. 761.
11 John S. Chipman, "A Survey of the Theory of International Trade: Part 1, The Classical Theory," *Econometrica*, 1965, p. 486. Chipman shows that Mill had set up and correctly as well as ingeniously solved a problem in non-linear programming. For a critique and extension of this discussion, see the article by D. R. Appleyard and J. C. Ingram, "A Reconsideration of the Additions to Mill's 'Great Chapter'," with reply by Chipman, in *HOPE*, 1979, pp. 459–504.
12 J. S. Mill, *Principles of Political Economy*, hereafter cited in the text as *Principles*, in *Collected Works*, vol. III (Toronto, 1965), p. 607.
13 Gary Becker and William J. Baumol, "The Classical Monetary Theory: the Outcome of the Discussion," *Economica*, 1952, pp. 355–76, reprinted in J. J. Spengler and W. R. Allen (eds), *Essays in Economic Thought: Aristotle to Marshall* (Chicago, Ill., 1960).
14 See D. P. O'Brien, *J. R. McCulloch: A Study in Classical Economics* (London, 1970), p. 148.
15 Details of their Platonic romance and of her effect on him are given in F. A. Hayek, *John Stuart Mill and Harriet Taylor* (Chicago, Ill., 1951); M. St J. Packe, *The Life of John Stuart Mill* (New York, 1954); and Bruce Mazlish, *James and John Stuart Mill* (New York, 1975). The latter is a psychohistory, with a chapter on Harriet Taylor.
16 Schwartz, *The New Political Economy of J. S. Mill* (London, 1972), p. 237.
17 George J. Stigler, "The Scientific Uses of Scientific Biography, with Special Reference to J. S. Mill," in *James and John Stuart Mill: Papers of the Centenary Conference*, edited by John M. Robson and Michael Laine (Toronto, 1976).
18 See Schumpeter, *History of Economic Analysis*, p. 529; Mark Blaug, *Ricardian Economics* (New Haven, Conn., 1958); George J. Stigler, "The Nature and Role of Originality in Scientific Progress," in his *Essays in the History of Economics*; Stigler, "The Scientific Uses of Scientific Biography"; and Samuel Hollander, "Ricardianism, J. S. Mill, and the Neo-classical Challenge," in Robson and Laine, *Centenary Conference*.
19 Hollander, "Ricardianism."
20 Schumpeter, *History of Economic Analysis*, p. 643.
21 See James H. Thompson, "Mill's Fourth Fundamental Proposition: A Paradox Revisited," *HOPE*, 1975, pp. 174–92. On the importance of fixed factor proportions, two articles by Samuel Hollander are crucial: "Technology and Aggregate Demand in J. S. Mill's Economic System," *Canadian Journal of Economics and Political Science*, 1964, pp. 175–84, and "The Role of Fixed Technical Coefficients in the Evolution of the Wages-Fund Controversy," *Oxford Economic Papers*, 1968, pp. 320–41.
22 See Maurice Dobb, *Political Economy and Capitalism* (New York, 1945), pp. 43ff.
23 The review, which appeared in 1869, is in vol. V of Mill's *Collected Works, Essays on Economics and Society*; the recantation appears on pp. 643ff.
24 "Economic Theory and Wages," in *Collected Scientific Papers*, vol. II, pp. 1561–2.
25 "Mill on Economics and Society," *University of Toronto Quarterly*, 1968, pp. 98–9.

26  J. S. Mill, "Thornton on Labour and its Claims," in *Collected Works*, vol. IV, *Essays on Economics and Society* (Toronto, 1967), p. 646.

27  R. B. Ekeland, Jr, "A Short-Run Classical Model of Capital and Wages: Mill's Recantation of the Wages Fund," *Oxford Economic Papers*, 1976, pp. 66–85, has a neat diagram of the wages fund as well as a discussion of the assumptions behind it. There is an extensive literature on the wages fund which the student can mine. It includes E. G. West and R. W. Hafer, "J. S. Mill, Unions and the Wages Fund Recantation: A Reinterpretation," *Quarterly Journal of Economics*, 1978, pp. 603–19; R. B. Ekelund, Jr, and W. F. Kordsmeier, "J. S. Mill, Unions, and the Wages Fund Recantation – Comment," with reply by West and Hafer, *Quarterly Journal of Economics*, 1981, pp. 531–49; William Breit, "The Wages Fund Controversy Revisited," *Canadian Journal of Economics and Political Science*, 1967, pp. 509–28; Scott Gordon, "The Wages Fund Controversy: The Second Round," *HOPE*, 1973, pp. 14–35; Hollander, "Role of Fixed Technical Coefficients"; and Pedro Schwartz, *New Political Economy of J. S. Mill*. These papers also have citations to some important nineteen-century books and papers by Taussig, Stuart Wood, and others.

28  See T. W. Hutchison, "The 'Marginal Revolution' and the Decline and Fall of English Classical Political Economy," *HOPE*, 1972, p. 452.

29  Schumpeter, *History of Economic Analysis*, p. 671.

30  Viner, "Bentham and J. S. Mill," p. 380. For a detailed analysis of the reception of the book and why it was so popular, see N. B. de Marchi, "The Success of Mill's *Principles*," *HOPE*, 1974, pp. 119–57.

31  Robert Lekachman, *A History of Economic Ideas* (New York, 1959), p. 177.

32  M. Blaug, *Economic Theory in Retrospect*, 4th edn (Cambridge, 1985), p. 220.

33  The chief source for this view is Pedro Schwartz, *New Political Economy of J. S. Mill*. The discussion is carried on by Robert B. Ekelund, Jr, and Robert D. Tollison, "The New Political Economy of J. S. Mill: the Means to Social Justice," *Canadian Journal of Economics*, 1976, pp. 213–31; E. G. West, "J. S. Mill's Redistribution Policy: New Political Economy or Old?" *Economic Inquiry*, 1978, pp. 570–86; and a reply to the article by E. G. West, Ekelund and Tollison, "J. S. Mill's New Political Economy: Another View," *Economic Inquiry*, 1978, pp. 587–92.

34  William Stanley Jevons, *The Theory of Political Economy* (New York, 1970).

# 11
# Marx and Engels

This chapter violates shamelessly two of the commonest prejudices of Marxists (and, to a degree, of Marxologists). The first is that the doctrines of Marx and Engels are a "holistic" set of ideas, that Marx's economics cannot be separated from his sociology, from his politics, and from his history. Thorstein Veblen, not in general a sympathetic interpreter of Marx, expressed it this way: "Except as a whole and except in the light of its postulates and aims, the Marxian system is not only not tenable, but it is not even intelligible."[1] The other is that comment and criticism has to be from the perspective of Marxist economics itself. Paul Sweezy, an eminent radical and expositor of Marx, will not even consider criticism from the outside. After first pointing out that Marxism is the only coherent intellectual tradition to which the radical Left can relate, Sweezy asks what value or importance a non-Marxist critic of radical economics can have. The obvious answer, he says, is "very little if any."[2]

By contrast with these points of view, the emphasis here is on Marx's economics and how it is related to previous and subsequent economic reasoning. Marx, from one point of view, was the last of the great classical economists. Also, it has been persuasively argued that the proposition that Marx's economics cannot be understood apart from his entire system should be stood on its head: his entire vision cannot be understood except in terms of its economic content, on which he lavished twenty years of hard work and thousands of pages of writing.[3] Marx was of course a major thinker with a lasting influence on world affairs as well as on millions of people; Professor Bronfenbrenner quipped that *Das Kapital* is still the most influential unread book in existence.[4] Because this chapter is deliberately focused on one aspect of Marx, the student wishing to see the complete picture should refer to one of the many surveys or anthologies of Marx.[5]

Both Karl Marx (1818–83) and his devoted friend and collaborator Friedrich Engels (1820–95) were born in Germany and both spent the major part of their working lives in England. Karl Marx – whose middle name, Heinrich, must rank with the least-used middle names of all time –

came from a family of rabbis, although his father became a Protestant in order to protect his position as a practicing lawyer. (Psychohistorians have speculated that this may be the source of Marx's feelings of marginality and ambivalence toward society.) As a university student Marx's chief interests were poetry and philosophy, pursued with his characteristic energy to such an extent that his father thought he was in danger of being consumed both physically and morally. His philosophic tastes were radical; Marx was a leading member of the Young Hegelians, a group who were radicals in both religion and politics. Although he obtained his PhD at the age of twenty-three and had decided on a university career rather than on law, this was a time when the conservative authorities were dismissing unorthodox thinkers rather than hiring new ones. His solution was to go into journalism; between 1842 and 1849 he wrote for and edited radical newspapers in Cologne, Paris, Brussels, and Cologne again, with censorship and expulsion sooner or later putting an end to his career in each place. Along with his journalism he fitted in marriage to his long-term fiancée and inspiration for much of his college poetry, Jenny von Westphalen; much study which resulted in an early work, *The Economic and Philosophic Manuscripts of 1844*[6]; the beginning of his life-long association with Engels; and his association with the Communist League which resulted, among other things, in the drafting of the *Communist Manifesto* by Marx and Engels in 1848. (This was the year of the first edition of J. S. Mill's *Principles of Political Economy*; Mill's point of view at that time was that "There has never been imagined any mode of distributing the produce of industry, so well adapted to the requirements of human nature on the whole, as letting the share of each individual ... depend in the main on that individual's own energies and exertions.... It is not the subversion of the system of individual property that should be aimed at, but the improvement of it."[7] Contrast this with Marx and Engels: "The proletarians have nothing to lose but their chains. They have a world to win.")

Exiled to London in 1849, Marx entered a period of poverty which lasted until he received an inheritance in 1864. During these years Marx survived by grants from Engels, who was a successful industrialist, and by writing articles for American newspapers including Horace Greeley's *New York Herald-Tribune*. During this time he studied economics with his usual complete devotion to an enterprise; he spent thousands of hours in the British Museum library. His studies eventually resulted in a number of books: the *Grundrisse* (an outline of political economy), the *Theories of Surplus Value* (actually a history of economic thought from Marx's perspective), and the famous three-volume *Capital*. Marx actually completed only the first volume; Engels edited the other two from manuscript, and *Theories of Surplus Value* was edited by Karl Kautsky after Marx died. These books were only a part of his output; there were many pamphlets, letters, and articles – so many that the English language publication of the complete works of Marx will require fifty volumes (Adam Smith's complete works take only six volumes and Ricardo's ten). In addition, he devoted an immense amount of time during 1864–72 to revolutionary politics, throwing himself into the International Working Men's Association (the First International). Soon after this group split up because of doctrinal disputes, Marx became ill, and during the last decade of his life was unable to work with his previous intensity. He died in 1883.

Friedrich Engels shared Marx's opinions but led an altogether different kind of life. His father owned cotton mills and Engels was the manager of the family mill in Manchester, England, which gave him the funds to support himself and Marx. Engels was early impressed with the contrast between the working class and the middle class of his home town of Barmen, Germany. He became a Young Hegelian and wrote for a number of radical publications, which led to his acquaintance with Marx and to their collaboration. Engels's early writings, in addition to his descriptions of the poor (for example, *The Condition of the Working Class in England in 1844*) included some theoretical economics, especially on the business cycle, which Marx used in *Capital*. And as mentioned already, he was a co-author with Marx of the *Communist Manifesto*. During the 1850s and 1860s Engels devoted himself to radical agitation and to military study in order to be ready for military leadership in the future revolution. At the same time he was helping Marx with encouragement, money, and favors such as assuming the paternity of Marx's illegitimate son. (His own family life centered on a twenty-year liaison with an Irish working girl; after she died, he lived with her sister for the next fifteen years.) Engels served as Marx's literary executor, editing the last two volumes of *Capital*. He delivered the graveside speech for his old friend, pointing out Marx's two foremost scientific discoveries – the materialist foundation of history and the law of surplus value – and summarizing his career with the phrase "Marx was before all else a revolutionist."[8]

Although this chapter focuses on Marx's economics rather than on the whole Marxist structure, a brief sketch of the rest of the system is needed as a background. In the first place, Marx used many Hegelian concepts and much of his terminology came from Hegel. Of these, the idea of emphasizing dynamic processes and the dialectical method – proceeding through successive levels of abstraction from the "essence" to the appearance – seem particularly important. Secondly, there is Marx's broad concept of historical change, the doctrine of historical materialism. This theory holds that such aspects of human culture as art, religion, law, and politics are the result of the "mode of production," and in a dynamic fashion, changes in the mode of production lead to changes in culture. The "mode of production" is visualized as including both productive forces such as technology and resources, and also such social aspects of production as property rules and the control of production. A final major concept, on the interface of history, sociology, and economics, is that of classes and the class struggle. Classes are economic groups, defined by their position in the ownership and control of the process of production. The antagonism between classes, the exploited struggling against the exploiters, leads to historical change, to the changes in the mode of production which change all the rest of human culture.[9] Marx analyzed capitalism in the framework of these ideas.

Marx began his analysis in *Capital* by distinguishing between two aspects of the value of commodities. Use-value is their capacity to satisfy wants; exchange-value is the proportion in which commodities are exchanged. Marx does not accept exchange-value as determined by supply and demand as in the standard economic theory of today. Anyone can see what prices as determined by markets are, but Marx wants to get at the essence of exchange. This essence is found in the fact that the one thing common to all commodities is human labor. When people exchange commodities they are really engaging in the social relationship of exchanging labor. Ignoring this, and instead analyzing exchange as only a relationship between things, is called "commodity fetishism." Defining value as the total of "socially necessary labor time" involved in the production of a good calls attention to this social relationship. It is also relevant for the Marxist theory of exploitation of labor. Profits, interest, and rent appear in general economic theory to be returns to factors of production other than labor. But if labor is considered to be the social source of production these other factor payments should be attributed to labor. Marx called the payments to capital "surplus value." Using the Marxist terminology of value and surplus value dramatizes the exploitation Marx felt adhered in capitalism. As we shall see shortly, Marx knew that value in his sense was not the same as market price, but he thought the two were related in a specific way. Before looking at that, however, we need to look at value a little more deeply.

If production required no capital, the value of a commodity would be the number of hours of labor it takes to produce it. But in such an economy under a capitalistic mode of production workers would in general receive less value in wages than they contributed in production. The reason is that workers themselves are valued at the socially necessary labor time required for their production – i.e., workers are valued at the subsistence wage for them and their family. As an illustration, if the working day is ten hours long, but it only requires six hours to produce the wage goods necessary for the survival of the laborer and his family, then the workers will produce four hours worth of surplus value every day. The competition of laborers for jobs insures that wages equal subsistence; the desire of employers for profits drives them to lengthen the working day as much as possible to get as much surplus value as possible.

In standard Marxist terminology, the amount of wages paid by employers is called variable capital and denoted by $v$; surplus value is denoted by $s$. Thus the value of a good requiring no fixed capital is $v + s$, and the rate of surplus value is $s/v$. The existence of surplus value explains why in capitalist production one can start with money, change it into a commodity by hiring labor, and sell the commodity for more money than was started with. Marx created a famous piece of symbolism to distinguish the production process in capitalism, which focuses on monetary gain, from other systems where the exchange of commodities is an exchange of use-value. Let $M$ stand for money and $C$ for commodities; and $M'$ for the larger sum of money that the capitalist winds up with at the end of his chain of transactions. Then capitalist production is symbolized by $M$–$C$–$M'$, and non-exploitative production by $C$–$M$–$C$ (where a commodity is exchanged for money, and that for a commodity of the same value as the original one).[10] In capitalism, although everything is bought and sold at its value, a gain to the capitalist results from his exploitation of the surplus value of the worker.

The essence of modern capitalism is the use of machines, and machines contribute to the value of a commodity in this way: suppose the machine requires 200 labor-hours to produce and that the machine is worn out after it produces 400 units of the commodity. Then the contribution of the machine to the value of one unit of the commodity is $1/400 \times 200 = \frac{1}{2}$ hour of congealed labor time. This depreciation charge on the machine is called $c$, for constant capital. (It is actually the flow of labor services provided in the past and congealed in the machine.) Thus the total value of the product is $c + v + s$. Although surplus value depends only on variable capital, with the rate of surplus value defined as $s/v$, the rate of profit as computed by the capitalist depends on all the capital he uses and is defined by Marx as $s/(c+v)$. (Note that this is correct only if capital only lasts one year; otherwise the flow of congealed labor is less than the value of fixed capital.)

Thus Marx's value theory is a labor theory. Although Marx's favorite economist was Ricardo, and one of Professor Samuelson's classic lines is that in economics Marx was a minor post-Ricardian auto-didact,[11] in fact the labor theory of value in Ricardo and in Marx are quite different. Ricardo, as explained in chapter 8 above, had an empirical rather than an analytical theory: he knew that allowing for the different amounts of capital used in different industries would give production costs which are not proportional to labor costs, but he believed that labor was so large a part of the cost structure than an insignificant error was involved in ignoring capital. (This is the "93 percent labor theory of value" of Professor Stigler.) Marx, too, knew that market prices were not determined by labor content; however, he used labor value, not as a first and useful approximation as Ricardo did, but because labor is the relevant *social* source of production. As Schumpeter puts it, for Marx the quantity of labor embodied in commodities does not merely determine their value; it *is* their value. Ultimately this is a metaphysical point.[12]

From the definitions of the rate of surplus value ($s/v$) and the rate of profits [$s/(c+v)$], it is obvious that equal rates of surplus value between two industries do not imply equal rates of profit, unless the two industries just happen to use the same amount of capital. (Marx said that the organic composition of capital, defined as $c/(c+v)$, had to be the same.) Here, as Marx realized and discussed at length in volume III of *Capital*, is a contradiction between the labor theory of value and the theory of price which had evolved out of classical economics: in standard price theory, competition equalizes the returns on total investment, not merely on the outlays on labor.

The argument may be illustrated using Marx's own numbers from volume III. Suppose we have two industries, with the following data:

| | Capital | $s/v$ | $s$ | $s/(C+v)$ | $c$ | $c+v+s=$value |
|---|---|---|---|---|---|---|
| I | $80C+20v$ | 100% | 20 | 20% | 50 | $50+20+20=90$ |
| II | $70C+30v$ | 100% | 30 | 30% | 51 | $51+30+30=111$ |

In this table, $C$ is the total amount of fixed capital in terms of labor hours, while $c$ is the depreciation charge, the amount of fixed capital used up this year. By assumption, the rate of surplus value is the same in each industry (this is the assumption used throughout volume I of *Capital*). However, in capitalist accounting what is relevant is not the rate of surplus value but the rate of profits, given in the fourth column as the capitalists' earnings ($s$) divided by his investment ($C+v$). Since the first industry has a 20 percent profit rate while the second has a 30 percent rate of profits, capital will flow into the second industry, output will expand, and prices will fall in the second industry, bringing its profit rate into equilibrium with the first industry. (To change the last column, value in labor hours, into a monetary unit which may be compared with price, simply assume some monetary rate of wages, such as $1 per hour; then the value of the output of industry I is $90 and of industry II is $111 before any transformation into prices occurs.) Because of the flow of capital and the fall in price in the second industry, Marx demonstrates that actual observed prices in the economy are not equal to and are not determined by labor time, but, he claims, labor value and capitalist prices are related and the contradiction between them resolved by the process called transformation (volume III, chapter IX). Transforming values into prices is rather easily done: find the average rate of profit in the whole economy by dividing total surplus value by the total amount of constant plus variable capital. Multiply the $C + v$ of each industry by this average profit rate to get the total amount of profits. Add this amount to $c + v$ to get the "price of production" or capitalist price. Suppose, for example, that the average rate of profit for all industries is 22 percent. Then in industry I $22 is added to $50c + $20v to get a price of $92, and in industry II $22 is added to $51c + $30v for a price of $103. In the first industry price is above value, in the second it is below value, and in Marx's examples the positive deviations exactly equal the negative ones. (Later writers pointed out that Marx should have recomputed $C$ into prices rather than left it at labor value.)

The divergence between value and price and the question of whether they are related has been one of the major bones of contention between bourgeois economists and Marxists for a century. Keynes, for example, repudiated Communism because, he asks, "How can I accept a doctrine which sets up as its Bible, above and beyond criticism, an obsolete economics textbook which I know to be not only scientifically erroneous but without interest or application for the modern world?"[13] Eugen von Böhm-Bawerk, a prominent Austrian theorist of the late nineteenth century, wrote a book about the contradiction between value and price which concluded that "The specific theoretical work of Marx and Engels was a most ingeniously conceived structure, built up by a fabulous power of combination, of innumerable stories of thought, held together by a marvelous mental grasp, but – a house of cards."[14] On the other hand, Marx himself was convinced that there was no contradiction between value and price; value could be transformed into price by the technique used above.

It is generally agreed, however, that the definitive treatment of the transformation problem was provided by Ladislaus von Bortkiewicz in 1907. Bortkiewicz was a professor of economics and mathematical statistics at Berlin; he wrote several articles on Marx and in the process developed an algebraic technique for transforming values into prices.[15] His first point was that Marx had commited an error by not transforming the constant and variable capital into price terms; instead he left them at the original value levels. Properly done the transformation is handled as follows.

If $r$ is the rate of profits, $P_1$ the price of constant capital, $P_2$ the price of wage goods consumed by the workers and paid for by variable capital, and $P_3$ the price of luxury goods paid for by the surplus value earned by capitalists, equations can be set up for each of the three industries (the fixed-capital industry, represented by equation (1); the wage goods industry, which is equation (2); and the luxury goods industry, shown as equation (3)). In these equations, the left-hand side is the total cost of production including profits, and the right-hand side is the value of the output. It is assumed that the third industry, luxury goods, does not produce anything which enters into the cost side; also note that the subscripts on $c$ and $v$ indicate which industry is using the output, whereas the subscripts on $s$ indicate in which industry the surplus value originates.

The equations are:

$$(P_1 c_1 + P_2 v_1)(1+r) = P_1 (c_1 + c_2 + c_3) \tag{1}$$

$$(P_1 c_2 + P_2 v_2)(1+r) = P_2 (v_1 + v_2 + v_3) \tag{2}$$

$$(P_1 c_3 + P_2 v_3)(1+r) = P_3 (s_1 + s_2 + s_3) \tag{3}$$

These three equations may be solved for the relative prices, since there are three equations to solve for three prices and for the rate of profits. Marxist scholars have attempted to provide one more equation to allow for the determination of absolute prices. Three important suggestions are to set the price of one of the industries (the gold producer) equal to one; to set total output in value terms equal to total output in price terms; and to set the total surplus value equal to total profit in price terms. Although Marx at different places espoused all three ideas, theoretical analysis shows that in fact they cannot all three be true at the same time unless the economy is not growing (what we call later simple reproduction) and unless the gold industry happens to have the same proportions of $c$ to $v$ and $c$ to output that the economy as a total has.[16] Such assumptions are so restrictive as to make the analysis, although valid, at the same time uninteresting.

Professor Paul A. Samuelson, in a series of papers (most notably "Understanding the Marxian Notion of Exploitation: A Summary of the So-Called Transformation Problem between Marxian Values and Competitive Prices,"[17]) adds that the transformation is logically unnecessary; both values and prices are determined by the fundamental technological and labor data of the system; each can be determined independently of the other, and rather than transforming value into price, one *erases* the values and replaces them with the prices. The debate continues in a heavy cloud of ideology, but it is worth re-emphasizing that for Marx himself the purpose of the "law of value" was to recognize the "inner essence and inner structure" behind the "outer appearance."[18] Profits arise from surplus value; it took (in his view) Marx himself to point out that capitalist profit rate equilibrium obscures this fundamental social fact.[19] It is also suggested that the theory of transformation was paralleled by a historical development. Did, at one time in pre-capitalist days, products exchange for their value, and did the rise of the exploiting capitalist convert actual pricing from Marxian value into the prices of production paradigm? Some Marxists – maybe even Marx himself – believe so.[20]

*Capital* is a dynamic analysis of the progress of capitalism, past and future, leading to the conclusion that capitalism will collapse and the expropriators will be expropriated. In the process of the analysis Marx looked at the economics of growth of a capitalist system, to see what conditions were necessary if the system continued to grow and to show the conditions would not be met. The model he used, developed in volume II of *Capital*, is called by Marx the system of capitalist reproduction.

In capitalist reproduction, Marx looked at an economy's behavior, first one with no growth, doing the same thing year after year (simple reproduction), and then an economy which grew from year to year (extended reproduction). The example used by Marx is of an economy with two industries or "departments" – a capital goods department (I) and a consumer goods department (II). In the case of simple reproduction, the example given in volume II, chapter XX of *Capital* is the following:

Capital goods      $4,000c_1 + 1,000v_1 + 1,000s_1 = 6,000$

Consumer goods   $2,000c_2 + \phantom{0}500v_2 + \phantom{00}500s_2 = 3,000$

For each department, the total value of output in labor hours is given, with breakdown into constant and variable capital and surplus value. This is an economy in equilibrium, for the total constant capital used up (4,000 in department I and 2,000 in department II) equals the total produced, and the total consumer goods purchased (the $v+s$ of department I plus the $v+s$ of department II) equals the value of the total output of consumer goods. The equilibrium condition, as Marx pointed out, is that $c$ of department II equals $v+s$ of department I; he called this the great exchange between the two classes and went on to elaborate how crises and prosperities interfered with the achievement of this condition. In arriving at this presentation, Marx made ample acknowledgment of debt to Quesnay's *Tableau Économique*, with its circulation of spending between the two main industries in the economy (although Quesnay found the source of surpluses in the economy in land and Marx found them in labor).

But Marx went far beyond Quesnay when he developed his model of extended reproduction (i.e., a growing capitalist economy). As an illustration, suppose that the economy – which means each industry in the economy in blanced growth – is growing at 10 percent per year. The first two years of history might then appear as follows:

First year

| | | | | |
|---|---|---|---|---|
| Capital goods | $4,400c_1 +$ | $1,100v_1 +$ | $1,100s_1 =$ | $6,600$ |
| Consumer goods | $1,600c_2 +$ | $400v_2 +$ | $400s_2 =$ | $2,400$ |
| | $6,000c$ | $1,500v$ | $1,500s$ | $9,000$ |

Second year

| | | | | |
|---|---|---|---|---|
| Capital goods | $4,840c_1 +$ | $1,210v_1 +$ | $1,210s_1 =$ | $7,260$ |
| Consumer goods | $1,760c_2 +$ | $440v_2 +$ | $440s_2 =$ | $2,640$ |
| | $6,600c$ | $1,650v$ | $1,650s$ | $9,900$ |

The basis for this table is that a growing economy requires net investment, while equilibrium (as Keynes taught us) requires that investment equals saving. Assume that saving equals half the surplus earned by capitalists the first year (saving equals 750), while the proletariat saves nothing. Investment the first year has to equal 750. Part of the investment is the excess amount of the production of capital goods (6,600) over the amount of capital goods used up (6,000); and part of the investment is the addition to the inventory of consumer goods. Consumer goods produced in the first year are 2,400; consumer goods used up are the entire income of the proletariat ($1,500v$) and one-half the surplus value earned by capitalists ($750s$). Thus the addition to inventory, production minus consumption, is 150. This makes it possible to advance 1,650 consumer goods to the proletariat in the second year, compared to 1,500 in the first year; and there are 600 more capital goods available the second year compared to the first year. Everything has grown by 10 percent. For the third year, simply multiply all the second-year numbers by 1.1, and so on for the rest of history.

Modern economic growth theorists see in this model pioneering work that deserves high praise.[21] For Marx himself, the important point was that growth required very precise conditions which crude, planless capitalism could achieve only by accident. Disproportion between supply and demand (or between saving and investment) would cause price fluctuations and trade crises. These crises were viewed as inevitably getting worse over time as capitalism developed, eventually getting so bad that workers would arise in revolt. Actually not only did the crises get worse, but they also occurred over a falling secular trend of profits. (This is one of Marx's predictions which has not come true.)[22]

The increasing severity of business cycles as capitalism developed had implications – mostly bad – for all people in the economy. For the capitalists, there was a tendency toward a falling rate of profit. Capitalists, as we saw in the model of extended reproduction, save ("Accumulate! Accumulate! That is Moses and the Prophets," said Marx).[23] But saving increases the ratio of capital to labor. If the rate of surplus value is kept the same, the rate of profits must fall. In order to prevent this, the employer squeezes more labor time out the workers; the workers became more exploited. In chapter X of *Capital* volume I, Marx displays at length the result of his many years' sitting in the British Museum reading reports of the Inspector of Factories and other sources on the incredibly long hours and young ages of workers in the early days of the Industrial Revolution. The reader unfamiliar with Marx should look at this chapter to see the conditions that roused Marx's easily awakened ire.[24] The result is that while capitalists suffer because of the falling rate of profits, workers suffer a peculiarly Marxian form of immiseration. That is, even though the accumulation of capital and technical progress produce vast quantities of goods very cheaply (in the *Communist Manifesto* Marx and Engels said that "The bourgeoisie, during its rule of scarce one hundred years, has created more massive and more colossal productive forces than have all preceding generations together"), the workers are worse off in several ways. It does not matter that their real income, as we measure it – the absolute amount of goods and services that the workers can purchase – rises. What counts for Marx, and what he believes counts for others, is their relative position. If they spend fewer hours per day working for themselves, and more hours per day working for others generating surplus value, then the value of wages has fallen. Furthermore, the worker becomes a mere appendage of the machine, unable to develop his full potentiality, and in this sense capitalism impoverishes the worker no matter how high his real income.[25] So it is possible to have both capitalists and workers feeling worse off as capitalism develops.

On the side of the capitalists, one of the reactions Marx predicted was an increasing concentration of industry as crises became more severe and some businesses collapsed during depressions. This gave more power to the ones who were left. For the workers, a crucial development was that depressions and technological change created a reserve army of the unemployed. The reserve army helps keep down wages. Marx, like Malthus, considered overpopulation a problem but Marx criticized Malthus severely for blaming it on the tendency of people to have too many children. Rather he considered it as coming from the demand side; it was deplorable but inevitable in capitalist development that labor demand lags behind population growth because of the increasing use of constant capital relative to the use of variable capital.[26] The result of the accumulation of capital, with its attendant crises, immiseration, reserve army, and depressions is:

> Along with the constantly diminishing number of the magnates of capital, who usurp and monopolise all advantages of this process of transformation, grows the mass of misery, oppression, slavery, degradation, exploitation; but with this too grows the revolt of the working-class, a class always increasing in numbers, and disciplined, united, organised by the very mechanism of the process of capitalist production itself. The monopoly of capital becomes a fetter upon the mode of production, which has sprung up and flourished along with, and under it. Centralisation of the means of production and socialisation of labour at last reach a point where they become incompatible with their capitalist integument. This integument is burst asunder. The knell of capitalist private property sounds. The expropriators are expropriated.[27]

As a scenario of the history of advanced countries this clearly fails. Still, Marx remains, as our earlier reference from Sweezy put it, the only coherent intellectual tradition to which the radical Left can relate. It is the vision rather than the empirical congruence or the usefulness of surplus value as a theoretical concept which makes it so.[28]

## Notes

1 "Veblen on Marx," in H. W. Spiegel (ed.), *The Development of Economic Thought* (New York, 1952), p. 314. For the same thought by a modern Marxologist, see David McLellan, *Karl Marx* (New York, 1975), p. 50.

2 Paul M. Sweezy, "Comment," in "Symposium: Economics of the New Left," *Quarterly Journal of Economics*, 1972, p. 659.

3 Mark Blaug, *A Methodological Appraisal of Marxian Economics* (Amsterdam, 1980), p. 2. This book, by the way, has an excellent bibliography of recent writing on Marxist matters.

4 Martin Bronfenbrenner, "Marxian Influences in 'Bourgeois' Economics," *American Economic Review Papers and Proceedings*, May, 1967, p. 624.

5 An excellent anthology is Robert C. Tucker (ed.), *The Marx–Engels Reader* (New York, 1972). Paul M. Sweezy, *The Theory of Capitalist Development* New York, 1968) is a highly regarded exposition of Marx's economics. A rather different approach is taken by Anthony Brewer, *A Guide to Marx's "Capital"* (Cambridge, 1984). This is a brief chapter by chapter guide in extremely short and simple sentences, a rarity among Marxist commentators. The centenary of Marx's death, 1983, saw many books, among which one of the most intriguing titles was Isaac D. Balbus, *Marxism and Domination: A Neo-Hegelian, Feminist, Psychoanalytic Theory of Sexual, Political and Technological Liberation* (Princeton, NJ, 1983).

6 This was a rather romantic effort by comparison with the later works such as *Capital*; it has appealed to many "new Marxists' who suffer from a similar

disillusion with society. Murray Wolfson, "The Day Karl Marx Grew Up," *History of Political Economy* (*HOPE*), 1971, pp. 335–52, traces the change in Marx's point of view from his romantic period to the more analytical later work.

7 Mill, *Principles* (Ashley edn, London, 1909), p. 985.

8 A convenient reference for Engels's share of Marxism is T. W. Hutchison, "Friedrich Engels and Marxist Economic Theory," *Journal of Political Economy*, 1978, pp. 303–19, which is a review article of W. O. Henderson, *Life of Friedrich Engels* (London, 1977).

9 Each of these points was extensively developed by Marx and Engels, and each has generated an immense literature. Two accessible references are a short discussion by Joseph Schumpeter, *Ten Great Economists* (New York, 1951), and a book-length study, M. M. Bober, *Karl Marx's Interpretation of History* (Cambridge, Mass., 1927).

10 Those interested in a Freudian interpretation of Marx should consult W. A. Weiskopf, *The Psychology of Economics* (Chicago, Ill., 1955) for a discussion of the significance of the prime in $M'$.

11 Paul A. Samuelson, "Wages and Interest: a Modern Dissection of Marxian Economic Models," *American Economic Review*, 1957, pp. 884–912. However, recent authoritative research stresses that Marx's debt to Ricardo was as much negative as positive, since he tried to correct Ricardo's errors in both theory and methodology. See J. E. King, "Marx as an Historian of Economic Thought," *HOPE*, 1979, pp. 382–94, and M. C. Howard and J. E. King, *The Political Economy of Marx* (London, 1975).

12 See J. Schumpeter, *History of Economic Analysis* (New York, 1954), p. 596. G. L. S. Tucker, "Ricardo and Marx," *Economica*, 1961, pp. 252–69, develops the thesis that Marx owed relatively little to Ricardo.

13 J. M. Keynes, *Essays in Persuasion* (New York, 1963), p. 300.

14 E. von Böhm-Bawerk, *Karl Marx and the Close of His System* (New York, 1949), p. 118.

15 He also studied the probability of a soldier dying from the kick of a mule in a Prussian regiment and found that it followed the Poisson rather than the normal distribution.

16 F. Seton, "The 'Transformation Problem'," *Review of Economics and Statistics*, 1957, pp. 149–60, contains a proof using matrix algebra.

17 Samuelson, "Understanding the Marxian Notion of Exploitation," in *Journal of Economic Literature*, 1971, pp. 399–431.

18 *Capital*, vol. III, (New World Paperbacks, International Publishers, New York, 1967), p. 168.

19 A very scholarly exegesis of this is Samuel Hollander, "Marxian Economics as 'General Equilibrium' Theory," *HOPE*, 1981, pp. 121–55.

20 See M. Morishima and G. Catephores, "Is There an 'Historical Transformation Problem'?," *Economic Journal*, 1975, pp. 309–28, and Ronald L. Meek, "Is There an 'Historical Transformation Problem'? A Comment," *Economic Journal*, 1976, pp. 342–52.

21 See Paul A. Samuelson, "Marx as Mathematical Economist," in G. Horwich and P. A. Samuelson (eds), *Trade, Stability and Mathematical Economics* (New York, 1974). A book which emphasizes the role of the surplus over costs in

generating economic growth in classical economics, including Karl Marx, is Walter Eltis, *The Classical Theory of Economic Growth* (New York, 1984); the theories are analyzed and put into equations.

22 Paul A. Samuelson, in another of his interesting papers on Marx, has analyzed the notion that the rate of profits must fall, and finds that it depends on the "arbitrariness of the airy presumption that the rate of surplus value is *constant* through the dramatic changes of the industrial revolution." See "Marx without Matrices: Understanding the Rate of Profit," in Padma Desai (ed.), *Marxism, Central Planning and the Soviety Economy* (Cambridge, Mass., 1983), p. 11. Marxists, however, although they may agree that the law of the falling rate of profits has not been satisfactorily (to them) formulated yet, still insist that it provides extremely useful insights into capitalist accumulation and crises. See Jens Christiansen, "Marx and the Falling Rate of Profit," *American Economic Review Papers and Proceedings*, May 1976.

23 *Capital*, vol. I, p. 595.

24 Marx's far-reaching scholarship did not stop at the study of early-day capitalism; the curious may wish to check his researches into the relation between Lady Orkney and King William (vol. I, p. 723).

25 An excellent analysis of this is Thomas Sowell, "Marx's 'Increasing Misery' Doctrine," *American Economic Review*, 1960, pp. 111–20. Also, William J. Baumol, "On the Folklore of Marxism," *Proceedings of the American Philosophical Society*, 1979, pp. 124–8, who documents the many places where Marx shows that wages are far above subsistence under capitalism.

26 This thesis is explored at length in Samuel Hollander, "Marx and Malthusianism: Marx's Secular Path of Wages," *American Economic Review*, 1984.

27 *Capital*, vol. I, p. 837.

28 Blaug, *Marxian Economics*, is particularly severe on Marxists who revise Marxist theory to accommodate growing anomalies and repeated falsification of Marx's predictions (e.g., revolutions have occurred in non-proletariat states like Russia and China, but not in advanced capitalist countries). His methodological position is that if the theory is falsified it should be abandoned, not stretched to allow for the anomalies.

# 12
# Precursors of the Marginal Revolution

An eminent reader of bygone economists once warned that "Walras or Keynes or Slutsky may have had their precursors, but one must not read into succinct or even incidental remarks in earlier writings a full-blown comprehension of the ideas of their successors."[1] With this warning in mind, we proceed to to look at the ideas of writers who anticipated to some degree the propositions of Jevons, Walras, and Menger, the great trio of what some call the marginal revolution. This revolution was in fact a process rather than an abrupt change. The various precursors wrote before the 1870s when the revolution is generally dated (Jevons's first publication was in 1862, so that he was in a way a precursor of himself). And after the major books of the great trio it took about twenty years for the new ideas to become generally accepted.

In order to have some perspective, it is worth while summarizing the classical system, which was replaced, and the neo-classical system, which did the replacing. The chief concern of the classical system was the wealth of the nation, the way it grew over time, and how the distribution of income changed with growth. The classical economists were most interested in the long run, in "normal" rather than market prices, and in the aggregate incomes of classes such as laborers or landlords rather than in the wages paid a given laborer. In matters of policy the classical economists were reformers, and they based their proposals on the newly developed science of political economy.[2]

By contrast, neo-classical economics deals with maximizing behavior when tastes and resources are given. It assumes that consumers try to maximize utility and producers try to maximize profits, and shows how their actions establish equilibrium prices. The prices of factors of production are included in this via marginal productivity theory. In general the marginal technique (in the hands of some, differential calculus) was the theoretical tool. Policy was not discussed in the main theoretical books; although Jevons's book was called *The Theory of Political Economy*, and Walras's title was *Éléments d'Économie Politique Pure*, they treat with what we would call economics rather than political economy. (Marshall changed the name of the subject from Political Economy to Economics single-handedly. He said: "The nation used to be called 'the Body Politic'.

So long as this phrase was in common use, men thought of the interests of the whole nation when they used the word 'Political'; and then 'Political Economy' served well enough as a name for the science. But now 'political interests' generally mean the interests of only some part or parts of the nation; so that it seems best to drop the name 'Political Economy', and to speak simply of *Economic Science*, or more shortly, *Economics*."[3]) Although at the time it seemed to people such as Jevons that their contribution was the marginal utility theory of value (specifically, in equilibrium in a competitive market the equation price of good $a$/price of good $b$=marginal utility of good $a$/marginal utility of good $b$ is true for every consumer), the opinion today is that what was important in the theory was the marginal concept per se rather than the specific application of marginal utility. In such a case, it is correct to start a survey of important precursors of neo-classical economics with von Thünen and Cournot rather than with the early marginal utility theorists.

Both Johann von Thünen (1783–1858) and Augustin Cournot worked in a vacuum as far as the economists of their day were concerned but made what later were regarded as important contributions. Von Thünen was a German agriculturalist with a good education in academic disciplines. He developed an almost fanatical interest in economics, at which he worked very hard both as a theorist and a compiler of data. After conceiving the ideas on rent and location which later appeared in the first volume of his book *Der isolierte Staat* (*The Isolated State*), he decided he needed data. So for the next ten years he put aside his theorizing to collect data from his own farming operations, keeping three accounts: in money, in labor inputs, and in wheat. It was this attention to empirical knowledge which later influenced Alfred Marshall, who once said that it was because of this that he loved von Thünen beyond all his other masters. (Posterity, in the form of Joseph Schumpeter, believes that Marshall owed more to Cournot, however.) Today von Thünen is more likely to be remembered because of his location theory and because of his attempts to formulate the theory of marginal productivity.

Von Thünen's first work was in location theory. He assumed a central city, with no foreign trade (hence it was an "isolated state," like the remote, backward area in which his farm was located); crops are grown on the surrounding farm land. Industrial goods are produced in the city, which sells them for different kinds of farm goods (fresh milk, fresh vegetables, grain). Unlike the classical economists, von Thünen did not emphasize land fertility differences in plotting the location of the production of different kinds of farm goods, but instead he focused on transportation costs. Fresh vegetables and milk had, in his day, a high transportation cost (counting spoilage from long-distance travel without refrigeration); grain, although heavy, had a lower cost. The high-cost-of-transportation production was located nearest the city, to enable farm labor to earn the same return everywhere. Furthermore, because there is a transportation cost of manufactured goods outward from the city, workers at a distance from the city have to earn a higher gross wage than those nearer in order to have the same net income, measured in terms of consumption. But this means that there must be fewer workers per acre, the further out from the city the farm is located, in order to give each worker a higher gross productivity. In turn, the land further out earns less rent, because it has fewer workers and their higher gross wages leave less of a residual for rent.[4] This theory, conceived by a lone scholar remote from the centers of action in economics, had elements of the theories of many economists of his day and later. Professor Samuelson summarizes them thus:

1   The theory of comparative advantage, developed early in the nineteenth century by Torrens and Ricardo. (Von Thünen's was not a *foreign* trade model, but the comparative advantage shows up in the location of domestic production in response to transportation cost differentials.)

2   The theory of rent, developed by Ricardo, West, and Malthus. As already mentioned, von Thünen did not develop the different productivities of land as stemming from differences in fertility, as did Ricardo; for him they stemmed from different intensities of cultivation, with land nearest the city supporting much more labor per acre. As a result, total output in excess of wages paid is higher nearer the city. (See figure 17.1 in the discussion of J. B. Clark for a diagram of this situation.)

3   The Heckscher–Ohlin theory of factors-and-goods pricing. This foreign trade model was developed in the twentieth century; it is a general equilibrium model in which countries with different endowments of the factors of production begin with different costs and prices of goods, but in equilibrium with trade the prices of the factors of production as well as of goods are equalized around the world. In von Thünen's model, the prices of goods and of factors of production are mutually determined in a similar general-equilibrium way.

4   The "Marx–Dmitriev–Leontief–Sraffa system of input–output." That is, farm products require manufactured goods as inputs; manufactured goods (such as bread) use farm goods as input. This is similar to the models surveyed in the previous chapter on Marx, where industry I's output is used as an input by industry II, and where the workers of industry I consume the output of industry II (see pp. 127–8). Quesnay should be added to the list of those who used similar models. (Dmitriev was a Russian writer of the early 1900s who used this model;[5] Leontief used it in the 1930s and Sraffa in 1960).

A noted economic theorist himself, with a keen appreciation of the accomplishments of the past, Professor Samuelson concludes that on the basis of his location theory "Thünen belongs in the Pantheon with Léon Walras, John Stuart Mill, and Adam Smith. As Schumpeter would say, it is the inner ring of Valhalla they occupy."[6]

But Thünen spent many years of his life on another economic theorem which was not so well received. That is what he called the doctrine of the natural wage. It was actually a marginal analysis, a mixture of the calculus technique which later became popular, together with a misconceived idea of what workers try to maximize and a slip in his idea of how the economy works – his mathematics is based on the idea that workers produce the same amount no matter what their wages are (i.e., that the supply curve of labor is perfectly inelastic with respect to wages).

In order for the student to see for himself the reason for these criticisms of Thünen's wage theory (which he himself was so impressed with that he had the final result, "$w = \sqrt{(ap)}$", engraved on his tombstone), let us work out a simple example. The wage, $w$, is equal to the annual subsistence wage, $a$, plus a surplus of saving available for investment, $y$. Therefore $w = a + y$. The other variables are $p$, the average product of the worker; $q$, the average amount of capital he uses; and $z$, the percentage rate of interest. $w$ is expressed as so many bushels of wheat and $q$ as so many units of a family's annual wage. Multiply $q$ by $(a+y)$ to get total $q$ in wheat units. The income from capital will be the rate of interest times the total amount of capital, or $q(a+y)z$. The total income of the worker, assuming that rent equals zero, is his wage income plus his interest income, and his income is in turn equal to the product $p$. Hence, $p = a + y + q(a+y)z$.

Next, express the rate of interest $z$ as the amount earned on capital divided by the amount of capital, or $z = (p-a-y)/[q(a+y)]$. Thünen says that the prudent family takes its savings, $y$, each year, invests it, and earns $zy = y(p-a-y)/[q(a+y)]$. It wants to earn the most it can on its savings, and to find the maximum, everyone knows that the calculus rule is to take the first derivative with respect to $y$ and make that equal to zero. The result is, as Thünen said, that $a + y = \sqrt{(ap)}$, the magical formula important enough to put on his tombstone.

But modern commentators join in several criticisms: the proper maximand for a rational worker is his total income, not the income from the capital he has saved; $a$, the subsistence level of income, is usually not a physiological limit, but a socially determined and hence imprecise number; $p$, the result of the worker's effort, varies with $w$, so that it is not correct to hold it constant while taking the derivative with respect to $w$.[7] Why, granting that the formula is incorrect as a desirable level at which to set wages, did von Thünen think it was so important? It was because he thought, as a result of his analysis, that it really would make the workers the best off; and, a lone scholar on his remote German farm, he had no one to try his theory out on or to give him criticism. Unlike Ricardo with his friend Malthus and unlike later economists with the paraphenalia of journals, libraries, and conventions, he did his thinking in solitude for nearly fifty years.[8]

Augustin Cournot (1801–77) was trained in science and mathematics, and spent most of his working life as a university administrator. He wrote more than ten books, three of them on economics, the rest on mathematics (calculus and probability) and on the philosophy of science and of history. Of his economics books, only the first, *Recherches sur les principes mathématiques de la théorie des richesses* (1838),[9] is regarded as important. Modern theorists call it "a true gem of economic analysis" (Baumol) and say it displays "a professional competence ... an analytical power and freshness that was breathtaking" (Samuelson). But the book was completely ignored for many years, as economists tended to be untrained in mathematics. It was not until the days of Marshall and Walras that Cournot came to be respected, and even then both these leading figures credited Cournot with giving them the idea of using calculus, continuity, and the like, while reserving to others the credit for influencing the substance of their ideas (von Thünen for Marshall, his father for Walras). These perhaps are early expressions of the sentiments of what is said to be J. Willard Gibbs's only speech before the faculty senate at Yale: "Mathematics is a language." In any event, the 1838 book was a fiasco at the time of publication, and Cournot remained an isolated figure for many years.

Cournot began his economic theorizing from a basis of reading Smith, Say, Ricardo, and such French economists as Canard and Auguste Walras. From these writings he understandably got the idea that "the definition of value, and the distinction between absolute and relative value, are rather obscure" (*Researches*, p. 18). By comparing values of commodities to the problem of assigning positions to bodies in space or on a line he decided that "What is really important is to know the laws which govern the variation of values" and that "there are only relative values" since the idea of value in exchange means the idea of a ratio between two terms (*Researches*, p. 24). He was thus able to proceed without having to solve the problem of what an invariable measure of value might be. And his procedure was simplicity itself: he makes the hypothesis that "each one seeks to derive the greatest possible value from his goods or from his labor" (*Researches*, p. 44). (This has been a serviceable hypothesis; the title of Professor Samuelson's 1970 Nobel Memorial Lecture was "Maximum Principles in Analytical Economics.")

To deduce the consequences of this hypothesis, we need data. The first important piece of data is the demand curve. Because empirical data was hard to come by in Cournot's day, he simply used general experience as the basis for drawing the demand curve for a commodity – the first time in the history of economics that anybody had done so. Generally the amount purchased increases when price falls, says Cournot, with things like diamonds (what we now call Veblen goods) as unimportant exceptions. This curve is (he assumes) continuous, monotonically decreasing, and differentiable. Unlike later writers, he does not try to justify the negative slope by appeal to utility considerations.

Cournot used his maximization hypothesis and his demand curve to analyze a variety of problems: monopoly, duopoly, perfect competition, taxation. To show the brisk straightforwardness of the analysis, Cournot wrote the demand function as $D=F(p)$, total revenue as $pF(p)$, marginal revenue as $F(p)+pF'(p)$, and the monopoly equilibrium as determined by marginal revenue equals marginal cost. And, to make sure that this is an equilibrium where profits are at a maximum rather than a minimum, he checks the sign of the second derivative of the profit function (it has to be negative). It was not until a century later that this sort of analysis became common.

For the average economics student today, Cournot is likely to be synonymous with duopoly. He defined the problem of small numbers of sellers: the decision of seller *a* will depend on his hunch about how his rival seller *b* will react to the price set by *a*. Cournot's assumption, that each duopolist believes his rival will hold his sales volume constant while meeting the price set by the first person, gave rise to much criticism and numerous other hypotheses about how duopolists might react. But his formulation of the problem and his technique of drawing reaction curves to show how the rivals respond is still used today. It may be of little consolation to the ghost of Cournot, but his book, which was a flop in 1838, is now called a book that "for sheer originality and boldness of conception has no equal in the history of economic theory."[10]

Turning to precursors of utility theory, the idea of marginal utility as opposed to total utility was proposed by some writers in the 1830s, in particular William Lloyd and Nassau Senior.[11] But these writers did not use the concepts once they were enunciated. No doubt more important as an influence on Jevons, in particular, was Jeremy Bentham, whose relationship to the Mills and Ricardo was discussed in chapter 10. Bentham's theories of pleasure and pain and his "felicific calculus" were influential in the development of the theory of marginal utility, although Bentham himself did not deal specifically in marginal terms. As a legal and institutional reformer, Bentham wished to have a general principle to test proposed changes. He found this in the principle that changes should provide the greatest pleasure and the least pain to society, and he listed a number of factors to help determine whether the pleasure/pain from one action is greater than from another: one should compare their intensity, duration, certainty, remoteness, chance of generating similar feelings or opposite ones, and the number of persons affected. It is this idea, that "the greatest happiness of the greatest number" should be the basis of social decisions, that is called utilitarianism.[12] These ideas were very influential to Jevons when he came to develop his theory of political economy many years later. For example, he starts his chapter on the theory of utility by stating "Pleasure and pain are undoubtedly the ultimate objects of the calculus of economics," and he cites Bentham's definition of utility as "the property in any good, whereby it tends to produce benefit, advantage, pleasure, good or happiness . . ." Of course Jevons applied the theory to individual exchange rather than to social aggregates as Bentham had done, and he based his theory on marginal rather than total utility.[13] With this tool he was able to show how exchange increased utility, and what was needed to achieve maximum utility.

An economist who was just as unrecognized in his own day as were Cournot and von Thünen was H. H. Gossen (1810–58). Gossen conceived the marginal utility notion all by himself. In his book *Entwickelung der Gesetze des menschlichen Verkehrs* (1854).[14] Gossen, like Cournot and von Thünen, used diagrams and mathematics, but he focuses specifically on utility. He postulated that as one consumes more of a product, the marginal utility (the addition to total utility) diminishes; this has been named Gossen's First Law. Much of his fame, however, rests on his Second Law: that to maximize utility, a person must spend his money so that the last dollar spent on each good yields the same utility; i.e., $MU_1/P_1 = MU_2/P_2$. It is through this relationship that utility is used to derive the demand curve, although Gossen himself did not take this step.

His book and ideas were completely ignored; he was not one of the circle of German economists, but had been a civil servant and in the insurance business. The dominant German economic fraternity of his day was the group of historical economists (see chapter 13 on Menger), who had no liking for work such as Gossen's. Because of the failure of his book, Gossen withdrew the unsold copies from his publishers, so that when many years later Jevons and Walras heard that Gossen had anticipated them, they had difficulty in running down the book to verify the rumor. But when they did, Jevons said in the preface to the second edition of his *Theory of Political Economy*, "It is quite apparent that Gossen has completely anticipated me as regard the general principles and method of the theory of economics" and Walras prepared an essay, published in the *Journal des Economistes*, to treat "with the respect which he deserves an original and profound thinker who is not adequately appreciated in his own country."[15]

The nineteenth-century German economist who held a regular university appointment and was a theorist rather than an historian was a rare bird. Such a person was H. K. E. von Mangoldt (1824–68). He was a liberal at a time when that point of view got people into trouble with the authorities (recall Marx's political exile). As a result, Mangoldt had a turbulent time, living in Switzerland for a while and moving in and out of government service and journalism. Eventually, in 1855, he procured a post as a university teacher after he submitted a book on entrepreneurial profit. During his university years he also wrote many encyclopedia articles and an outline book on the principles of political economy. He was not especially influential during his lifetime, but long after his death Francis Y. Edgeworth was very impressed by Mangoldt's international trade theory and Frank Knight by his theory of entrepreneurship.

His outline or *Grundrisse* (1863) was a rigorous book, using geometrical diagrams (one of the earliest to use supply and demand curves) as well as tables. It discussed pricing of goods and factors of production, using utility as an explanation of demand and using marginal productivity in the treatment of the payment to factors of production. It also dealt with money and business cycles. Since part of his economics resembles that of John Stuart Mill, he has been called a "classical and quasi-neoclassical economic theorist."[16]

The contribution of Mangoldt to the theory of international trade was to extend Ricardo's theory of comparative advantage to cases of more than two goods. The costs of production of all the goods are arranged in a side-by-side table for each country; the table for one country is moved up if its wage rates rise, or down if its wage rates fall, so that comparison of which goods are more expensive in which country is easy. Edgeworth substituted a diagram in which the logarithms of the costs of production are put on side-by-side scales for each country, and then the scale slides if wages change, permitting visual comparison of the relative costs of production.

One of the most perceptive and important predecessors was the French engineer, Jules Dupuit (1804–66). He was an active civil engineer but also had a keen interest in economics, publishing about an equal number of articles in each subject. His major contribution, the idea of consumer surplus, was ignored in England (until rediscovered by Marshall) but it attracted a good deal of attention among continental writers. Jevons thought that Dupuit must probably be credited with the "earliest perfect comprehension" of the theory of utility, but that as far as he (Jevons) knew, no English economist ever knew anything about these remarkable memoirs.[17]

What Dupuit did in his first article, "On the Measure of the Utility of Public Works,"[18] was attempt to provide a measure of the social utility of things like bridges and highways in order to know whether to advise that they be constructed. He argued that J. B. Say's measure of utility, which was the price that a person would pay, was wrong, the reason being that if a reduction in costs enables the price to fall, the measure would indicate a lower utility for the good. Dupuit's solution was to measure total utility by what a person would pay rather than go without the good. In other words, he identified the demand curve with the marginal utility curve. Total utility of the amount of goods $q_1$ in figure 12.1 is defined to be the area under the demand curve, $0Pnq_1$, since by charging the maximum price the consumer would pay for each unit of the good between 0 and $q_1$, this area would be the amount collected. If the consumer pays the price $p_1$ for each unit he buys, his total expenditure is $0p_1nq_1$. Subtracting expenditure from total utility leaves the area $p_1Pn$, which Dupuit called relative utility and which Marshall later called consumers' surplus. The proper toll to charge for using a public work, he concluded, was the one which provided the greatest utility together with a sufficient revenue to pay the maintenance and interest on the capital. In some of his writings he used the tool of relative utility to analyze pricing policies for private and public monopolists, how discriminatory pricing would enable an otherwise unprofitable firm to convert losses into profits, and why a small general sales tax is better than high excise taxes on a few goods. (The latter result depends on sufficiently high elasticities of demand.)[19]

A British writer whom we can class among our precursors in the sense that his contributions, although known, were more or less ignored, was H. C. Fleeming Jenkin (1833–85). (The correct pronunciation of Fleeming is "Flemming.") Jenkin was an electrical engineer and an inventor, and

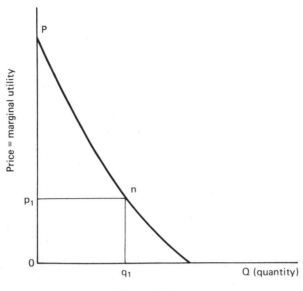

**Figure 21.1**

held the chair of engineering at Edinburgh University from 1868 on. He wrote three papers on economics, one on trade unions, one on "The Graphic Representation of the Laws of Supply and Demand and their Application to Labour," and one on the incidence of taxes.[20] The article on trade unions included a footnote with equations of supply and demand; these caught Jevons's eye and he began a correspondence with Jenkin. Then Jenkin's paper on supply and demand appeared in 1870. Jevons's son, H. S. Jevons, later reported that his father might well have postponed his writings on economic theory for several years had it not been for the articles by Jenkin "which are distinctly mathematical in method and contain a number of very ingenious geometrical diagrams illustrating the laws of supply and demand."[21] Fearful of losing his priority, Jevons hastened to get his ideas into print.

Jenkin drew his supply and demand curves as shown in figure 12.2. In the short run demand depends on considerations existing in the minds of the purchasers; stocks are fixed in the short run but holders will withhold some products in the expectation of higher prices. The higher the current price the less will be withheld from the market. In the long run, supply depends on the cost of production, with decreasing returns leading to a rising supply curve. Jenkin was the first British writer to use supply and demand diagrams and to discuss demand as a function.

He went on to apply his supply and demand analysis to the labor market, both long and short run (deciding, by the way, that the wages fund doctrine of the classical economists was wrong). In the analysis of taxation, he showed how a tax on a commodity changes the price paid by the consumer

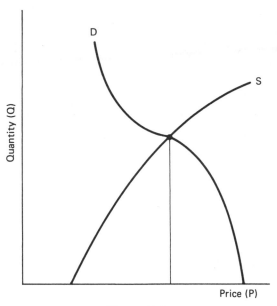

**Figure 12.2**

and received by the seller, and furthermore he showed what the tax did to consumer surplus. He defined consumers' surplus exactly as did Dupuit, and made an analogous definition for producer surplus (the area under the supply curve between its intersection with the price axis and the equilibrium price). Taxes, he showed, reduce both consumers' and producers' surplus. He thus predated Marshall in the publication of the analysis of partial equilibrium supply and demand and consumers' surplus, although Marshall claimed (as with other pieces of theory which other people did) to have developed and given lectures on these topics before Jenkin appeared in print.[22] Jenkin was no doubt an original thinker, but he had little influence on the rising profession of economics.

America's contribution to our roster of precursors was a man of even less influence. This was Charles Ellet, Jr (1810–62), a civil engineer whose writing included a mathematical analysis of the theory of discriminating monopoly and the theory of canal and railway rates. His book, *An Essay on the Laws of Trade, in Reference to the Works of Internal Improvement in the United States* (1839), was, it is said, found by a young economist who excitedly told Jacob Viner he had found an undiscovered nineteenth-century American mathematical economist. When Viner rejoined that it must be Charles Ellet, the crushed young discoverer wanted to know how Viner knew. Viner answered, "That's simple – Ellet is the only undiscovered nineteenth-century American mathematical economist."[23]

As a mathematical economist, Ellet was not in Cournot's class, not only because his work was restricted to transportation economics and freight rates, but also because rather than using general functions he used linear equations, claiming that for practical purposes this assumption is applicable. His technique essentially was to define a profits function in terms of the distances carried along feeder roads and new trunk lines as well as in terms of the freight charges, then to differentiate with respect to the freight charges to find the maximum profits. He did this in hypothetical situations of monopoly, of duopoly, and for goods and for passenger hauling services. Although his work was for long completely ignored, Ellet provides an example of the affinity between engineering training and mathematical economics which we have seen already in the cases of Dupuit and Jenkin.[24]

## Notes

1 William Baumol, "Jacob Viner at Princeton," *Journal of Political Economy*, 1972, p. 13.
2 Chapter VI of Lionel Robbins, *The Theory of Economic Policy* (London, 1953), is very good on this.
3 Alfred Marshall, *The Economics of Industry* (London, 1879), p. 2.
4 Paul A Samuelson, "Thünen at Two Hundred," *Journal of Economic Literature*, 1983, pp. 1468–88, presents a modern mathematical version of Thünen's location theory. It is detailed, thorough, and involves a lot of calculus. Robert Dorfman and Professor Samuelson worked over the natural wage and agreed that with von Thünen's assumptions it is valid; see Dorfman, "Comment: P. A. Samuelson, 'Thünen at Two Hundred,'" and Samuelson, "Yes to Robert Dorfman's Vindication of Thünen's Natural-Wage Derivation," *Journal of Economic Literature*, December, 1986. Mark Blaug, "The Economics of Johann von Thünen," in Warren J. Samuels (ed.), *Research in the History of Economic Thought and Methodology*, vol. 3, 1985 (Greenwich, Conn.) is a good review of all aspects of von Thünen's work.
5 Dmitriev's book was translated and published as V. K. Dmitriev, *Economic Essays on Value, Competition, and Utility* (New York and London, 1974), ed. D. M. Nuti, trans. D. Fry. Dmitriev was unable to fulfill his ambition to be a physician, studied economics as second best, was only a minor tax official, but did write a pioneering mathematical economics book. Its argument, that the total labor requirement in a situation where good $a$ requires some of good $b$, which requires some of good $a$, can be solved by simultaneous equations, and costs and prices thereby determined, is summarized in a book review by Professor Samuelson in the *Journal of Economic Literature*, 1975, pp. 491–5.
6 Samuelson, ibid., p. 1482.
7 See Arthur H. Leigh, "von Thünen's Theory of Distribution," *Journal of Political Economy*, 1946, pp. 481–502.
8 An interesting account of von Thünen's life is provided by Erich Schneider in H. S. Spiegel (ed.), *The Development of Economic Thought* (New York, 1952), pp. 445–57. More details and an interpretation of $w = \sqrt{(ap)}$ as an attempt at formulating a just wage rather than a positive description of the equilibrium

wage as set by the market is provided by H. D. Dickinson, "Von Thünen's Economics," *Economic Journal*, 1969, pp. 894–902.

9  Translated into English in 1897 as *Researches into the Mathematical Principles of the Theory of Wealth* (New York). Subsequent citations in the text are from this edition.

10  Mark Blaug, *Economic Theory in Retrospect*, 4th edn (Cambridge, 1985), p. 317. Expository and evaluative articles in English are scarce. Irving Fisher had one in the *Quarterly Journal of Economics* in 1898. More recently, see C. L. Fry and R. B. Ekelund, Jr, "Cournot's Demand Theory: A Reassessment," *History of Political Economy (HOPE)*, 1971, pp. 190–7; George F. Rhodes, Jr, "A Note interpreting Cournot's Economics by his General Epistemology," *HOPE*, 1978, pp. 315–21; Claude Ménard, "Three Forms of Resistance to Statistics: Say, Cournot, Walras", *HOPE*, 1980, pp. 524–41; and a book in French by Claude Ménard, *La Formation d'une Rationalité Économique: A. A. Cournot* (Paris, 1978).

11  There is a minor piece of controversy over whether or not to include Montifort Longfield; the latest study argues that he never made an explicit statement of the law of diminishing marginal utility, although he was certainly interested in the demand side of the market. See Laurence S. Moss, *Mountifort Longfield: Ireland's First Professor of Political Economy* (Ottowa, Ill., 1976), pp. 39ff.

12  There is a tale that an administrator of British India, following this principle, advocated breaking up the Taj Mahal and selling the marble, using the funds for economic growth, on the basis that this action would result in a good to a greater number of people than those who could afford to travel to the Taj Mahal to admire its architectural glory.

13  Jacob Viner, "Bentham and J. S. Mill: the Utilitarian Background," *American Economic Review*, 1949, pp. 360–82, is very good on utilitarianism. R. D. C. Black, "Jevons, Bentham, and De Morgan," *Economica*, 1972, deals with Bentham's influence on Jevons. T. W. Hutchison, "Bentham as an Economist," *Economic Journal*, 1956, pp. 288–306, covers Bentham's strictly economic writings in monetary theory and *laissez-faire*, noting that like Gossen and Cournot these writings were virtually unknown and of no influence in his day.

14  In English, the title is *Development of the Laws of Human Relations*.

15  This essay is translated and published in H. W. Spiegel (ed.), *The Development of Economic Thought* (New York, 1952).

16  Carl G. Uhr, "H. K. E. von Mangoldt's Contributions to Economic Theory," University of California at Riverside, *Working Papers Series*, No. 38, 1979, p. 1.

17  Jevons, *Theory of Political Economy* (Penguin edition, New York, 1970), p. 57.

18  Which appeared in 1844 in the *Annales des Ponts et Chaussées*, and is translated in *International Economic Papers*, No. 2, 1952. Dupuit's article "On Tolls and Transport Charges," is translated in *International Economic Papers*, No. 11, 1962.

19  Dupuit's work is summarized by R. W. Houghton, "A Note on the Early History of Consumer's Surplus," *Economica*, 1958, pp. 49–57, and in a remarkably detailed textbook treatment by Robert B. Ekelund, Jr, and Robert F. Hébert. *A History of Economic Thought and Method*, 2nd edn (New York, 1983), chapter 12. These same two authors detail how Dupuit's concepts arose out of an empirical engineering background rather than out of a reworking

of classical economics in "Dupuit and Marginal Utility: Context of the Discovery," *HOPE*, 1976, pp. 266–73.

20 These essays were reprinted by the London School of Economics in 1931.

21 Jevons, in preface to the fourth edition of *The Theory of Political Economy*.

22 For an exposition of Jenkin's work and his relations with Jevons and Marshall see A. D. Brownlie and M. F. Lloyd Prichard, "Professor Fleeming Jenkin, 1833–1885, Pioneer in Engineering and Political Economy," *Oxford Economic Papers*, 1963, pp. 204–16.

23 W. J. Baumol and S. M. Goldberger, *Precursors in Mathematical Economics* (London, 1968), p. 171.

24 Ellet's life and writing is surveyed in C. D. Calsoyas, "The Mathematical Theory of Monopoly in 1839: Charles Ellet, Jr.," *Journal of Political Economy*, 1950, pp. 162–70. Christopher Ross Bell, "Charles Ellet, Jr., and the Theory of Optimum Input Choice," looks at a primitive production function and associated cost function derived by Ellet in "Charles Ellet, Jr., and the Theory of Optimum Input choice," *HOPE*, Fall, 1986.

# 13
# Carl Menger and the Austrian School

Carl Menger (1840–1921), although one of the trio credited with the marginal revolution of the 1870s, differed in many significant ways from both Jevons and Walras. The content of his theory, the way it was formulated, his attitude towards mathematics, and his subsequent influence are among these differences.

Menger's father was a lawyer and young Carl studied law at three universities – Vienna, Prague, and Cracow. His early career was in journalism, including a stint in the press office of the prime minister of Austria. He later claimed that his interest in economics came from having to write market reports in that job. During the years 1867–71 he worked out his value theory; although he stressed the role of utility, he did not, interestingly enough, stumble upon Gossen, although he used many other German references.[1] He published his theory in 1871, but, although it led to his appointment at the University of Vienna, where he and his pupils built up a body of doctrine distinguished enough to become known as the Austrian School, the book remained untranslated into English until 1950.[2]

Menger devoted most of his career to teaching economics to students of law, although two men whom he influenced, Wieser and Böhm-Bawerk, did go on to become distinguished economists of the Austrian School. Beginning in 1883, however, he became embroiled in a controversy with German historical economists over the goals of economic study and the proper way to pursue them. This developed into a bitter battle, called the *Methodenstreit*, details of which will be covered later in the chapter. Apart from his teaching, Menger found time to write many articles and memoranda, as well as testimony on Austrian currency reform in the 1890s, and he also collected an imposing library of some 25,000 volumes (now in Hitotsubashi University in Tokyo).

Menger, as mentioned, differed significantly from Jevons and Walras. On the level of technique, he objected to the use of mathematics, which could not help discover the "essence" of economic transactions. As for the aims of his *Principles of Economics*, he said he wished to establish whether and under what conditions the following held: if a thing is useful; if it is a good;

if it is an economic good; if it has value and what the measure of value is; if an economic exchange will take place; and finally the limits within which a price can be established (*Principles*, p. 48). However, with the benefit of hindsight, it can be seen that what Menger emphasized compared to his colleagues from England and Lausanne are considerations dealing with economic progress, with changes in the range and quality of goods because of changes in information standing out as a major part of his exposition. What Menger stressed was the *formation* of price, not the determination of the equilibrium conditions for competitive prices, according to Professor Moss.[3] Menger did not stress static price theory as did Jevons and Walras because "market price is merely a superficial and incidental manifestation of much deeper forces at work in the exchange of goods and services."[4] These deeper forces are the subjective comparisons which people make in deciding how scarce resources that may be used for many different ends are actually to be employed.

Menger put his value theory in the center of a pattern of economic development from primitive life to modern capitalism. Modern (i.e., 1870) man must plan and control production, which is based on scientific knowledge and on the use of capital. Capital is viewed as a collection of goods at various stages or distances from the final consumer – the retailer's counter is close to the consumer but the drills and shovels in the coal mine are further away (at a higher stage, in Menger's orientation). The science and the capital increase productivity and the need for planning and coordination. At the same time that there are more goods, there are more people so that needs continue to outrun means. Private property encourages people to economize and allows them to avoid conflict over the disposition of the scarce means. It also allows producers to produce in anticipation of need, since they can own the stocks which will be desired by consumers; this is a much smoother economy than one where consumers must put in orders and wait for them to be filled. It is obvious that Menger took pains to establish the institutional background for his value theory, something which contemporary microeconomics takes for granted.

In the market economy, trade enables one to give up something on which he places a low value in return for something which has, for him, a higher value. Menger explained that goods are valued differently both because they satisfy different needs (food as compared to a good filling a less significant niche; Menger used tobacco to illustrate, not appreciating its addictive quality), and because increasing the supply of the same good fills less pressing requirements for the same need. His table illustrating his idea is famous (*Principles*, p. 127). Needs are labelled I, II, III, etc., with the most significant having the lower numbers (food is I). The columns under each need show the additions to total satisfaction of additional units of the good meeting that need.

Technically, this is called a lexicographic ordering, and it appears that Menger had in mind that the numbers in the ordering represented an ordinal rather than a cardinal scale of marginal utility. He discussed at

| Needs | I | II | III | IV | V |
|---|---|---|---|---|---|
| | 10 | 9 | 8 | 7 | 6 |
| | 9 | 8 | 7 | 6 | 5 |
| Marginal | 8 | 7 | 6 | 5 | 4 |
| utilities | 7 | 6 | 5 | 4 | 3 |
| | 6 | 5 | 4 | 3 | 2 |

length how to allocate a good that meets several needs; for example, if good $x$ could be used for both needs I and II, and if a consumer has five units of $x$, he should use 3 units for the first need and 2 for the second, as this equates the marginal utilities at 8. Using 4 for the first need and 1 for the second is wrong, as the next unit in need II would give a satisfaction of 8 rather than the 7 yielded in need I. Although he claimed that this sort of valuation was related to price, he did not consider the opposite problem, of several goods meeting the same need. In this case, says Professor Georgescu-Roegen, Menger's theory cannot explain prices.[5] Indeed, Menger made no attempt to derive demand curves from the underlying utility functions; he stated that "The value of a particular good or of a given portion of the whole quantity of a good at the disposal of an economizing individual is thus for him equal to the importance of the least important of the satisfactions assured by the whole available quantity and achieved with any equal portion" (*Principles*, p. 139)[6] and that "the *prices* of actual labor services are governed, like the prices of all other goods, by their *values*" (p. 171). But he attempted no formal proof.

If his theory of demand was weak, his theory of the supply blade of the scissors was non-existent (to use Marshall's analogy that, like a pair of scissors, the theory of price needs both a supply and a demand blade). This was because he believed that value depends only on the utility of the last unit: "Whether a diamond was found accidentally or was obtained from a diamond pit with the employment of a thousand days of labor is completely irrelevant for its value" (p. 146). Jevons once put the same thing more pithily: "In commerce by-gones are forever by-gones." Since in fact both costs and demands must be studied in the theory of price it is Marshall rather than Jevons or Menger who fathered partial-equilibrium theory, and Walras who is the parent of general equilibrium.

But although Menger did not utilize costs in the determination of value, he did make important contributions to the theory of production and to the determination of the values of the factors of production. One of these was that the proportions in which inputs are combined are not fixed but variable. Another was his development of the idea mentioned above in the summary of his views of economic development, that in capitalism there is a heirarchy of production, in which consumer goods (called goods of the first order) are produced by other, higher-order goods as well as by labor and land. For example, gunpowder is produced by "saltpetre, sulphur, charcoal, specialized labor services, appliances, etc." (*Principles*, p. 150). (In Austrian production theory there is only a one-way flow in production;

goods of lower order are never used to produce goods of higher order, by contrast with today's input–output theory, where for example, coal may be needed to produce coal.) The higher order goods' value is derived from the value of the consumer goods they produce; this is called the theory of imputation. This value is prospective as far as the producer is concerned, since production takes time. The value of one unit of a particular higher order good is equal to "the difference in importance between the satisfactions that can be attained when we have command of the given quantity of the good of higher order whose value we wish to determine and the satisfactions that would be attained if we did not have this quantity at our command" (*Principles*, p. 165). (Sir Alexander Gray once said that Menger's sentences and paragraphs, which are sometimes indistinguishable, frequently seem to call for dynamite.[7] No wonder Menger remained untranslated so long!) This theory, which was more extensively developed by such followers as Wieser, is "unquestionably superior to any preceding explanation of the determination of the value of productive agents."[8] The theories of the classical economists, deriving from Adam Smith, had been related to the returns of social classes (rent to landowners, wages to labor, profits to capitalists), and each class got a separate analysis. Thus, in Ricardo rent was the residual after the returns to capital and labor together had been determined, wages were (broadly) determined by the iron law, and capitalists got what was left of the returns to the dose of capital and labor together at the margin. Menger's difference was that he made the value of productive goods and services part of the general theory of value.

While Menger did not emphasize the market price as being the center of economic science, he did discuss it, warning that it is only an "incidental manifestation," that it is simply the "symptom of an economic equilibration between the economies of individuals" (*Principles*, pp. 191–2). He discussed the formation of this market price between two individuals, in what is now known as bilateral monopoly, showing how the final terms of trade depend on bargaining strength. Then he discussed the effect of more traders entering the market and how the limits of bargaining are lessened, because the final terms of trade must lie between the amount offered by the individual who offers the least and still participates in trading and the amount that would be offered by the individual who offers the most of those excluded from the trade. The more people in the market, the closer are the offerings of these two people. When markets become large in developed economies speculators and middlemen keep the market price close to a genuine competitive equilibrium.[9]

Menger's interests did not remain with the sort of theory he attended to in the *Principles*. His next substantial effort was a book whose title in English is *Problems of Economics and Sociology*.[10] Part of the book explains Menger's conception of economic theory, that it should proceed by determining the essence of phenomena; part of it is called "The Organic Understanding of Social Phenomena," and explains how some unplanned social institutions can unintentionally but effectively serve society. This is a similar idea to Adam Smith's invisible hand, but Smith applied the notion to markets, whereas Menger applied it to the state, language, law, morals, and other social institutions. But what the book is mainly remembered for is its attack on the German historical school, the beginning of the *Methodenstreit* mentioned above.

To understand the *Methodenstreit* it is necessary to realize that "the interests of German economists had been fastened on social reform, on altogether practical questions, and on problems of administrative techniques, and that the purely scientific interest, so far as it existed at all, had concerned itself exclusively with economic history."[11] This scientific interest was expressed in the methodological proposition that scientific economics should consist in the results of historical monographs. If any generalizations were made, they would be made from these monographs, not from abstract principles. What is called "the Older Historical School" – Wilhelm Roscher, Bruno Hildebrand and Karl Knies – looked for the laws of economic development in comparisons between societies at different times and at different locations at the same period of time. Their approach was to study the nation as a whole in comparison to other nations. The Younger Historical School, in particular Gustav Schmoller, denied any non-empirical laws in economics; Schmoller concentrated on institutions and their inter-relations within a given national economy. His goal was to derive the "essence" of economic phenomena by deriving empirically all the characteristics of the economic institutions involved in these phenomena. Because economic laws are empirical, and change as more experience is examined, there is no absolute economic law; all such laws are relative to the situation from which they were derived.[12]

Menger had been influenced by the Historical School; indeed his *Principles* is dedicated to Roscher. Furthermore, the chapter on money in the *Principles* is developed on Historical School lines, tracing the development of money from the earliest societies. But after his *Principles* was published he found a complete lack of interest and understanding in Germany; he also became concerned by the complete one-sidedness of the German approach.[13] His epistemological position has been called that of a "moderate realist" or "Aristotelian" by Samuel Bostaph. He looked for the "essence" of real things by abstracting them down to their simplest elements. He would then explain more complicated phenomena by showing how they arose from the simple essences. The laws he derived from these were considered to be exact, in contrast to the relative sort of historical laws derived by Schmoller. Furthermore, Menger concentrated on the individual, in contrast to the concentration on the nation or on social institutions as a whole favored by the Historical School.

These completely opposed epistemological positions set the stage for the battle. Menger, in his book *Problems of Economics and Society* (1883), wrote such things as

The vagueness about the nature of political economy and of its subdivisions; the lack of any really strict distinction of the historical, the theoretical and the practical point of view in research in the economic field; the confusion of individual orientations of theoretical research and of the philosophy of economic history in particular with theoretical economics and with political economy at large; the vagueness about the nature of the exact orientation of theoretical research and its relationship to the empirical–realistic orientation; the opinion that the historical–philosophical orientation is the only one justified in political economy and is analogous to historical jurisprudence; the failure to recognize the true nature of the historical point of view in our science, especially as regards its theoretical aspects; the exaggerated importance which is attributed to the so-called historical method; the vagueness about the nature of the organic approach in economy and about the problems resulting therefrom for social research – all these methodological errors and one-sided emphases appearing already to no small extent in Roscher's youthful writings are also found in his later writings, in which, to be sure, he is more and more frequently likely to designate his method as "historical or (!) physiological."[14]

Schmoller reviewed this book, adversely; Menger replied in the form of a series of letters, highly polemical and full of invective; Schmoller sent Menger an insulting letter which he also published in his journal. In the course of these publications and others which continued to flow, the respective methodological positions were thoroughly set out. Many later writers concluded that the debate was a waste of time, as both theoretical and historical methods are necessary in the pursuit of economic knowledge. Bostaph's contention is that if the epistemological issues had been more clearly spelled out in order to justify the contrasting methodologies, the project would not have been so inconclusive and frustrating for the participants, and would have been more valuable for the later development of economics.

Parenthetically, in Britain at about the same time there was what has been called a historist movement, but it came from the writings of Auguste Comte and the legal historian Sir Henry Maine rather than from the German Historical School. For twenty years between 1870 and 1890 there was a considerable attack on the remains of orthodox classical economics by such writers as Bonamy Price, John Kells Ingram, Walter Bagehot, Cliffe Leslie, and others. They questioned whether economics was a science, claimed its scope was too narrow, appealed for more induction, and in general raised a turmoil in British economics which was ended when Marshall's *Principles* became the dominant influence after 1890. It was a much less acrid affair than the *Methodenstreit*, and had, it is judged, only a modest and subtle influence on the development of economics. It did, however, lead to the development of a new field, economic history.[15]

Menger's *Principles* may have had little effect in Germany, but Austrian students developed and disseminated his ideas. One of these disciples was Friedrich von Wieser (1851–1926), whose interest in history and social evolution was changed to an interest in economics when he read Menger's book. Initially in government service, Wieser then taught at Prague and eventually took over Menger's chair in Vienna. The doctrines which are particularly associated with Wieser are, first, the proposition that cost is not determined by the discomfort of labor or the agonies of abstinence, but instead by the marginal utility of the alternatives foregone. This is an idea often applied to wartime economics, that the cost of the guns produced is the butter which would otherwise have been produced by the resources shifted into war production. In the economics of his day this doctrine was disputed by the real cost theories of the classical economists and of Alfred Marshall (see chapter 16 on Marshall for discussion and evaluation).

Secondly, Wieser developed and expanded Menger's idea that the value of the final product could be imputed back to the higher order goods and factors of production.[16] His exposition was confused because he did not clearly distinguish between fixed and variable proportions in the combining of inputs, but he seemed to emphasize fixed proportions. The difference between imputation and marginal productivity theories is this: to say that wages equal $(\partial x/\partial L) \cdot P_x$ (wages equal the change in output resulting from a change in labor, times the price of the output) is a marginal productivity theory of the demand for labor; while $\partial U/\partial L = \partial U/\partial x \cdot \partial x/\partial L$ (the utility contributed by another unit of labor equals the utility of the extra product times the marginal product of the extra labor hired) is an imputation concept, and economists like Wieser and Menger believed there was a deeper meaning in the latter.[17] If marginal utility is measured by the price of the product, the two concepts become the same, and imputation may be analyzed as the process of dividing up the price of the product among the inputs. For this purpose, Wieser's fixed coefficients approach was very clumsy, as well as ignoring diminishing returns.[18] In terms of modern theory, his imputation problem is the equivalent of setting up the linear programming problem of maximizing national income subject to given product prices and fixed resource constraints, and finding the shadow prices of the resources. The comment that his fixed coefficients approach was clumsy refers to the awkwardness of attempting to find shadow prices in a literary exposition.

Neo-Austrian theory is now very much in vogue among followers of Ludwig von Mises.[19] Most of this discussion is in terms of how the market system can cope with uncertainty. However, standard neo-classical economists have not been as interested in that aspect of Austrian economics as in the capital theory of the last of the trio of Austrians of the late nineteenth century, Eugen von Böhm-Bawerk (1851–1914). Expository articles and essays on his capital theory have recently been written by eminent theorists, and his capital model figured prominently in the Cambridge–Cambridge controversy (see p. 155).

Böhm-Bawerk, like his brother-in-law Wieser, was a law student at Vienna who was greatly impressed by Menger's *Principles*. His career was a combination of academic and government service. Between 1881 and

1889 he was a professor at Innsbruck; in 1889 he entered the Austrian finance department where he was concerned with currency reform. Later he became minister of finance on three occasions. In 1904 he resigned to become a professor at Vienna. Although he wrote on the usual Austrian topics – alternative cost, utility, imputation – it was his capital and interest theory which made him famous. He published a long, detailed and highly critical survey of previous writers in the field in 1884; his own contribution, *The Positive Theory of Capital*, appeared in 1889; and comments and rebuttals of criticisms of the *Positive Theory* made up what was in effect a separate volume that appeared as an appendix to a new edition of the *Positive Theory* in 1909.[20]

There are two major aspects of his interest theory: an analysis of the causes of interest, and a model of the determination of interest rates.[21] The first part on the causes of interest is definitely Austrian: a concern with the essence of the concept, and the notion that the value of present goods as well as of future goods as perceived at the present depends on their marginal utility. His problem was, why is the value of present goods higher than that of future goods of like kind and number (i.e., if you will pay $1 for a loaf of bread today, why will the maximum you will give someone for a promise to give you a loaf of bread a year from now be less than $1)? His answer was the famous three causes of interest:

1 You may well not be in the same circumstances today and tomorrow. You might be in temporary distress today, or you might expect that your income will be rising over time. If you expect to be able to buy more loaves of bread next year than today, it is rational to pay more for today's loaf – its marginal utility is higher. Böhm-Bawerk claimed that there are more people who will get more goods tomorrow than there are people who will get fewer goods (these people would pay a negative rate of interest) so that on balance society has a positive rate of interest.

2 The first cause of interest is subjective and rational; the second is subjective and irrational: people systematically undervalue future wants and the utility of the goods which satisfy them. There is a myopia about the future. Imagination is incomplete; the will-power to save today's candy and eat it tomorrow is weak; and life is uncertain.[22]

3 Present goods have a higher marginal utility than future goods because they have a technological superiority. Roundabout, time-consuming processes are more productive, he says; compare, for example, walking to the spring each time you want a drink of water, or taking time to make a pail, or taking still more time to make and lay a pipe-line. Although the last two alternatives take more time today, they will save you many more hours over their lifetime than you invest today (*Positive Theory*, pp. 10–11).

For illustration of this last point, suppose a month's labor is invested in 1888, and yields a product of 280 in 1890; a month's labor invested in 1889 yields 200 in 1890; and a month's labor invested in 1890 with no roundabout process involved yields only 100. Then the goods which support the labor are worth more delivered to you in 1888 than if you wait to accept delivery in 1889 (although paying for them in 1888), because of the productivity of time-consuming processes.

Later theorists such as Irving Fisher dealt with the interaction of the three reasons; for example, if the first two reasons are absent, the third reason will result in a higher physical product for present goods but not a higher value product.

In discussing the third ground for interest, roundaboutness, Böhm-Bawerk tried to devise a measure for how much roundaboutness was actually present in an economy. Using the Austrian stage scheme of production, he argued that, for example, in making cloth it might take five years between growing the wool and making the cloth. The economy would need to provide five years' subsistence for the person who grew the wool; four years' subsistence for the one in the next stage, say spinning; three years of provisions for the weavers, and so on. The average amount of subsistence needed would be $(5+4+3+2+1)/5=3$. (*Positive Theory*, p. 318). Böhm-Bawerk worked with considerably more complicated examples, but this gives the flavor of his work.[23]

Some economists argue that this way of viewing capital is the same as Ricardo's in essence. Ricardo had stages of production and roundabout processes, although he certainly did not calculate periods of production.[24] This was just as well, for the concept of the period of production proved to be one of the more confusing and controversial concepts in economics. Irving Fisher argued that a geometric rather than an arithmetic mean should be used. Wicksell pointed out that compound interest should be charged on the labor invested, in which case the labor in the earlier stages would be weighted more heavily than that of later stages.[25] Modern commentators argue that Böhm-Bawerk oversimplified by considering only the quantity of labor bound up in his roundabout processes. There is in fact another primary factor of production involved whenever machines are used, and this is sometimes called "waiting".[26] Resources tied up in machines can be converted to consumer goods in the present if the machines are not maintained; keeping the stock of machines intact involves the social cost of waiting to get the consumer goods from the productivity of the machines. Dorfman, in the cited article, presents the complicated calculations necessary to compute the period of production in waiting and also, as Böhm-Bawerk did, the amount of labor invested when part of the labor is tied up in machines. Then he points out that the overall period of production is something in between the period of production in waiting and the period of production of labor. This concept, which has now moved far beyond Böhm-Bawerk, can be calculated, although many past theorists had claimed that it could not, particularly if machines are used to make machines. In any event, the only simple and intuitive use of the period of production concept is the case where only labor is used, as in the planting of trees and the maturing of wine. Although the concept has had a stormy past, it has not much of a present.

When he stops asking questions about the fundamental reasons and the essence of the rate of interest and begins actually determining the rate of interest, Böhm-Bawerk becomes a productivity theorist. He relates interest to the marginal productivity of time – that is, to an extension of the roundaboutness of production. But how is the period of production determined? Given a stock of capital to serve as subsistence to the workers, and given the size of the labor force, notice that an increase in wages will reduce the length of time that can be taken in production. The reason is that the subsistence fund will be exhausted sooner at a high wage rate, and the new production had better be ready. Secondly, notice that wages plus interest are the total of national income, and the entrepreneur would like to maximize his return from interest. This is equivalent to requiring that labor be paid its marginal product, where the marginal product depends on the length of the period of production. So what is needed is a wage that will fully employ labor and that will equal the marginal product of labor. There will be one period of production which gives this wage, and the marginal product of extending this period of production will be the rate of interest.[27]

Böhm-Bawerk's model has long been thought to be of historical interest only, having been superseded by Wicksell and Irving Fisher. But it was recently called on to demonstrate some points in the Cambridge–Cambridge controversy. This was a lively debate about the fundamentals of the theory of capital and of the distribution of income. It prompted a reexamination of the validity and usefulness of some of the long-standing theories which had originated in the nineteenth century, and so it remains interesting in the history of economic thought even though it is no longer a fashionable topic for research. Briefly, Joan Robinson and some colleagues at Cambridge University, England, objected to the economic growth theories of Paul A. Samuelson and Robert M. Solow of the Massachusetts Institute of Technology, Cambridge, Massachusetts. A simple neoclassical growth model of the MIT variety expressed output ($Y$) as a function of the inputs of labor ($L$) and capital ($K$) with a given technology, $Y = f(L,K)$. The growth of $Y$, $dY/dt$, where $t$ stands for time, depends on the growth of the inputs, $dL/dt$ and $dK/dt$, and on changes in technology. Changes in wages and the interest return on capital are determined by the marginal products, $\partial Y/\partial L$ and $\partial Y/\partial K$. Mrs Robinson objected that this theory was faulty because a unit in which to measure capital at the aggregate level for the whole economy could not be found, that marginal products may not have a unique relation to the amounts of labor and capital, and that in the real world wages and interest depend on the economic and social power of labor and capital, not on marginal products.[28]

The Cambridge–Cambridge controversy covered considerable ground in the theory of capital, but the relevant points for Böhm-Bawerkian capital theory are this: do the following propositions hold in comparing one long-run steady state with another:

1  Lower interest rates lead to more roundabout, capital-using processes.
2  As the processes get more roundabout, there are diminishing marginal returns to capital (which is why it takes a lower interest rate to induce their use).
3  As the process gets more roundabout, output per worker rises.
4  The capital–output ratio rises as the interest rate falls and more roundabout processes are used.

As it turns out, analysis shows that in a simple neo-classical model none of the above is necessarily true. Here is the example used by Professor Samuelson on the occasion when he conceded that the simple parables of capital theory were inadequate: suppose there are two ways to make product $x$. In one technique, 7 units of labor are invested in 1978 and the product appears in 1980 (perhaps $x$ is wine or a live tree). In the other technique, 2 units of labor are invested in 1977, 6 units in 1979, and $x$ appears in 1980. The cost of production by the first technique, assuming wages equal \$1, is $7(1+r)^2$, where $r$ is the rate of interest and the term $(1+r)$ must be squared because the 7 units of labor are in process for two years. The cost of using the second technique is $2(1+r)^3 + 6(1+r)$. If $r$ is zero, the first technique is the cheapest. As $r$ rises, the costs of the two become closer together, and they become equal at \$15.75 when $r=50$ percent. At higher interest rates the second process is cheaper, and firms will switch their techniques. But they will not stay with that when interest rises to more than 100 per cent; at $r=100$ percent both techniques cost \$28 and at higher rates than that the first technique is again cheaper. There will be a switch from the first to the second technique, then a switching back to the first.[29]

The significance of re-switching is that none of the four propositions listed above is true when it occurs. In that case, lower interest rates will sometimes lead to lower instead of higher output per worker; they may reduce instead of raising the capital–output ratio; and the first two propositions may similarly be violated.[30] There are various reactions to this theoretical development. Some would drop neo-classical theory in favor of various neo-Keynesian theories enunciated by Lord Kaldor, or some of the theories of the late Joan Robinson. These theories stress class differences in savings behavior or in power. Others say that "in real life" the distribution of income does depend significantly on the relative supplies of labor and of diverse capital goods, and if the simplified parables have logical holes in them, then better theories involving the empirical realities are needed. For this chapter, the interesting thing is that Böhm–Bawerk served as a tool for digging the grave of the simplified theory which he had helped form.

# Notes

1 Hayek, in his biography of Menger, points out that there was a complete absence of influence of Austrian economists "for the simple reason that, in the early part of the nineteenth century in Austria, there were practically no native economists." Friedrich von Hayek on Menger, in H. W. Spiegel (ed.), *The Development of Economic Thought* (New York, 1952), p. 531.

2 Carl Menger, *Principles of Economics* (Glencoe, III., 1950), hereafter cited in the text as *Principles*. The translators, James Dingwall and Bert F. Hoselitz, suggest that a partial explanation for the long delay in getting a translation into English is the unusually difficult and cumbersome German prose style Menger had developed as a government official, with sentences half a page long involving clauses within clauses.

3 Laurence S. Moss, "Carl Menger's Theory of Exchange," *Atlantic Economic Journal*, 1978, special issue, pp. 17–30. This is one of the most helpful articles on Menger's value theory.

4 William Jaffé, "Menger, Jevons and Walras De-homogenized," *Economic Inquiry*, 1976, p. 521. See also Erich Streissler, "To What Extent was the Austrian School Marginalist?", *History of Political Economy* (HOPE), 1972, pp. 426–41.

5 See his article "Utility," *International Encyclopedia of the Social Sciences*, vol. 16 (New York, 1968), p. 251.

6 That is, if you have two units of a good satisfying need I, its value is 9.

7 Gray, *Development of Economic Doctrine* (London, 1980), p. 350.

8 George Stigler, *Production and Distribution Theories* (New York, 1941), p. 153.

9 Moss, "Carl Menger," has a good discussion of some of the subtleties of Menger's discussion and of how it relates to Cournot and Marshall.

10 Originally published in 1883; the English translation was published in 1963 by the University of Illinois Press.

11 Joseph Schumpeter, *Ten Great Economists* (New York, 1951), p. 148.

12 The theory of knowledge lying behind such an approach is called nominalism; for an article explaining the epistemological (or theory of knowledge) differences between Menger and the Historical School see Samuel Bostaph, "The Methodological Debate Between Carl Menger and the German Historicists," *Atlantic Economic Journal*, 1978, special issue, pp. 3–16; the foregoing description of the approach of the Historical School is drawn from this article.

13 See T. W. Hutchison, "Some Themes from *Investigations into Method*," in J. R. Hicks and W. Weber (eds), *Carl Menger and the Austrian School of Economics* (Oxford, 1973), p. 32.

14 *Problems of Economics and Society* (Glencoe, Ill., 1963), pp. 187–8. Two footnotes, each more lengthy than the quoted sentence, have been omitted.

15 For a discussion of the English historist movement, see A. W. Coats, "The Historist Reaction in English Political Economy 1870–90", *Economica*, 1954, pp. 143–53; chapter 1 of T. W. Hutchison, *A Review of Economic Doctrines, 1870–1929*; and G. M. Koot, "T. E. Cliffe Leslie, Irish Social Reform, and the Origins of the English Historical School of Economics," *HOPE*, 1975, pp. 312–36, and "English Historical Economics and the Emergence of Economic History in England," *HOPE*, 1980, pp. 174–205.

16 It has been argued that a rather obscure Irish economist named Isaac Butt was an unacknowledged precursor of this theory. See Laurence S. Moss, "Isaac Butt and the Early Development of the Marginal Utility Theory of Imputation," *HOPE*, 1973, pp. 317–38.

17 See J. Schumpeter, *History of Economic Analysis* (New York, 1954), pp. 941–2. Schumpeter suggests a genuine Austrian would use deltas instead of partial derivatives; i.e. small finite changes rather than infinitesimals.

18 Stigler, *Production and Distribution Theories*, chapter VII, expounds and criticizes Wieser.

19 The interested student is referred to a bibliography in H. W. Spiegel, *The Growth of Economic Thought*, rev. edn (Durham, NC, 1983), p. 819.

20 Although the first two volumes had been previously translated in the nineteenth century, a convenient modern translation is *Capital and Interest* (South Holland, Ill., 1959), which contains all three of the volumes mentioned above and from which text citations are taken.

21 Stigler, *Production and Distribution Theories*, p. 194, quotes Wicksell's recollection of a conversation with Böhm-Bawerk on the reason why there are different emphases in the two parts of his book. Böhm-Bawerk claimed that the first part of the book was at the printers before the second half was written so that he was unable to revise the first part in light of later thoughts.

22 Sometimes the uncertainty is not large; the French eighteenth-century scientist Buffon claimed that all probabilities smaller than 0.0001 equal zero, since that was the probability of a man of fifty-six dying during the day and people treat this probability as negligible. See George Stigler, *Essays in the History of Economics* (Chicago, 1965), p. 112.

23 For the interested student: Let $L_t$ be the amount of labor invested in period $t$ (measuring $t$ as the length of time between the labor input and the time at which the output of consumer goods becomes available). If there are $N$ divisions of time in the production process, the period of production, $\theta$, is defined as $\theta = (\Sigma L_i t)/\Sigma L_t$. If one unit of labor is invested each period for $N$ periods, the formula becomes $\theta = (1+2+ \ldots +N)/N = [(1/2)N(N+1)]/N = (N+1)/2$. For the example in the text, where $N = 5$, $(N+1)/2 = 3$, just as Böhm-Bawerk calculated.

24 Victor Edelberg, "The Ricardian Theory of Profits," *Economica*, 1933, pp. 57–74, relates Ricardo to Austrian capital theory.

25 A good reference is Robert E. Kuenne, *Eugen von Böhm-Bawerk* (New York, 1971), pp. 68ff.

26 Robert Dorfman, "Waiting and the Period of Production," *Quarterly Journal of Economics*, 1959, pp. 351–72.

27 Robert Dorfman, "A Graphical Exposition of Böhm-Bawerk's Interest Theory," *Review of Economic Studies*, 1959, pp. 153–8, shows the complicated diagramming needed to convert the model into geometry. J. Hirschleifer, "A Note on the Böhm-Bawerk/Wicksell Theory of Interest," *Review of Economic Studies*, 1967, pp. 191–9, argues that Böhm-Bawerk would have included his time preference theory from the first two causes of interest, so that the stock of capital would have been a variable rather than a given, if he had only had the technical equipment to be able to do it; this article shows how. P. A. Samuelson, "A Summing Up," *Quarterly Journal of Economics*, 1966, pp. 568–83,

shows that in this model a fall in the interest rate always goes along with a rise in the real wage.

28 G. C. Harcourt, "Some Cambridge Controversies in the Theory of Capital," *Journal of Economic Literature*, 1969, pp. 364–405, presents a review which is sympathetic to the Cambridge, England, position; Mark Blaug, *The Cambridge Revolution* (London, 1974) is critical of that position.

29 See Samuelson, "Summing Up."

30 A good exposition of these points is William J. Baumol, *Economic Theory and Operations Analysis*, 4th edn (Englewood Cliffs, NJ, 1977), chapter 26.

# 14
# William Stanley Jevons and the Marginal Revolution

Two of the problems connected with the marginal revolution of about 1870 is, in the first place, whether it can be regarded of an example of a "paradigm change," and, secondly, whether the marginal utility theory can be regarded as a multiple discovery in the same sense as the independent, nearly simultaneous discovery of calculus by Leibnitz and by Newton. Thomas Kuhn in his book *The Structure of Scientific Revolutions*[1] used the term paradigm to mean the choice of problems and the techniques for analyzing them,[2] and suggested that the progress of science was a history of abrupt, discontinuous changes from one paradigm to another. However, as discussed in chapter 12, the judicious view is that during the years 1870–1900 the major concern of economic theory became comparative static pricing and allocation problems, the concern with economic growth and classical macroeconomics fading away in an evolutionary rather than revolutionary change. In this process, Jevons, Walras, and Menger had predecessors, as we have seen, but these three remain the major early figures in the shift of research interests. At the same time, the differences among the three heroes are sufficiently great that there is some difficulty in citing them as an example of sociologist Robert Merton's proposition that multiple discoveries in science are to be expected rather than to be surprised at in an institutionalized science.[3] Walras emphasized the general equilibrium, Jevons concentrated on the relation of utility to value in exchange rather than the determination of the value in exchange in inter-related markets, while Menger focused on the structure of wants in relation to people's evaluation of goods, not in relation to market values.[4] They did have in common an emphasis on marginal utility.

The first of the trio to publish on marginal utility was William Stanley Jevons (1835–82), although Menger's ideas became influential before Jevons was recognized. While he was attending University College in London as a science student the family business went bankrupt, so Jevons took a job at the age of nineteen as assayer of the mint in Sydney, Australia. During his time in Australia he followed an ambitious program of study and research in meteorology, urban problems, and economics (in which he had originally become interested as a result of concern about London's poor). His *Papers and Correspondence*[5] gives an extremely interesting picture of his intellectual development. He read Smith's *Wealth of Nations* (which he called "the best work though rather old" and "perhaps one of the driest texts"), and Archbishop Richard Whateley's *Introductory Lectures on Political Economy*. From the latter and from an Australian professor, John Wooley, whose lectures he attended, he derived the proposition that competition produced the greatest happiness and maximized wealth, and that man should be conceptualized as calculating how to maximize pleasure and minimize pain. He sharpened his ideas in a series of letters to newspapers about a burning issue in Australia at the time: should railway construction be subsidized? Those in favor of subsidies cited external economies and benefits to society which could not be recouped in charges for railway services. These benefits included a stimulus to production, a rise in land prices, and economic development. Jevons took the side of those opposed, arguing that prices reflected all benefits and that unimpeded competition provided maximum happiness and wealth. In this argument he followed the lead of Professor Pell, a professor of mathematics and a wealthy man who was on many Australian governmental commissions and part of the power structure.[6]

When he returned to England in 1859 Jevons completed his college work, then became first a tutor and later a professor of logic and mental and moral philosophy and of political economy at Manchester. (Clearly a man of multiple talents!) This wide-ranging appointment was reflected in his publications; while he was writing on a wide range of economic subjects he also published important works on logic and scientific method. In 1882 he drowned while swimming, cutting short at forty-seven a very productive career.

One of the fields of economics in which Jevons worked to great effect was economic statistics. Keynes was very impressed with Jevons's talents here, remarking that "Jevons was the first theoretical economist to survey his material with the prying eyes and fertile, controlled imagination of the natural scientist."[7] One of his important early papers was published in 1863 – "A Serious Fall in the Value of Gold Ascertained, and Its Social Effects Set Forth" (it was later reprinted in a collection of Jevons's papers, *Investigations in Currency and Finance*). Here Jevons attempted to determine the effects on the general price level of the then recent gold discoveries in California and Australia. There was a dispute between John Elliot Cairnes (sometimes called the last of the classical economists) and William Newmarch as to whether the new gold had caused an inflation, the former claiming on quantity theory grounds that it had whereas Newmarch claimed that real incomes rather than prices had risen. Jevons's contribution was to compile price statistics into index numbers, solving, as Keynes said, the problem of price index numbers practically from the beginning. His conclusion was that indeed there had been an inflation, of at least 9 percent, but the exact number he calculated was perhaps less important than the pioneering methodology. To quote Keynes once more, "For unceasing fertility and originality of mind ... this pamphlet stands unrivalled in the history of our subject."[8]

But although now recognized as a major piece of work, at the time it aroused little interest. Jevons decided that he needed to do something to make himself known, so his next piece of statistical work was deliberately designed to be shocking. He wrote a study of *The Coal Question*, in which he projected a geometric rate of increase of the demand for coal for industrial purposes, showed this bumping up against the ceiling of coal reserves, predicted a shift of industrial might to the United States, and discussed various policies with the conclusion that Britain had to make the momentous choice between brief greatness and longer-continued mediocrity. Keynes thought the book did not survive cool criticism and that it reflected Jevons's instinct for hoarding (he thought paper would become scarce and bought such a supply that his children were still using it fifty years after his death), which was the psychological basis for the book. With recent experience of an energy crisis we may think more of his book, although his model – essentially the Malthusian model, with industrial use of coal taking the place of population growth and with coal supply taking the place of food supply – is definitely an antique compared to the energy models of today.

Jevons's final foray into economic statistics was his famous (or infamous) theory that business cycles were caused by a regular recurrence of sunspot activity. A burst of sunspots every eleven years or so was reflected in poor harvests – after some hesitation Jevons decided that the harvests in India were the most affected – which through a kind of multiplier process produced cyclical downturns in production, employment, and incomes. The theory did not generate widespread adherence.

But it was Jevons's theoretical work which makes him a marginal revolutionist. During his return to college at the end of his Australian experience he worked out a theory which, as he said in a letter written in 1860, "I have no doubt is *the true Theory of Economy*, so thorough-going and consistent, that I cannot now read other books on the subject without indignation."[9] This indignation remained for the next two decades; in the preface to the 1879 edition of *The Theory of Political Economy* he referred to his belief that "it will be seen that that able but wrong-headed man, David Ricardo, shunted the car of economic science on to a wrong line – a line, however, on which it was further urged towards confusion by his equally able and wrong-headed admirer, John Stuart Mill."

Jevons first presented his theory in a paper called "Notice of a General Mathematical Theory of Political Economy," which was read at a meeting of the British Association for the Advancement of Science in 1862 and was published four years later. This paper was completely ignored, and Jevons turned his attention to the coal and monetary studies already described. He returned to his work on theory after Professor Fleeming Jenkin of Edinburgh published his paper on "The Graphic Representation of the

Laws of Supply and Demand" in 1870 (see chapter 12 on the precursors of the marginal revolution for a description of Jenkin's work). In order not to lose his priority as a mathematical theorist Jevons quickly wrote *The Theory of Political Economy*, which appeared in 1871.

The theory of which Jevons had such high hopes begins with Bentham's calculus of pleasure and pain, described in chapter 12 above. Economics, says Jevons, must be founded on the theory of utility. Utility itself is the aggregate of the feeling of pleasure created and pain prevented by consuming a commodity. Jevons carefully distinguished between the total utilities from consuming a good, denoted by $u$, and the increment of utility, $du$, contributed by an additional amount of the good, $dx$. (Here $d$ stands for "a small change in"). He believed several things to be true about utility; that it depends only on the amount of the particular good which is consumed, independently of the amount of other goods consumed; that utility of different people cannot be compared; that utility can, in principle, be measured; and that as more $x$ is consumed, less $du$ is contributed by an additional $dx$. The fraction $du/dx$ thus diminishes as $x$ increases; this is the law of decreasing marginal utility, as it is now called. Jevons, however, did not speak of marginal utility; he called $du/dx$ the degree of utility, and referred to the degree of utility of the last increment of $x$ consumed as "the final degree of utility." Diagrammatically, Jevons's picture of consumer psychology is shown in figure 14.1 (which corresponds to figure 4, chapter 3, of *The Theory of Political Economy*).

Jevons used his utility theory to handle several problems in economics. For example, if a good has several uses, how much of the good do you employ in each use? Answer: enough to make the final degree of utility equal in each use. (This is Gossen's Second law, rediscovered by Jevons.) He also sorted out Adam Smith's confusion between value in use and value in exchange (the diamond–water paradox, that water which is useful has such a low exchange value, while the converse is true for diamonds). Value in use is really total utility, while the urgency of the desire for more is the final degree of utility; and value in exchange is the ratio of exchange of one good for another, which is equal to the ratio of final degrees of utility.

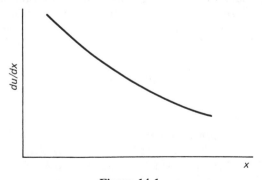

**Figure 14.1**

Water has a high total utility but a low marginal utility and hence a low exchange value. However, the basic application of Jevons's theory is to the analysis of trading. The case taken by Jevons is two people[10] bartering from a fixed supply of goods. They trade because the marginal utility of the goods received exceeds the marginal utility of the goods given up; as they trade, the marginal utility of the former falls and that of the latter rises until they become equal, and then trading stops.

The analysis of this trading situation, assuming price-taking behavior, is the following: if the goods traded are $x$ and $y$, the marginal utility of trading a small amount $dx$ is $(du/dx)dx$, and the same is true for $y$ – i.e., the marginal utility of a small amount traded is $(du/dy)dy$. In equilibrium these are equal:

$$(du/dx)dx = (du/dy)dy.$$

This can be converted into:

$$\frac{(du/dx)}{(du/dy)} = \frac{dy}{dx}.$$

Because of the law of one price (called by Jevons "the law of indifference") the barter of the small amounts $dx$ and $dy$ is on the same terms as the total amount traded in the market:

$$dy/dx = y/x.$$

And since the equilibrium condition is true for both people in the market, by the use of small letters for the first person and capital letters for the second person we can state the equilibrium condition.

$$\frac{(du/dx)}{(du/dy)} = \frac{y}{x} = \frac{(dU/dX)}{(dU/dY)}.$$

Thus there are two equations to determine the two unknowns, the amounts of $x$ and $y$ traded. This is, as intermediate microeconomics texts demonstrate, equivalent to determining the price ratio, since $y/x = p_x/p_y$.

Jevons concludes that his utility theory has destroyed the labor theory of value, insisting that labor once spent has no influence on the future value of any article: "In commerce bygones are forever bygones." Labor's influence, he claimed, was indirect, as expressed in what is called a catena:

Cost of production determines supply;
Supply determines final degree of utility;
Final degree of utility determines value.

Marshall, in his review of Jevons's book (actually the first of Marshall's writings to be published), says that Jevons is confused, that the amount of the wages and the exchange value of the products are varying elements, each affecting the other. Later he put it more memorably: it takes both

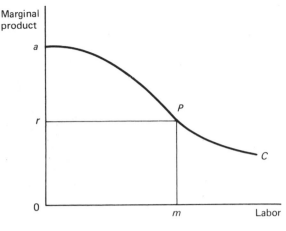

**Figure 14.2**

blades of the scissors (supply and demand) to do the cutting, and Jevons had only looked at one blade. He had not even done that completely, since he did not derive a demand curve from his utility curve. And he certainly did not investigate the theory of the firm at all, even though a book which he had studied in Australia (Lardner's *Railway Economy*) had cost and revenue functions in it.[11]

The last part of Jevons's *Theory of Political Economy* includes chapters on the theory of rent, the theory of labor, and the theory of capital. Each of them has something interesting; none of them is anywhere near a complete treatment. In the rent chapter he gives the classical theory of rent, and for the first time in the literature gives the diagram showing the rent triangle (see figure 14.2).

If the curve *apc* is the marginal product of labor (in classical economics, of a dose of capital and labor in fixed proportions), the marginal product of *m* units of labor is *mp*. This in turn is the payment to a unit of labor. The total earned by all labor is the rectangle *Orpm*, which is the wage times the quantity of labor. The total product is the area under the curve *Oapm*. The difference between the total product and total wages is the amount of rent, *arp*.

He made more than a geometrical contribution in the labor chapter; Professor Blaug calls it Jevons's most important contribution to the main stream of neo-classical economics. That is the theory that the supply of labor depends on a comparison between the marginal utility of the return to labor and the marginal disutility of the effort expended. As long as the marginal utility of the reward exceeds (in absolute value) the marginal disutility of the effort, the worker will continue to supply labor; equilibrium is where they are equal.

The graphical version of the theory is shown in figure 14.3. Here the upper curve is the marginal utility of the product; the lower is the marginal

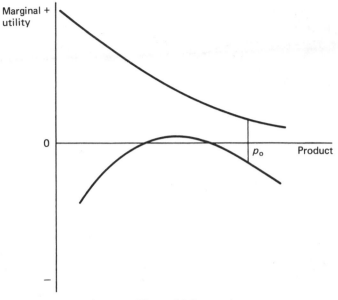

**Figure 14.3**

disutility of the labor needed to produce the output, and the equilibrium supply of labor is whatever is needed to produce $P_o$. This was used by Marshall in his *Principles of Economics* as the simplest illustration of equilibrium between desire and effort in the form of a parable of a boy picking blackberries for his own eating (Book V, chapter II), as well as, and more importantly, the basis for his theory of labor supply (Book IV, chapter I).

Jevons abstracted very severely in his capital theory. He defined capital as only commodities needed to sustain labor: food and clothing. Capital enables labor to be expended in advance of the time of output, and the more capital you have the longer the time that may elapse between beginning to work on the output and the time it is finished. This concept was very similar to the Austrian theory of capital associated with Böhm-Bawerk. (Jevons did not, however, deal with what Böhm-Bawerk called the systematic undervaluation of future wants and the means which serve to satisfy them – i.e., with time preference. He focused on the production aspect of roundabout methods.) With this theory of capital, Jevons developed a theory of the rate of interest: interest is the rate of increase of produce divided by the whole produce.

In all of these sections Jevons makes use of marginal concepts but does not give complete theories and has been said to supplement rather than supplant classical ideas.[12] Although one of the marginal revolutionists, in the field of marginal productivity theories of distribution he was more a fore-runner. Professor Black argues that the reason Jevons treated distribution the way he did was the result of his fundamental notion that economics was a calculus of pleasure and pain. The pleasure and pain show up clearly in the labor chapter; the rent chapter shows how a surplus over the compensation for pain (i.e., labor disutility) emerges, and the chapter on capital shows how capital increases total utility.

Jevons's book was not received with open arms by the reviewers. As has been mentioned, Marshall was critical of it (Marshall later reminisced how the angry phrases kept creeping in to the draft of his review and how he had to cut them out) because he did not really believe that Jevons had upset Ricardo's and Mill's theory of value. John Elliot Cairnes did not believe the theory was any good because utility could not be measured, and he had no sympathy with the use of mathematics. Only the American scientist and economist Simon Newcomb praised it. In general it took twenty years or so before the theory became widely accepted, but when it did, it became the new orthodoxy. "To a man like Edgeworth, steeped as he was in the Utilitarian tradition, individual utility – nay social utility – was as real as his morning jam."[13]

## Notes

1  Chicago, Ill., 1970.
2  See M. Blaug, "Kuhn vs. Lakatos, or Paradigms vs. Research Programmes in the History of Economics," *History of Political Economy* (*HOPE*), 1975, p. 402.
3  Robert Merton, "Singletons and Multiples in Scientific Discovery: A Chapter in the Sociology of Science," *Proceedings of the American Philosophical Society*, 1961, pp. 470–86.
4  The major source for discussion of topics such as multiples and paradigms in connection with the marginal revolution is R. D. C. Black, A. W. Coats, and C. D. Goodwin, (eds), *The Marginal Revolution, Interpretation and Evaluation* (Durham, NC, 1973). William Jaffé, "Menger, Jevons and Walras De-homogenized," *Economic Inquiry*, 1976, pp. 511–24, goes into detail on the differences among the three men.
5  Edited by R. D. C. Black (London, various dates).
6  For a detailed study of this period of Jevons's life see Michael V. White, "Jevons in Australia: a Reassassment," *The Economic Record*, 1982, pp. 32–45.
7  John Maynard Keynes, *Essays in Biography* (London, 1933). Keynes's essay on Jevons should not be missed.
8  Ibid., p. 271.
9  The letter is reproduced in part on p. 13 of the edition of *The Theory of Political Economy* edited by R. D. C. Black (New York, 1970).
10  Jevons discussed the theory in terms of two "trading bodies" which might be people, or countries, or industries considered as a whole. Edgeworth pointed out in *Mathematical Psychics* (1881) that this would be a case of bilateral monopoly with an indeterminate price. The traders have to behave as perfect competitors (i.e., as price takers) to have a determinate equilibrium. Also note

the difficulties in arguing that a trading body bigger than one person has a utility function; how do you aggregate the functions of the members of the body?

11  It is interesting that Jevons's chapter on labor has much more of a general equilibrium approach in its section "Relation of the Theories of Labour and Exchange." But although he said he hoped in the future to explain his theory in more detail, he never did, and the catena, rather than the few pages in the labor chapter, seems to reflect what Jevons thought his contribution was.

12  George J. Stigler, *Production and Distribution Theories* (New York, 1941), chapter II, summarizes Jevons's ideas on distribution and explains how many of the changes Jevons says he makes from classical positions are "typical Jevonian half-truths."

13  Paul A. Samuelson, *Foundations of Economic Analysis* (Cambridge, Mass., 1947), p. 206. A summary of the contemporary criticisms of Jevons is given by Jacob Viner, "The Utility Concept in Value Theory and its Critics," *Journal of Political Economy*, 1925, pp. 369–87, 638–59.

# 15
# Léon Walras

Léon Walras[1] is today famous as the father of the general equilibrium system, although as recently as 1941 it was stated authoritatively that he was best known as one of the discoverers of marginal utility theory.[2] This change in reputation is a result of the tremendous amount of work done on general equilibrium models in economic theory since the 1930s, when such writers as Wald, Hicks, and Samuelson began the current stream of theorizing.[3]

Walras's father, Auguste, was an administrator in the educational system in France, but he always had a keen interest in economics (he had, in fact, been a classmate of Cournot's). He wrote on economics but had unpopular views – that value depended on utility rather than on the cost of production, that land should be nationalized, and that taxes should be reformed so that landowners bore the burden of taxation (what was later called the single tax) – which together with opposition to the church kept him out of any university teaching job. Léon Walras, attempting to synthesize his father's reform ideas and his own theory of general equilibrium, later pushed the same causes, and was similarly kept out of teaching in France. Eventually, though, he got a post at the University of Lausanne, in Switzerland, in 1870.

But before that happened he had a life of struggle. He was sent to Paris to the School of Mines, his mathematics being too skimpy for admission to the École Polytechnique (the engineering institute). This fact is not only ironic for one who spent many years working out a mathematical economic theory but also shows why he had so much trouble with his theory and why his translator called his mathematics "primitive." He was bored at the School of Mines, preferring to lead the Bohemian life of artistic and literary Paris. His own efforts at literature were undistinguished, but important in that they showed how ingrained was economic thinking. The hero of one of his stories had this experience: "After falling dumbly in love at the age of eighteen, he came to Paris and took up with a mistress. But then he left her, *decently* to be sure, on becoming more alarmed about the future than dissatisfied with the present, when one day he cooly weighed the pleasure his mistress afforded against the loss of time and money she occasioned, and discovered there was a net deficit."[4]

Deciding eventually that his career lay in economics rather than in literature, he worked variously in journalism, as a white-collar worker for the railroad, and in banking, while writing and lecturing in economics. At this stage he was interested in social reform, economic justice, an ideal tax system, and the like, rather than the pure theory which later made him famous. An example of the sort of thing he was interested in is the proposition he put to an International Tax Conference in 1860: the single tax on land rent conforms to the principles of justice, but is tantamount to confiscation of land and therefore contravenes the rights of landowners; hence the problem of the single tax is insoluble.[5] But his ideas were not welcome to the French professors, who formed what has been called a "closed semi-official self-recruiting academy, stimulated by a measure of political dogmatism."[6] The academy vigorously rejected mathematical economics and embraced *laissez-faire* policies. The result was that what we now consider the best economics in nineteenth-century France was ignored by the academy and done by people outside it: Cournot, Dupuit, and Walras. But if the orthodox French economists were not impressed by Walras, an influential Swiss lawyer was, and the latter helped Walras to get his professorship at the University of Lausanne.

At Lausanne Walras intensified his work in economic theory which resulted eventually in his book *Eléments d'Économie Politique Pure* (1874). The book went through four editions before the definitive edition of 1926 (translated into English by William Jaffé, 1954), but the number of editions is not a signal of a roaring success. Walras sold only a few more than 500 copies of the first edition and actually financed most of the publication himself.[7]

Because the book is rather difficult, the strategy in this chapter will be to go through a very simple Walrasian model, not reproducing Walras's own complicated notation.[8] The central vision is that of the economy as composed of inter-connected markets, where events in each market influence what goes on in other ones. This is very evident at times of great and sudden changes, such as the modern-day oil embargo of 1973–4, but it is true all the time. The price of a product depends on the prices of its substitutes and complements, as well as on the income of its purchasers, their tastes, the technology, and the available resources. In turn, the income of the purchasers depends on the resources they own and on the price of the things made with those resources. So everything depends on everything else. Walras provided a precise specification of how things depend on each other.

In the simple model of this chapter, we will take a certain number of consumers who also own the resources of the economy – say, $n$ consumers. There are two goods, $X_1$ and $X_2$, and two types of productive services, $Y_1$ and $Y_2$. Capital letters will stand for totals in the economy, and small letters for quantities purchased or supplied by individuals. For simplicity in presentation assume that each person has a fixed supply of productive services, which he sells to the entrepreneur no matter what the price. What the economy does is to determine how much $X_1$ and $X_2$ will be produced, what the price $p_1$ and $p_2$ of the goods will be, and how much each person will earn by selling his productive services at the factor prices $w_1$ and $w_2$. There are therefore six unknowns in this economy.

There are some things given for the economy, in addition to the given resources. For one thing, it is assumed that people behave as though all markets were competitive. Secondly, the consumer tastes are given. Walrus, as one of the famous marginal utility trio, assumed that each person has a marginal utility function (he called it a *rareté* function) for each good. Thirdly, we assume that each person's spending equals the earnings from his given $y_1$ and $y_2$ – there is no saving or borrowing. So for each person the "budget equation" holds:

$$p_1x_1 + p_2x_2 = w_1y_1 + w_2y_2.$$

Finally, the technology is known. For this chapter we assume a very simple fixed proportions technology, so that a constant amount of input per unit output is always used no matter what the factor prices are. We express this technology by means of the four coefficients:

$$a_{11} = y_1/x_1 \qquad a_{12} = y_2/x_1$$
$$a_{21} = y_1/x_2 \qquad a_{22} = y_2/x_2$$

Now to determine the six unknowns mathematically we need to set up a system of equations. Walras was guided in setting up his system by a text in mechanics, Louis Poinsot's *Eléments de Statique*. "Walras kept the 1842 edition of Poinsot's book constantly by him throughout his life. When I managed to locate a copy of this edition, I discovered in it an almost perfect analogue of Walras's equilibrium system and, what is more remarkable, the derivation of Walras's naive method of solution which consists in simply equating the number of independent equations with the number of unknowns."[9]

The first task in setting up the system is to find the demands for products. Walras, unlike Cournot, did not take demand as an empirical fact; instead he built it up from the underlying utility functions. This is what originally linked Walras with the marginal utility revolution of the 1870s. Walras had inherited some basic notions about utility from his father who was, Sir John Hicks has said, "one of those excellent people (they seem to have existed since very near the dawn of history) who taught the true but unhelpful doctrine that value depends on scarcity (rareté)."[10] But a professor of mechanics at Lausanne, Paul Piccard, showed Walras how to apply the calculus technique of maximization and thereby convert the idea of *rareté* into the much more precise tool of marginal utility.

To show how one may derive demand curves from marginal utility functions, consider the following simple example. We have the *rareté* functions for the two goods for one person, $r_1 = 5 - x_1$ and $r_2 = 15 - 2x_2$. As Jevons, unknown to Walras, had already showed, maximum satisfaction requires that $r_1/p_1 = r_2/p_2$. At this point Walras introduced the concept of the *numéraire*, an arbitrary standard commodity which is just like any other except that it is the standard in terms of which all other prices are expressed. In effect, he sets $p_1 = 1$, and then $p_2 = p_2/p_1 = p_2/1$. One effect is that the number of unknowns in the system is now five instead of six. Another is that this procedure makes very clear that what counts in this system, where money and inflations are unknown, is not the absolute price level but relative prices.[11]

Using the *numéraire* and the equation for maximization of utility we have

$$5 - x_1 = (15 - 2x_2)/p_2.$$

Solving for $x_1$,                 $x_1 = 5 - (15 - 2x_2)/p_2.$

This solution for $x_1$ is substituted in the budget equation. For concreteness, assume $y_1 = 10$ and $y_2 = 4$. The budget equation, with the substitution of the solution for $x_1$ and with $p_1 = 1$ is

$$5 - (15 - 2x_2)/p_2 + p_2 x_2 = 10w_1 + 4w_2.$$

Solve this for $x_2$, to derive

$$x_2 = [p_2(10w_1 + 4w_2 - 5) + 15]/(p_2{}^2 + 2).$$

This is, in fact, the demand function for $x_2$, showing the quantity demanded as a function of all the prices in the economy, including the prices of factors of production. Once the demand for $x_2$ is known, it is easy to find $x_1$ from the budget equation:

$$x_1 = 10w_1 + 4w_2 - p_2 x_2.$$

Finally the total market demands in the economy are found by summing the individual demands; these equations are so important that we shall number them.

$$X_1 = w_1 Y_1 + w_2 Y_2 - p_2 X_2$$
$$X_2 = f(p_2, w_1, w_2) \tag{15.1}$$

Turning from the demand to the production side of our tiny economy, Walras assumed that there would be full employment – if there is excess supply of factor services, the prices of the factors fall until all available factors are used. Using the definitions of the coefficients of production given earlier, the full employment condition may be expressed as:

$$a_{11}X_1 + a_{21}X_2 = Y_1$$
$$a_{12}X_1 + a_{22}X_2 = Y_2. \tag{15.2}$$

These equations say that the amount of the first factor used in producing the first good, plus the amount of the same factor used in producing the second good, equal the total available amount of the factor, and the same for the second factor. Observe how these equations tie the factor markets in with the product markets in the sense that the use of the factors depends on how much of each product is made. The two types of markets are also tied together because the prices of factors and of goods are related. In competitive markets the average and marginal cost of production equals the price, when the technology is the constant returns to scale type used in this example (otherwise price may equal marginal cost but exceed average cost in the short run when one factor is fixed, but the other is variable, for example). This equilibrium condition is expressed as:

$$a_{11}w_1 + a_{12}w_2 = 1 \ (= p_1)$$
$$a_{21}w_1 + a_{22}w_2 = p_2. \tag{15.3}$$

Equations 15.1, 15.2 and 15.3 total six in number, which is one more than the number of unknowns (two $X$'s, two $w$'s, and $p_2$). In general, systems with more equations than unknowns are overdetermined, but in fact in this system there are only five independent equations. One of them is redundant because it may be derived from the others and therefore gives no independent conditions.[12] Walras concluded that therefore he had solved the problem of how to formulate a general-equilibrium theory of the economy, in which he had demonstrated exactly how the price of every-thing depends on the price of everything else, and of course on the utility, technology, and factor supply conditions.

In fact, Walras was mistaken in believing that equality between the number of equations and the number of unknowns was all that he needed to solve his problem. It was not until the 1930s that Abraham Wald provided the first rigorous proof that the solutions to a properly formulated general equilibrium model exist. His papers are translated, and useful comments on the history of existence proofs are provided in Baumol and Goldfeld's *Precursors in Mathematical Economics*.[13] But nevertheless Walras's work was so basic that we may agree with Professor Stigler that here was "One of the few times in the history of post-Smithian economics that a fundamentally new idea has emerged."[14]

In his years of working on his general equilibrium model Walras contributed many ideas, some of which are still used. One of these is the theory of *tâtonnement* or groping, which he developed in an attempt to show how real markets find equilibrium prices which are the same as the equilibrium prices determined in his model. He argued that if any random set of prices is tried, there will be some products and factors for which demand is greater than supply, some for which it will be less. If prices rise when there is excess demand and fall if there is excess supply, the markets come closer to equilibrium. That is because for any one market the change in its own price has a larger effect than the simultaneous changes which are going on in other markets (a rise in the price of shoes affects the shoe market more than does a rise in the price of cloth). So the market gropes its way to equilibrium. The trouble with this theory is that if trading is actually done at the disequilibrium prices, then people's incomes change, hence their demands change, and the market result is not the same as the static solution to the general equilibrium equations. In the fourth edition he added the notion of *bons* or tickets: when a set of prices is tried, producers and purchasers issue tickets showing what they would buy and sell at those prices. If supplies do not equal demands, the tickets are not binding and another set of prices – higher if there is excess demand, lower if there is excess supply – is tried. Eventually the price where all excess demands are zero is discovered. This theory is certainly not realistic, as Walras himself said; it was not supposed to be a dynamic approach to market equilibrium, but an attempt at a formulation of a static equilibrium.[15] Some subsequent users of the model have both criticized and improved the idea of a *tâtonnement* process, and Don Patinkin thinks the theory is one of Walras's "most imaginative and valuable contributions to economic analysis."[16]

Walras is also regarded as having made significant contributions to the theory of capital and as being important in monetary theory. The complete statement of his capital theory had better be left to more specialized texts (e.g., Stigler's *Production and Distribution Theory*), but it should be noted that he clearly distinguished between stocks of capital goods and the flows of services from them, a basic distinction not made before him. Similarly, a complete statement of his monetary theory is rather involved,[17] but it is a theory of the transactions demand for money, with interest as the price of money and real balances yielding a marginal utility. In one respect, however, Walras's monetary theory is still alive: Patinkin identified and named "the invalid neoclassical dichotomy," which, in his view, was promulgated by such writers as Walras, Fisher, Pigou, and Cassel.[18] This led to much discussion – as a result of which neo-classical monetary theory was reformulated more tightly than it had been by the original writers – as well as to considerable debate as to whether in fact people had held the invalid dichotomy.

The idea of a dichotomy is that the relative prices of goods and factor services are determined in one set of markets in response to real forces such as utility functions, technology, and available resources. This is exemplified by our earlier review of a simple Walrasian general equilibrium model, where $p_1$, the *numéraire*, was set equal to 1. But actual economies have an absolute price level. The invalid dichotomy says that this price level is determined by means of an equation like $MV = PY$, used by Irving Fisher, or $M = kPY$, used by Marshall. If $Y$ (real income), $M$ (the money supply), and either $V$ (velocity of circulation) or $k$ (the proportion of income people demand as cash balances) are known, the price level $P$ is determined. If there is an increase in $M$, other things remaining the same, the price level $P$ is increased. What does this do to relative prices as determined in the Walrasian model? If the real market is completely separate from the money market, nothing. But according to modern writers such as Patinkin, it is necessary to include the real value of an asset (remembering that money is an asset) in the demand functions for goods. When the price level increases, the real value of cash goes down (the real value is defined as $M/P$). Then the demand for goods will be affected, and so will their relative prices. Absolute and relative prices are both affected simultaneously.[19]

Professor Samuelson believes another dichotomy is important: that between the literary views of the old timers and the attempts to capture in mathematics what was being said in words. He also points out that earlier writers should not be blamed for not formulating their theories in the excess demand and stability analysis made popular by Hicks's *Value and Capital*. He therefore tends to believe that the basic neo-classical tradition did not involve the invalid dichotomy.[20]

Walras has also been studied as a protagonist in the Cambridge–Cambridge controversy discussed in chapter 13. Those who object to the neo-classical theory of distribution, instead proposing that "institutional factors determine a historical division of income between residual and non-residual shareholders, with changes in that distribution depending on changes in the growth rate,"[21] often cite Walras as an originator of the type of theory they deplore. In fact, however, Walras did not aggregate capital goods into a single category and indeed was highly critical of Wicksteed for doing so. And while Walras did believe that a free capital market yielded the greatest satisfaction, as a theorem, he did not therefore follow a *laissez-faire* attitude. In fact, as seen earlier, he favored land nationalization and the single tax. He would have preferred to have the distribution of income at least partly determined by political power.[22]

As Walras worked on his general equilibrium theory over the decades, he developed his ideas on marginal productivity and its relation to factor prices. In the presentation of the simple six-equation Walrasian model earlier in the chapter, constant coefficients of production were used, partly for simplicity and partly because Walras himself used them in Lesson 20 of his *Eléments*. With constant coefficients there is no marginal product, as one factor cannot be varied by itself. The manufacture of one unit of $X_1$ requires $a_{11}$ units of $Y_1$ and $a_{12}$ units of $Y_2$; additional units of $Y_1$, holding $Y_2$ constant, do not give additional output. In the first three editions of his book Walras said that the production coefficients could be variable, but he did not include variable coefficients in his formal theory before 1896. However, he asked one of his colleagues at Lausanne, Herman Amstein, how to find the minimum cost of production when the coefficients are variable and linked together with a production function. Amstein solved the problem as a constrained maximization problem, using a Lagrange multiplier (a technique still used in the more rigorous microeconomics courses). But Walras apparently did not understand it then and only incorporated it in his book in 1900. But he did insist that Wicksteed was wrong in 1894 when the latter claimed that his book was the first to state the marginal productivity theory of factor prices; in fact, he "flew into a rage." Although Walras claimed that some of his passages on Ricardian rent were identical to Wicksteed and that therefore he (Walras) actually had the theory first, Stigler points out that Walras did not analyze the production function, nor hint that $\partial Q/\partial K = P_k$ (i.e., the additional product contributed by another unit of capital is equal to the price of a unit of capital's services). Although first with the general equilibrium theory, Walras's claim to be also the first with the marginal productivity theory is unfounded.[23]

## Notes

1  The name often gives students trouble. It is a French corruption of a Dutch name, Walravens; the W is pronounced as V and the final s is sounded. Details on the history of the Walravens–Walras family are to be found in a posthumous article by the great authority on Walras, William Jaffé, "The Antecedents and Early Life of Léon Walras," *History of Political Economy* (*HOPE*), 1984, pp. 1–57.

2  George Stigler, *Production and Distribution Theories* (New York, 1941), p. 228.

3  An excellent summary is Kenneth Arrow, "Economic Equilibrium," in *International Encyclopedia of the Social Sciences*, vol. 4 (New York, 1968).

4  William Jaffé, "Biography and Economic Analysis," *Western Economic Journal*, 1965, p. 232.

5  See William Jaffé, "Léon Walras, An Economic Advisor Manqué," *Economic Journal*, 1975, p. 811. This article and T. W. Hutchison's chapter on Walras in *A Review of Economic Doctrines, 1870–1929* (Oxford, 1953), are good sources on what Walras called his applied and social economics.

6  Hutchison, ibid., p. 198.

7  An interesting account of Walras's struggles to get his book published, distributed, and reviewed is William Jaffé, "The Birth of Léon Walras's *Eléments*", *HOPE*, 1977, pp. 198–214. For the scholar the three volumes of *The Correspondence of Léon Walras and Related Papers*, edited by Jaffé (Amsterdam, 1965) give a detailed account of Walras's efforts to convince economists all over Europe and America of the importance of his theories.

8  This presentation of the general equilibrium model follows George Stigler, *The Theory of Price*, rev. edn (New York, 1952), pp. 290–5.

9  Jaffé, "Biography and Economic Analysis," p. 229.

10  "Léon Walras," *Econometrica*, 1934, reprinted in H. W. Spiegel (ed.), *The Development of Economic Thought*, (New York, 1952), p. 531.

11  Professor Jaffé points out that Walras got the idea of the *numéraire* as well as the framework of a general equilibrium economic model from a little known book called *Traité des Richesses* by A. N. Isnard, published in 1781. Isnard was another of the French engineers who wrote on economics. The book is mostly about what is wrong with the Physiocratic doctrine but does contain a general equilibrium model which was a starting point for Walras. See W. Jaffé, "A. N. Isnard, Progenitor of the Walrasian General Equilibrium Model," *HOPE*, 1969, pp. 19–43, and R. D. Theocharis, *Early Developments in Mathematical Economics* (London, 1961), for details.

12  To prove this, multiply the first equation in 15.1 by $X_1$, the second equation by $X_2$, and add these two expanded equations together. Now multiply the first equation in 15.2 by $w_1$, the second equation by $w_2$, and add these two

expanded equations together. Observe that the left-hand sides of the equations derived from the operations on 15.1 and on 15.2 are equal, so that their right-hand sides are equal. Then observe that these equal right-hand sides are the budget equation, which in turn is the first equation in 15.1.

13 W. J. Baumol and S. M. Goldfeld (eds), *Precursors in Mathematical Economics: An Anthology* (London, 1968).

14 Stigler, *Production and Distribution Theories*, p. 242.

15 See William Jaffé, "Another Look at Léon Walras's Theory of Tâtonnement," *HOPE*, 1981, pp. 313–36.

16 Patinkin, *Money, Interest and Prices*, 2nd edn (New York, 1965), p. 531.

17 See Patinkin, ibid., supplementary note C.

18 Ibid., p. 183.

19 If the theory that relative prices are determined in goods markets and the absolute price level in the money market is an invalid dichotomy, the student may well ask what is a valid dichotomy. Patinkin (ibid., p. 181ff) suggests that one valid dichotomy is to study things like shifts in taste and technology in the goods market and shifts in liquidity preference in the money market. Gary Becker and William J. Baumol provide another one: if impact effects are ignored and only equilibrium positions are compared, an economy in which the money supply has doubled will have all prices doubled and the real value of the money stock unchanged when the final equilibrium is achieved (there will be twice as much money, each unit of which is only worth half as much). In this case it is correct to say that $P$ is determined only in the money market and does not affect the goods market. See their article, "The Classical Monetary Theory: the Outcome of the Discussion," *Economica*, 1952, pp. 355–76.

20 See his papers "What Classical and Neoclassical Monetary Theory Really was," and "Samuelson on the Neoclassical Dichotomy: A Reply," *Canadian Journal of Economics*, 1968, pp. 1–15, and 1972, pp. 283–92, respectively.

21 Alfred S. Eichner and J. A. Kregel, "An Essay on Post-Keynesian Theory: a New Paradigm in Economics," *Journal of Economic Literature*, 1975, p. 1305.

22 See D. Collard, "Léon Walras and the Cambridge Caricature," *Economic Journal*, 1973, pp. 465–76.

23 See Stigler, *Production and Distribution Theories*, pp. 368–70. For an explanation of the final version of Walras's marginal productivity theory see pp. 550ff of *Eléments* (London, 1954), in which Jaffé clears up ambiguities and shows how to use the Lagrangean multiplier in proving that cost of production is minimized when marginal productivities are proportional to factor prices (essentially the same first-order condition which is necessary to maximize utility). For details on the Walras–Wicksteed quarrel, see W. Jaffé, "New Light on an Old Quarrel," *Cahiers Vilfredo Pareto*, 1964, pp. 61–102.

# 16
# Alfred Marshall

Alfred Marshall (1842–1924) was the dominant figure in British and American economics from roughly 1890 until 1925. His father, a cashier in the Bank of England, was himself a dominating figure, with a severe control of his family's life and an Evangelical approach to religion.[1] The young Marshall was slated to go to Oxford and prepare for the Anglican ministry, which would have required him to study classical languages and literature. Instead he preferred to go to Cambridge and study mathematics; he was one of the top honors students in his class and became a teacher of mathematics at Cambridge. Thus he was much better trained in mathematics than either Walras or Jevons, but unlike them he did not think that mathematics was the key to progress in economics. In fact, he came to economics from a conviction that knowledge of it was essential to be able to cope with the social problems of the poor which worried him all his life, and the kind of economics he thought useful was very detailed studies of historical and contemporary factual and institutional affairs.

His first venture into economics, after friends kept refuting his proposals to cure poverty by telling him that he would not say such things if he knew economics, was to study John Stuart Mill's *Principles* and to "translate it into mathematics" (this was in 1867). He then turned to Ricardo, von Thünen, and Cournot, and completed by 1870 most of the mathematical theory which is in the appendix to his *Principles of Economics*. He devoted the decade of the 1870s to historical and empirical studies, including such writers as Richard Jones (who tried to refute Ricardian rent doctrines in the 1830s on the basis of studies of rent in many different societies) and Roscher, a member of the German Historical School. But he was also a firm believer in on-the-spot visits, not only to British industrial firms but even to America in 1875, to see for himself how the policy of the protective tariff had worked out. During this decade he switched his teaching from mathematics to economics (still covered as part of the Moral Sciences at Cambridge at this time; it did not become a separate subject until 1903). One of his pupils was Mary Paley, one of the first women allowed to study at Cambridge; and when he married her in 1877 he was forced to resign his fellowship under the rules prevailing at the time. He taught for five years at Bristol (with a year off in Italy to improve his health), a year at Oxford, and then returned to Cambridge as professor until 1908.

Marshall was not one to rush into print with his ideas. Left to himself, he would probably have published relatively little until he had completed volume I of his *Principles* in 1890.[2] But Mary Paley Marshall had started a little book on *The Economics of Industry* for extension classes in 1879, to which he decided to contribute a great deal – although he later regretted the premature statement of his views and had the book withdrawn. And Henry Sidgwick had privately printed and circulated some of Marshall's theoretical work (*The Pure Theory of Foreign Trade and the Pure Theory of Domestic Values*) in order to protect Marshall's right of priority. This issue of right of priority has been a topic that has exercized historians of economic thought since Marshall's day. In connection with the origin of the theory of marginal utility, for example, Professor Howey, after a detailed review of the evidence, concludes that "Marshall never published any statement of his belief in his own originality, although he felt no qualms in hinting at it in print, and in correspondence he did go so far as to state it baldly."[3] But the independent evidence for Marshall's claim is not strong, and Professor Howey concludes that "No writer ought to presume to claim priority in the origin of ideas simply on the basis of what he recalls that he thought at a much earlier period." But although priority in the use of marginal utility may be in question, there is an astounding amount of other material in Marshall's *Principles*.

He began the *Principles* in 1879 and it was published in 1890, eventually going through eight editions (the last one in 1920). During the time of its composition he put a great deal of effort into testimony before the Gold and Silver Commission, and in the 1890s he was associated with the Royal Commission on Labour. Eventually, toward the end of his life, he published two other books, *Industry and Trade* and *Money Credit and Commerce*, both of them based on work done many years before.[4]

Marshall's biography is quite pertinent for a study of his economics, as it explains many of the characteristics of his writing. His early mathematical training, his Victorian moral upbringing, and his belief in the importance of realistic studies are all obvious in the *Principles of Economics*. Reading that book is indeed a shock to students reared on the current type of microeconomics textbook. People now do not believe that statements such as "The most valuable of all capital is that invested in human beings; and of that capital the most precious part is the result of the care and influence of the mother, so long as she retains her tender and unselfish instincts, and has not been hardened by the strain and stress of unfeminine work"[5] have any business in an economics book, but the *Principles* are full of them.[6] And his empirical studies are called on constantly. The theoretical parts are drastically downplayed. Marshall wished his book to be understood and read by businessmen, so he presented his ideas verbally in the text, with diagrams in the footnotes, and by brief mathematical treatment in the appendix. But the restrained use of mathematics not only came from a desire to have the book widely read; it was also the result of a methodological point of view. The following statement from a letter of Marshall's is often quoted:

> But I know I had a growing feeling in the later years of my work at the subject that a good mathematical theorem dealing with economic hypotheses was very unlikely to be good economics; and I went more and more on the rules – (1) Use mathematics as a shorthand language, rather than as an engine of inquiry. (2) Keep to them till you have done. (3) Translate into English. (4) Then illustrate by examples that are important in real life. (5) Burn the mathematics. (6) If you can't succeed in 4, burn 3. This last I did often.[7]

Marshall's avoidance of mathematics and his desire for wide readership resulted in writing which made hard things look easy, as Harry Johnson claimed that Keynes (who was Marshall's student) also did in the *General Theory*: "There is also the non-rigorous Cambridge style of theorizing, the didactic Marshallian style, in which awkward complications are hidden in plain view and common sense is allowed to run away with the argument ..."[8]

A final characteristic of his book is that unlike Jevons and Walras he did not consider himself a revolutionary, but rather a developer of classical doctrine. For example, in commenting on Ricardo's alleged neglect of demand, he says (no doubt with Jevons in mind) that there is growing belief that "harm was done by Ricardo's habit of laying disproportionate stress on the side of cost of production ... although he and his chief followers were aware that the conditions of demand played as important a part as those of supply in determining value, yet they did not express their meaning with sufficient clearness ..." (*Principles*, p. 84). This sort of comment led to Marshall's acquiring a reputation as a compromiser, which made him angry: "Such work seems to me trumpery. Truth is the only thing worth having, not peace."[9]

A result of the Marshallian didactic style was that much subsequent work was devoted to controversy about what he really meant. As late as 1949 an extended controversy broke out about the proper interpretation of the Marshallian demand curve, stimulated by an article in the *Journal of Political Economy* by Milton Friedman. Friedman pointed out that because Marshall gave no complete definition, often letting the context explain his meaning, the reader had to infer the contents of *ceteris paribus* (that is, what things are to be held constant while prices vary). Prior to Friedman's article the standard interpretation (actually stemming from Edgeworth) was that tastes, money income, and the prices of other goods were to be kept constant while the price of the good in question varied; the quantity of other goods purchased would also vary (unless the demand curve had unit elasticity) because the amount of money available to purchase those goods would change when total spending on the good in question varied. But in this interpretation real income varied with changes in the price of the good under consideration. Friedman argued that Marshall really meant to hold real income constant, which would require compensating changes in money income or in the prices of some other (not closely related) goods. Friedman developed the implications of his interpretation and backed them up by many citations from the *Principles*, incidentally illustrating the dangers of the Marshallian didactic style. A lively controversy developed, much of it reprinted in 1972 in *The Evolution of Modern Demand Theory*.[10] However, one of the best articles refuting Friedman was not included in that collection, and the student is referred to it to see how an alternative interpretation can be justified by quotation from the *Principles*.[11] There is no consensus as to what Marshall really meant; the student is left on his own.

Since the *Principles* is a huge book, covering many topics, it is necessary to be selective and try to comment on only the most important matters. Even so, because of the influence of Marshall's work on subsequent economists, there is a lot of ground to cover.

As already noted, Marshall was early in the marginal utility field (even if not the first). He based his theory of consumer's demand on a marginal utility function in which the marginal utility of good $x$ depends only on the amount of $x$ consumed and not also on the amount of $y$ because the latter sort of function "seems less adapted to express the every-day facts of economic life" (*Principles*, p. 845). This is called an additive utility function since the total utility of a consumer is the sum of the utilities derived from each separate good or service. And, in terms of later development, it was a cardinal utility function, in which utility is measurable. Naturally, the marginal utility was held to be diminishing. Writing the total utility function as $U_x = f(x)$, $dU/dx$ decreases as more $x$ is consumed.

Another important aspect of Marshall's theory of utility is his proposition that the marginal utility of money (actually, of income rather than of the stock of money held as an asset) is constant.[12] Denote the utility of money as $\mu$ and money as $m$; then the marginal utility of money is $d\mu/dm$. When the consumer is buying the equilibrium quantity of $x$, the marginal utility per dollar spent on a unit of $x$ is equal to the marginal utility of money. If the former is greater than the latter he should buy more $x$, and if less, he is buying too much $x$. The equilibrium condition is thus $(dU/dx)/p_x = d\mu/dm$. Now suppose the price of $x$ falls, and hold the marginal utility of money constant. Obviously to keep the equilibrium condition the marginal utility of $x$ has to fall, which means the consumer must buy more $x$. Voilà! We have deduced that the demand curve has a negative slope.[13] Actually, if the marginal utility of money were literally constant and the utility functions were additive, the price elasticities of demand would be unity and so would the income elasticity. But Marshall, with his preference for realism over rigor, would say that he meant an approximate constancy of the marginal utility of income, and proceed to discuss elasticities either greater or less than one.[14] (Marshall, by the way, was the originator of the elasticity concept, a feat which led Schumpeter to remark that "the cases must be rare in which so modest a contribution has met with such applause."[15] This was in reaction to Keynes's contention that in the provision of concepts Marshall did no greater service than in his elasticity definition. Of course differences in the responsiveness of quantity demanded to price had long been noted;[16] Schumpeter's judgment that the concept was modest perhaps comes from the mathematical simplicity of the definition $-(dx/x)/(dp/p)$ rather than from the extensive use people make of it.)

As already noted, Professor Milton Friedman and others have raised questions about exactly what Marshall was doing with his demand curve. It is clearly a partial equilibrium concept, in which one consumer or one industry at a time is studied. The *Principles*, indeed, is a partial equilibrium book, although Note XXI in the Mathematical Appendix discusses general equilibrium when there is joint demand and composite supply, and Marshall once said that his career had been the working out of the implications of that note. The partial equilibrium demand curve is also a *ceteris paribus* concept, in which other things are held constant while the price is allowed to vary. Exactly which other things are held constant is disputed, as already noted; Marshall clearly said that custom, the supply price of rival commodities, and the number of commodities in existence must be held constant (*Principles*, p. 100), but was ambiguous on how to treat real incomes and the prices of goods other than close substitutes or complements.

Although Marshall had derived, as we saw, "the one universal rule" of demand, that the demand curve declines negatively throughout the whole of its length, this turns out to be "universal" only because it is true when the marginal utility of money is constant, and there are very few practical cases where that is not approximately true in his judgment. But he did notice and make famous one exceptional case: the Giffen paradox. As he explained it,

> For instance, as Sir R. Giffen has pointed out, a rise in the price of bread makes so large a drain on the resources of the poorer labouring families and raises so much the marginal utility of money to them, that they are forced to curtail their consumption of meat and the more expensive farinaceous foods: and bread being still the cheapest food which they can get and will take, they consume more, and not less of it. (*Principles*, p. 132)

This, besides being a beautiful example of Marshallian prose, seems untrue both as to factual content and authorship; at least, Professor Stigler could not find any place where Sir Robert made such a statement, and no one else has definitely pinpointed a source.[17] But revised into modern theory as the case where the income effect of a price change for an inferior good outweighs the substitution effect, the Giffen paradox lives on in microeconomics textbooks.

Turning to the supply blade of the scissors, Marshall began by defining the "real cost" of a commodity: it is the exertions of the labor and the sacrifice involved in the abstinence (or the waiting, a term which Marshall preferred) necessary for capital formation. Thus the real cost is a subjective psychological cost, a matter of disutility, either because labor is painful or because waiting involves a sacrifice of current consumption, and this disutility has to be paid for or else the supply of the factor of production is not forthcoming.[18] These real costs are of course not the concern of the employing firm; it is interested in the money costs. Marshall warns that the correspondence between the two is not to be assumed lightly; the real costs, which are what counts when measuring the social costs of production, are not always accurately measured by money costs. (*Principles*, p. 350). But he went ahead and assumed that the correspondence was there.

Of course, not only is the firm interested in money costs, it is interested in the least money cost for a given output. It achieves this by following "the principle of substitution," a principle whose applications "extend over almost every field of economic inquiry" (*Principles*, p. 341). Marshall gave many illustrations of substitution at the margin, where the marginal cost of hiring a resource is equal to the value of its marginal product. This is the formulation of Mathematical Note XIV; the literary formulation is the much simpler statement that the entrepreneur substitutes cheaper for more expensive resources, measuring the cheapness by product divided by money cost.

Although many pages are devoted to increasing and decreasing returns, complete with examples of both the hypothetical and the historical variety, as a major factor influencing the costs of production, here was one of the fuzzy parts of theory left for others to clean up. One area of confusion was that diminishing returns sometimes was framed as diminishing marginal returns to successive doses of capital and/or labor applied to fixed land, and sometimes as a fall in the average product (also referred to as proportional diminishing returns). Francis Y. Edgeworth systematically and patiently sorted out the difference, pointing out that average returns can be rising while marginal returns are falling, in 1911.[19]

Secondly, Marshall was not clear about the distinction between returns to scale, when all factors are increased simultaneously, and the marginal returns to one factor when it alone is increased, holding others constant. "The law of or statement of tendency to Diminishing Return" (*Principles*, p. 150) is treated in a very classical way, as applying to the historical situation in agriculture where land is the constant factor. On the other hand, increasing returns to scale are the province of industrial organization. Here Marshall made a fundamental distinction which was very important in the subsequent discussion of his theories. This was the famous division of the economies of scale into cases of internal and external economies.

Marshall was led into the idea of external economies because his model was that "the forces of demand and supply have free play; . . . there is no close combination among dealers on either side, but each acts for himself,

and there is much free competition" (*Principles*, p. 341).[20] But if there are
economies of scale the firm that first gets started can achieve a monopoly
simply by expanding output and having lower costs than the newcomers.
Cournot had long before pointed out that the marginal cost of manufactured articles is generally decreasing as output expands because of
better organization of the work, discounts on the price of raw materials
when purchased in large volume and the reduction of "general expense" (a
term he does not define but presumably it is some sort of overhead cost).[21]
Marshall developed this idea by dividing the causes of decreasing costs into
two categories, internal economies which lead to the monopoly power of
large firms and external economies in which lower costs from expanded
production are compatible with competition. Internal economies are the
sort mentioned by Cournot, the organization and efficiency of the individual houses of business. External economies, by contrast, are those
dependent on the general development of the industry, in which the
average cost curve of each firm is lowered as industry output expands, so
that no one firm gets the advantage of the others (*Principles*, p. 266). Such
developments as a larger pool of skilled labor, growth of knowledge and
invention which is shared by all firms, and the rise of subsidiary firms
producing equipment or using by-products, are suggestions made by
Marshall. Although externalities and one particular subset of them, public
goods, are one of the growth industries of economics today, the important
refinement and development of Marshall's ideas which is covered by all
microeconomics texts was contributed by Jacob Viner in 1931.[22] In this
article, which developed the geometry of short-run and long-run cost
curves and their relationship to supply curves, Viner made the important
distinction between "pecuniary" and "technological" economies and dis-
economies. Discounts for volume purchasing is an example of the first;
improved organization an example of the latter. The price theorist who
judged Marshall's analysis of external and internal economies "ambiguous" also allowed that they seemed to have considerable serviceability as
a tool in the explanation of economic history.[23] This affinity of Marshall's
ideas to the real world is exemplified in the literature on economic
development, where it is claimed that "internal technological and external
pecuniary economies have real importance."[24]

But Marshall did not rely exclusively on external economies as an
explanation of how a firm's costs could fall without it becoming the
monopolist of the industry. He also invented the concept of the "representative firm." He argued that one could not get an accurate idea of the
normal cost of producing a commodity if one sampled the cost of a
struggling newcomer, or of an inordinately successful, extraordinarily large
firm, but rather the appropriate one to study was a firm managed with
normal ability, with normal access to economies of scale (*Principles*,
p. 317). The picture is that individual firms in an industry go through a life
cycle, from young to representative size to maturity to eventual decay, and
that the falling costs they experience in youth are cancelled out by rising

costs in old age so that no one can achieve a permanent control over the industry. In equilibrium the industry price is at a level where the representative firm will earn normal profits. If demand increases, the supply price will change as internal and external economies affect the representative firm – it can become bigger in a growing industry without becoming monopolistic.

Marshall's representative firm was one of his theoretical constructs which did not survive. For one thing, theorists of the next generation found it too vague, imprecise, and unsubstantial. "It lurks in the obscurer corners of Book V like some pale visitant from the world of the unborn waiting in vain for the comforts of complete tangibility."[25] And for another thing, the development of the theory of imperfect competition by Joan Robinson and of monopolistic competition by E. H. Chamberlin in the early 1930s offered other solutions to one of the problems which Marshall used the representative firm to solve: "the fact that the relations between the individual producer and his special market differ in important respects from those between the whole body of producers and the general market" (*Principles*, p. 459) and "when we are considering an individual producer, we must couple his supply curve – not with the general demand curve for his commodity in a wide market, but – with the particular demand curve of his own special market. And this particular demand curve will generally be very steep" (*Principles*, p. 458, n. 1).[26] The fate of the concept of the representative firm is tied up intimately with Professor Samuelson's judgment that "no one can understand the history of the subject if he does not realize that much of the work from 1920 to 1933 was merely the negative task of getting Marshall out of the way."[27] Now with the perspective of a little more time there is an interesting reversal, with the feeling that this negative task was carried too far.[28]

But one concept of Marshall's has stood the test of time, and that is the division of the analysis of pricing problems into different time periods depending on which things are being held constant. Marshall provided the three familiar periods: the market or temporary equilibrium period, in which the stocks actually in the market are sold at whatever price equates demand with the supply on hand; the short period, in which the "stock of appliances for production" is taken as fixed; and the long period, in which people adjust the flow of the appliances for production (i.e., fixed capital) to the expected demand (*Principles* p. 374). The version found in contemporary microeconomics texts corresponds to Marshall's stationary state, in which "income earned by every appliance of production [is] truly anticipated beforehand" (p. 810), but Marshall gave his attention rather to the world in which we live, as he put it, and was greatly concerned with the dynamics of changing expectations and uncertainty in the long run. His creed was that "economic problems are imperfectly presented when they are treated as problems of statical equilibrium, and not of organic growth" (p. 461).[29]

Another of Marshall's concepts which the student of microeconomics often meets today is that of stable as opposed to unstable equilibrium in the market, and here the question is how Marshall's approach differed from that of Walras. Figure 16.1 illustrates the difference. We assume that the supply curve S slopes downward to the right as the result of external economies. At output $x_1$ Marshall argued that the demand price along the demand curve D was higher than the supply price; entrepreneurs therefore made a profit, more firms were attracted to the industry, and output expanded in the direction of equilibrium E. E is therefore a stable equilibrium: if the industry is at E and a random movement reduces the output, the industry moves back toward E. To Walras, by contrast, E is unstable: at price $P_1$ more of $x$ is demanded than will be sold. Therefore the price rises as unsatisfied demanders scramble for the scarce supply. A random rise of price above that at equilibrium E will lead to higher prices and the market moves away from E. Thus the analyses associated with our eminent neo-classical authors lead to contrary conclusions in this case.[30]

Marshall's use of continuous curves, as in figure 16.1, and his use of calculus in his Mathematical Notes, are not just a matter of convenience, it should be noted. It was his conviction that, as the motto of his book put it, "Natura non facit saltum": nature does not make leaps. This idea appears not only in his mathematics but also in his history of economic thought – there was no revolutionary change away from the classical economists, only a development of their ideas and a change of emphasis. It further appears in his statement that there is no sharp division between normal and abnormal economic conduct nor between market and long-run normal prices (*Principles*, p. vii). Marshall adopted the Latin motto from Charles Darwin, who held that evolution and natural selection operated by slight variations rather than by radical discontinuities.[31]

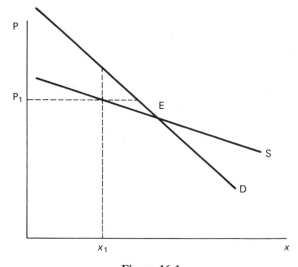

**Figure 16.1**

Although as we saw in chapter 12 Dupuit and Fleeming Jenkin had developed the concept of consumer surplus, Marshall made it popular and used it as a tool of welfare analysis.[32] Defined as the excess of the price which a consumer would be willing to pay rather than do without the good over the price actually paid (*Principles*, p. 124), consumers' surplus is illustrated in figure 16.2 as the area $P_0EB$. Producers' surplus is the excess of the price received over the supply price, and is the area $P_0EA$. Marshall pointed out that the surplus for individual consumers could be aggregated (and consumer's surplus replaced by consumers' surplus) if the same sum of money represented the same amount of pleasure for different people, although as a matter of fact the marginal utility of money is higher for poor people than for rich. But since most events in economics "affect in about equal proportions all the different classes of society" (*Principles*, p. 131), this consideration can be neglected in practice. One can also neglect the fact that the demand curve is not actually known except around the customary price, but that range is indeed the range in which the applications of consumers' surplus are made. So Marshall swept away the difficulties, including the additional one that his measure is valid only if the marginal utility of money is constant.

Marshall used consumers' surplus in the first place to show that consumers benefited from their environment, from being able to buy cheaply things for which they would pay a higher price. Secondly, he used it in the analysis of *laissez-faire*, the proposition that a stable equilibrium of demand and supply is generally a position of maximum satisfaction (*Principles*, pp. 470ff). Looking at figure 16.2, it is easy to see that if output is less than $x_0$, moving in the direction of equilibrium increases both

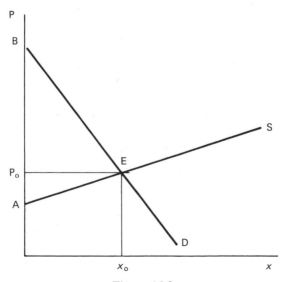

**Figure 16.2**

consumers' and producers' surplus, and hence the total satisfaction in the community.[33] This demonstration of the optimum qualities of competitive markets is subject to two reservations: it holds for the existing distribution of income, and it may be possible by judicious juggling of taxes and bounties to increase the total amount of surplus. Suppose, for example, that we have an increasing returns situation in a given industry, as in figure 16.3. If a subsidy of CB is offered per unit of output, the equilibrium shifts from E to B. Consumers' surplus increases by the area FEAB, while the cost of the subsidy is the area DACB. Consumers have a net gain of FEDC. Ideally, the tax would be raised by taxing decreasing returns industries, in which, as the supply price falls when output is reduced, the loss in consumers' surplus can be less than the tax proceeds. (Marshall's tax and bounty analysis is in chapter XIII of Book V.)

This superficially neat analysis has not survived. With the change away from cardinal utility to ordinal utility and indifference maps, with their emphasis on income effects as well as substitution effects, it turns out that there are four measures rather than just one of the gain or loss to a consumer from a change in price.[34] Indeed, so thoroughly has consumers' surplus been expunged from modern theoretical welfare economics that a recent authoritative text does not even mention it.[35] But empirical workers in the field of cost–benefit analysis have found it a useful tool, and have continued to use the area under the demand curve with suitable apologies. The error involved in using this measure as compared to one of the four measures established from indifference curves has been shown to be small in most cases, and in any case the limits within which the error lies can be calculated from income and income elasticity data. So today the empiricist has been given the green light to use "Consumers' Surplus without Apology."[36]

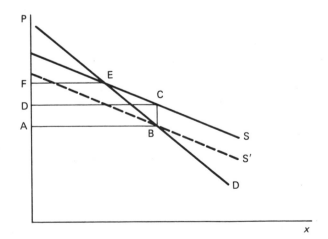

**Figure 16.3**

The last of the major topics covered in the *Principles* is the distribution of the national product. As a first approximation Marshall used fixed coefficients of production, exactly as we did in chapter 15 on Walras. For example, if a knife is being manufactured, it requires one handle and one blade. Since the employer cannot find the marginal product of an input by hiring a little more of it, keeping other inputs the same, in the fixed proportions case, another approach is needed. Marshall used the concept of "derived demand" in discussing factor pricing in this case: the demand for an input is derived from the demand for the final product. Total the supply prices of the other inputs, subtract that total from the demand price for the final product, and the difference is the amount that will be paid for the input under consideration. This is however only for simplified exposition; it is not the general case. In general, substitution among inputs is possible, and indeed it is the job of the businessman to substitute until the cheapest technique is found. In this case the employer hires additional inputs as long as the net product of an additional worker, machine, or piece of land is greater than its cost so that in equilibrium "the wages of every class of labour tend to equal to the net product due to the additional labour of the marginal labourer of that class." Marshall claimed that this was not a theory of wages, but only a useful part of one; however, his claim is not accepted by commentators.[37] One aspect of Marshall's objection to calling the analysis of marginal productivity a theory of wages was that one also has to consider the supply of the factor. Another, perhaps more major one, was that in line with his interest in the doctrines of classical economics Marshall wanted to analyze aggregate totals in the economy: wages as a whole, the total share of rent in the economy, and so on. But marginal productivity theory of the partial equilibrium kind is no good here, because the value of the marginal product depends on the demand curve for the product being produced. The product demand curve changes when wages and hence incomes change. All the general equilibrium equations, including the marginal productivity ones as a subset, are needed when looking at the economy as a whole. The proposition that wages $= (dx/dL)p_x$ is a microeconomic partial equilibrium theorem, applicable to the industry but not to the economy.

Marshall's long analyses of aggregate wages and rent and of capital theory will not be reviewed here; they are very much tied to the long period and to historical developments. But one of his contributions was indeed a new concept: that the idea of rent can be applied to fixed investments. Since the capital goods in existence are in fixed supply in the short run, the return to them resembles the rent of land. In both cases the return is a surplus in the sense that the factor of production would be in existence whether the rent was paid or not. But in the long run for capital goods, the return in one industry must equal that generally attainable in the economy or the investment will not be replaced. The difference in the long-run behavior of capital goods as compared to land is the reason why the return to land is called rent but the return to capital is "quasi-rent."

This is one Marshallian concept which should be familiar; it is discussed in nearly all current microeconomics and principles of economics texts.

One of Marshall's early interests, and a subject in which he became famous, was the theory of money. But he did not write about it in the *Principles*, and his ideas were the subject of an "oral tradition" for many years. In fact, the major printed source for them was testimony before various Royal Commissions in the 1880s before he finally published *Money Credit and Commerce* in 1923, a work containing the ideas he had worked out fifty years previously. This was the monetary theory which Keynes learned and later taught at Cambridge, and from which the composition of *The General Theory* was a "long struggle of escape".[38]

There are two main aspects of the Cambridge monetary theory: the cash-balances equation and the credit cycle. The cash-balances theory is a theory of the demand for money; it is based on the idea that people hold money as a convenient form of general purchasing power. Having cash on hand smooths commercial life and personal consumption purchasing, but at the expense of foregoing an investment or at the expense of the foregone marginal utility of a consumer good. The demander of money weighs the advantages against the disadvantages and decides what fraction of his income[39] he wishes to hold as cash. The Cambridge equation is $M = kPy$, where

$M$ = money
$k$ = the desired ratio of cash to income
$y$ = real income (Pigou's resources)
$P$ = the price index indicating the level of prices.

When the supply of money is given – arbitrarily fixed by the government, or a function of the price level if the country is on the gold standard – the price level $P$ is determined by the equation of money supply with its demand. The major theoretical problem is what determines the size of the ratio $k$. It was not considered constant from year to year – there was nothing mechanical about applying the equation – but rather it varied with things like "the expected fruitfulness of industrial activity" and expectations about which direction future price changes would take. This theory, with embellishments to take account of different values of $k$ for holdings of cash and of bank deposits and of banks' holdings of cash as reserves against deposits, was developed by such notable British monetary theorists as Hawtrey, Pigou, Robertson, and J. M. Keynes in his writings up to *A Tract on Monetary Reform* (1923). After that Keynes began going his own way.[40]

The other important aspect of Marshall's monetary thought is the relation between real and money rates of interest, and the way divergences between them generate a business cycle. Starting from equilibrium, where the supply and demand for capital and the real and money rates are all equal, suppose there is an influx of money (e.g., gold, under the gold standard). Then the money rate of interest falls below the real return on capital. Speculative investors borrow money and buy goods, raising the price of goods and starting the upturn of a credit cycle. Eventually prices rise so much that some of the borrowed funds cannot be repaid, credit becomes shaky, the money rate of interest rises, borrowing is restricted and hence fewer goods are bought, so prices begin to fall.[41] As in the case of the Cambridge equation, the Marshallian theory of the credit cycle was further developed by his pupils. Knut Wicksell, a Swedish economist of approximately Marshall's vintage, also had a theory involving real and monetary rates of interest, much more carefully worked out than Marshall's, and very influential on Continental but not British economics. But Marshall's monetary theories were put into the shadows by the Keynesian revolution, at least until Milton Friedman led the University of Chicago into modern monetarism.

Marshall, with his great humanitarian interest in the problems of poverty and his general interest in real world problems, naturally had things to say about the policy problems of his day. On poverty, he thought that "financial socialism," defined as "a cautious movement towards enriching the poor at the expense of the rich" (or Reaganism in reverse), was a suitable policy, along with increased education. But socialism in the form of government ownership and control of industry would mean that management would become bureaucratic. The desirable leadership talents of modern businessmen (1890 businessmen, which were modern to Marshall) would vanish, as bureaucracies have little scope for initiative and forethought. Thus he concluded that under socialism real incomes would not rise as fast as they had done in Great Britain in the late nineteenth century.[42]

Unemployment, the great policy problem of the 1930s, was also a problem in the Great Depression of the 1880s. Marshall's policy here followed from his analysis of the credit cycle in his monetary theory: if the credit boom is moderated, the resulting downturn and unemployment will be less. Keeping a stable monetary system and a stable price level was the thing to do.

Another policy issue of the time was the tariff. Although England had repealed the Corn Laws and adopted free trade in the 1840s, by the 1890s sentiment for protection, with special preference for trade with the British empire, was building up. Britain's industrial joints were creaking and leadership was passing to Germany and the United States, much as it seems to be passing to Japan today. Tariff protection seemed the answer, as it does to such industries as steel today. But Marshall, who had made a study of the infant industry protectionism in the United States, thought that the tariff had been misapplied and that the secret of industrial growth was not protectionism. Indeed he thought that free trade would increase the alertness of British manufacturers.[43] He was also opposed to the tariff because Britain's demand for imports was relatively inelastic compared to the foreign demand for British goods, and therefore, according to John Stuart Mill's reciprocal demand curve analysis, the incidence of the tariff would be on British consumers, mainly the poor. As it turned out, the tariff with Imperial Preference (i.e., free imports from the British empire) was not adopted in Marshall's day, but under the pressures of the world depression it was adopted in 1932.

To conclude: Marshall was the commanding figure of his day and had a profound influence on the subsequent development of economics. Although from the standpoint of contemporary theory the *Principles* has many deficiencies, Professor Stigler reminds us that "A true appreciation is best secured by comparing the *Principles* with the standard works on political economy current in 1890. Marshall was almost incomparably superior to his immediate predecessors and his early contemporaries in the profundity and originality of his thought, in his consistency, and in the breadth of his vision."[44]

# Notes

1 The Evangelicals held the doctrines of man's sinful condition and need of salvation, of God's grace in Christ, and the necessity of spiritual renovation and redemption through faith. Marshall's was obviously a rather repressive religious background. His mother was the daughter of a butcher, but because this was an inferior social background his father's family concealed this as much as possible. See Ronald H. Coase, "Alfred Marshall's Mother and Father," *History of Political Economy*, (*HOPE*), 1984, pp. 519–28.

2 The checklist of Marshall's publications between 1872 and 1890 in J. K. Whitaker (ed.), *The Early Economic Writings of Alfred Marshall 1867–1890*, vol. 1 (New York, 1975) includes book reviews, articles, lectures, and prefaces. Perhaps seven or eight of them are substantial articles.

3 Richard S. Howey, *The Rise of the Marginal Utility School* (Lawrence, Kansas, 1960), p. 87. Cf. Whitaker, *Early Economic Writings*, pp. 37–52, for a careful analysis and skeptical conclusion on Marshall's claims to priority.

4 The two major sources of biography for Marshall are Keynes's essay "Alfred Marshall, 1842–1924", which appears in Keynes's *Essays in Biography* as well as in the very useful four-volume collection *Alfred Marshall: Critical Assessments*, John Cunningham Wood (ed.) (London, 1982), and the letters and reminiscences which are reprinted in A. C. Pigou (ed.), *Memorials of Alfred Marshall* (London, 1925). Mary Paley Marshall also wrote of their life together in a charming little book, *What I Remember* (Cambridge, 1947).

5 *Principles of Economics*, 8th edn (London, 1920), p. 564, hereafter cited in the text as *Principles*.

6 Theodore Levitt has rounded up and analyzed the moral strictures in "Alfred Marshall: Victorian Relevance for Modern Economics," *Quarterly Journal of Economics*, 1976, pp. 425–43. R. F. Harrod tells of a Rhodes scholar at Oxford who refused to read "all that drivel" when he was assigned Marshall. Harrod was horrified until he realized that the student was not quarreling with Marshall's economics but with his Victorian morality, and Harrod reports that he had to find other means for the student to acquire economic wisdom. See Harrod, *The Life of John Maynard Keynes* (London, 1951), p. 117.

7 *Memorials of Alfred Marshall* (London, 1925), p. 427.

8 Harry G. Johnson, *"The General Theory* after Twenty-Five Years," *American Economic Review*, 1961, p. 3. Lawrence E. Fouraker also compares Keynes to Marshall in "The Cambridge Didactic Style," *Journal of Political Economy*, 1958, pp. 65–73.

9 Quoted in T. W. Hutchison, *A Review of Economic Doctrines 1870–1929* (Oxford, 1953), p. 67.

10 R. B. Ekelund, E. G. Furubotn and W. P. Gramm (eds), *The Evolution of Modern Demand Theory* (Boston, 1972).

11 R. F. G. Alford, "Marshall's Demand Curve," *Economica*, 1956, pp. 23–48.

12 *Principles*, p. 95, where he says it is a fixed quantity if a person's material resources are unchanged. It is constant with respect to price changes but decreases as income rises. The mathematical implications of "Constancy of Marginal Utility of Income" are interesting; they have been worked out by P. A. Samuelson and reprinted in *The Collected Scientific Papers of Paul A. Samuelson* (Cambridge, Mass., 1966).

13 Marshall deviated from standard mathematical practice when he drew his demand curve. If the quantity purchased depends on price, $x = f(p_x)$, usually $x$ would be placed on the vertical axis and $p_x$ on the horizontal axis. That is the way Cournot drew the original demand curve. Marshall, however, reversed this procedure, as in the accompanying familiar diagram.

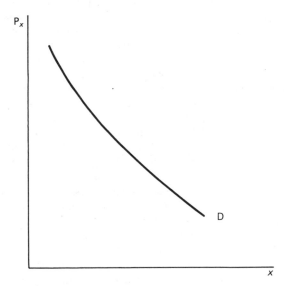

14 Hutchison suggests that those who wish to indulge a possibly pedantic taste for lucidity and precision in fundamental matters do not always find Marshall easy to follow. *Review of Economic Doctrines*, p. 73. N. Georgescu-Roegen, "Revisiting Marshall's Constancy of Marginal Utility of Money," *Southern Economic Journal*, 1968, pp. 176–81, is an example of a sympathetic interpreter; he submits that Marshall intended $d\mu/dm$ to be quasi-constant, not literally constant in every conceivable situation. In particular, if he was thinking of a

middle-class consumer making numerous purchases of conveniences it is appropriate to regard the marginal utility of income as constant, to a first approximation; but it is not appropriate to do so for low incomes, where marginal purchases are a high proportion of income, nor for high incomes if the marginal purchase typically is so large as not to be negligible.

15 J. Schumpeter, *History of Economic Analysis* (New York, 1954), p. 993.

16 For example, Cournot, *Mathematical Principles of the Theory of Wealth* (New York, 1897), pp. 46–7.

17 George J. Stigler, "Notes on the History of the Giffen Paradox," in his *Essays in the History of Economics* (Chicago, Ill., 1965).

18 In Marshall's day, and even later down into the 1930s when Professors Viner and Haberler were debating the theory of international trade, there was a vigorous debate between the real cost theorists and the devotees of the Austrian theory of opportunity cost. The Austrians – particularly Wieser and Böhm-Bawerk – contended that the cost of producing $x$ is the payment needed to attract resources from their next most gainful employment, commodity $y$. Since $y$'s value depends on its marginal utility, the Austrians argued that a real cost theory was not needed: all value depends on utility, including the value of resources. The outcome of the debate was that the opportunity or alternative cost theory, as formalized in the transformation curve between $x$ and $y$, is valid only for given amounts of the factors of production and only if the factors are indifferent among different uses – otherwise a premium over the value of the foregone opportunity would have to be paid. The final pronouncement was that "Inevitably, therefore, when the opportunity cost doctrine is carefully stated and qualified, it degenerates into the full conditions of general equilibrium in which factor supply and preference equations must be introduced if only as inequalities. This is not to imply that one must accept the dubious psychological language and interpretations of classical real cost theorists." Paul A. Samuelson, *Foundations of Economic Analysis* (Cambridge, Mass., 1947), p. 234. Jaroslav Vanek, "An Afterthought on the 'Real Cost-Opportunity Cost' Dispute and Some Aspects of General Equilibrium under Conditions of Variable Factor Supplies," *Review of Economic Studies*, 1959, pp. 198–208, shows a geometrical combination and reconciliation of real and opportunity cost theories.

19 See F. Y. Edgeworth, *Papers Relating to Political Economy* vol. 1, (London, 1925), pp. 61ff; he thought this analysis was necessary to introduce a series of articles called "Contributions to the Theory of Railway Rates."

20 Marshall, the keen student of economic life, knew that "though monopoly and free competition are ideally widely apart, yet in practice they shade into one another by imperceptible degrees; that there is an element of monopoly in nearly all competitive business: and that nearly all the monopolies, that are of any practical importance in the present age, hold much of their power by an uncertain tenure; so that they would lose it ere long, if they ignored the possibilities of competition, direct and indirect" (*Industry and Trade*, (London, 1923), p. 397). Marshall's understanding of what was later known as imperfect or monopolistic competition is surveyed by H. H. Liebhafsky, "A Curious Case of Neglect: Marshall's *Industry and Trade*," *Canadian Journal of Economics and Political Science*, 1955, pp. 339–53. The "free competition" of the *Principles* is a model, a tool of analysis, and not intended to describe every industry.

21 *Mathematical Principles*, p. 59.

22 Viner, "Cost Curves and Supply Curves," *Zeitschrift für Nationalokonomie*, 1931, pp. 23–46. This article, among other things, is the source of the famous Viner–Wong paradox. Professor Viner told his Chinese draftsman, Mr Wong, to draw the long-run average cost curve through the minimum points of the successive short-run average cost curves, and to draw the long-run curve so as never to be above any portion of any short-run curve for a given output. Mr Wong said he could not do both; Viner says that Wong "saw some mathematical objection to this procedure which I could not succeed in understanding. I could not persuade him to disregard his scruples as a craftsman and to follow my instructions, absurd though they might be" (Viner, *The Long View and the Short*, Glencoe, Ill., 1958, p. 66). Mr Wong was of course correct; at the minimum point of $SRAC_1$ there will be a cheaper way to produce in the long run by building a somewhat larger plant and operating it at a capacity less then the output needed for least short-run average cost of the larger plant.

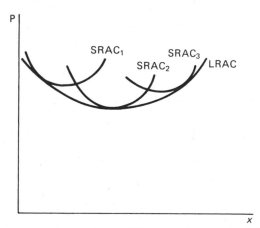

23 Stigler, *Production and Distribution Theories* (New York, 1941), p. 76.

24 C. P. Kindleberger and Bruce Herrick, *Economic Development*, 3rd edn (New York, 1977), p. 149.

25 Lionel Robbins, "The Representative Firm," *Economic Journal*, 1928, p. 387.

26 For a development of this theme, see Samuel Hollander, "The Representative Firm and Imperfect Competition," *Canadian Journal of Economics and Political Science*, 1961, pp. 236–41.

27 P. A. Samuelson, "The Monopolistic Competition Revolution," in R. E. Kuenne (ed.), *Monopolistic Competition Theory: Studies In Impact* (New York, 1967).

28 For example, an unpublished paper by Vivian C. Walsh, "The Rehabilitation of Alfred Marshall," and Lawrence A. Boland, "Difficulties with the Element of Time and the *Principles of Economics* or Some Lies My Teachers Told Me," *Eastern Economic Journal*, 1982, pp. 47–58.

29 One of Marshall's generalizations about the different periods has an interesting counterpart in modern science. He pointed out that the shorter the period being considered, the more influence demand has on value, and the longer the period,

the more influence the cost of production has. He said this was because the influence of changes in cost of production takes a longer time to become effective than does that of changes in demand (*Principles*, p. 349). Actually the longer the time period the more elastic the supply curve, because more factors of production can be varied; consequently, a given change in the demand curve will have more of an impact on price and less on quantity in the market period and the short run than it will in the long run. The generalization is the Le Chatelier Principle, which Professor Samuelson took over from thermodynamics and fitted to problems of maxima and minima in economics. One form of the Le Chatelier Principle is that the reactions of the equilibrium position of a variable to changes in a coefficient of one of the constraints in a problem is less, the more constraints are added. Thus in the market period, which has the most constraints, changes in the equilibrium quantity are less than in the long period for a given change in demand. See Samuelson, "The Le Chatelier Principle in Linear Programming," in *Collected Scientific Papers*, vol. 1, for the most accessible of his discussions of the Le Chatelier Principle.

30  Check to see that they also lead to contrary conclusions if the negatively sloping supply curve cuts the demand curve from above, but to the same conclusion if the supply curve has a positive slope. Marshall's diagram is on p. 806 of *Principles*. The association of Marshall with the assumption that firms adjust output when there is a gap between demand and supply price and of Walras with the assumption that firms raise price if there is an excess quantity demanded is too facile; as a matter of fact, Marshall sometimes used Walras's model and Walras sometimes used the Marshall model. For citations and discussion see David G. Davies, "A Note on Marshallian versus Walrasian Stability Conditions," *Canadian Journal of Economics and Political Science*, 1963, pp. 35–40.

31  See Laurence Moss, "Biological Theory and Technological Entrepreneurship in Marshall's Writings," *Eastern Economic Journal*, 1982, pp. 3–13.

32  Just a year before the first edition of the *Principles*, in 1889, two Austrians, Rudolph Auspitz (a sugar magnate) and Richard Lieben (a banker) published a book whose English title is *Investigations of the Theory of Prices (Untersuchungen über die Theorie des Preises)*. This book had many of the Marshallian concepts – partial equilibrium, consumers' surplus – as well as diagrammatic analysis using total and marginal curves, indifference curves, and monopoly analysis. Their work was appreciated by such competent theorists as Edgeworth, Pareto, and Irving Fisher, but had no great general influence. Hutchison, *A Review of Economic Doctrines*, pp. 188–91, covers Auspitz and Lieben briefly.

33  It was not only his theory that led Marshall to favor market decisions over collective economic decisions. Rita McWilliams-Tullberg documents the proposition that Marshall's rejection of socialism was not intellectual but emotional. His excessive fear of change meshed with his missionary zeal to improve the condition of the poor to bias him toward the position that the existing system would solve the problems of poverty with the very minimum of interference, according to McWilliams-Tullberg's article "Marshall's 'Tendency to Socialism'," *HOPE* 1975, pp. 75–111.

34  Mark Blaug, *Economic Theory in Retrospect*, 4th edn (Cambridge, 1985), chapter 9, surveys these measures, which were originally developed by Sir John Hicks, in detail.

35  James Quirk and Rubin Saposnik, *Introduction to General Equilibrium Theory and Welfare Economics* (New York, 1968).

36  This is the title of an article by Robert D. Willig, *American Economic Review*, 1976, pp. 589–97.

37  Such as Stigler, *Production and Distribution Theories*, chapter 12. A much more sympathetic interpretation is H. M. Robertson, "Alfred Marshall's Aims and Methods Illustrated from his Treatment of Distribution," *HOPE*, 1970, pp. 1–65, who says that the reader must follow the subtle nuances, and that while Marshall's statements about marginal productivity lack precision, they may not be quite so lacking in common sense. The latter point, it will be recalled, is one of Harry Johnson's objections to the Cambridge didactic style. In case the student wonders what is wrong with common sense, Professor Samuelson once explained that common sense says "Absence makes the heart grow fonder" and it also says "Out of sight, out of mind". You need something to enable you to decide which version of common sense is right.

38  J. M. Keynes, *The General Theory of Employment, Interest and Money* (London, 1936), p. viii.

39  In chapter IV of *Money Credit and Commerce* Marshall states that the demand for cash balances is a function of both income and wealth; Pigou, in what is regarded as an authoritative statement of Cambridge monetary theory, has the demand a function of "the total resources ... that are enjoyed by the community." See A. C. Pigou, "The Value of Money", *Quarterly Journal of Economics*, 1917, pp. 38–65.

40  The story is traced out in Eprime Eshag, *From Marshall to Keynes* (Oxford, 1963).

41  Marshall's writings on this subject are very scattered; they have been collected and analyzed by J. N. Wolfe, "Marshall and the Trade Cycle," *Oxford Economic Papers*, 1956, pp. 90–101.

42  See Donald Winch, *Economics and Policy: A Historical Study* (New York, 1969), chapter 2.

43  *Official Papers*, (London, 1926), p. 408. As T. W. Hutchison points out, this has remained a major British problem until the present day. See "Economists and Economic Policy in Britain after 1870," *HOPE*, 1969, pp. 231–55.

44  Stigler, *Production and Distribution Theories*, p. 61.

# 17
# American Economics: Benjamin Franklin to Irving Fisher

Since this book deals with the history of economics rather than with contemporary economics there have been very few American economists referred to so far. It is generally agreed that before the days of John Bates Clark and Irving Fisher at the end of the nineteenth century only John Rae really made much of a contribution to economics, and he was ignored by contemporary European economists. (However, John Stuart Mill was an exception; he made several flattering references to Rae.) Nevertheless, there was a large volume of writing on economic subjects by Americans.[1] We shall look at its general characteristics as well as the specific ideas of some of the better known writers.

Benjamin Franklin and Alexander Hamilton are the two eighteenth-century Americans whose economic writings appear today to be significant. Both, of course, were busy at other things and their attention to economics was incidental. Franklin's first pamphlet was *A Modest Inquiry into the Nature and Necessity of a Paper Currency* (1728). When the Commonwealth of Pennsylvania decided to follow his advice and print money, Franklin got the job of doing the printing. His argument was that too little money resulted in high interest rates, low prices, discouragement of trade and employment, and he claimed that if the bills were issued on the security of land they would maintain their value. This idea was to be found in Sir William Petty's writings in the previous century, and also was part of John Law's monetary notions. A more widely known book by Franklin was *Observations Concerning the Increase of Mankind and the Peopling of Countries* (1755). This book was the source of Malthus's data on the doubling of an unchecked population in twenty-five years. It also contained the proposition that one of the checks to population was late marriage, which Malthus adopted as one of his "moral restraints." After visiting France, where he met a number of Physiocrats, Franklin's writings began to reflect Physiocracy more than mercantilism, as they had previously done. He began praising agriculture as the "honest way" and the activity that is truly productive of new wealth, by contrast with manufacturing, which only changes forms.

Hamilton's contribution, which Schumpeter calls "applied economics at its best," is contained in papers which he wrote as Secretary of the Treasury under George Washington. These included a report on the public credit, on a national bank, and, most importantly for subsequent influence, the *Report on Manufactures* (1791). This advocated a protective tariff on infant industry grounds, and in making his case, Hamilton in fact anticipated to a large extent the economic development arguments put forward by Raúl Prebisch and the Economic Commission for Latin America (ECLA) in the 1950s. Hamilton argued that an agricultural producer such as the United States faced an unstable, "rather casual and occasional" foreign demand. It could not exchange on equal terms with Europe, the manufacturing country, which would drain the United States of its wealth. To escape this, the United States had to promote its own industry. It could not rely on *laissez-faire* to do this, because habit, slowness to make changes, fear of risk, and the natural disadvantage of trying to compete with established manufacturers would all keep the United States an agricultural country. Therefore government intervention in the form of protective or prohibitive tariffs as well as bounties on exports was urged. Also Hamilton pushed the development of the infrastructure – such things as roads and canals. The comprehensiveness of his report leads one recent student to say that "It seems that since Hamilton, the world's first modern statesman of 'economic development', not much has been learned about development policy."[2] This may be something of an exaggeration, but it is true that Hamilton's ideas were influential in American policy-making and on later writers. Among contemporary development experts, however, the strategy of export-led growth is now popular, because experience with protective programs shows that "Only with the most meticulous economic planning and in situations in which domestic competition is present can the import-substitution strategy lead to real economic development."[3] Hamilton would have approved of the large-scale import-substitution proposals in energy which emerged during the energy crisis of the 1970s (but which turned out not to be needed in the 1980s).

In the nineteenth century there was, naturally, a great increase in the volume of writing by Americans on economics. Professor Samuelson, in a convenient short essay on "American Economics,"[4] lists the characteristics of most of this work: optimistic, theological, protectionist, nationalistic, pro-business, and anti-theoretical. Henry C. Carey (1793–1879), one of the most famous economic writers of the period, illustrates several of these characteristics. His father, Mathew Carey, was an Irish immigrant who founded a successful Philadelphia publishing firm, and, beginning at age sixty, wrote voluminously in favor of a protective tariff to support the industrialists who were faced with foreign competition when the war of 1812 ended. A measure of his influence is the sales figure for one of his books, more than 10,000 copies, an enormous number for that time.[5] The son, Henry C. Carey, worked for the publishing firm from the age of eight until forty-two, and then began writing – his output totalled thirteen books and 6,000 pages of pamphlets and newspaper articles. Carey's optimism appears in his rejection of the Malthusian population arguments and in his doctrine of harmony. According to this idea, capital accumulation at a faster pace than population growth raises both profits and wages, while the landowners' rents are regarded as a return to capital so that there is no conflict between his interests and those of society at large. In fact, Carey claimed that the historical movement of agriculture is from inferior to superior land (the opposite of Ricardo) so that increasing returns are found in agriculture. A major part of his writing was devoted to pleas for protective tariffs; among other arguments, he claimed that the South could develop an industrial base and put an end to slavery with tariff protection. Although famous in his day, Carey's long-run impact was not significant; a recent biographical sketch concludes that "Carey had some academic adherents, especially in Philadelphia, but his influence on the later development of a more disciplined and specialized economic science was slight."[6]

Another exponent of nationalism and protectionism, perhaps less famous in his day in the United States but resurrected in recent economic development literature, was Friedrich List (1789–1846). List was a German whose advanced political views got him into trouble with the authorities. He went to Pennsylvania in the 1820s and was a success at coal mining and short-line railroading. His experience and observation led him to believe that industrially underdeveloped countries needed protective tariffs. He returned to Germany as an American consul and wrote his major work, *The National System of Political Economy* (1841), in which he claimed that the nation is the most important link between the individual and mankind and that it is necessary to protect the nation from destruction at the hands of free-traders during its underdeveloped stage. In discussing the growth of the nation List introduced two ideas found in economic development theory: balanced growth of the sectors of the economy, and the importance of social overhead capital. Although List was known in Germany for years as the greatest German economist, author of the German system of political economy, he really only exported "the American system."[7]

The "theological" character of earlier American economic thought was stressed by T. E. Cliffe Leslie, a British historical economist, in an essay on "Political Economy in the United States," written in 1880 and published in his book *Essays in Political Economy*. Theology, he said, was for many American textbook writers the backbone of economic science; exchange was designed by God for the welfare of man, and the Malthusian moral checks to population were contrary to the commandment to replenish the earth. Cliffe Leslie suggests that this religious element is partly explained by the fact that colleges were founded by religious groups, and political economy was typically taught by ministers of religion as part of the moral philosophy course. Examples of influential people of this sort include Francis Wayland (1796–1865), a Baptist minister who was president of Brown University from 1827 to 1855, and who wrote a text that sold 50,000 copies. He derived specialization and international trade from the will of the Creator in distributing resources. Francis Bowen (1811–90), who taught natural religion, moral philosophy, and civil polity at Harvard, was another believer that the principles of political economy manifest the wisdom of the Deity. John McVickar, who held the first chair of political economy in the United States, at Columbia University, was another clergyman.[8]

The untheoretical or anti-theoretical character of most of American economic writing was noted by Charles F. Dunbar, who celebrated the one-hundredth birthday of the United States by surveying "Economic Science in America, 1776–1876."[9] Dunbar concluded that "the United States have, thus far, done nothing toward developing the theory of political economy, notwithstanding their vast and immediate interest in its practical applications." One notable exception, broadening the geographical horizon to include Canada, was John Rae, mentioned earlier in this chapter. He studied medicine at Edinburgh, but did not finish his degree, and after his father's business failed he migrated to Canada. There he taught school, studied agricultural conditions and economic geography and geology, and wrote his book on economics, *Statement of Some New Principles on the Subject of Political Economy, Exposing the Fallacies of the System of Free Trade and of Some Other Doctrines Maintained in the "Wealth of Nations"*.[10] He wrote widely on scientific, literary, and philosophical matters as well, but he lost his job because of church politics. He headed for California to hunt for gold in 1850, and moved on to Hawaii the next year. There he stayed for twenty years, farming, serving as a medical agent for the board of health, and doing geology. Finally he retired to the house of a friend on Staten Island, New York, where he died in 1872. His breadth of interest was incredible, like Benjamin Franklin or Jevons, and his book on economics was just a small part of his life's work. Perhaps if it had been better received he would have been encouraged to do more, but it got poor reviews in the United States (where it was published) and was pretty much ignored in Europe. Nassau Senior accidentally ran across a copy of it, was impressed by it, and recommended it to John Stuart Mill, who, as we have mentioned, made favorable comments about it, but Rae was not following economics closely and did not know this until five years after Mill's *Principles* was published.

Rae's capital theory has long been regarded as the high point of his contribution, although Joseph Spengler has suggested that it is really a book about economic development which depends both on capital accumulation and on technological progress.[11] Rae pointed out that capital instruments involved a lapse of time between their formation and their yield of want–satisfying events. Capital goods can be ranked in terms of their yield; Rae did it by ranking them according to the number of years it took to achieve a yield equal to twice the cost of production (the shorter the number of years the more productive the capital instrument). A formula to calculate $x$, the number of years, where $r$ = the percentage rate of return, is $(1+r)^x = 2$. Increased durability of capital instruments typically increases both the rate of return and the cost; Rae argued there were decreasing returns to more durability, as well as a greater chance of technological obsolescence. On the side of the demand for capital, capital formation requires the sacrifice of present goods for the sake of a future return. People generally prefer the present goods but are willing to make the sacrifice for the sake of their family or country, or, in a healthy climate, a safe occupation and the prospects of a long life for their own sake. The greater the demand for capital, the lower would be the yield of the instrument at which capital accumulation stopped, when ranked as above. But not only is the amount of investment important in determining the yield of capital, so is the rate of invention. Invention increases the return and lowers the cost of capital, so that a given rate of capital formation is more productive and the development of the society is speeded up. This is the most important factor in long-run economic growth, and it requires that inventors be treated well, that arts and materials be numerous and diverse, and that people not be prone to be mere imitators of the past.

The role of government in fostering economic development is fairly obvious from this theory. It should foster the security of the people, not only by preventing crime, but also by providing such helpful institutions as banks and schools. It should help provide for inventions by means of tariffs (this is a version of Hamilton's infant-industry argument for tariffs, but Rae emphasized that the protected industry should be one in which invention would take place). And finally capital formation would be advanced by preventing luxury spending. In connection with this, he made statements which sound similar to the ideas Thorstein Veblen later promoted about conspicuous consumption being the motivation for spending on luxury goods. Scarcity and high prices often are the motive for people buying one particular good rather than another.

Although as we have seen Rae's ideas did not have very much influence in his own day, they were later important in Irving Fisher's work on capital and interest. His book *The Theory of Interest* (1930) was dedicated "To the Memory of John Rae and of Eugen von Böhm-Bawerk who laid the Foundations upon Which I have Endeavored to Build," and in his preface he states that every essential part of his own theory was at least foreshadowed by Rae. However, we shall see that Fisher's theory was a much improved version.[12]

While John Rae looked at economic growth and wrote a solid but neglected book about it, another nineteenth-century American looked at it and wrote an impassioned book about the injustices which he perceived resulted from growth. Henry George (1839–97) held a variety of jobs in California between the 1850s and 1880, and he was struck by the fact that the rapid growth of the state and its cities did not seem to make any difference in wages, but that land values increased spectacularly. His hypothesis was that increases in rent ate up all the increase in productivity, which he spelled out in detail in his book *Progress and Poverty* (1879). His solution was to nationalize land or to tax away all the increments in value (this proposal was known as the "single tax" because it was thought that the revenue from the land tax would be enough to support all government spending, making other taxes needless). The book was a great success, partly because of the fiery way in which George expressed his ideas. For example, he explains how one may become rich by buying land in a village just before it takes off into the growth which will make it a great city; you need do nothing but just hold onto the land.

> You may sit down and smoke your pipe; you may lie around like the lazzaroni of Naples or the leperos of Mexico; you may go up in a balloon, or down a hole in the ground; and without doing one stroke of work, without adding one iota to the wealth of the community, in ten years you will be rich. [13]

Henry George became popular with intellectuals (e.g., John Dewey, the philosopher; Leo Tolstoy; and George Bernard Shaw, who claimed that George converted him to socialism); with the public (he ran for mayor of New York City in 1886 and just barely lost); but not with professional economists. Spiegel quotes Francis A. Walker, an American economist who became president of the Massachusetts Institute of Technology, that George's work was "a precious piece of villany" and a project "so steeped in infamy."[14] Alfred Marshall criticized the book in three lectures he gave while teaching at University College in Bristol.[15] Marshall and George met in a debate at Oxford University on George's trip to Britain in 1884. This meeting, which Paul Samuelson picked as the historical moment in economics at which he would have liked to have been present,[16] was reported in the *Oxford Journal* under the heading "Mr. Henry George at Oxford, Disorderly Meeting". Among other comments, Marshall said that George had not in any single case understood the authors he criticized, that he had not proved that the way to remedy poverty was to divide up land, that there was no doctrine in George's book which was both new and true. The report makes hilarious reading and gives a picture of Marshall which does not come out in his writings.[17]

But the enthusiasm Henry George generated did not last on any wide scale. There is still a Henry George School of Social Science listed in the Manhattan telephone directory, and in 1981 a Henry George research program in business, economics, and taxation was established at Pace University's Lubin Schools of Business in New York, but no lasting influence on American economics comparable to John Rae or to the late nineteenth-century and early twentieth-century economists, John Bates Clark and Irving Fisher, may be attributed to George.

An American economist of the late nineteenth century who was much less famous at the time, and, indeed, is so even today, but who had a more substantial influence was a mathematician and astronomer, Simon Newcomb. Newcomb had heard Carey's work praised, but when he read it he was very disappointed. After a couple of decades of thinking about it he published his *Principles of Political Economy* in 1885, a book which has

won praise from Schumpeter, Keynes, and Irving Fisher, and of which it
has been said that one would have to go back to the seventeenth century to
find a distinguished natural scientist doing such a useful service to political
economy.[18] In particular, Newcomb made the distinction between stocks
and flows absolutely clear, showed the circular flow of income and the
counter-flow of goods and services which is now commonplace in principles
textbooks, and presented the equation of exchange ($MV=PT$) together
with a discussion of the psychological forces behind changes in velocity and
the distinction between what people would like to do and what actually
does occur. (This is now known as the distinction between ex ante and ex
post.) His work was taken over and developed by Irving Fisher in his
monetary studies. An intriguing aspect of Newcomb's presentation is that
instead of the usual form of the circular flow, which shows aggregate
quantities per unit of time, Newcomb drew a lot of individuals, with arrows
representing payments going from one individual to several others, and
payments from several individuals going to each one. The whole drawing
looks like stars in the night sky and must reflect his astronomical training.[19]

Toward the end of the nineteenth century professional economists with
substantial graduate training began to replace the self-taught and part-time
practitioner. Because graduate seminars in economics did not exist in
either British or American universities around 1870, but were quite
plentiful in Germany, it became common to do graduate work there. Of
seventy-six economists in twenty-eight leading American schools in the
period 1870–1900, fifty-three had studied in Germany.[20] British universities were basically undergraduate institutions, while German research and
scholarship in general and economics in particular were greatly admired.
One of the most famous American economists to go through German PhD
training was John Bates Clark (1847–1938). (His middle name is always
cited to avoid confusion with his son, John Maurice Clark, an eminent
economist of the following generation.) He finished his German studies in
1875, and taught at various colleges until he went to Columbia in 1895. The
contributions which made him famous fall into two parts: the marginal
productivity theory and the capital theory. His first book, however, The
Philosophy of Wealth (1885), was a work of protest against so-called
Ricardianism, with its premise of economic man, and its concentration on
competition when really that form of economic organization had disappeared (especially in the labor market). The book called for arbitration
in labor disputes, profit-sharing, and producers' cooperatives. His second
book, The Distribution of Wealth (1899), was completely different. For one
thing, it was designed to show that the existing system of property rights
provides a fair distribution of income in the sense that each man gets what
he produced (i.e., he gets his marginal product). This he demonstrated by
being as abstract as Ricardo, focusing on the static state and holding
constant the factors which account for dynamic change in the real world:
changes in population, capital, technology, consumers' wants, and the
elimination of inefficient businesses. Other assumptions are full employment

and competition. Finally, there is the crucial law of diminishing returns, which is held to be a universal phenomenon, applicable to all factors of production. If additional units of a resource (e.g., labor) are added to fixed amounts of other resources, the result is smaller and smaller additions to output, because of the crowding and eventual overcrowding of fixed resources. The wage will be set by the market at the marginal product of the last worker hired (the employer cannot pay more, and if he does not pay that much, the worker can go to work for someone who will). In competition each worker gets the same wage. Does that mean that the intramarginal workers, who produced higher marginal products before the last worker was hired, are being exploited? No, because the higher marginal product when there are only a few workers is the result of there being more capital for each one to use, not because of any superiority of the workers. Workers are really interchangeable.

Another feature of Clark's approach was his use of generalized decreasing returns and the idea of the residual payment, which was behind Ricardo's rent theory. This generalization is shown in figure 17.1.[21] Total product is the area under the marginal product curves, and must be the same whether you consider capital as the fixed factor and labor as the variable, or the reverse (the left and right hand diagrams, respectively). If labor is the variable factor, wages per worker are the marginal product of the amount of labor, $L_o$, and total wages are the rectangle so labelled. Interest payments are the residual triangle, the difference between total product and the wages bill. You could just as well regard capital as the variable factor, in which case interest is the rectangle and wages the residual triangle. The total wages and interest must be equal, whichever way you view them.

Clark's other contribution to economics was his analysis of capital; this

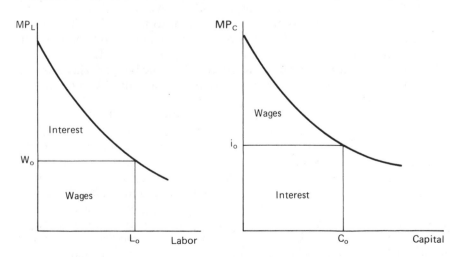

**Figure 17.1**

was still being quoted during the Cambridge–Cambridge controversies discussed earlier. In this context, Clark's theory has been called a "parable." Clark distinguished between capital as concrete capital goods, and pure capital or social capital, which is the permanent value of the concrete capital goods. The former wear out; the latter remains permanently because the product of the capital goods includes the depreciation and maintenance costs which allow the fund to maintain its value. As for the determination of interest, it is the marginal product of the capital *fund*, not of the capital *goods*.

J. B. Clark was an extremely important theorist in his day, not because he was the only marginal productivity theorist (von Thünen, Wicksteed, Walras, and Alfred Marshall are well known, and Stuart Wood, who got the first American PhD in economics at Harvard but was primarily a businessman, is a less well-known contributor), but because of his extensive and lucid exposition. But his aggregation and his capital parables did not survive the Cambridge criticism nearly as well as the Walrasian general-equilibrium approach.[22]

Germany contributed not only the formal training of people like J. B. Clark; it also contributed a model for an organization of economists. Some German economists had formed an association called the *Verein für Sozialpolitik*; it was a social reform organization. (This is the origin of the wicked definition of an economist quoted by Schumpeter, that an economist is one who measures the dwelling-houses of workmen and pronounces them too small.) Richard T. Ely, a reformer and Christian socialist and a professor at Johns Hopkins, started in 1885 what he intended to be a similar oganization in the United States, the American Economic Association. The *laissez-faire* believers among American economists were not happy with the reformers' emphasis on the role of the state, and the theorists were not happy with the organization's insistence that its platform recognize the importance of institutional and historical studies. There was a long battle over whether the AEA would be a scientific body or a reform group. According to a recent study of the origins of the AEA, it was not until 1904 that it was firmly established as a scientific body.[23] This was one signal that economics was now a separate and thriving discipline in the United States.

Towards the beginning of the twentieth century two outstanding figures appeared in the world of economics who were trained in American universities: Thorstein Veblen (1875–1929), critic of social institutions and orthodox economics alike, and Irving Fisher (1867–1947), theorist and health crusader. Veblen, whose parents were Norwegian immigrants who settled in Minnesota, attended Carleton College and took John Bates Clark's economics courses there. He got a PhD in philosophy at Yale in 1884, then was unable to get a job and spent six years at home, reading widely. In 1890 he started graduate work in economics at Cornell, and went to Chicago as a teacher at the university in 1892. His academic career brought a series of moves – Stanford, the University of Missouri, the New

School for Social Research (in New York City) – because of his radicalism and his penchant for other men's wives. Throughout this time he was turning out a stream of books, of which *The Theory of the Leisure Class* (1899) and *The Theory of Business Enterprise* (1904) are the best known today.[24]

One distinguishing feature of Veblen's work was his style, characterized by Professor Boulding as combining weapons of irony and sarcasm and sardonic innuendo.[25] For example, referring to the snobbery of the respectable middle class, Veblen says that "'Snobbery' is here used without disrespect, as a convenient term to denote the element of strain involved in the quest for gentility on the part of persons whose accustomed social standing is less high or less authentic than their aspirations."[26] Another example is his categories of the ways in which the rich spend their money: Conspicuous Consumption, Conspicuous Leisure, and Conspicuous Waste.

The basic message of Veblen was that economics should be an evolutionary subject, studying what he called institutions – widely prevalent habits of thought and action. Veblen wished to study how these institutions evolve, rather than make a static analysis which takes the institutions for granted. He used the tools of anthropology and psychology, but focused them on economics because that is the activity which occupies most of people's time and exercises the most influence on the mind. In *The Theory of the Leisure Class* Veblen's contention was that money-making was the test of success in life, and that people's propensity toward emulation therefore is based on pecuniary factors. We do things that are costly so as to seem successful. This is the basis of the conspicuous waste and all the foibles of the wealthy which he listed in detail in *The Theory of the Leisure Class*. Of course, the life he described is that of what is called "The Gilded Age," when the great mansions of the Vanderbilts, the Morgans, the Astors, and so on were being built and filled with treasures at Newport, on Fifth Avenue, and elsewhere. The lifestyles of the wealthy have changed today to be somewhat less conspicuous.

In *The Theory of Business Enterprise* two more institutions are examined, that of the machine process, the modern technological apparatus for making goods, and the business enterprise, which organizes the making and selling of goods but whose fundamental interest is in making money rather than in making goods. Business enterprise establishes monopolies and restricts production, because that way it can make more money, and it thereby frustrates the engineers who develop and operate the technology. Left to themselves, the engineers would produce more than the monopolistic businessmen let them.

Part of the legacy of business enterprise is the business cycle, says Veblen. In good times, with high prices and profits, businesses borrow freely. Output expands, but so do costs and it becomes more difficult to keep on borrowing as profits fall and interest rates rise. So a few firms fail and creditors start pushing for payment from the rest. There comes a crisis and a depression, all from the push for profits.

Another of Veblen's conclusions was that the engineers would become tired of having their productivity sabotaged by the financiers who managed business, and a new institutional form of organizing production would ensue. Veblen could not decide whether the new form would be socialistic or a right-wing police state (what we would now call Fascism). Since labor unions as well as the engineers would become critical of the traditional private property institutions, they might develop enough power to lead to socialism. But the clergy, the lawyers, and the military do maintain power, and they might keep enough power to thwart the unions and bring about a police state. This is a fuzzy theory, full of normative elements, personal bias, and emotions. It contains elements that are not subject to verification, such as his contention that the technical change which transforms industry at the hands of the engineers does not come from their pecuniary greed but basic, inborn instincts, the instincts of workmanship and of idle curiosity. Professor Walker points out that this proposition is untestable because it covers all eventualities: if you observe behavior and see that it is workmanlike (no shoddy output, no restriction of production) then the instinct of workmanship is shown to exist; if you observe behavior and see that there is waste, poor design and construction, idle machines, then you conclude that the instinct of workmanship is thwarted by the decisions of the businessmen in the interests of profits. [27]

Veblen's emphasis on institutions was shared by others, giving rise to a small school, Institutionalism. The other important members of the school were Wesley Mitchell, a student of Veblen's, who did statistical work on business cycles and founded the National Bureau of Economic Research, still a thriving empirical establishment, and John R. Commons, interested in the institutions of collective action and legal institutions in particular. The work of these people has been summed up by Kenneth Boulding: "The institutionalists may not have given the right answers, but they did ask some very right questions." [28]

Our last eminent American economist to be discussed in this chapter is Irving Fisher, whose career was pretty much the opposite of Veblen's. He spent his entire academic career, both as student and professor, in one place, at Yale. He was wealthy rather than poverty-stricken like Veblen, because of his invention of a visible card-index filing system. His research was in orthodox economic theory and statistical investigation rather than in institutionalism. While Veblen prophesied broad social change, Fisher was a crusader for all kinds of reforms: for world peace, for health through diets, no cigarette smoking, and no drinking, and for the "compensated dollar" (the weight of gold behind each dollar would vary so as to keep the purchasing power of a dollar constant. If prices rose, more grains of gold would be added to the definition of a dollar.)

Fisher's PhD dissertation was "Mathematical Investigations in the Theory of Value and Prices." It was a study of general equilibrium involving utility theory – independent cardinal utilities, cases where utility is a cardinal function of all goods consumed, and ordinal indifference curve analysis. This work, which Samuelson calls the greatest PhD dissertation ever written,[29] has some innovations which stuck, such as indifference curves and the use of vectors, and one which did not. This was Fisher's use of sketches of a hydraulic machine which showed visually how the general equilibrium works. Tanks of different shape and size represent the utility functions of different people, and the settling of water to the same height in each tank shows the equilibrium condition, that marginal utility per dollar has to be equal. Fisher constructed and used such machines in his classes for years. In the midst of all his other activities, Fisher kept up his interest in utility theory by trying to devise empirical ways of measuring cardinal utility.

In his day he was better known for his work on money and on index numbers. His 1911 book, *The Purchasing Power of Money*, contains his version of the quantity theory of money: $MV=pQ$, where $M$ is money, $V$ is velocity (the number of times money turns over in a year), $p$ is the average price, and $Q$ the total quantity of goods purchased. (For the Marshallian version, which emphasizes the demand for money as a fraction $k$ of the total payments which people hold as money on hand, see chapter 16.) Much of the book is made up of a study of the short-run effects of changing the supply of money. The long-run effect is easy. Double $M$ and in the long run $p$ is doubled. But in the short run there are all sorts of transition effects. For example, while prices are rising, the real rate of interest is below the nominal rate because of lags. The nominal rate is whatever the market sets, such as 5 per cent. The real rate is the nominal rate corrected for the expected rate of inflation. If you expect prices to be rising, the real rate of return will be less than the nominal rate. Borrowing for new business construction is stimulated; bank loans are expanded and bank deposits (called $M'$ by Fisher) increase. This leads to a further rise of prices. Thus in Fisher's hands the quantity theory is not mechanical but involves an analysis of the whole macroeconomic process. In working on this theory, Fisher got deeply involved in index numbers, as the statistical verification of the quantity theory required both price and quantity indices. Fisher attempted to develop what he regarded as an ideal index number, but, as Professor Frisch of Norway later proved, no index can meet all of Fisher's criteria.[30]

But the pundits all agree that Fisher's central contribution was his theory of interest. Originally published in 1907 as *The Rate of Interest*, the book was revised and published in 1930 as *The Theory of Interest*, with the subtitle *As Determined by Impatience to Spend Income and Opportunity to Invest It*, and with a dedication to John Rae and to Böhm-Bawerk. This theory is a general equilibrium supply and demand model.

A diagrammatic version of Fisher's interest theory is given in figure 17.2. The productivity of capital goods is shown by the "opportunities for investment" curve, OP. By sacrificing some of this year's income and investing it rather than consuming it, some return will result. At point E in the diagram the return is shown by the tangent line, whose slope is $-(1+r)$,

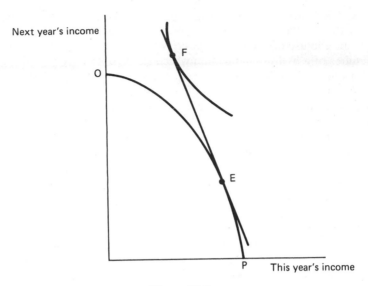

Next year's income

F

O

E

P    This year's income

**Figure 17.2**

where *r* is the rate of interest. For the given rate of interest the consumer will arrange his investment so that he is at E. The combination of this year's and next year's income shown at E is the highest budget line that the consumer can obtain.

The second factor in determining interest rates is the consumer's preference between incomes today and tomorrow. This preference is shown by a set of indifference curves. The one tangent to the budget line at point F shows that in equilibrium this consumer will lend some of his today's income to someone in return for a payment which adds to next year's income. In the market this is a supply of loans. For equilibrium to exist in the market, another consumer would have to wish to borrow exactly that much. Otherwise the rate of interest would change.[31]

Schumpeter called this book "a wonderful achievement, the peak achievement, so far as perfection within its own frame is concerned, of the literature of interest."[32] The features which theorists had emphasized in their literary discussions – the preferences of people for present rather than future goods, and the productivity of capital goods – can be shown in the shape of the indifference curves and the production possibility curves. The conditions for market equilibrium, that the supply of loans equals the demand for them, can also be shown.

It is convenient to cover the next important American economist, Edward H. Chamberlin, in a separate chapter devoted to the monopolistic competition revolution, so with Irving Fisher we close this chapter.

## *Notes*

1  This writing is surveyed in great detail by Joseph Dorfman, *The Economic Mind in American Civilization* (New York, 1946–59). It is much easier to get the pattern of this story from H. W. Spiegel, *The Rise of American Economic Thought* (Philadelphia, 1960), a short volume with excerpts from typical writers preceded by the editor's comments. A long bibliography is contained in Daniel Horowitz, "Historians and Economists: Perspectives on the Development of American Economic Thought," *History of Political Economy* (*HOPE*), 1974, pp. 454–62. Paul K. Conkin, *Prophets of Prosperity: America's First Political Economists* (Bloomington, Ind., 1980) looks at some twenty-two early nineteenth-century economic writers from the point of view of an intellectual historian.

2  Joseph Grunwald, "Some Reflections on Latin American Industrialization Policy," *Journal of Political Economy*, 1970, p. 827. This article contains lengthy excerpts from Hamilton's *Report* and makes point by point comparisons with ECLA reasoning.

3  Charles P. Kindleberger and Bruce Herrick, *Economic Development*, 3rd edn (New York, 1977), p. 285.

4  In R. E. Freeman (ed.), *Postwar Economic Trends in the United States* (New York, 1960).

5  Spiegel, *Rise of American Economic Thought*, p. 47.

6  Henry W. Spiegel, "Henry C. Carey," *International Encyclopedia of the Social Sciences*, vol. 2 (New York, 1968), p. 305.

7  Dorfman, *The Economic Mind*, vol. 2, pp. 575–84. For an extensive discussion of List's life and ideas, see W. O. Henderson, *Friedrich List: Economist and Visionary, 1789–1846* (London, 1983).

8  A very detailed survey is E. R. A. Seligman, "The Early Teaching of Economics in the United States," in J. H. Hollander (ed.), *Economic Essays Contributed in Honor of John Bates Clark* (New York, 1927). Seligman's "Economics in the United States: a Historical Sketch," in his *Essays in Economics* (New York, 1925), is a comprehensive listing of authors and books with a bare minimum of commentary holding the list together.

9  Reprinted in Dunbar's *Economic Essays* (New York, 1902).

10  The book was originally published in 1834. A new edition was published in 1905 as *The Sociological Theory of Capital* (C. W. Mixter, ed.). A photographic reproduction of the original edition was published by the University of Toronto Press as volume II of *John Rae, Political Economist* (R. W. James, ed.) in 1965. Volume I of this edition contains a life of Rae and a summary of his work, as well as some selected papers and letters of Rae's.

11  J. J. Spengler, "John Rae on Economic Development: A Note", *Quarterly Journal of Economics*, 1959, pp. 393–406.

12  The student looking for material on John Rae may also find useful R. W. James, "The Life and Work of John Rae," *Canadian Journal of Economics and Political Science*, 1951, pp. 141–63.

13  This quotation is included in the excerpt from *Progress and Poverty* which is reprinted in Spiegel, *Rise of American Economic Thought*, p. 157.

14  Ibid., p. 154.
15  The lectures are reprinted in *The Journal of Law and Economics*, 1969, with an introduction by George J. Stigler.
16  "Economists and the History of Ideas," *American Economic Review*, 1962, p. 16.
17  The report is reprinted in the *Journal of Law and Economics*, 1969, in the article cited in n. 15 above.
18  T. W. Hutchison, *A Review of Economic Doctrines 1870–1929* (Oxford, 1953), p. 269. Presumably the natural scientist in question was Sir Isaac Newton.
19  It is reproduced in Spiegel, *Rise of American Economic Thought*, p. 174.
20  John B. Parrish, "Rise of Economics as an Academic Discipline: The Formative Years to 1900," *Southern Economic Journal*, 1967, p. 5.
21  The figure is adapted from *The Distribution of Wealth* (New York, 1899), p. 201.
22  See Mark Blaug, *The Cambridge Revolution: Success or Failure?* (London, 1974).
23  A. W. Coats, "The First Two Decades of the American Economic Association," *American Economic Review*, 1960, pp. 555–74.
24  the most convenient source for information on Veblen's life and work is the introduction by Wesley Mitchell to *What Veblen Taught* (New York, 1936). A more detailed life of Veblen is Joseph Dorfman, *Thorstein Veblen and His America* (New York, 1934).
25  Kenneth Boulding, "A New Look at Institutionalism," *American Economic Review Papers and Proceedings*, May, 1957, p. 2.
26  *The Theory of Business Enterprise* (New York, 1904), p. 388.
27  See Donald A. Walker, "Veblen's Economic System," *Economic Inquiry*, 1977, pp. 213–37. This is a highly recommended study of Veblen.
28  Boulding, "A New Look at Institutionalism," p. 12. This article is an interesting statement of the role of the institutionalists in contemporary economics.
29  Paul A. Samuelson, "Irving Fisher and the Theory of Capital," in W. Fellner et al., *Ten Economic Studies in the Tradition of Irving Fisher*, (New York, 1967).
30  Ibid.
31  Joseph W. Conard, *An Introduction to the Theory of Interest* (Berkeley, Ca., 1959), gives a patient exposition of Fisher's interest theory in its graphical version.
32  Joseph Schumpeter, *Ten Great Economists* (Oxford, 1951), p. 230.

# 18
# The Monopolistic Competition Revolution

There were two "revolutions" in economics in the 1930s. The Keynesian revolution will be studied in chapter 19; this chapter is devoted to the revolution in microeconomics whose high point was the publication in 1933 of E. H. Chamberlin's *The Theory of Monopolistic Competition* and Joan Robinson's *The Economics of Imperfect Competition*. Some people, indeed, rate Chamberlin's book as "the most influential single work ever produced by an American economist."[1]

Actually, the reworking of price theory from the way it was formulated by Marshall had begun earlier, in the 1920s. However, interest in monopolistic competition theory was at its height in the 1930s and 1940s (by 1948 Chamberlin had compiled a bibliography of 691 items). Since then analytical work has been increasingly devoted to general equilibrium problems with the emphasis on elegant mathematical formulations rather than on realism dealing with market imperfections.[2] Much of the detailed work on the problems emphasized by Chamberlin – oligopoly, product differentiation, selling costs – is pursued in the field of industrial organization. The originators of this field, notably Edward Mason and Joe Bain, were heavily influenced by Chamberlin, but it has not been a strictly abstract field. Instead it has included institutional, legal, and empirical studies along with considerable use of and contribution to price theory.[3]

Chamberlin explained that the origins of his theory went back to his graduate school days at the University of Michigan, where he wrote a paper on a controversy between Taussig (of Harvard) and Pigou (of Cambridge) over the explanation of the practice of railroads of charging different freight rates for coal and for copper. Pigou claimed it was because railroads had monopoly power, and Taussig that it was because of joint costs. (This goes back to John Stuart Mill's explanation of the price of wool and mutton, where the joint cost is the cost of raising the sheep. In the railroad case, the joint cost is the roadbed, the rolling stock, etc.) Chamberlin declared that a "slight element" of monopoly would be enough to allow the discrimination to persist, since the fewness of carriers would check price-cutting on the good carrying the higher rate. This was the origin of the study of the effects of blending competition with monopoly which he pursued in further graduate work at Harvard and which he finally published in 1933.[4]

While Chamberlin was pursuing his solitary researches at Cambridge, Massachusetts, a far from solitary concern with the inadequacies of Marshallian price theory was agitating Cambridge, England. J. H. Clapham, an economic historian, opened fire with an article, "Of Empty Economic Boxes," on the concept of increasing and decreasing returns industries, claiming that it was practically impossible to say which industries belonged to which class and of little practical usefulness even if you could.[5] Another and even more influential article was Piero Sraffa, "The Laws of Returns under Competitive Conditions," which appeared in the *Economic Journal* in 1926. Sraffa argued that diminishing returns really applied to cases where only a fixed amount of a factor of production was available (land, in classical economics), and in modern economics was applicable only to very broad definitions of industries. In fact, he says, only a minute class of commodities employs the whole of a factor of production, and therefore decreasing returns, or its equivalent, rising supply price, is not often found. On the other hand, what are called, following Marshall, internal economies of large scale production are found in "a very large number of undertakings", most of which would be delighted to expand production if it were not for the fact that in order to do so they would have to reduce price or increase selling costs. "It is necessary, therefore, to abandon the path of free competition and turn in the opposite direction, namely, towards monopoly."[6] In turning toward monopoly, it is not ordinary monopoly but rather industries in which each firm has a more or less particular market to which attention must be given. The demand prices of such firms will be determined by the price at which the goods could be purchased from other firms as well as by the value which the purchaser puts on his preference for the firm in question. This may allow high profits which are maintained because of the large marketing expense that would be necessary for new firms to break into a situation where existing firms have established their goodwill. This marketing difficulty may also mean that firms have to remain small and have limited profits simply because they cannot get the financial credit for the large expenses needed to break into someone else's market. Sraffa's article, written independently of Chamberlin, is very similar in spirit, and may be an example of one of Merton's multiple discoveries of a scientific theory.[7]

During the next few years a series of writers in the *Economic Journal* carried out Sraffa's suggestion to turn toward monopoly theory, in the process developing the theory of the monopoly firm that students learn in intermediate microeconomics courses today. In order to maximize profits, the monopolist whose cost and demand functions are shown in figure 18.1 will select the output at which marginal revenue (MR) becomes equal to marginal cost (MC), and sell it at the price which is shown on the demand curve (D) for that output. The important tool here was marginal revenue,

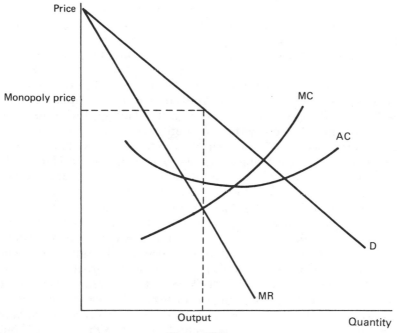

**Figure 18.1**

the idea that the monopolistic decision-maker looked not at price but at price corrected by the fall in price necessary to sell the additional output, multiplied by the previous output.[8] Now this idea was actually a hundred years old when T. O. Yntema, Sir Roy Harrod, and Joan Robinson worked it out (again) in the period around 1930. Cournot had developed the theory in chapter V of his book *The Mathematical Principles of the Theory of Wealth* in 1838, and the book had been translated into English in 1897. Although Cournot did his differentiation with respect to price rather than output, and although he was sloppy in his verbal formulation, stating on p. 59 of the 1897 translation that "the increase in gross receipts" (i.e., marginal revenue) was price times the change in output, neglecting the other term in the derivative, he did analyze the monopoly firm in a modern manner. Cournot's contribution led Professor Samuelson to the exasperated comment "That grown men argued seriously in 1930 about who had first used or named the curve that we now call 'marginal revenue' is a joke."[9] Marshall discussed monopoly in Note XIV of the Mathematical Appendix to his *Principles of Economics*, deriving marginal revenue by using calculus. But he certainly did not emphasize the concept, and to the mathematically illiterate it took the intricate verbal analysis of Roy Harrod in "Notes on Supply" in the *Economic Journal* in 1930 to give insight into the marginal analysis of the monopoly firm.[10]

The work at Cambridge, England, which most definitively carried out

Sraffa's program of turning toward monopoly and away from competitive theory was Joan Robinson's *The Economics of Imperfect Competition*.[11] It is a rigorous book, based in technique on the geometry of the relationships among average and marginal curves and definitions of elasticities, and it is represented in its second sentence as "a box of tools." It is based on the idea that "the existence of a perfect market is likely to be extremely rare in the real world" (p. 89) and that all kinds of markets, including oligopolies as well as monopolistic factor markets, can be analyzed with the tools of monopoly theory. Indeed, perfect competition is regarded as only a special case of monopoly (p. 307). Although an extremely important pioneering book in converting the literary formulations of Sraffa and Harrod about the ubiquity of monopoly into rigorous models, the amount of work left for others to do was considerable. To take two examples: Joan Robinson admitted twenty years later that she neglected oligopoly in the book because she could not solve it and tried to fence it off by a "fudge" in the definition of the demand curve.[12] The fudge was the definition of the demand curve for the individual firm: it included the full effect upon its sales of a change in the price it charged, whether it caused a change in the prices charged by others or not. This completely ignored the very problem at hand in oligopolies: will a change in firm A's price change the other firms' prices or not? Another example is the discussion of equilibrium when there are a number of imperfectly competitive firms in the industry (chapter 7); among other simplifying assumptions, it is assumed that all firms are alike both in their costs and in the conditions of demand for their individual outputs (p. 98). This enabled her to draw what Shackle calls the fundamental diagram of imperfect competition.[13] The diagram displays the two conditions of equilibrium: for each firm marginal revenue (MR) equals marginal cost (MC), and, in order for there to be no entry or exit of firms, profits must be normal; i.e., average revenue (AR), which is the same as the demand curve (D), equals average cost (AC). Figure 18.2 illustrates these conditions.[14] The equilibrium bears out Sraffa's contention: if there are increasing returns (decreasing costs) the industry cannot be competitive, for in such an industry equilibrium will be along the downward sloping AC curve. Hence there will be a downward slope to the demand curve; the demand curve cannot be the horizontal demand curve of the competitive firm, and the theory of monopoly, rather than the theory of competition, is relevant.

In 1948 the American Economic Association surveyed the state of contemporary economics. Professor J. K. Galbraith noted that apart from the Keynesian revolution, no problem attracted more attention from economists than that of monopoly, and Robinson's and Chamberlin's books were the texts of this revolution. Joe S. Bain, surveying the field of "Price and Production Policies" (what today is called Industrial Organization), claimed that in the reformulation of price theory to make it more congruent with actual business behavior, Chamberlin's work was by all reckonings the most important. Mrs Robinson's book, he says, was of a

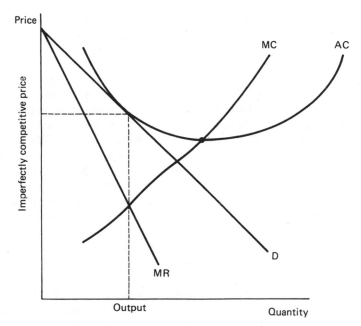

**Figure 18.2**  From Joan Robinson, *The Economics of Imperfect Competition*, Macmillan, 1934. Reproduced by permission of the publishers.

more formalistic character and was also influential.[15] Mrs Robinson claimed that she herself was never able to grasp the nature of the distinction between imperfect and monopolistic competition.[16] Professor Chamberlin, however, insisted that his theory was a blending or fusion of the hitherto separate theories of monopoly and competition, whereas Mrs Robinson left the dichotomy as sharp as ever.[17] "Almost all other students of the matter have agreed with each other that in describing the structure and mechanism of equilibrium in firms and groups of firms when oligopoly and selling expenditure are absent, the two books present identical theories."[18]

Chamberlin's two key concepts for his blending were product differentiation and the number of sellers. Each firm has some unique features which make its product different from those of other firms – location, selling costs, the personality of the manager. Thus each firm has some monopoly power (its demand curve is not horizontal like that of a perfect competitor). And the number of firms competing against each other obviously makes a difference in the price and output of the firms. Chamberlin's career was devoted to an attempt to formulate theory out of these concepts. He made three different attempts.[19] In the original edition of his *Theory of Monopolistic Competition* (1933) he focused attention on the group, a number of producers whose goods are close substitutes for each other, and he worked out most fully the case of the large group under the "heroic" assumption that both demand and cost curves are uniform throughout the group. This gives a tangency equilibrium like that of figure 18.2, for with a large group there must be sufficient ease of entry that any excess profits are eroded by the entry of new firms which shifts the demand curve into the tangency position. It is this formulation and construction which typically appears in microeconomics texts as the theory of monopolistic competition. But Chamberlin insisted that the theory is much broader, and attempted to make it so in his subsequent formulations.

His second attempt was made in response to criticism of his large group presentation, particularly that of Nicholas Kaldor in *Economica* in 1935. Chamberlin had used a *ceteris paribus* (i.e., other things held constant) demand curve, which is not appropriate where firms are competing by product differentiation and sales expenses. What Chamberlin changed in a chapter added to the fifth edition of his book in 1946 was the emphasis on the group; that idea was dropped and instead it was urged that each producer has a monopoly of his own product, and faces the competition of substitutes which brings in interrelations of other monopolists who are in some appreciable degree of competition with him.[20] This is essentially Sraffa's contention, made in 1926.

On reconsideration, however, Chamberlin decided that it was not possible to cover all of price theory, including competition, in terms of ordinary monopoly. Since he insisted that monopolistic competition did embrace all market situations, he had to try again. In his final attempt, in chapter 3 of *Towards a More General Theory of Value* (1957), he emphasized oligopoly, claiming that oligopolistic elements are very general in the economic system, that economic study must be increasingly concerned with them (p. 61), and that the basis for a general theory to replace that of pure competition is one in which oligopoly emerges with great force (p. 69). Now oligopoly theory is very difficult, but it is receiving much attention, particularly with the aid of game theory. Its practitioners believe that "the contributions of game theory to economics are major and continuing," particularly in refining the concepts of oligopoly equilibrium.[21] So far the work gives insight rather than directly applicable models. It is interesting that this work merges into Chamberlin's notion of a general theory coming from oligopoly in the theory of what is called the core of an economy. In *n*-person game theory, groups of two or more players can join together in a coalition against the others, as one possible strategy. Some outcomes or allocations of resources can be blocked by coalitions of players; the set of allocations which cannot be so blocked is called the core. One of the theorems proved by game theorists is that every competitive equilibrium is in the core. Hence, the theory of games, which began with Oskar Morgenstern and John von Neumann's applications to duopoly situations, has developed into a tool to study the mathematics of competitive economies.[22]

There were two historically important developments in the literature on monopolistic competition which we have not yet discussed. One was the publication in 1940 of Robert Triffin's *Monopolistic Competition and*

*General Equilibrium Theory.*[23] Triffin argued that monopolistic competition had eliminated the significance of the concept of an industry or of Chamberlin's group of related firms. When the elasticity of substitution between two products is imperfect, the sellers can pursue independent price policies. For example, the competition between two differentiated makes of cars is the same as that between cars and tailoring (p. 88). But there are differences in how much competition exists between firms selling different things, and Triffin proposed to analyze these differences and classify various degrees of competition empirically on the basis of the "cross-elasticity" of demand (pp. 97–112). Ordinary elasticities measure the percentage change in one firm's output which results from a given percentage change in its price. The cross-elasticity measures the percentage change in firm I's output which results from a given percentage change in firm II's price. If the cross-elasticity is high, there would be considerable competition between the two firms. There was much subsequent writing on the subject, which led to the conclusion that it was necessary also to include in the analysis a factor showing the number of sellers as well as the degree to which customers of firm I respond to price changes by firm II.[24] This rather extensive line of development came to an end eventually, with the outcome that it had become too complex for empirical use and that "in describing the market structures it may therefore be preferable to fall back on simpler concepts . . . "[25]

Another offshoot of Chamberlin's work was a long discussion of methodology, hinging on the role of realism in the assumptions as well as the conclusions of theory. This got its start in the "Chamberlin vs Chicago" controversy, in which George Stigler and Milton Friedman attacked the theory of monopolistic competition.[26] Stigler argued that the Chamberlin theory of the group was substantially the same as the Marshallian industry when he assumed uniformity and symmetry among firms, and was indeterminate, like oligopoly, when he does not. Abandoning the group, as does Triffin and Chamberlin at a later stage of the development of his thought (see above) leads only to *ad hoc* empiricism. The reason for this failure, says Stigler, is that Chamberlin started by rejecting the (pure) competition and monopoly models on the ground that their assumptions were unrealistic – they did not consider the pervasive product differentiation, selling costs, and similar facts of business life. But, says Stigler, the test of a theory is not whether its assumptions are realistic but whether there is "concordance between its predictions and the observable course of events." Stigler thought that monopolistic and pure competition theories gave essentially the same predictions in the large group, uniformity case. In general Chamberlin's theory warned people to pay more attention to monopoly, but had no specific contribution of its own to make.

Milton Friedman pushed the argument further; concentrating on the role of assumptions as opposed to testing hypotheses, he argued that in general significant theories would have wildly inaccurate premises because they must abstract crucial elements from complex circmstances.[27] It was this defense of unrealistic assumptions that set off the methodological controversy about the "F-twist," as Samuelson named this particular philosophy of science.[28] Samuelson's argument was that "the validity of the *full* consequences of a theory implies the validity of the theory and so of its *minimal* assumptions."[29] The student who reads this controversy will be much more aware of the role of assumptions and conclusions. As for the conclusion of the specific Chicago attack on Chamberlin, it did not succeed in eliminating monopolistic competition theory from the face of the earth. "The survival of Chamberlinian economics testifies to the apparent superiority of relevance over logical consistency."[30]

# Notes

1 William J. Baumol, "Monopolistic Competition and Welfare Economics," *American Economic Review Papers and Proceedings*, May 1964, p. 52.
2 See Paul A. Samuelson, "The Monopolistic Competition Revolution," in Robert E. Kuenne (ed.), *Monopolistic Competition Theory: Studies in Impact* (New York, 1967), pp. 116 and 130. These comments should not lead students to believe that the field has been completely abandoned, as articles on it continue to appear from time to time.
3 Joe S. Bain, "The Impact on Industrial Organization," *American Economic Review Papers and Proceedings*, May 1964, pp. 28–32.
4 Edward H. Chamberlin, "The Origin and Early Development of Monopolistic Competition Theory," *Quarterly Journal of Economics*, 1961, pp. 515–43.
5 This article, originally published in the *Economic Journal* in 1922, has been reprinted along with other articles in the "cost controversy" of the 1920s in American Economic Association, *Readings in Price Theory* (Homewood, Ill., 1952).
6 Ibid., p. 187.
7 See Samuelson, "Monopolistic Competition Revolution," p. 107.
8 Total Revenue $= pq$, where $p$ is price, $q$ is output, and $p = f(q)$. Marginal revenue is the derivative of total revenue with respect to output, $MR = d(pq)/dq = p + q(dp/dq)$. Since $dp/dq$ is negative, $MR < p$.
9 Samuelson, "The Monopolistic Competition Revolution," p. 110.
10 G. L. S. Shackle, *The Years of High Theory* (Cambridge, 1967), has an excellent chapter on the history of the concept of marginal revenue.
11 Joan Robinson, *The Economics of Imperfect Competition* (London, 1933).
12 See her article " 'Imperfect Competition' Revisited," *Economic Journal*, 1953, reprinted in her *Collected Economic Papers* (Oxford, 1957), vol. 2, p. 228.
13 Shackle, *High Theory*, p. 51.
14 See Robinson, *Imperfect Competition*, p. 95.
15 Howard S. Ellis (ed.), *A Survey of Contemporary Economics* (Philadelphia, 1948), pp. 99–100 and 130–1.
16 See her *Collected Economic Papers*, vol. 2, p. 222.
17 E. H. Chamberlin, *Towards a More General Theory of Value* (New York, 1957), p. 66.

18 Shackle, *High Theory*, p. 62.
19 Romney Robinson, *Edward H. Chamberlin, Columbia Essays on the Great Economists*, No. 1 (New York, 1971), is the best source on the evolution of Chamberlin's thought. A. S. Skinner and M. C. McLennan, "Oligopoly and the Theory of the Firm," in J. Creedy and D. P. O'Brien (eds), *Economic Analysis in Historical Perspective* (London, 1984), briefly reviews Robinson and Chamberlin before examining in detail the theoretical developments since their day.
20 Chamberlin, *The Theory of Monopolistic Competition*, 5th edn (Cambridge, Mass., 1946), p. 206.
21 J. W. Friedman, *Oligopoly and the Theory of Games* (Amsterdam 1977), p. 8.
22 Friedman's book (ibid.) contains an expository chapter.
23 Robert Triffin, *Monopolistic Competition and General Equilibrium Theory* (Cambridge, Mass., 1940).
24 See Joe S. Bain, "Chamberlin's Impact on Microeconomic Theory," in Kuenne (ed.); *Monopolistic Competition*, pp. 154ff for a review of the literature.
25 William Fellner, "The Adaptability and Lasting Significance of the Chamberlinian Contribution," in Kuenne (ed.); *Monopolistic Competition*, pp. 9–10.
26 George J. Stigler, "Monopolistic Competition in Retrospect," in *Five Lectures on Economic Problems* (New York, 1949); Milton Friedman, *Essays in Positive Economics* (Chicago, 1953), pp. 7ff.
27 Friedman, *Positive Economics*, p. 14.
28 A series of articles in the *American Economic Review* for May, 1963, September, 1964, and December, 1965, contains this controversy.
29 P. A. Samuelson, in *American Economic Review*, 1965, p. 1165.
30 Romney Robinson, *Columbia Essays*, p. 58.

# 19

# John Maynard Keynes

The most famous and most influential economist of the twentieth century was beyond a doubt John Maynard Keynes (named Baron of Tilton in 1942). While the modern student, tutored in the Keynesian concepts in every macroeconomics class in his career, may not really appreciate it, *The General Theory of Employment, Interest and Money* (1936) was indeed revolutionary.[1] As Professor Patinkin puts it, "the basic structure of the book . . . defined the framework of both theoretical and empirical research in macroeconomics for decades to come – truly a scientific achievement of the first order."[2]

In previous chapters describing the economics of Alfred Marshall, Knut Wicksell, and Irving Fisher, the background of the neo-classical monetary theory (which Keynes referred to as the classical theory) has already been developed. Business cycle literature was also a relevant part of pre-Keynesian macroeconomics. The business cycle theorists generally agreed that there was a cumulative process which would keep an economy moving up or down once a trend was established but disagreed on what caused the crises that heralded the beginning of depressions. The cumulative process on the upswing was based on the effect of rising prices which would generate profits and hence encourage more investment to keep the economy in a prosperous state. The opposite cumulative reaction occurred in depressions. Falling prices and falling output led to gloomy expectations, a cut-back in investment, and a continuing fall in economic activity. The debates in this field centered on the causes of crises: whether they stemmed from under-consumption, over-consumption, over-investment, building up of excessive credit, or Jevons's agricultural fluctuations which reflected sunspot cycles.[3] Much of this research was done by continental rather than British or American writers.

The monetary theory which determined the static equilibrium around which the business cycle fluctuated was the quantity theory in one or another guise. The Cambridge form, as developed by Marshall, was $P = (kR)/M$.[4] $P$ and $M$ are prices and money, $k$ is the fraction of "total resources" that the community wishes to hold as legal tender and $R$ is the resources enjoyed by the community. In this formulation, which looks odd to modern eyes, $P$ is the resources (e.g., bushels of wheat) that can be commanded by one unit of currency; it is, in fact, the reciprocal of the price level.

Marshall made the demand for currency a function of both income (a flow) and wealth (a stock), using as his example a country whose citizens demanded currency equivalent to the tenth part of their annual income and a fiftieth part of their property.[5] Pigou did not say whether resources were to be thought of in terms of income or of wealth, but Keynes, who had the benefit of the Cambridge "oral tradition," claimed that the context implied that $R$ meant income over a period of time.[6] Then if the number of units of money increased, with $k$ and $R$ held constant, prices would rise. But the quantity theory was a theory, not a tautology, and the theory consisted in the spelling out of the mechanism that made the two sides of the equation equal. Pigou, for example, claimed that in the real world causes of change often acted on both the supply and demand for money at the same time. On the side of demand, a change would often affect both $k$ and $R$ at the same time. Finally, a change in demand introduces a series of changes in the value of money, different according to the time elapsed since the original change.

Pigou's formula is often re-written as $M = kpR$, where $p$ is the money price of the resources (remember that in the original formulation $P$ was the amount of resources per unit of currency; in this formulation, $p = 1/P =$ the number of units of currency one unit of resources is worth). In this form, the theory is called the cash balances approach, since it regards the demand for money as a demand for cash balances proportional to the money value of income.

Irving Fisher, in his book *The Purchasing Power of Money* (1911), presented the alternative transactions approach. His equation of exchange was $MV = \Sigma pQ$, where $M$ is the amount of money in circulation (the average over a year), $V$ is total money expenditure for goods divided by $M$ (i.e., the velocity of circulation of money), $p$ is the price of a given good, and $Q$ is the amount of the good purchased over a year. As in the case of the Cambridge cash balance theorists, Fisher did not apply his theory mechanically. For example, here is his analysis of the effects of an increase in $M$:

1  Prices rise.
2  The rate of interest rises, but not enough to eliminate the increase in profits. (He claimed that the adjustments in the rate of interest lagged price changes for reasons of psychology, law, and custom.)
3  Entrepreneurs increase their borrowing.
4  This expands bank deposits and hence $M$ increases still more.
5  Prices continue to rise and the whole sequence is repeated until the rate of interest rises enough to restore profits to normal.[7]

While Fisher had the rate of interest as part of his monetary analysis, it was Knut Wicksell among the neo-classical monetary theorists who really made the rate of interest central. Wicksell and his great predecessor of nearly a century earlier, Henry Thornton (*The Paper Credit of Great Britain*, 1803), are the expositors of what is called the indirect mechanism, in which changes in the supply of money affect economic activity through their effects on the rate of interest rather than through direct action on the demand for money, as in the case of Hume and all his followers. Wicksell argued that there were two rates of interest to be compared: the real rate (what Keynes called the marginal efficiency of capital), which is the yield to be expected from new investment,[8] and the loan rate. At any time there is a normal or natural real rate. This is the rate at which the demand for loan capital and the supply of savings are equal, and also the rate which maintains equilibrium in the goods and services markets (wages and prices will not be changing). This natural rate changes with changing expectations, inventions, and so on. Suppose that we begin with the case where the loan rate equals the natural real rate, and then suppose that banks expand credit. The loan rate falls below the natural rate, with two results. Savings are discouraged, consumption is expanded, and the pressure of demand makes prices rise. At the same time profits rise so that investment spending is encouraged and once again prices and wages rise. This continues in a cumulative fashion until the increased incomes absorb all the currency for exchange purposes, leaving no cash reserves against which banks can expand credit. The loan rate will then rise back to the natural rate, reflecting the reduced supply of credit.[9]

Wicksell noted that the data seem to contradict the theory: according to the theory, when the rate of interest falls, prices rise and vice versa. However, the data collected by Thomas Tooke in the nineteenth century show that prices and the rate of interest move together.[10] Wicksell's explanation was that the real rate of interest was unobserved, and that what happened when the loan rate was rising (along with prices) was that the real rate had previously risen because of technological change, population growth, or some other dynamic cause. The loan rate was being pulled up because of the increased demand for loans, together with the leakage of cash into transactions, which reduced the relative supply of loans.

In the longest run, however, neo-classical monetary theory held that money was neutral, since, if long-run equilibrium was ever reached, real outputs, inputs, and price ratios depended only on tastes, endowments, technology, and whatever other real factors were important.[11] This, then, was the monetary theory which Keynes inherited and within which he worked until the early 1930s, when, dissatisfied with the theory he had presented in *A Treatise on Money*, he began the rethinking which culminated in *The General Theory*.[12]

Before getting involved with the details of *The General Theory* it is worth looking at Keynes's career, to see how he became the most influential economist of his generation. He was born on June 5, 1883, in

Cambridge, England, where his father, John Neville Keynes, taught both philosophy and economics.[13] Maynard, as his friends referred to him, attended Eton and then Cambridge University, where he met people such as Leonard Woolf and Lytton Strachey. They invited Keynes to join the Apostles, a philosophical group whose creed was to respect truth and nothing else, and later all of them belonged to the *avant-garde* literary and artistic group called the Bloomsbury Set. Details of the free living and free thinking of this group have recently become available through the publication of letters and from studies of such members of the group as Strachey and Virginia Woolf.[14]

At Cambridge Keynes studied mathematics and then put in a year after graduation taking economics to prepare for the civil service examination. Since he was ranked only second in the examination he did not get the best job at the Treasury, but instead he went into the India Office. There he gathered the material for his first book, *Indian Currency and Finance* (1913). At the same time he started work on a prize fellowship dissertation on probability theory which was eventually published in 1921, but which had won the prize before that. In 1908 he returned to Cambridge and to lecturing in economics, specializing in lectures on money.

A very important aspect of his career was his service in the British Treasury during World War I. In fact he became the senior Treasury official in the negotiations over the peace treaties, including reparations, relief, war debts, and other financial matters. He was completely at odds with the decision made to impose extremely large reparations on Germany, and resigned to write *The Economic Consequences of the Peace* (1919). D. E. Moggridge, one of Keynes's biographers, says that this book "ranks as one of the finest pamphlets written in the field of political economy and is, perhaps, a classic in the English language, both for its contents and for its influence on affairs."[15]

Throughout the 1920s and 1930s Keynes continued to have an influence on affairs, as a member of government committees and councils, a frequent writer to newspapers, author of *A Tract on Monetary Reform* (1923), bursar at King's College, Cambridge, patron of the theatre and the ballet,[16] chairman of the board of an insurance company, speculator on the foreign exchanges, collector of art and of rare books – all this while continuing to write and to think about monetary theory and policy.

The recently published letters and manuscripts of Keynes, in particular volumes XIII, XIV, and XXIX of his *Collected Writings* which deal with the preparation of *The General Theory* and with its defense and development, make it possible to trace out the evolution of his thinking.[17] His first book of the 1920s, *A Tract on Monetary Reform*, was concerned with the inflation, deflation, and exchange disequilibrium problems of Europe in the post-war era. It was basically a policy book, and the monetary theory in it was straightforward Marshall and Pigou. Soon after its appearance in 1923 Keynes began to work on *A Treatise on Money*, a major two-volume work that dealt at length with theory and with empirical magnitudes as well as with policy. The basic theory of this book, which appeared in 1930, was that changes in output are caused by windfall profits and losses, and these profits and losses depend on different movements of prices compared to costs. The price movements were in turn related to savings and investment. In the course of this analysis he developed what he called the "fundamental equations" for the value of money. To show the difference between Keynes's 1930 approach and the completely different approach in *The General Theory* six years later, we can look at one of these equations:

$$\Pi = E/O = (I-S)/O.$$

Here $\Pi$ is the current price level for output as a whole, $E$ is current money income (= cost of production) exclusive of windfall profits, $O$ is money income at base period prices, $I$ is the current market value of investment goods produced, $S$ is the difference between $E$ and consumption spending. Thus price level changes depend both on changes in the cost of production (the $E/O$ term) and profit inflation which comes from the excess of investment over savings. (It is very important to note here that Keynes uses investment in *The General Theory* sense but savings are defined differently – here savings are the difference between income excluding abnormal profits and consumption spending.) The price change is assumed to hold for fixed output. Later output is assumed to adjust to the price change.[18] In general much of the criticism of the *Treatise*, both from book reviews and among his Cambridge colleagues, was that it offered no theory of the determination of output in the short run.

The fundamental equations are certainly not all there is in the *Treatise*; it includes a model of the financial system, a model of the foreign-trade sector (which is ignored in *The General Theory*), the beginnings of the theory of liquidity preference, and the beginnings of the emphasis on expectations which is in *The General Theory*. Keynes also discussed the effect of changes in money on interest rates and hence on investment, but in a less satisfactory manner than Wicksell had. Rather than relating the market rate of interest to the natural rate defined as the marginal product of capital, Keynes related the market rate to the rate of interest which would make $I = S$ and therefore rule out price changes due to profit inflation (in the fundamental equation, the second term would drop out). But while the book was regarded as a contribution, the criticisms were sufficiently damaging to lead Keynes to begin to work his theory out all over again from the beginning.

Volume XIII of the *Collected Writings* shows the way this was done and traces out, by way of many letters, drafts of lectures, and so on, how Keynes arrived at the concepts he used in *The General Theory*. One of the more colorful parts of the process was the Circus. This was a group of young economists (Joan and Austin Robinson, R. F. Kahn – one of those who invented the multiplier – James Meade, Piero Sraffa, and others) who held a seminar on the *Treatise* in 1931. R. F. Kahn regularly reported to

Keynes on what they were talking about (the multiplier, costs of investment, relation of prices to output changes) and brought Keynes's ideas back to the group. Although the Circus lasted only one year, Keynes continued to discuss his evolving ideas with its members and with other luminaries such as R. F. Harrod, Ralph Hawtrey, and D. H. Robertson. Robertson was later to fall out with Keynes over the theory of interest developed in *The General Theory*.

The result of this five years of hard work was *The General Theory*, a book which, as Keynes told his readers in the preface, contained much controversy, might well strike the reader as a confusing change from the *Treatise*, and reflected a long struggle of escape from previous models and terminology. Later commentators, noting that the book turned out to be a difficult one to read and interpret, trace much of the difficulty back to Keynes's Marshallian roots. Part of the difficulty was that Keynes used the Marshallian didactic style (see chapter 16 on Marshall), which he defended by claiming that if rigorous mathematical methods were used, the author could not keep in mind all the reservations and qualifications and allowances needed in economic thinking (*The General Theory*, p. 297). Also Marshallian in spirit is the distinction between short- and long-term expectations. Furthermore, Keynes's definition of income (the value of sales minus the "user cost", which is the reduction in the value of capital equipment) was derived from the short-period theory of the firm, as was his assumption of fixed capital stock and increasing costs. Another difficulty was that instead of presenting his model as a general equilibrium model, Keynes tried to show it as a one-directional line of reasoning, beginning with demand and supply of money and winding up with level of income (*The General Theory*, pp. 247–9).[19]

But in spite of the difficulties, *The General Theory* is a great book, a classic within a few short years of its publication, and the student knows from his first economics course something about the fundamental building blocks of Keynesian theory. Keynes claimed that money wage cuts would not be effective in restoring full employment, in contrast to the "classical" economists who theorized that if there is unemployment, it is because real wages are too high and they can be reduced by money wage cuts. We shall see the basis for Keynes's belief shortly. In the meantime, Keynes replaced a labor supply and demand approach to full employment with his theory of effective demand. The level of national income and hence the level of employment is determined by the intersection of aggregate supply with aggregate demand. Aggregate demand is the total of consumption and investment spending. (Actually Keynes, in another Marshallian carryover, speaks of aggregate supply price and aggregate demand price.) Aggregate supply, the total national income (denoted by Y) produced, is the 45-degree line in the familiar "Keynesian cross" diagram in figure 19.1. Since a 45-degree line is the diagonal of a square, a given national income such as $Y^1$ whose production is shown on the horizontal axis is also shown on the diagonal line immediately above it. The production of Y on the horizontal axis

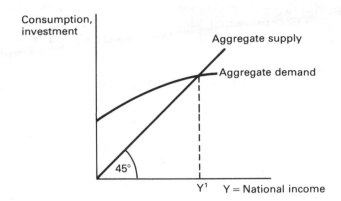

**Figure 19.1**

may thus be compared with the demand for Y shown on the vertical axis. National income is determined at the intersection of aggregate demand and aggregate supply.[20]

The consumption component of aggregate demand was analyzed by Keynes in his concept of the consumption function. Keynes held that consumption depended mainly on aggregate income, following the psychological law that consumption increased when income did, but by a smaller amount – that is, $dC/dY$, the marginal propensity to consume, is less than 1 (*The General Theory*, p. 96). While Keynes discussed the psychological factors leading people to save some of their incomes (under the headings of precaution, foresight, calculation, improvement, independence, enterprise, pride, and avarice) and the motives for business saving (funds for investment, liquidity, prudence, and improvement), he also discussed what he called the objective factors influencing consumption. These included changes in fiscal policy, windfall gains, changes in expectations, and changes in the rate of interest. However, in the short run he argued that the subjective psychological factors were stable while the objective factors were generally of secondary importance, so that consumption changes depended on income changes – in other words, the economy would move along a given consumption function rather than shifting the function.

Figure 19.2 shows the Keynesian consumption function. The marginal propensity to consume, i.e., the slope of the consumption function, decreases as income rises; that was one of Keynes's specific assumptions (*The General Theory*, p. 127).

The study of the consumption function was one of the major developments in macroeconomics after the Keynesian revolution, particularly when forecasts of post-World War II depression in the United States based on the simple Keynesian function were completely wrong. Econometric study of the consumption function went along with study of the investment

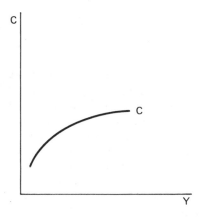

**Figure 19.2**

and liquidity functions and with empirical models of the Keynesian system as a whole. In the process not only was factual knowledge of these macroeconomic variables developed, but so were the tools of economet-rics. And *The General Theory* added impetus to a statistical movement that had already started when it was published (and on which Keynes drew for some of his data) – the collection of measures of national income and its components by Colin Clark and by Simon Kuznets.[21]

Keynes made immediate application of his formulation of the consump-tion function in his version of the multiplier.[22] Since Keynes had defined consumption as a function of income, $C = f(Y)$, he was able to use its deriv-ative, the marginal propensity to consume $(dC/dY)$ to show that a change in investment, $dI$, led to a multiple change in income, $dY$, because the $dI$ led to subsequent changes in $C$ which increased $Y$ in turn. Formally, let

$$Y = C(Y) + I,$$

where $I$ is treated as a parameter. Then

$$dI/dY = 1 - dC/dY, \qquad \text{or}$$

$$dY/dI = 1/(1 - dC/dY).$$

Finally,

$$dY = [1/(1 - dC/dY)] \, dI$$

The term $1/(1 - dC/dY)$ is the multiplier, and is often symbolized by $k$. Although Harry Johnson in his twenty-fifth anniversary lecture on *The General Theory* called the multiplier a tiresome way of comparing general equilibrium positions, it played a central part in the book itself and in the development of Keynesian economics in the years following 1936. Many articles and even books were written on foreign trade multipliers, balanced budget multipliers, and so on. As P. A. Samuelson wrote in 1948, "advanced students in business cycle theory have become proficient in calculating a large variety of different 'income multipliers'. In fact, the subject has become something of a black art."[23]

But in *The General Theory* the art was not so black; based on Kuznets's data, Keynes calculated the multiplier as around 2.5 and the marginal propensity to consume as about 60 – 70 percent in the United States. He went on to argue that the multiplier showed how pyramid building, wars, or filling bottles with banknotes, burying them, and leasing the rights to dig them up would increase wealth, since the consumption induced via the multiplier would add to employment even if the original activity did not. But of course useful improvements (i.e., public works) would be much better and they would be provided if only statesmen did not try to follow the principles of classical economics.[24]

The other part of aggregate demand is investment. Keynes argued that, given the state of expectations of future income by entrepreneurs, investment was determined by the rate of interest in the following way: the discounted present value of the expected future income stream is

$$R_1/(1+r) + R_2/(1+r)^2 + \ldots + R_n/(1+r)^n,$$

where $R_i$ is the anticipated return in year $i$, $r$ is the discount rate (the rate of interest) being applied, and $n$ is the number of years the equipment is expected to last. What rate of interest, $r$, should be applied? Keynes said that the entrepreneur took the rate which made the discounted present value equal to the supply price of producing the capital equipment which provided the income stream. This rate of discount he called the "marginal efficiency of capital." (Irving Fisher had earlier called the same concept the internal rate of return.) As more investment is made, for a given state of expectations, the marginal efficiency of capital falls, as in figure 19.3. That

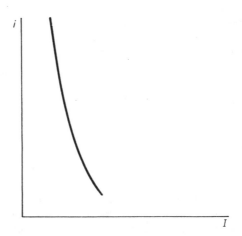

**Figure 19.3**

is because the supply price of the equipment rises (rising marginal cost) and because the $R_i$ terms fall (decreasing marginal revenue). As expectations change, the whole marginal efficiency of capital schedule shifts to the left or to the right; but, for a given state of expectations, the amount of investment is determined at the point when the marginal efficiency of capital, $r$, equals the market rate of interest, $i$. If the marginal efficiency of capital exceeds the market rate, it pays to borrow money and increase investment.

So far, then, we have national income equal to the sum of consumption and investment spending ($Y = C + I$), with $C = f(Y)$ and $I = F(i)$, where $i$ is the market rate of interest. The next step is to determine the market rate of interest.

Keynes argued that interest was a monetary phenomenon and had no business at all in a book such as Marshall's *Principles*, which dealt with the real side of economics. He was thus completely against the tradition of Böhm-Bawerk, Fisher, Marshall, and so on, who analyzed the rate of interest as the outcome of the productivity of capital and the reward for waiting, impatience, time-preference, or some other expression of the preference for present rather than future goods. Keynes expressed this stream of analysis as the proposition that the rate of interest was determined by the demand for investment and the supply of saving; in fact, he said, the classics believed that the rate of interest adjusts so as to make investment equal saving, since a fall in the rate of interest increases $I$ and reduces $S$, in the classical view. By contrast, Keynes argued that interest was really the payment needed to make people willing to part with liquidity. If you hold your savings in bonds rather than in cash, there is the chance that the price of the bond will fall and you will suffer a loss. In fact, the lower the rate of interest, the higher the price of your bond will be, and the more chance of suffering a loss; therefore the quantity of money

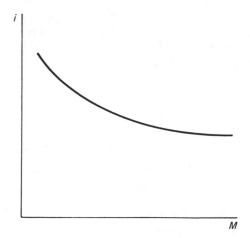

**Figure 19.4**

demanded for liquidity purposes will be higher, the lower the rate of interest. Figure 19.4 shows this relationship. Keynes called this relationship "liquidity preference".

But the demand for money does not depend solely on the psychology outlined above, which Keynes called the speculative motive. People also demand money for transactions purposes and as a precaution for emergencies or to take advantage of bargains. These two motives are functions of income, while the speculative motive is a function of the rate of interest.

We are now in a position to analyze the economy as Keynes did. Given the amount of money available to satisfy liquidity preference, the rate of interest is determined in figure 19.4; with this rate of interest, the amount of investment is determined in figure 19.3; given this amount of investment, the national income and hence the level of employment will be determined via the multiplier. (Alternatively, the level of income must be such that the amount of savings, $Y-C$, will equal the amount of investment.) But this is an equilibrium only if the amount of money used to determine the rate of interest in the first step is equal to the total supply of money less the amount of transactions money demanded as a function of the income determined in the last step; otherwise, there will be what Keynes called repercussions. You can go through the circuit of the diagrams again, using the new supply of money available for liquidity purposes, until the system converges to equilibrium if the system is stable. This is an example of attempting to present a general equilibrium model as a system of one-way causation, and later theorists abandoned it in favor of the $IS-LM$ analysis of J. R. Hicks and Alvin Hansen.[25]

Suppose we have determined the level of income and employment, and find that it is too low for full employment. Keynes cautioned that in the 1930s there would be difficulty eliminating the unemployment. He believed that manipulating the amount of money would not bring the rate of interest low enough to bring a full-employment level of income because, in the first place, the minimum level of interest established by liquidity preference was above the marginal efficiency of capital at full employment (i.e., the curve in figure 19.4 becomes elastic at low rates of interest) (*The General Theory*, pp. 308–9). But even if the rate of interest could be changed, it would not be associated with much change in the rate of investment (i.e., figure 19.3 is inelastic) (p. 252). Therefore full employment will require a "somewhat comprehensive socialization of investment" (p. 378).

Because of the difficulty of *The General Theory*, a period of digestion was required, during which several notable controversies took place. One of these concerned Keynes's proposition on p. 63 of *The General Theory*, that saving was necessarily equal to investment. Since saving was done by both business and consumers, while investment (except housing) was done only by business, why were they necessarily equal? Eventually it was agreed that saving and investment must always be equal in one sense, that is, in the measured or ex post sense, since they are defined so that they must be identical. But in the desired or ex ante sense they are equal only in equilibrium, and when they are not equal national income changes so as to bring them into equality.

A second, extended controversy was over whether Keynes's liquidity preference theory of the rate of interest should be allowed to displace the loanable funds theory, according to which the rate of interest is determined by the intersection of the supply and demand for loanable funds.[26] By the 1960s it was agreed that if the problem is to determine the equilibrium level of the rate of interest the two theories are equivalent, because if the markets for goods and for factors of production are in equilibrium, then equality between the demand for and supply of money implies that the stock and flow demand for and supply of loans is equal, and vice versa. But the two theories are not the same in dynamic disequilibrium analysis, and recent developments in this field have not found it helpful to organize theories around either model. Specifically, the demand for money is now regarded as a special topic in capital theory, with income left out as a variable in favor of wealth and the rate of return as the arguments of the demand function.[27]

A third major controversy started by *The General Theory* was whether Keynes was correct in his interpretation of classical economics, and just what it was that distinguished Keynesian economics from the classics. This controversy was the more bitter because of Keynes's polemics; as Lawrence Klein said, Keynes was the winning economist but the losing gentleman. One definite winner in the Keynes–classics controversy, however, was John R. Hicks, who provided a diagrammatic interpretation that became standard. (Because Alvin Hansen of Harvard did much to popularize it, it has become known as the Hicks–Hansen diagram.) In the diagram (figure 19.5), the *IS* curve shows combinations of interest rates and levels of income which would give equilibrium in the goods and services market. Starting from a position of equilibrium along the *IS* curve, if income rises so will the amount of saving. In order to maintain equilibrium the amount of investment has to rise, which requires that the rate of interest fall. Similarly, the *LM* curve shows equilibrium positions in the money market. If the level of income rises with a given money supply, the transactions demand for money increases. Equilibrium requires that the liquidity demand for money be reduced, and the rate of interest must rise to achieve that. Therefore the *LM* curve has a positive slope, and the *IS* curve a negative slope. Their intersection gives the combination of interest rates and income for which both markets are simultaneously in equilibrium.[28]

Not only does this construction demonstrate that *The General Theory* is really a general equilibrium system, with the interest rate, income, and employment determined simultaneously, it also provided economists with an interpretation of the fundamental difference between Keynes and the classics. In Hicks's interpretation, the difference is in the shape of the functions. Suppose in figure 19.6 that equilibrium is at point A, involving unemployment because the level of income is so low. An attempt by the monetary authorities to reduce the interest rate by expanding the quantity

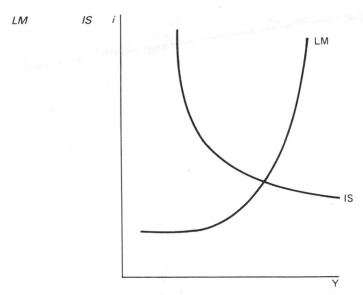

**Figure 19.5** From J. R. Hicks, "Mr Keynes and the Classics; a Suggested Interpretation". *Econometrica*, 1937, pp. 147–59. Reproduced by permission of The Econometric Society.

of money changes *LM* to *LM'*. Although in general the *LM* curve is shifted to the right, in the range where it is horizontal no change occurs because the economy has already reached what Keynes called "the minimal level of interest acceptable to the generality of wealth holders" (*The General Theory*, p. 309). However, in the part of the *LM* curve with a positive slope, monetary policy is effective.

Alternatively, even if the *LM* curve does respond to the change in monetary policy, the *IS* curve may be nearly vertical, as in figure 19.7. Then even though the rate of interest is reduced, income does not increase much. This is the case where the marginal efficiency of capital schedule is inelastic. Both figure 19.6 and figure 19.7 show the kind of arguments that led economists in the 1930s and 1940s to downplay monetary policy and to urge reliance on fiscal policy.

Keynes's antagonist Professor Pigou took a different route in reconciling Keynes and the classics. Keynes had argued that wage cuts would be ineffective in combating a depression because the money released from the transactions circulation would not lower the rate of interest. Pigou said that Keynes had overlooked the wealth effect (later called the Pigou effect): lower prices resulting from lower wages would increase the real value of money balances and thereby stimulate consumer spending.[29]

A different development of ideas in *The General Theory* led to the formation of a branch of economic theory that was very prominent in the period of the late 1950s to the early 1970s – the modern theories of

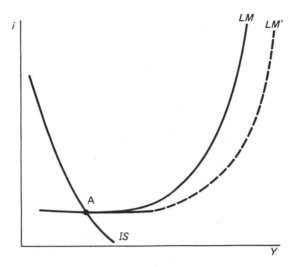

**Figure 19.6** From J. R. Hicks, "Mr Keynes and the Classics; a Suggested Interpretation". *Econometrica*, 1937, pp. 147–59. Reproduced by permission of The Econometric Society.

economic growth. The article which stimulated all this was R. F. Harrod's "An Essay in Dynamic Theory" in the *Economic Journal*, 1939. He assumed, with Keynes, that in equilibrium $I = S$. The savings function is $S = sY$, where $s$ is both the average and marginal propensity to save. The investment function is not the marginal efficiency of capital, but rather a dynamic function often used in business cycle analysis, the accelerator. According to this theory, $I$ is a function of the rate of change of $Y$: $I = vdY$. (Note that since $I$ is the rate of change of the capital stock $K$, the above relation can be written $dK = vdY$, which implies that $v = dK/dY$, the marginal capital – output ratio). Putting the savings and investment functions into the $I = S$ equilibrium condition, $sY = vdY$, or $dY/Y = s/v$. Since $dY/Y$ is the rate of growth of the economy, we have derived the condition that economic growth depends on the propensity to save and on the marginal capital–output ratio.

Harrod pointed out that $v$ could be interpreted as either the measured $dK$ divided by the measured $dY$, or as the $dK$ that would be required to satisfy entrepreneurs that the new capital stock was at the correct level for the new income. In the latter sense, using $v_r$ to show that we are thinking of the required $v$, $dY/Y = s/v_r = G_w$, called by Harrod the warranted rate of growth. Now the actual rate of growth does not have to equal the warranted rate of growth, and even if it did the rate of growth would not have to be the one that gave continuous full employment to a growing labor force. Harrod's essay, and his later book, *Towards a Dynamic Economics* (1948), were concerned with what happened when the actual rate of growth was either greater or less than the warranted rate. He found

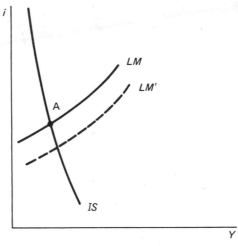

**Figure 19.7**

that if the two rates deviated, the effect was cumulative – the actual rate got further away from the warranted rate as time went on. This was called the "knife-edge" problem of growth.

This simple model of growth is actually called the Harrod–Domar model, because in 1946 Evsey Domar published an article[30] dealing with a different problem but which led to the same growth-rate equation. His approach was to argue that investment meant an increase in the capacity to produce national income, and to ask what rate of growth of investment would keep actual income produced equal to the full employment capacity. Interestingly, his answer was equivalent to Harrod's equation.

Growth theory rapidly became much more complex after Harrod and Domar, but they are the pioneers of a major field of economics.[31] The other contributions to economic growth theory, however, got away from the simple Keynesian concepts into neo-classical concepts such as the production function, and eventually the theory of growth became entangled in the Cambridge–Cambridge controversy.

To return to the influence of Keynes, there was a time in the early 1960s when economists like Walter Heller were successfully handling national economic policy on a Keynesian basis. But years of "stagflation" have raised unsolved questions about the proper policies to use and have pointed up the need for theories to understand the modern economy. People are working with alternative theories – disequilibrium macroeconomics and rational expectations, for two examples[32] – and some of these alternatives are actually different interpretations of Keynes.[33] Macroeconomics is in considerable ferment, but it cannot be understood without knowing Keynes.

While *The General Theory* was the high point of Keynes's career, it was by no means the end of it. He suffered a heart attack the year after *The General Theory* was published, so that his activity was considerably reduced. But he did publish a few interpretive articles on his book, and in 1940 published a pamphlet, *How to Pay for the War*, which showed how he applied his analysis to inflationary rather than depression conditions. He was very active during the war in making and negotiating post-war international monetary plans, including in particular his participation in the Bretton Woods conference at which the International Monetary Fund and the World Bank were established, as well as helping negotiate a major United States loan to Britain in 1945. In 1946 he had his fatal heart attack.

## Notes

1 Two quantitative measures of Keynes's impact: in the *Survey of Contemporary Economics* volumes published by the American Economic Association in 1948–52, Keynes had 98 index entries to 56 for the runner-up (see D. E. Moggridge, "The Influence of Keynes on the Economics of his Time," in Milo Keynes (ed.), *Essays on John Maynard Keynes* (Cambridge, 1975). Also, George J. Stigler and Claire Freidland, "The Pattern of Citation Practices in Economics," *History of Political Economy* (*HOPE*), 1979, pp. 1–20, found that Keynes was the most frequently cited economist (32, to 21 for the runner-up) in the sample of articles which they analyzed.
2 Don Patinkin, *Keynes' Monetary Thought: A Study of Its Development* (Durham, NC, 1976), p. 139.
3 Gottfried Haberler, *Prosperity and Depression* (League of Nations, 1937), is a source of detailed summaries of this literature. T. W. Hutchison, *A Review of Economic Doctrines 1870–1929* (Oxford, 1953), gives a good shorter treatment.
4 This is the formulation of A. C. Pigou, Marshall's pupil and the representative of classical economics who received the most severe criticism in *The General Theory*. See his article, "The Value of Money," *Quarterly Journal of Economics*, 1917–18, pp. 38–65, which is regarded as an authoritative source of neoclassical monetary theory and has been reprinted many times.
5 *Money Credit and Commerce* (London, 1920), Book I, chap. iv.
6 *A Treatise on Money* (London, 1930), vol. I, p. 231.
7 *The Purchasing Power of Money*, p. 60. The transactions and the cash-balances version are formally equivalent; $1/k \equiv V$. See Mark Blaug, *Economic Theory in Retrospect* 4th edn, (New York, 1985), p. 153.
8 In modern macroeconomics, the real rate of interest is defined as the monetary rate corrected for the expected rate of inflation.
9 This exposition follows Wicksell, *Lectures on Political Economy*, vol. 2, *Money* (London, 1935). Other sources for Wicksell's monetary theory are his book *Interest and Prices* (London, 1936), and a mathematical treatment by Ragnar Frisch, "Frisch on Wicksell," in H. Spiegel (ed.), *The Development of Economic Thought* (New York, 1952), pp. 652–99.
10 Keynes called this the "Gibson paradox" in volume II of *A Treatise of Money*, after A. H. Gibson who published similar data in the 1920s.

11  See P. A. Samuelson, "What Classical and Neoclassical Monetary Theory Really Was," *Canadian Journal of Economics*, 1968, pp. 1–15, for a mathematical exposition.

12  Actually the book Keynes singled out for attack as representative of "classical" theory was Pigou's *Theory of Unemployment*; Keynes attacked this as having nothing to offer in determining total employment. See *The General Theory*, in vol. VII of the *Collected Writings* (London, 1973), p. 260. All references are to this work, but the pagination is the same as in the original edition.

13  Adam Smith was also born on June 5.

14  Two recent biographies are Robert Skidelsky, *John Maynard Keynes: Hopes Betrayed, 1883–1920* (New York, 1983), and Charles H. Hessian, *John Maynard Keynes: A Personal Biography of the Man Who Revolutionized Capitalism and the Way We Live* (New York, 1984). The latter attempts to relate Keynes's unorthodox personal life to his accomplishments. Roy Harrod, *The Life of John Maynard Keynes* (London, 1951) is the standard biography, focusing on Keynes's professional life and accomplishments. D. E. Moggridge, *John Maynard Keynes* (New York, 1976), is an excellent short biography, including many insights gathered from the publication since 1970 of letters and other documents in the 30 volume series of *The Collected Writings of John Maynard Keynes* (London, 1971–82).

15  Moggridge, "Influence of Keynes," p. 55.

16  In 1925 he married Lydia Lopokova, a Russian ballerina. She had previously been married to Randolpho Barocchi, but a recent biographer of Lydia Keynes said that he had never asked her about Barocchi, knowing how ballerinas dislike reference to their first husbands. See Richard Buckle, "On Loving Lydia," in Milo Keynes (ed.), *Essays on Keynes*. Lydia Keynes died in 1983. Milo Keynes (ed.), *Lydia Lopokova* (New York, 1984) is a collection of essays by people who knew Lydia and Maynard.

17  In addition to Moggridge, "Influence of Keynes," this material has been exploited by Don Patinkin, *Keynes' Monetary Thought*. Patinkin's book is more detailed than is Moggridge's on the theory, but contains no biography. An even more detailed exposition of the theory is Victoria Chick, *Macroeconomics after Keynes: A Reconsideration of the General Theory* (Cambridge, Mass., 1983). This book is a chapter-by-chapter exposition which tackles all the concepts, the ones that have dropped out of the literature as well as the ones that remain.

18  This interpretation follows Patinkin, *Keynes' Monetary Thought*, chapter 4. It is a measure of the difficulty of interpreting this part of the *Treatise* that different interpretations are provided by J. R. Hicks, *Critical Essays in Monetary Theory* (Oxford, 1967) and by G. L. S. Shackle, *The Years of High Theory* (Cambridge, 1967).

19  Harry Johnson, "*The General Theory* after Twenty-Five Years," *American Economic Review Papers and Proceedings*, 1961, pp. 1–17, is particularly good on *The General Theory* as economic literature.

20  The 45-degree line can properly be called the aggregate supply curve only with the understanding that each point on the line reflects the real wage which corresponds to the marginal product of the quantity of labor required to produce the given amount of national income. See Don Patinkin, *Anticipations*

*of the General Theory?* (Chicago, Ill., 1982), p. 152. Chapter 5 of this book thoroughly discusses the errors and obscurities in Keynes' presentation of aggregate supply in *The General Theory*.

21 The econometric work on the Keynesian system is surveyed in chapters VIII and IX of the second edition of Lawrence R. Klein, *The Keynesian Revolution* (New York, 1966), and by Don Patinkin, "Keynes and Econometrics," *Econometrica*, 1976, pp. 1091–1123.

22 Keynes attributed the notion of the multiplier to R. F. Kahn, "The Relation of Home Investment to Unemployment," *Economic Journal*, 1931. Kahn, however, was by no means the first to develop the theory; Nicholas Johannsen, *A Neglected Point in Connection with Crises* (1908) was very clear on it, and there are 19th-century references as well. See Don Patinkin, "Keynes and the Multiplier," *The Manchester School*, 1978, pp. 209–23.

23 "The Simple Mathematics of Income Determination," in *Income, Employment, and Public Policy: Essays in Honor of Alvin H. Hansen* (New York, 1948).

24 *The General Theory*, pp. 128–9. Here Keynes was indulging in his polemical rhetoric. Actually economists had been calling for relief via public works since the beginning of the Great Depression. See J. Ronnie Davis, *The New Economics and the Old Economists* (Chicago, 1971) for the United States and Donald Winch, *Economics and Policy* (New York, 1969) for Great Britain. But they did not have the theory to draw on, which was what Keynes provided. And it is true that statesmen, together with one economist, R. G. Hawtrey, opposed public works; the "Treasury view" was that capital formed as public works would be subtracted from private capital, so that total employment would not change. Hawtrey's point was different; it was that public works raised employment only because credit was created, so the government could get the same effect by increasing credit to private borrowers. See K. Hancock, "The Reduction of Unemployment as a Problem of Public Policy, 1920–1929," *Economic History Review*, 1962, pp. 328–43.

25 *The General Theory*, chapter 18, is entitled "The General Theory Restated," and is the chapter where Keynes pulled all the threads together in the fashion outlined in this paragraph.

26 Harry Johnson relates the bitter debates over this at Cambridge, with Dennis Robertson taking a great deal of punishment because of his advocacy of loanable funds. See "Cambridge in the 1950s," *Encounter*, 1974, reprinted in Elizabeth S. Johnson and Harry G. Johnson, *The Shadow of Keynes* (Oxford, 1978).

27 D. J. Ott., A. F. Ott, and J. H. Yoo, *Macroeconomic Theory* (New York, 1975), chapter 9. As an exception, in a model which assumes that transactions are made even though markets are not cleared, both liquidity preference and loanable funds theories are used at the same time. See P. G. Korliras, "A Disequilibrium Macroeconomic Model," *Quarterly Journal of Economics*, 1975, pp. 56–80.

28 John R. Hicks, "Mr. Keynes and the 'Classics'," *Econometrica*, 1937, pp. 47–59. In this article, in a masterpiece of understatement, Hicks characterized *The General Theory* as a useful book.

29 A. C. Pigou, "The Classical Stationary State," *Economic Journal*, 1943, pp. 343–51.

30 "Capital Expansion, Rate of Growth, and Employment," *Econometrica*, 1946, pp. 137–47.
31 A good exposition is Hywel G. Jones, *An Introduction to Modern Theories of Economic Growth* (New York, 1976). I have used his notation, which conforms to general usage, rather than Harrod's. For a more detailed survey, F. H. Hahn and R. C. O. Matthews, "The Theory of Economic Growth: A Survey," *Economic Journal*, 1964, pp. 779–902, is notable.
32 See P. G. Korliras and R. S. Thorn (eds), *Modern Macroeconomics* (New York, 1979) for sample articles.
33 Axel Leijonhufvud, *On Keynesian Economics and the Economics of Keynes* (Oxford, 1968) is the most influential of these.

# 20
# Modern Times: Macroeconomics

The years since Keynes's *General Theory* have been a period of rapid development and considerable controversy in macroeconomics. From the late 1940s through the middle part of the 1960s the major focus was on the development of Keynes's ideas and the working out of their policy implications. The leader in this enterprise was Alvin Hansen, who at Harvard taught such leaders in macroeconomics as Paul Samuelson and James Tobin as well as making significant contributions of his own.

Hansen, born in 1887, was forty-nine years old when *The General Theory* was published. He had been a specialist in business cycles since the days of his PhD dissertation, written at the University of Wisconsin in an institutionalist setting. He moved on to absorb the European business cycle literature, which attributed the turning points of cycles to exogenous changes in innovations, population, and the like. Like Viner, Schumpeter, and others he wrote an unfavorable review of *The General Theory*, but, unexpectedly, when he was hired at Harvard he changed his mind and became a Keynesian convert. In 1948 he said that the publications which had changed the direction of economics were the *Wealth of Nations*, the books of the marginalists (Jevons, Walras, and Menger), and *The General Theory*.[1]

Hansen worked at great length on the problems of fiscal policy using the complete Keynesian system rather than simple multiplier models (his most influential book was *Fiscal Policy and Business Cycles*, 1941). His use of the *IS–LM* model was so pervasive that it became known as the Hicks–Hansen diagram (although created exclusively by Hicks). Among other ideas, he was the first to integrate the multiplier and the accelerator. Paul Samuelson analyzed the model using difference equations in a famous article, but credits Hansen with the idea and an initial numerical analysis.[2] The accelerator was a long-standing explanation of the fact that investment is much more variable than consumption.[3] If $B$ is the quantity of plant and equipment needed to produce one unit of consumer goods, and $C$ is the total amount of consumption, then the quantity of capital, $K$, required is $K = BC$, and $I = dK/dt = B(dC/dt)$, taking derivatives with respect to time. In difference equation form, $I = B(C_t - C_{t-1})$ where the subscripts refer to properly defined periods of time. The amount of this period's consumption is assumed to be determined by last period's income, a proposition made popular by Dennis Robertson. This is expressed as $C_t = AY_{t-1}$, where $A$ is the marginal propensity to consume. Since $Y_t = C_t + I_t$, we have

$$Y_t = AY_{t-1} + B(AY_{1-1} - AY_{t-2})$$

or          $$Y_t = A(1+B) \, Y_{t-1} - AB \, (Y_{t-2}).$$

Samuelson analyzed this second-order difference equation, showing that it could generate damped cycles, explosive cycles, exponential growth, or an asymptotic approach to a constant value of income, depending on the sizes of $A$ and $B$.[4] This was a popular type of dynamic analysis for many years.

In the late 1930s Hansen explained the low level of investment which brought on the Great Depression as the result of a chronic stagnation of the economy. This stagnation resulted partly from declining population growth, and partly, he said, from the closing of the frontier (which is usually dated as happening in 1890). No longer did westward expansion require large investments in farms, railroads, and towns. His remedy for the alleged stagnation was fiscal policy. Of course, World War II and its aftermath of inventory shortage, pent-up consumer spending, and the liquidity built up from accumulated war-time saving completely changed the picture, and the typical worry became inflation rather than stagnation (or, in the 1970s, the combination called stagflation: price inflation combined with high unemployment).

Detailed studies of parts of the Keynesian model formed a major part of the development of macroeconomics after World War II. The consumption function was a popular subject. The simple Keynesian formulation, $C = a + bY$, or its lagged version as expressed above in the multiplier-accelerator model, implies that $C/Y$, the average propensity to consume, falls as income rises. But Simon Kuznets, Nobel Prize winner in 1971, found that the average propensity was constant over a sequence of 30-year periods since 1869. Various extensions of the consumption function were proposed. One is the life-cycle theory of Nobel Prize winner Franco Modigliani in association with various colleagues.[5] According to this idea, people plan for a constant level of consumer spending over their lives. During the early years, while they are working, some of their income is saved to provide for the retirement years. The annual consumption is equal to expected life-time income ÷ expected years of life, which is equivalent to consumption = (working life/total life) (annual income). This equation has to be modified to include consumption out of inherited wealth, any desired level of wealth you wish to leave your heirs, interest earned on saving, and the like. Note that if this is true for each person, a population with a preponderance of young people will be saving in the aggregate, whereas a graying population (like the United States when the baby-boomers reach age sixty-five sometime after AD 2000) will be dis-saving. Thus a shifting short-run consumption function is compatible with a stable Kuznets-type long-run one.

Milton Friedman, whose major research was monetarism as an alternative to the Keynesian system, also worked on the consumption function to show that the Keynesian version was inaccurate. His approach was to say that consumption was proportional to *permanent* disposable income, $C = A$(permanent income). Permanent income is a weighted average of past and current incomes, on the theory that your expected income depends on the history of your past incomes (the present one gets higher weights). Any unexpected changes of income – windfall gains or losses – are not consumed but are saved, since they do not enter into your currently expected permanent income.[6] Modern research combines both Friedman's and Modigliani's version into one model.

While research into parts of the Keynesian model flourished (Nobel Prize winner James Tobin's detailed work on the financial markets expanded on the simple Keynesian liquidity preference function, for another example to complement the consumption work just reviewed), a major change in focus into an overall evaluation of the Keynesian system was provided by Axel Leijonhufvud.[7] He claimed that the standard Hicks–Hansen *IS–LM* model, being an equilibrium model, did not capture the essence of Keynes, which was disequilibrium. In Keynes's world information is not perfect (entrepreneurs work on the basis of animal spirits or hunches), markets do not clear rapidly but remain out of equilibrium for a long time, and while they are out of equilibrium prices remain sticky but quantities of output and employment change. The reaction to this book was both a long argument about what Keynes really meant (Joan Robinson, for example, weighed in with the claim that Hansen's followers were Bastard Keynesians; Keynes really dealt strictly with a Marshallian short period with expectations, uncertain, always changing, unrealizable, controlling the level of aggregate demand) and some attempts to model disequilibrium formally.[8]

Macroeconomics changed drastically with the onset of inflation in the 1960s. Some of the new tools and outlook had started earlier but became accepted by many economists with the need to move past what Sir John Hicks called the "fixprice" models of Keynes. The Keynesian model could explain "demand-pull" inflation, in which $C + I + G$ increased to a level greater than full-employment output at constant prices. This excess aggregate demand resulted in price increases. By contrast, in "cost-push" inflation the price of an input, such as labor or imported oil, rose exogenously, causing prices of final goods to rise as a result. In the former case policy may require higher taxes or lower government spending; in the latter a Reagan-type union-busting action (as in the case of the airline controllers' strike of 1981) might be suggested. One of the tools added to the model to help analyze inflation was the Phillips curve, originally developed as the result of empirical research in British economic history.[9]

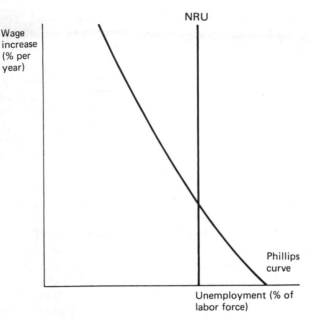

**Figure 20.1**

In this curve, the rate of change of wages is on the vertical axis, the rate of unemployment is on the horizontal. In Phillips's original research, higher wage increases were associated with less unemployment. There was, in fact, one rate of unemployment (about 6 percent) which would yield a zero increase in wages, or, in a cost-push model, no inflation. Adapting the Phillips curve to the modern American economy and more directly to inflation problems, Professors Paul Samuelson and Robert Solow plotted percentage annual price increases rather than wage increases on the vertical axis.[10] In this formulation, a policy choice is posed: how much unemployment do Congress and the President wish? How much inflation? The goal of full employment, the desideratum of the 1930s, might involve as much as a 5 or 6 percent annual rate of inflation. The alternative goal of no inflation might involve considerable unemployment.

If the reader gets a copy of *The Statistical Abstract of the United States* and tries to plot a Phillips curve for the United States from the 1960s to the present, there will be a pattern of dots running all over the place, with what seems to be one curve for the 1960s, another for the last half of the 1970s, and lots of noise. Such empirical confusion can be straightened out with the help of two concepts. One is the "expectations-augmented" Phillips curve – in a period of rising prices people expect price increases and build them into their wage and other price agreements. A given level of unemployment is associated with a higher rate of price increase than in an era of stable prices, such as the 1980s. The Phillips curve shifts around, depending on the expectations of the future rate of price change.[11]

The other development of Phillips-curve reasoning is that the curve is a short-run relationship. There is a long-run curve, which is vertical at what Friedman called the "natural rate of unemployment."[12] This is the amount of unemployment at which the average real wage and the price level is constant. In figure 20.1 this long-run Phillips curve is labelled NRU. Any attempt to reduce unemployment below the NRU will result in short-run inflation as the economy moves along a given Phillips curve. But the inflation changes expectations and shifts the Phillips curve up. In the process as prices rise real balances fall, aggregate real demand falls, and unemployment returns to the natural rate with a higher rate of inflation.

The introduction of Professor Friedman's views on the Phillips curve is a good place to turn to monetarism, which for long was the rival to Keynesian theory as the highly significant stream of macroeconomics after World War II. Monetarism is more or less Friedman's creation, in its theoretical, empirical, and policy aspects.[13] His theoretical contributions include a revision of the theory of the demand for money to include not only Keynes's theory that the liquidity demand for money depends on the yield from holding bonds but also equities, real physical wealth, and human capital. In empirical work he finds the substitution between money and these assets is low, so that changes in money affect nominal income directly rather than going into liquidity preferences as Keynes had it in *The General Theory*.[14]

Friedman's major empirical work on money was his long *A Monetary History of the United States, 1867–1960*, written with Anna Schwartz. The most controversial aspect of this turned out to be the Friedman–Schwartz contention that the Great Depression which started in 1929 was the result of mistaken Federal Reserve policy which allowed the monetary base to decline, rather than secular stagnation as proposed by Hansen or a sharp fall in the consumption function as Professor Peter Temin suggests. Another influential empirical paper, which resulted in much econometric work attempting to rebut it, was "The Relative Stability of Monetary Velocity and the Investment Multiplier in the United States, 1897–1958," written with David Meiselman and published in 1963 in Commission on Money and Credit, *Stabilization Policies* (Englewood Cliffs, NJ, 1963). The paper concluded that the money stock was a much better predictor of induced consumption spending than total autonomous spending ($G + I$, in a simple Keynesian model). If this is true, then policy-makers should rely on monetary rather than on fiscal policy. Taken altogether, Friedman's work and that of his disciples resulted in what Harry Johnson called "the monetarist counter-revolution."[15] But whereas the Keynesian revolution resulted in Keynesian domination of macroeconomics for many years, the Friedman monetarist revolution resulted in the absorption of monetarist ideas, albeit in a softened version (for example, rather than saying "only money matters" the eclectic macroeconomist says that "money matters, and of course other things do too"). Part of this accommodation is no doubt due to the fact that another pioneering group, the rational expectations theorists, came along. But Friedman's work was presented in a challenging form and many people responded to the challenge; because a good reference is available, the many exchanges between James Tobin and Friedman may be cited.[16]

While Friedman views monetary policy as much more potent than fiscal policy for controlling the economy, his empirical studies persuaded him that the lag between changing the money supply and the resulting impact on the economy was so variable that it would be a mistake to try to change the money supply in reaction to short-run changes in the economy. Instead, his policy recommendation was to provide the economy with a steady, constantly growing money supply at a rate corresponding to the long-run growth rate of output. This will give a monetary environment which does not provide shocks to the economy and which gives a steady base for expectations. Like other Friedman propositions, this one is influential and controversial. Certainly the behavior of the President and the Congress in the Reagan years more or less eliminated fiscal policy for the time being; whether it can be restored as an option is to be seen. And in response to the monetarists' emphasis on the money supply, the Federal Reserve changed its policy criterion from the short-term interest rate, which Keynesian analysis stressed, to setting targets for the stock of money.

Many ideas in economics flare brightly for a time; only history reveals whether they then die out or become as permanently ensconced as Keynesianism and monetarism. One such movement is post-Keynesian economics, which supports two journals (*Post-Keynesian Economics* and the *Cambridge Journal of Economics*) and has a sizeable number of adherents who quarrel with the standard Keynesian macro model. Their disputes include

1   The insistence that the pricing policies of large firms are crucial; because they hold that prices follow a policy of cost plus a percentage mark-up, adjustments in their view take the form of quantity rather than price changes.
2   Because the marginal propensity to save is low for workers compared to the more wealthy receivers of profits, the amount of saving in an economy depends on the distribution of income.
3   Investment depends, as Keynes said, on animal spirits, which leads to waves of optimism and pessimism and hence to a cyclical economy.
4   Investment by firms is largely self-financed so that investment may be brought to a halt by a lack of funds when the corporation has used up its accumulated cash. (Some post-Keynesians, such as Professor Hyman Minsky, allow for debt finance and analyze the relation of money to investment and the business cycle.)

Although writings in this vein date back to the early 1970s,[17] the movement remains distinct rather than widely incorporated into current research, as rational expectations has been.

Macroeconomists since Keynes have known that spending decisions, both on investment and on consumption, depend on people's views of the future. In the 1950s and 1960s a standard way to model these views for theory and empirical research was adaptive expectations, the idea that you predict the current level of, for example, prices will change next period by some fraction of the difference between the forecast you made last period and the actual prices which history brought forth. This makes a neat formula, $dp/dt_e = a(p - p_e)$, where the subscript $e$ refers to expected values, but it is a backward-looking formulation and the actual value of $a$ remains a question. In the 1970s an alternative proposition, rational expectations, came into prominence.

John Muth originally proposed rational expectations in 1961 in connection with research in the securities markets. He suggested that people use all available information and make a forecast whose expected value is the same as the solution to the correct structural model of the market (or the economy). However, because of random elements in the economy people do not have perfect foresight, and actual prices or outputs differ from the expected ones by random amounts. If they differed systematically, it would pay to improve your data collection or forecasting technique. This suggestion was taken up by R. E. Lucas, Jr, in the early 1970s in connection with research on inflation and business cycles, and, in combination with the assumption that markets function like competitive markets and clear rapidly, it provided some very striking results. Lucas, together with Thomas Sargent and Neil Wallace, created "the new classical economics," whose cornerstones were the theorems that money was neutral in the long run (you could not change real output by raising the money supply) and that only surprise, unexpected changes in the money supply could have any short-run effects.[18]

How can this be so? Suppose current output is equal to the trend rate of output (e.g., 1.8 per cent greater than last year), plus some fraction of the difference between actual and expected prices (if prices are higher than expected, output will be encouraged by the windfall), plus a random error term whose expected mean is zero. The price level is affected by monetary policy, but the public correctly anticipates the effect of the current monetary policy and any changes which are made in it. Since actual and (rationally) expected prices are equal except for the error term, current output must equal its trend value plus the error term. Monetary policy drops out as a determinant of output, and, since employment depends on output, of employment.[19]

While this conclusion is revolting to the common sense, as Francis Horner once remarked about some of Malthus's more outrageous ideas, it has attracted devotees because, unlike adaptive expectations, it is based on a market-clearing and utility-maximizing model rather than *ad hoc* (i.e., arbitrary and unexplained) conditions. It is part of a major contemporary attempt to base macroeconomics firmly on standard microeconomic assumptions such as utility maximization. It also has received a relativistic interpretation (recall from chapter 2 that relativists relate changes in economic thought to the conditions of the time): Professor Samuelson suggests that after 1973, with stagflation, "The mixed economy was sick; and it was that sickness that opened the way for the virus of the Lucas rational-expectationist new classical economics."[20]

From study of previous revolutions or paradigm changes we expect new (or revived old) ideas which challenge prevailing thought to generate debate, and this is true of the rational expectations idea. Of many critical articles, one by Alan S. Blinder is excellent for clearly outlining the contrasting positions of Keynesians and new classical economics. In particular, Blinder criticizes the market-clearing assumption ("It is hard, for me at least, to look at what has gone on in this country – not to mention in Europe – since 1974 and see clearing labor markets",[21] and declares that there is a scientific role for starting at the macro level and inductively deriving models from observations, as compared to the Lucas–Sargent preference for starting at the micro level and deducing behavior from maximizing principles. His reluctance to follow the microfoundations path is that this precludes "the colossal market failures that created macroeconomics . . . "[22] In the fury of current research it is not possible to predict the judgment of the future concerning the lasting role of rational expectations.

Although there is not space here to develop the topic in detail, the Keynesian model was used to develop growth models, and the reaction to these stimulated other growth models. Because of the stagnation of the 1930s in advanced countries and the post-World War II concern with underdeveloped countries, growth was a hot topic. The Keynesian model was converted into the Harrod–Domar model, whose conclusion is that the growth rate, $dY/Y$, is equal to the savings ratio divided by the capital–output ratio, $s/v$ (see Chapter 19 for a discussion of the Harrod model). A feature of this model is that if this growth rate is less than enough income growth to keep the growing labor force employed, there will be long-run stagnation. In reaction to this, Robert Solow in 1956, and others, developed a neo-classical growth model, in which there can be substitution between labor and capital and the capital–output ratio is no longer fixed constant.[23] Another influential alternative was the linear growth model with several different production processes; this was analyzed by John von Neumann in the 1930s but became a popular model only later. However important growth models are at a time when US economic growth is significantly below that of Japan and other economies, it is not feasible to do more than notice them now.

## Notes

1 Seymour Harris (ed.), *The New Economics* (New York, 1948), p. 133.
2 P. A. Samuelson, *Collected Scientific Papers*, vol. II (Cambridge, Mass., 1966), p. 1123.
3 Gottfried Haberler, *Prosperity and Depression* (League of Nations, 1937), p. 87, traces it back to Mentor Bounitian in 1903.

4  See the articles "Interactions between the Multiplier Analysis and the Principle of Acceleration" and "A Synthesis of the Principle of Acceleration and the Multiplier" in *Collected Scientific Papers*, vol. II.

5  See, for example, Franco Modigliani, "The Life Cycle Hypothesis of Saving, the Demand for Wealth, and the Supply of Capital," *Social Research*, vol. 33, no. 2, 1966.

6  Friedman, *A Theory of the Consumption Function*, (Princeton, NJ, 1957) is the source for the development of this idea.

7  Professor Robert Solow gives a handy guide to the pronunciation of this formidable name; it is "Axel." The book was *On Keynesian Economics and the Economics of Keynes*. As in Hansen's case, it is one of the rare examples where non-mathematical formulations are successful.

8  See E. Roy Weintraub, *Microfoundations: The Compatibility of Microeconomics and Macroeconomics* (Cambridge, 1979).

9  A. W. Phillips, "The Relation between Unemployment and the Rate of Change of Money Wages in the United Kingdom, 1861–1957," *Economica*, 1958, pp. 283–99.

10  "Analytical Aspects of Anti-Inflation Policy," *American Economic Review*, May 1960, reprinted in Samuelson, *Collected Scientific Papers*, vol. 2, pp. 1336–53.

11  See Milton Friedman, "The Role of Monetary Policy", *American Economic Review*, March 1968, pp. 1–17; Professor Edmund Phelps also independently stated this proposition in 1967.

12  Ibid.

13  Niels Thygesen, "Thygesen on Friedman", in H. W. Spiegel and W. J. Samuels, *Contemporary Economists in Perspective* (Greenwich, Conn., 1984), is an excellent source of information on Friedman's long career.

14  See Thygesen, "On Friedman," p. 326.

15  Johnson, "The Keynesian Revolution and the Monetarist Counter-Revolution," *American Economic Review Papers and Proceedings*, May 1971, pp. 1–14.

16  See Douglas Dale Purvis, "Purvis on Tobin," in Spiegel and Samuels, *Contemporary Economists in Perspective*.

17  See Alfred S. Eichner and J. A. Kregel, "An Essay on Post-Keynesian Theory: A New Paradigm in Economics," *Journal of Economic Literature*, December 1975, pp. 1293–1314. Three useful appraisals of post-Keynesian economics, some favorable, some not, are provided by L. Tarshis, Janet Yellen, and James R. Crotty in the *American Economic Review Papers and Proceedings*, May 1980, pp. 10–28.

18  A series of articles in the *Journal of Economic Literature* provide an accessible introduction: A. M. Santomero and John L. Seater, "The Inflation-Unemployment Trade-Off: A Critique of the Literature," June 1978, pp. 499–544; Bruce Kantor, "Rational Expectations and Economic Thought," December 1979, pp. 1422–41; and R. Maddock and M. Carter, "A Child's Guide to Rational Expectations," March 1982, pp. 39–51. The original papers are really at the graduate level.

19  D. K. H. Begg, *The Rational Expectations Revolution in Macroeconomics: Theories and Evidence* (Baltimore, Md., 1982), chapter 6, is very clear on this.

20 "What Would Keynes Have Thought of Rational Expectations," *Collected Scientific Papers*, vol. 5, p. 294.
21 A. S. Blinder, "Keynes, Lucas, and Scientific Progress," *American Economic Review Papers and Proceedings*, May 1987, p. 132. A more advanced critical analysis is Robert Shiller, "Rational Expectations and the Dynamic Structure of Macroeconomic Models," *Journal of Monetary Economics*, vol. 4, January 1978.
22 Blinder, ibid., p. 135.
23 See Robert M. Solow, "A Contribution to the Theory of Economic Growth," *Quarterly Journal of Economics*, 1956, pp. 65–94. Professor Solow received the Nobel Prize for this theory. For growth theory to the middle of the 1960s see F. H Hahn and R. C. O. Matthews, "The Theory of Economic Growth: A Survey," in American Economic Association and the Royal Economic Society, *Surveys of Economic Theory*, vol. II, 1965.

# 21
# Modern Times: Econometrics and Microeconomics

The direction of economics since the days of John Maynard Keynes can be neatly summarized by comparing the opening sentences of the articles on cost in the 1925 edition of Palgrave's *Dictionary of Political Economy* and in the 1988 edition. The earlier article begins, "The *real* cost of production of any commodity is held to be the 'sum of the efforts and abstinences' requisite to make it ready for consumption . . ."[1] and the recent survey starts with ". . . suppose that the firm's . . . cost is described by the function $K:R_+^n \times \Omega \to R_+$, where : . . .$K(PQv,PQw)$ is the cost incurred by the firm in employing the vector of input quantities $v \in R_+^n$, given the input market conditions $\omega \in \Omega$ . . ."[2] The fifty years since publication of *The General Theory* has seen the core of economics dominated by mathematics, some of impressive complexity. In this chapter we shall highlight some of the most important developments of this period in microeconomics and econometrics, which have used more rarefied mathematics than macroeconomics.

## *Econometrics*

Econometrics, a combination of formulating theories in mathematical terms with the use of statistical techniques to apply data to these theories, began as far back as 1911 when Henry L. Moore published *Laws of Wages: An Essay in Statistical Analysis*. While William Stanley Jevons had studied the statistics of inflation after the gold discoveries of the mid-nineteenth century and Irving Fisher had worked with the statistics of money and prices around 1900, the approach which distinguished Moore from their work was that Moore used the new theories of statistics being developed in Britain by Pearson, Yule, and the like. The techniques which Moore adopted were, in particular, multiple correlation and contingency tables. He followed his studies of wages with work on business cycles which involved the calculation of demand curves for specific commodities, and eventually he turned to the study of commodities in which, he claimed, supply depended on lagged price. (That is, changes in the quantity of land planted to a given crop depended on how big the price change was last year as a percentage of price two years ago.) This turned out to be the first dynamic econometric model.[3]

Other significant early work included the attempts to derive empirical demand curves by Henry Schultz in the 1920s and 1930s, and the famous study of production functions by Paul Douglas and Charles E. Cobb.[4] Such work had progressed far enough and there were enough people working in the field, including Ragnar Frisch (Norway) and Jan Tinbergen (Holland), to result in the formation of The Econometric Society in 1930. The contributions of Frisch and Tinbergen were so important that they were awarded Nobel Prizes in 1969, the first year that the Nobel awards were extended to the field of economics.

Frisch's work in economics was always quantitative and far-ranging, including micro- and macro-theory as well as statistical methodology (in fact, he is said to have coined the terms of micro- and macro-economics in 1933 in an article called "Propagation Problems and Impulse Problems in Dynamic Economics").[5]

While the early American work focused on microeconomic analysis such as the estimation of supply and demand curves, Jan Tinbergen became famous in the 1930s for modeling complete systems of the economy. His work for the League of Nations, called *Statistical Testing of Business Cycle Theories*, involved the formulation of theories of investment and output where the variables were functions of the differences over time of things like profits, prices, and outputs. The coefficients of these functions were estimated by least squares.

Keynes was not in the least impressed by this work, and published a critical review in *The Economic Journal* in 1939.[6] His criticisms were that multiple correlation depended on having a complete list of factors to correlate, that these factors should be measurable, that they should be independent of one another, that Tinbergen used linear correlations throughout, that he determined time-lags by trial and error trends in an arbitrary way, and that his statistical data were frightfully inadequate. Tinbergen, said Keynes, if only he were funded to carry on his project, would be quite ready and happy to go a long way toward admitting that the results probably have no value. He said Tinbergen probably agreed with much of his (Keynes's) criticism, but that his reaction would be to engage another ten computers and drown his sorrows in arithmetic. (How could one reply to a critic like that?)[7]

The replies to Keynes's criticism of econometric models were eventually formulated by a group of people including Jacob Marshak, Tjalling Koopmans, Lawrence Klein and others. (Koopmans won the Nobel Prize in 1975 and Klein in 1980. The Nobel Committee reminds us that the empirical application of the econometric models would not have been possible without reasonably reliable data to work with in its award of the prize to Sir Richard Stone of Cambridge, England, in 1984; his contribution was the development of systems of national accounts. This work was done in the United States in the 1930s in the US Department of Commerce.) Many of the developers of econometrics had come to the United States at the outbreak of World War II, and after working at various universities were brought together at the Cowles Commission for Research in Economics. This foundation had originally been formed to apply mathematical methods to the prediction of stock market behavior but broadened into mathematical economics generally. Under Marshak's direction the Cowles Commission group developed the theory of modern econometrics, which was published in 1950 as *Statistical Inference in Dynamic Economic Models*.[8]

While this material is too technical for review here, a feeling for what is involved is provided by a look at the aggregate economic models which were developed employing these tools.[9] The models contained a dozen or more equations describing a sector of the economy, or defining an accounting identity such as GNP. The others, the structural equations which set forth the structure of the economy, included behavioral equations (such as what determines consumption), restraints such as a production function, and adjustment process equations describing reactions to disequilibrium. These equations included a stochastic error term, assumed to be random, since they could not include all the items influencing the variables. The model could determine as many variables as there were equations; other variables had to be given exogenously, from outside the model. The variables to be determined, the endogenous variables, were affected not only by the exogenous variables but by lagged values of endogenous variables; hence, the models were dynamic, describing a time path. Such a model could be used for forecasting if the parameters (such as the marginal propensity to consume out of labor income, for example) could be estimated. The econometric problems involved the best statistical techniques for estimating the parameters, given that only a few observations are typically available. Professor Christ's conclusion from reviewing these early models was that they "leave much to be desired." This was only natural in pioneering work, but thirty years later it was still judged that "Empirical experience with structural estimation has been less satisfactory" than the development of statistical theory such as estimation procedures, test statistics, and finite sample theory. "There is little evidence that the large macroeconomic models estimated to date are consistently able to forecast out of sample better than very naive alternative methods. Furthermore, contending schools of macroeconomic theory have not yet been resolved by econometric studies."[10]

This state of affairs has not been for lack of trying. During the 1960s the econometric models became larger (several hundred equations) as computer technology improved and more research support became available, such as that provided by the Brookings Institution, a Washington think-tank which produced a large quarterly model.[11] The Federal Reserve Board and the Massachusetts Institute of Technology produced and operated another large model.

But the turmoil, inflation, and exchange rate depreciation following the huge OPEC oil price increase in 1973 made these models less usable (the parameters changed in radical, discontinuous ways) and model construction changed to smaller, more microeconomic systems. A major factor in this change was the famous Lucas critique, which pointed out a serious defect in the use of the existing models as guides to what would happen should the government change monetary or fiscal policy.[12] Lucas drew on rational expectations theory to point out that whenever a policy variable is in a parameter, a change in the policy will change the parameter. Since in the solution to the model (the reduced form) the policy change not only affects the equation describing the policy itself, it also affects whatever parameters in other equations it may have entered, one cannot predict the result of a policy change by assuming parameters derived under previous policies remain unchanged. For example: if the money supply has been growing rapidly people expect inflation and foreign exchange depreciation. If the econometrician wishes to predict how changing to slow monetary growth will affect the economy, including the foreign exchange and the money markets, he cannot leave unchanged the parameters describing the markets. They were formed under the expectation of high inflation. To evaluate the new policy, new parameters relevant to low inflation would be needed. Econometric models, however, are estimated using past data, and could not be used to predict the effects of the new policy.[13] Professor Epstein summarizes the impact of rational expectations on econometric research as the refocus of attention on the "analysis of underlying structural parameters to evaluate the real and lasting effects of any type of economic policy." This study should be "based on more detailed knowledge of economic behavior under institutional restraints."[14]

Another reaction to the problems presented for econometric model building by the difficult economic conditions of the 1970s was to abandon the estimation of structural equations in favor of the position that everything depends on everything else, and putting every variable in the equations. This procedure, called vector autoregression (VAR), was developed by Christoper Sims. It is criticized for abandoning any guidance from economic theory when the challenge is really to move from aggregative theory to a high level of institutional and period detail, according to Professor Epstein.[15]

## Microeconomics

The major thrust of microeconomics since the 1930s has been the competitive general equilibrium model with its associated spin-offs in fields such as welfare economics and international economics. Some of the work of the 1930s was done by European mathematicians such as Abraham Wald, Karl Menger, and John von Neumann, and became widely known among economists only later as mathematics became more and more widely required in graduate education.[16] These studies were principally concerned with answering the questions of how to prove that there is an equilibrium solution to the general equilibrium model, and whether this solution was unique. The developments which had wide impacts at the time were the work of John R. Hicks (later, Sir John) and Paul Samuelson, which was more concerned with whether the equilibria were stable or not.

J. R. Hicks studied mathematics and economics at Oxford in the 1920s and so was not under the direct influence of Marshall. His first teaching job was at the London School of Economics and there, under the influence of Lionel Robbins, he intensively studied European economists such as Knut Wicksell and Wilfredo Pareto, who wrote on general equilibrium theory and welfare economics.[17] Hicks' major work of the early part of this period in microeconomics was *Value and Capital* (1939). But earlier work was important, such as *The Theory of Wages* (1932). This book deals largely with the marginal productivity theory of wages, but also was very influential in focusing the study of technical progress and the impact of changes in the supply of a factor of production on the "elasticity of substitution." Recall that an isoquant measures the different combinations of two inputs, such as capital and labor, that can be used in producing a fixed quantity of output. The elasticity of substitution has as numerator the percentage change in the capital–labor ratio, as denominator the percentage change in the slope of the isoquant. If the isoquant is relatively flat the elasticity of substitution is high (it is easy to substitute one factor for the other). The relation of this to changes in factor shares as factor supplies change is obvious; it is also easy to see how a technical change which reduces the requirements of one or the other input can be analyzed with this concept.

On the demand side of microeconomics, Hicks's development of indifference curves and ordinal utility analysis was fundamental. In ordinal utility, unlike the utility theory of Jevons, Walras, and Marshall, it is not necessary to assume that one can at some point devise a quantitative measurement of utility. It is enough to be able to say that a consumer prefers one combination of goods to another; he does not have to say by how much he prefers them. While Edgeworth had introduced indifference curves in the late nineteenth century, Wilfredo Pareto had dealt with ordinal utility and indifference curves in the 1890s, and Eugen Slutsky had published theorems like those of Hicks in 1915 in an Italian journal, Hicks together with R. G. D. Allen in 1934 made ordinal utility popular in English-language economics. One major use of their indifference curve analysis was to distinguish between the income effects and the substitution effects of a price change (if the price of good $x$ rises, people substitute some cheaper good for it, so that the demand for $x$ falls; at the same time, the price rise has reduced their real incomes, and while normally people buy less of a good when their incomes fall, for some goods, called inferior goods, people actually buy more when their incomes fall.) It can also be used to give a more definitive answer to the old question of how to tell whether goods are substitutes, like hamburgers vs hot-dogs, or complements, like hamburgers and cheese. The Hicks–Allen answer is this: if the price of one good rises, you will fall to a lower indifference curve. To tell whether a good is a substitute you should stay on the same indifference curve, so assume that your income is increased by enough to put you back on the first indifference curve. Then see whether you buy more or less of the other good. The idea of compensated price changes has been very important in demand analysis. [18]

*Value and Capital* pushed forward the analysis of production and demand, and also provided a dynamic model in which a temporary equilibrium holds prices constant at the beginning of a week, depending on the price expectations in force at that time. If some of these expectations are wrong, they are revised and a new temporary equilibrium occurs the following week. This gives a time path toward full equilibrium as well as showing how money and securities fit in their roles as stores of values. [19]

The analysis of the stability of equilibrium was a very influential part of *Value and Capital*. Hicks worked this out because, he said, general equilibrium in the form left by Walras was rather sterile. The system would be useful if one knew what would happen if tastes or resources changed. But to make sure that the system would settle down to a new equilibrium after the change, one needed to know if it was stable. Hence his emphasis on the stability conditions, that to be stable – to return to equilibrium after a temporary dislocation away from it – a rise in price had to make quantity supplied greater than quantity demanded. [20] But in general equilibrium some goods are stable when prices in other markets are fixed, and others only when prices adjust to preserve equilibrium in all markets. The analysis of stability was a major part of the microeconomics of the 1940s, and other criteria were developed. [21]

While Hicks was developing his ideas in England, Paul Samuelson, having gone through the University of Chicago graduate courses by the age of twenty, moved on to Harvard to complete his education and then to the Massachusetts Institute of Technology where he has had a long and distinguished career combining rigorous use of mathematics with a widespread coverage of many aspects of theoretical economics, a detailed knowledge of the history of economic thought, and a continued interest in questions of public policy. The 388 articles listed in the five volumes of *The Collected Scientific Papers*, plus the twelve editions of his elementary textbook, and the two advanced books, *The Foundations of Economic Analysis* (1947) and *Linear Programming and Economic Analysis* written jointly with Robert Dorfman and Robert Solow, pose a formidable, indeed impossible, task of summarizing. The following are some of the major fields he has worked in:

1   General equilibrium. Some of his early work was to improve on Hicks's stability analysis by pointing out that not only did you need to know that a price rise made the excess demand negative; you needed to know the dynamic sequence of the movement back towards equilibrium.

For example, if the rate of price increase is proportional to the excess demand, a differential equation system results from which one may deduce the income effects necessary for stability. Another important application of general equilibrium theory was in international trade, where two major theorems, the Stolper–Samuelson theorem and the factor–price equalization theorem, are cornerstones. The general equilibrium model used was a formalization of the Heckscher–Ohlin model, in which countries' pre-trade prices differ because they have different supplies of the factors of production although their tastes and technologies are the same. Using constant returns to scale technology, Wolfgang Stolper and Samuelson showed that a tariff on the good making intensive use of the scarce factor would improve that factor's income. And Samuelson showed that in his model international trade would completely equalize the prices of the factors of production – a labor-plentiful country which had low wages before trade would wind up with the same wage rate as a labor-scarce trading partner. An unexpected result of this rigorous analysis was to make the Heckscher–Ohlin model a less popular trade theory because its factor–price implications are so unrealistic.

2    Consumption theory. Samuelson pushed the Hicks–Allen ordinal indifference curve analysis one layer deeper in abstraction. Rather than assuming that people would tell the investigator which combinations of goods they preferred, the economist could infer the preferences by observing what combinations they purchased. The principle of "revealed preference" is that if a combination of goods is purchased, that combination is revealed to be preferred to all others which are cheaper at the prevailing prices. Those other combinations can never be revealed to be preferred to the first one at other prices, or else a serious inconsistency is involved. Why do this? It is related to the next topic, methodology.

3    Methodology. In the *Foundations of Economic Analysis* Samuelson proposed that economic theory should be operationally meaningful in the sense that it could conceivably be refuted by empirical data, if only under ideal conditions. Thus the revealed preference indifference curve could be refuted by observing that someone purchases combination $A$ at a higher total cost than $B$, when he had previously purchased $B$ at prices which made it cost more than $A$. As a model for how to do research, however, Milton Friedman's "positive economics" became more popular than operationalism after he published his *Essays in Positive Economics* in 1953. Friedman's proposition was that the proper way to construct theories was to test their conclusions against evidence, not their assumptions. In fact, said Friedman, "Truly important and significant hypotheses will be found to have 'assumptions' that are wildly inaccurate descriptive representations of reality, and, in general, the more significant the theory, the more unrealistic the assumptions (in this sense)."[22] Samuelson objected to this "F-twist", but, says Professor Blaug, the apparent mainstream view is that direct verification of the postulates or assumptions of economic theory is unnecessary and misleading.[23]

4   Welfare economics. A general equilibrium model might show what quantities of goods would be produced and what amounts of resources would be used; but would there be some better economic result? Welfare theorems work with this problem. For example, a Pareto-optimum is a point from which you cannot make one consumer better off without making another one worse off. (In an Edgeworth–Pareto box diagram the indifference curves are tangent and the consumers are on their contract curve.) Samuelson gives much credit to Abram Bergson for developing the concept of a social welfare function which would rank all the possible Pareto-optimum points. This function is formulated individualistically rather than dictatorially; it "ethically orders the various states of the world and ... lets 'individual tastes' [count] in the sense of agreeing with individuals' orderings *when those orderings are unanimous* and *resolving them ethically* when they are not unanimous."[24]

5   Capital theory and growth. We have previously utilized some of Samuelson's contributions in connection with the famous Cambridge–Cambridge controversy over reswitching in the neo-classical capital model of, for example, Böhm-Bawerk. This is only a fairly minor part of the total body of work. Important aspects include capital theory for well-defined, heterogeneous capital goods. In addition, Samuelson shows how a determinate price of capital can be achieved even if it is not possible to define an *aggregate* capital stock, as Joan Robinson continued to insist. So the distribution of income can be considered even though there is no aggregate capital factor to compare with labor. A different line of thought is the "consumption–loan" model, where the allocation of goods among generations achieves the support of the young by their parents (a loan) and, later, the support of the aged parents by their now-productive offspring (the repayment of the loan). Another aspect is the relation of the growth of capital and labor to the growth of the economy; here the "turnpike theory" is particularly well known.[25] Start with capital stocks of each of two goods in the simple two-good model, and specify what amount of the stock of one of these goods you desire at the end of the process. Let the initial stocks grow at the same percentage rate each year into the future (balanced growth). There will be one set of initial stocks which will give the highest growth rate. The turnpike theorem says that in an infinite-time context if you don't start at the maximum growth set of stocks and don't wish to possess the capital stocks which result from following the highest growth rate path, it still pays society to rearrange its capital stock, follow the highest growth rate path most of the time, and only near the end of the process change the investment pattern in the two goods to get the desired final capital stock composition. There will be more capital that way than if the growth path had followed the final composition all along.[26] Many subsequent articles by Samuelson and others have been written on the turnpike theory.

6   Others. Samuelson's other output includes the famous macroeconomic articles; many important articles in the history of economic

thought, including analyses of Ricardo and Marx; many articles on stochastic theory and speculative price; articles which started much current research in public goods and free rider problems; articles on mathematical biology; and that important category, miscellaneous. It is a formidable body of work. In all this vast output, according to Assar Lindbeck, Samuelson has done more than anyone else to raise the general analytical and methodological level of central economic theory.[27]

The next and so far definitive generation of economists to work on general equilibrium theory included the Nobel prize winners Kenneth Arrow and Gerard Debreu. Arrow won his initial fame on a different problem, however – the famous impossibility voting theorem.[28] Under the conditions that all combinations of preferences had to be considered, that some people changing their mind and deciding to vote for an option which previously was the winner would not change the outcome, that some people changing their mind about a third alternative would not affect the ranking of two other alternatives, that there cannot be a social preference for only one given alternative no matter what the combination of individual preferences, and that there cannot be a dictator, it turns out there cannot be a non-contradictory voting mechanism that will rank social choices. Many interesting attempts have been made to salvage the basic theory of voting by changing Arrow's axioms.

Arrow is also an outstanding contributor to the theory of risk-taking. Here his idea is that the general equilibrium model should be extended to include contingent commodities – those that will be delivered only in a given state of the world. Thus you might specify a demand for a new pane of plate glass if there is a hurricane in Georgia on July 20, 1990. Obviously there can be many potential states of the world. If there are $C$ commodities and $S$ possible states of the world, there could be $C \times S$ markets. But this can be reduced to $C + S$ by saying there are $C$ spot markets for the commodities and $S$ securities markets which pay one dollar in the event state $S$ occurs. The general equilibrium then determines the price on each of these markets in such a fashion as to allocate goods and risks optimally. In addition, Arrow has worked with risk-aversion, medical economics, and other topics in the field of uncertainty.

In collaboration with another Nobel Prize winner, Gerard Debreu, Arrow produced what is currently the accepted formulation of the general equilibrium model. This appeared in 1954, and Debreu later published a version in *The Theory of Value* (1959). Their formulation was an abstract, set theory version, designed to give a much easier proof of the existence of equilibrium than had been achieved. In the process, they made use of what is called a fixed-point theorem.[29] Their model assumes that the production side of the economy is a convex set (i.e., has no indivisibilities or increasing returns), can make no outputs without inputs, and cannot make inputs from outputs. Consumers have well-defined, ordinal preferences, and have a limit on how many services they can supply but are able to supply a positive amount of each good. Using these assumptions, and proofs from topology, the authors gave a much neater proof than had Wald in the 1930s that there was a solution to a rigorously formulated general equilibrium model, and thereby they proved that the economy did function in deciding what goods to produce and what incomes to pay as though it were guided by an invisible hand, just as Adam Smith had said. Arrow, using the same set-theory tools, had previously proved that the market equilibrium was Pareto-optimal. However, since the world is full of economies of scale and since there are no securities markets for every state of the world, what relevance have such models, asks the skeptical student. One answer is "What we shall gain from the work is a deeper understanding of how a market-guided economy operates, and a sharper view of which economic problems free markets can contend with and which ones should be dealt with by other means."[30] Another is that it gives a secure basis for others who work with the general equilibrium model, which Walras had failed to do. As a recent survey of general equilibrium theory explains, "a growing number of papers in the applied areas adopt a variant of the Arrow–Debreu–McKenzie framework. Only in this context can they discuss the importance of interactions among markets and the distribution of wealth."[31]

One person who has made a notable contribution to empirical use of the general equilibrium model is Nobel Prize winner Wassily Leontief. Leontief, born in Russia and trained at Berlin, has been in the United States since the 1930s, first at Harvard and then at New York University. His most famous work has been in input–output economics, which utilizes the production side of the general equilibrium model. Although Leontief has split the American economy into as many as 400 industries, we can show the essence of the model by assuming there are two industries, each of which uses the output of the other as an input (as well as using its own output, as in the case of the coal mine which uses coal to make the steam that runs its machinery). The outputs are $X_1$ and $X_2$. Inputs per unit of output are called $a_{ij}$, where $i$ denotes the input and $j$ the output industry. Suppose we know the total amount of output needed by consumers (which might be the army or a state-owned industry needing a stated amount of wheat to export). Call these final amounts needed $C_j$. Then the total output is the sum of the intermediate goods plus the final output, or

$$a_{11}X_1 + a_{12}X_2 + C_1 = X_1$$

$$a_{21}X_1 + a_{22}X_2 + C_2 = X_2$$

$$a_{01}X_1 + a_{02}X_2 = X_0$$

where the last line shows the total labor ($X_0$) needed in the economy. Notice these are true general equilibrium equations, where everything depends on everything else; notice however that Leontief assumed constant returns to scale. These equations, which may be as many as 400 equations, each with 400 variables, can now be solved with computers, although when Leontief started hand labor was required. The answers, the

$X_j$'s, have been used in many different situations. They have been used in helping plan for the conversion of the American economy to peace-time after World War II; in many plans for less-developed countries and planned economies; in analyzing US and other nations' foreign trade (surprisingly, it turned out that the United States exported labor-intensive goods, by contrast with the reasonable assumption that the United States had so much capital that it exported capital-intensive goods); and in studying inflation and environmental problems.[32]

While Leontief was using his input–output model in large-scale empirical work, Piero Sraffa was putting in many years' work polishing a theoretical volume based on an input–output model, *Production of Commodities by Means of Commodities: a Prelude to a Critique of Economic Theory* (1960). Sraffa presents the input–output equations, including the labor requirements, and shows that if wages are fixed at subsistence, relative prices and profits will be determined. With wages at a different level, a different price structure is determined; Sraffa uses a standard commodity, which is composed of outputs in the same proportion as the non-labor inputs which are used in producing them, in order to find what Ricardo called an invariable measure of value. Using the standard commodity we can tell, says Sraffa, whether any particular price change is the result of the peculiarity of the commodity being measured or of the measuring standard. The model received much attention because, unlike the standard marginal productivity theory of the distribution of income, it does not determine the distribution of income. It provides a theoretical basis for those who think income distribution is the result of the class struggle or of economic power.[33]

Finally, no survey of modern general equilibrium theory is complete without a look at the theory of games. This theory was presented by John von Neumann and Oskar Morgenstern in 1944 in their book *The Theory of Games and Economic Behavior*. The book presents many important results, including a version of a cardinal utility function suitable for cases involving probabilities rather than completely certain outcomes. Its basic purpose was to analyze decision-making where the outcomes depend on decisions made by other people, such as the Sherlock Holmes–Dr Moriarity problem. Holmes, pursued by Moriarity, takes a train to Dover, but gets off at a way station where he watches Moriarity steaming by in hot pursuit in a special train. Holmes remarks that it would have been a coup "had he deduced what I deduced and acted accordingly." This multilateral decision-making is the essence of the theory of games. It may be used in models of oligopoly pricing, such as the Cournot duopoly problem; it may also be used in models of negotiation, where the strategy may involve threats or collusion. A simple game is matching pennies, where the outcome depends on the side of the coin shown by each player. Here the correct strategy involves a random probability of showing each side, because the other player can always win if he detects a pattern of which side you will show (always heads, or alternating heads and tails, etc.).

General equilibrium theorists became interested in game theory when it was shown that what was called the "core" of a game was the same as the contract curve in an Edgeworth model, which is the set of equilibria from which no movement making one person better off without making another worse off is possible. The core in a game is a set of solutions that leaves no coalition of players in a position to improve the payoffs of all its members. With an infinite number of economic actors, both the Walrasian model and the game theoretic model converge to the same equilibrium. Game theory is also used in bidding models, in studying institutions that make plans for "satisfactory" outcomes, for voting mechanisms where the problem is to make sure voters truthfully report their preferences, and for public goods models. It is also used in biology where the problems of evolution can be studied as strategies in games against nature. Game theorists believe their subject has a lively future because it is not tied to one institutional form, as is the study of competitive markets.[34]

There is much else in modern economics, far too much to give even a rapid survey. Radical economics, a product of the 1960s, was a Marxist-based movement, critical of both the society and of mainstream economics (too narrow, not enough attention to social and economic classes). Its members continue to do research and writing. James Buchanan was a recent Nobel Prize winner for his material, much of it in collaboration with Gordon Tulloch, on the economics of public choice and the calculus of consent. This is an attempt to formulate a theory of constitution-making. Economic history, including "cliometrics" (use of econometric methods in the study of that part of history which has left any data behind), is another branch of economic research, one that crosses disciplinary boundaries. So do the many applications of economic theory to the family, to divorce, and to other sociological topics by Gary Becker of the University of Chicago.[35] There is a group called the "neo-Austrians" who emphasize the market, entrepreneurship, prices as information devices, and the like. The theory of the firm and of different types of markets, the domain of Professor George Stigler, another Nobel Prize winner from the University of Chicago, continues to be an important field of economics. New ideas of what it is that firms maximize, what their natural decision-making processes are, how their behavior is influenced by property rights, how they process information, all form part of a growing literature.[36]

Keynes called economics "the most pleasant of the moral sciences," and the large and increasing number of economists attests to the fact that, as in the past when people like Ricardo studied economics for pleasure, economics today continues to be fascinating.

## Notes

1  Palgraves's *Dictionary of Political Economy* (London, 1926), vol. I, p. 437.
2  *The New Palgrave: A Dictionary of Economics* (New York, 1988), vol. I, p. 681.

3  Roy J. Epstein, *A History of Econometrics* (Amsterdam, 1987) is an excellent source for a historical survey of the subject. An article-length review is A. C. Darnell, "Economic Statistics and Econometrics," in J. Creedy and D. P. O'Brien (eds), *Economic Analysis in Historical Perspective* (London, 1984). Carl Christ, "Early Progress in Estimating Quantitative Economic Relationships in America," *American Economic Review*, vol. 75, no. 6, December 1985, gives more detail on the actual models used than does Darnell.

4  Paul Samuelson, "Paul Douglas's Measurement of Production Functions and Marginal Productivities," *Journal of Political Economy*, October 1979, tells how Douglas and Cobb found the immortal production function $P = bL^kC^{1-k}$ and comments on some of the statistical problems.

5  Frisch's work is surveyed in Leif Johansen, "Johansen on Frisch," in Henry W. Speigel and Warren Samuels (eds), *Contemporary Economists in Perspective* (Greenwich, Conn., 1984), vol. 1. This article, and others in the book, originally appeared in the *Scandinavian Journal of Economics*.

6  Reprinted in vol. XIV of J. M. Keynes's *Collected Works* (London, 1977), pp. 306–18.

7  After World War II Tinbergen became interested in planning, both for the Dutch economy and for less developed countries. His contributions are surveyed by Bent Hansen in "Hansen on Tinbergen," in Spiegel and Samuels, *Contemporary Economists*.

8  Cowles Commission Monograph no. 10.

9  A review of five models, describing their construction, is contained in Carl F. Christ, "Aggregate Econometric Models," *American Economic Review*, vol. XLVI, June 1956.

10  Epstein, *History of Econometrics*, p. 224.

11  See James Duesenberry et al., *The Brookings Quarterly Econometric Model of the United States*, 1965.

12  R. E. Lucas, Jr, "Econometric Policy Evaluation: A Critique," in Karl Brunner and A. H. Meltzer (eds), *The Phillips Curve and Labor Markets*, supplement to the *Journal of Monetary Economics*, 1976.

13  For a clear illustration of the Lucas critique in the context of a little three-equation model, see David K. H. Begg, *The Rational Expectations Revolution in Macroeconomics* (Baltimore, Md., 1982).

14  Epstein, *History of Econometrics*, p. 199.

15  Ibid., p. 220.

16  This work is very clearly summarized in E. Roy Weintraub, *General Equilibrium Analysis: Studies in Appraisal* (Cambridge, 1985).

17  Pareto's work has now been translated; *Manual of Political Economy*, trans. Anne S. Schwier (Clifton, NJ, 1971).

18  For a very interesting discussion, see Paul Samuelson, "Complementarity: An Essay on the 40th Anniversary of the Hicks–Allen Revolution in Demand Theory," *Journal of Economic Literature*, December 1974, pp. 1255–89.

19  For the current state of temporary equilibrium theory, see Kenneth Arrow and F. H. Hahn, *General Competitive Analysis* (San Francisco, 1971), pp. 136–51. Note that this requires knowledge of set theory.

20  J. R. Hicks, *Value and Capital* (Oxford, 1939), pp. 61ff.

21  The modern formulation is in Arrow and Hahn, *General Competitive Analysis*.

Two convenient surveys of Hicks's contributions are Brian Morgan, "Sir John Hicks's Contributions to Economic Theory," in J. R. Shackleton and G. Lockesley, *Twelve Contemporary Economists* (London, 1987), and William Baumol, "Baumol on Hicks," in Spiegel and Samuels, *Contemporary Economists*.

22  Friedman, *Essays in Positive Economics* (Chicago, Ill., 1953), p. 14.

23  Mark Blaug, *The Methodology of Economics* (Cambridge, 1980), p. 127.

24  Paul Samuelson, "Bergsonian Welfare Economics," in Steven Rosefielde (ed.), *Economic Welfare and the Economics of Soviet Socialism: Essays in Honor of Abram Bergson*, (Cambridge, 1981), reprinted in *Collected Scientific Papers* vol. 5 (Cambridge, Mass., 1986). Actually the next article in vol. 5 of *Collected Scientific Papers* is easier to understand for the mathematically non-sophisticated; it is called "Reaffirming the Existence of 'Reasonable' Bergson–Samuelson Social Welfare Functions," and provides a neat geometric treatment, showing how an ethical system resolves problems of how to distribute goods between persons to achieve maximum social welfare.

25  The theory got its name because the fastest way between two points by car may not be the direct way. It may be optimal to go out of your way to get on a turnpike road and follow that for most of the way to your destination.

26  R. Dorfman, P. A. Samuelson, and R. Solow, *Linear Programming and Economic Analysis* (New York, 1958), pp. 325–34.

27  "Lindbeck on Samuelson," in Spiegel and Samuels, *Contemporary Economists*, p. 6.

28  Arrow *Social Choice and Individual Values* (New Haven, Conn., 1951).

29  William J. Baumol, *Economic Theory and Operations Analysis*, 4th edn (Englewood Cliffs, NJ, 1977) gives a very good illustration of fixed-point theorems and how they are used to solve problems of the Arrow–Debreu variety.

30  Robert Dorfman, *The New York Times*, October 23, 1983.

31  William Novshek and Hugo Sonnenschein, "General Equilibrium with Free Entry: A Synthetic Approach to the Theory of Perfect Competition," *Journal of Economic Literature*, September 1987.

32  See Robert Dorfman, "Dorfman on Leontief," in Spiegel and Samuels, *Contemporary Economists*.

33  See chapter 8, appendix I, of this text for a more extensive treatment of Sraffa's model.

34  Martin Shubik, *Game Theory in the Social Sciences*, (Boston, Mass., 1982), gives a reasonably accessible mathematical treatment. Andrew Schotter and Gerhard Schwödiauer, "Economics and Game Theory: A Survey," *Journal of Economic Literature*, June 1980, explain all the many subjects where the theory of games is relevant.

35  Jack Hirshliefer, "The Expanding Domain of Economics," *American Economic Review*, vol. 75, no. 6, December 1985, looks at a number of applications of economics in political behavior, charity, biology, conflict, and anthropology.

36  A good reference is Oliver E. Williams, "Firms and Markets," in Sidney Weintraub (ed.), *Modern Economic Thought* (Philadelphia, 1977).

# Index